The Shell Guide
to Spain

*For my brother Lorne
and his family*

The Shell Guide to Spain

Angus Mitchell

SIMON & SCHUSTER

LONDON · SYDNEY · NEW YORK ·
TOKYO · TORONTO

Angus Mitchell has lived in Spain for the last five years
working as a freelance writer and journalist.
He is the author of Spain: Interiors, Gardens, Architecture and Landscape
and has worked for many publications on both sides of the Atlantic.

First published in Great Britain by
Simon & Schuster Ltd in 1992

The information contained in this book is believed correct
at the time of printing. While every care has been taken to ensure that
the information is correct, Shell UK cannot accept responsibility for any
errors, omissions or changes in the details given.

The name Shell and the Shell emblem are registered trademarks.

Simon & Schuster Ltd
West Garden Place
Kendal Street
London W2 2AQ

Simon & Schuster of Australia Pty Ltd
Sydney

British Library Cataloguing-in-Publication Data available

ISBN 0-671-71020-6

Design and layout: Susie Home
Maps: Ian Foulis Associates

The Publisher would like to thank all the people and
organizations who loaned transparencies for use in this book.

Front cover picture: Montefrio, Andalusia. Tony Stone Worldwide

Typesetting: Ace Filmsetting Ltd, Frome, Somerset
Printed and bound by: Butler & Tanner Ltd, Frome, Somerset

Contents

Preface

SPAIN: the warm African south against the green Atlantic north veiled in mist, the crowded beaches of the Mediterranean *Costas* protecting the boundless empty expanses of the interior; the dazzling light and quenching shade; the heat of the summer and the biting winds blowing off the snow-capped sierras of winter. On average, more than a million foreigners fly into Spain each week and, though the boom years of coastal tourism are on the wane, Spain is the most popular holiday destination in the world.

It is strange therefore that most of the country remains unknown to foreigners; a wilderness populated by thousands of beautiful, sometimes forsaken villages, which survive on little except the strength of rural traditions. This Spain is composed of different languages, customs, lifestyles and traditions. When you begin to know the country you will appreciate these differences, which often divide not only one region from another but pueblo from pueblo. The topography of Spain makes its regions individual: regional autonomy is therefore deeply rooted. It is balanced by the attractive force of Castile and its cultural values, now represented by Madrid. Since 1479 Castile has been the unifying factor of Spain as a whole: General Franco from 1939 to 1975 took centralization to its extreme. Basque and Catalan separatism has been the natural reaction, and recognition of the regional differences is now enshrined in the constitution of King Juan Carlos signed on 27 December 1978.

Spain was the first authoritarian state of post-war Europe to move into democracy: an example for Eastern European countries to follow. Monarchy and autonomy have developed with astonishing ease, and the opening of European borders on 1 January 1993 reflects the country's new mood of freedom. Regional government will be firmly re-established in the new European Spain. There are seventeen autonomous regions, sixteen of which are covered in this book. The Canary Islands are omitted, but their historical importance as a launching pad for the exploration of Africa and the New World should not be forgotten.

Spain is a country of pilgrimage, and every region has at least one sacred place: a succession of Romanesque monuments leads to Santiago de Compostela and its shrine of St James the Apostle; in the south there is the Mezquita in Córdoba, a focus of Islamic civilization in Western Europe; in between, there are a multitude of other places for the modern pilgrim to discover, where the spirit of Spain and its regions and its place in the world can be understood.

CHAPTER ONE

Introduction

History and Chronology

THE BEGINNING of Iberian civilization can be seen in the Neanderthal flint tools and Paleolithic cave art dating from between 25,000 and 15,000 BC, concentrated in the limestone mountains of the north of the country and along the coast of Valencia. The cave at Altamira in Cantabria is the most astonishing example (see p. 133). Between 6,000 and 2,000 BC, Neolithic hunter-gatherer tribes migrated north from the Sahara and established small agricultural communities along the river courses of the interior. Several megalithic standing stones and dolmens mark the emergence of the 'pot or beaker culture' stretching through the Danube basin and as far north as the Orkney Islands: the unique testaments are Los Millares in Almería and the stone cupola ceiling in the burial chambers at Antequera north of Málaga.

With the Bronze Age (c. 2,000–1,000 BC), stable and well-defended communities developed in the south and central *Meseta*, where they mined the rich sources of copper and tin. In about 1,000 BC Indo-European tribes crossed the Pyrenees, and Celtic peoples settled in the north. The country became a network of separate tribes: among them, the '*castro*' clans of Galicia and Asturias, the Urnfield people of Catalunya, and the Vascones or Basques.

At about the same time the history of the Peninsula becomes less speculative. Attracted by the area's minerals, Phoenician traders from the eastern Mediterranean founded a city at Gadir (Cádiz), and for the next six centuries they spread along the south coast, tapped the rich mineral resources of the interior and helped to 'orientalize' the indigenous people through the introduction of more sophisticated mining and farming methods. Their cultural influence was equally important: in the province of Huelva and along the Costa del Sol archeologists have unearthed grave-goods that show an advanced level of metalwork, including gold and silver bracelets, gold pectorals and necklaces inlaid with green and pink glass.

This was the age of Tartessos, a partly fabulous but in essence histori-cal kingdom. According to classical

Spanish regions and provincial capitals

Greek writers, this was located at the end of the habitable world and was terrorized by Geryon, a monster with three heads and three bodies, whose pet oxen devoured human flesh. The myth of Tartessos holds as much fascination as the Abyssinia of Prester John locked away in the highlands of Ethiopia, and its precise location has intrigued archeologists for well over a century. A plausible explanation is that a rich Bronze Age community, strongly influenced by Phoenician culture, did exist somewhere near the Guadalquivir between Huelva and Cádiz, whose enormous wealth derived from the mines of Río Tinto.

Though the Greeks traded extensively with the Tartessians, they preferred to colonize Iberia through their settlement at Massilia (Marseilles). From the sixth to the fourth centuries BC, Greek communities rose all along the eastern coast and in the Balearic Islands, of which the most important remains are to be seen at Empúries and Rhode, on the Costa Brava in Catalunya.

The Carthaginians, descendants of the Phoenicians, developed similar trading societies in the third century BC. They subjugated most of the Penin-

The Bardenas Reales in Navarre is an extreme case of the **Meseta***'s arid, karstic landscape. Miles of windscorched landforms hint at the burning summers and freezing winters that make up the harsh Iberian climate.* Incafo

sula south of the Ebro and founded a new capital at Cartago Nova (Cartagena, Murcia) after their retreat from Sicily. They were eventually defeated by the Romans in the second Punic War (218–201 BC), precipitated by Hannibal's attack on Saguntum in 219 BC, thereby leaving the way open for the Roman conquest of Spain.

By this stage Iberia had developed into a network of sophisticated and quite affluent societies. Village fortifications had been influenced by Greek military architecture; the *varracos* – stone bulls or boars found throughout the Peninsula, especially in the province of Avila – suggest animal-inspired cults; while strange carved stone priestesses testify to a high level of artistic ability, influenced by the artisans of Phoenicia and Carthage. The most intriguing riddles are the undeciphered scripts and the Iberian steles (gravestones) which no epigraphist has yet been able to read.

The Roman conquest of Iberia took nearly 200 years of continuous military campaigns to complete, and involved a succession of Rome's greatest commanders, including Scipio, Pompey, Julius Caesar and Augustus. In 197 BC the Romans divided their Iberian territory into two separate provinces – Hispania Citerior (Tarraconensis), comprising the east coast between Cartago Nova and the Pyrenees, with Tarraco (Tarragona) as its capital; and Hispania Ulterior (Baetica), which corresponded roughly with modern-day Andalusia. The Romans' main opponents were the Celts of Lusitania (Galicia and Portugal) who continuously raided their territories until full-scale war broke out between 155 and 139 BC. In 133 BC Scipio the Younger ended the campaign after the long

siege of the Celtiberian tribes at Numancia (see p. 197), on a promontory overlooking the early course of the River Duero. By the time of Augustus even the remotest recesses of the north, inhabited by the Cantabri and Astures, had been pacified.

Rome's control and pacification of Iberia was followed by the exploitation of the Peninsula's rich mineral resources to pay for wars in other parts of the Roman Empire. The *Via Plata*, joining the Río Tinto and Emerita (Mérida) with the mines of the north and the Atlantic ports, opened up vast stretches of new territory. The scale of these operations can be seen in the gold mine below the artificial sierra of Las Médulas in León and by the bridges of Extremadura. The *Via Augusta* connected the *Meseta* and Mediterranean with Gaul and Italy. Tarragona was the centre of seaborne trade and, along with Mérida, preserves the best urban remains of the age. Zaragoza, whose name derives from Caesarea Augusta, was the most important of the new interior capitals. Hispania was transformed from an importer of luxury goods into a large exporter of olive oil, wine, fish sauce, silver, horses, ceramics, weapons and wheat, considered to be the best in the Mediterranean. The historian Tacitus, rhetoricians Seneca and Lucan and the Emperors Trajan and Hadrian were all Spaniards.

The first barbarian invasions swept across the Pyrenees between AD 264 and 276, but not until the early fifth century did the invasion of Germanic peoples and other tribes lead to significant settlement. The first of these were the Vandals, who gave their name to Andalusia, followed by the Sueves and Alans in Galicia. The Visigoths came some time after their expulsion from southern Gaul in 490, and established a tribal kingdom round their capital at Toledo. Visigothic government took time to establish roots in a still-Roman Hispania. Its loose tribal institutions and heretical Arian religion caused constant tension with the Hispano–Romans, and their numbers were not sufficient to control the provinces effectively. Their early history before the conversion of King Reccared to Catholic Christianity in 587 was a chronicle of instability and betrayal.

Under Visigothic rule, Catholic Spain flourished. Monasticism arrived from Egypt and a series of bishoprics were established. Civilization peaked in the reign of King Leovigild (569–586) and in the early decades of the eighth century when the influence of Bishop Isidore of Seville, who wrote what may be considered the first encyclopedia, was considerable. Visigoths and Romans merged into a truly Spanish society. In spite of this growing unity, however, the Moorish conquest was able to sweep through the Peninsula like a Muslim *blitzkrieg*.

In 711, Tariq-ibn-Ziyad, a captain of Governor Musa of Mauretania, crossed the strait dividing North Africa from Gibraltar with a force of around 7,000 men, and defeated the last Visigothic king Roderic at the Battle of Guadalete. Within ten years, all Iberia save a few of the more inhospitable northern sierras had fallen under Arab control, and the inhabitants were subjected to the new religion of Islam. The conquereors called the kingdom Al-Andalus, and it became part of the vast Muslim empire that stretched from the Pyrenees to the Punjab. The ease of the conquest showed how brittle Visigothic government had been. Reli-

gious toleration, however, was granted to the Christians, who were permitted to practise their faith under penalty of taxation. They were known as Mozarabs from the Arabic *musta 'rab* (arabicized). Jews were also able to follow their religion openly and, in this atmosphere of *convivencia*, a considerable degree of cultural exchange took place.

Muslim government suffered many vicissitudes in its early years – disagreements between the Arab governors, revolts among their Berber mercenaries and spasmodic guerrilla attacks by Christians in the north. In 718 or 722 Pelayo, the leader of a small group of Christian guerrillas, routed a small Muslim force at Covadonga in the mountains of Asturias and created a kingdom. In these trivial events the *Reconquista*, or Christian reconquest, was effectively born.

This conflict between Muslims and Christians lasted more than 700 years, until the defeat of the kingdom of Granada in 1492, but the exchanges were not always hostile. Christian kings sent their sons to be educated in Arab courts; mixed marriages were made between the two cultures; Christian women wore the veil; kings dressed as caliphs. Muslim theologians wrote treatises on Christian theology, and Christians emulated the poetry of the Arabs.

The Arab advance north was finally repulsed by Charles Martel at Poitiers in 732. The Arabs retreated south of the Pyrenees to consolidate their territories with *alcázars* and interior fortresses. In 756 Abd-ah-Raman, the last of the Ummayad line and the successor of Mohammed, fled Damascus following the assassination of his family by the Abbasid dynasty. He eventually established an independent Emirate at Córdoba. It flourished and, by the tenth century, Muslim Spain reached its zenith under Abd-ah-Raman III (912–61) who in 929 proclaimed himself Caliph of an independent Western Islamic Empire. Córdoba became 'the jewel of the world' – the most advanced city of Europe; a centre for scholarship and science; and a leader in the fields of architecture, medicine, astronomy and poetry.

As long as unity was maintained, the Muslim kingdom continued to thrive. Just before the millennium, Al-Mansur usurped power from the young caliph Hisham II and embarked on a long campaign against the strengthening Christian kingdoms of the north, which virtually wiped them out and ended only on his death at Medinaceli in 1002. As a consequence of his death the Arab kingdom fell into a long period of factional struggle and gradually weakening government. Al-Andalus was splintered into several small, internally competitive kingdoms (*Reinos de Taifas*), which were incapable of presenting a unified front against the increasingly powerful Christians.

By this time the independent Christian Kings of León, Navarre and Aragón, together with the Counts of Castile and Barcelona, had advanced to the rivers Duero and Ebro, and fortified their territory with a vast line of military and monastic defences. Their frontier tax, the *paria*, levied on the *taifas*, generated considerable wealth, especially for the Counts of Castile who from 1037 were Kings of both Castile and León.

With the capture of Toledo by the Christians in 1085, and the continuing advances of Alfonso VI, the *taifa* kings in desperation sought help from the Almoravids, or 'people of the Ribat': fanatical Muslim warriors who had recently conquered Morocco. By 1086 these fierce nomads from the region near the mouth of the River Senegal who controlled the trans-Saharan gold trade had conquered southern Spain, founded a dynasty and absorbed something of Andalusian civilization before their power waned. In 1147 they were followed by more fanatics, the Almohads, but the Christians retaliated by enlisting the resources of the Crusading Orders, the Knights of Calatrava, Santiago, Alcántara and the Knights Templar, and gradually the Moorish hold on the Peninsula diminished.

The balance of power was decisively shifted in 1212 following the victory of the united Christian kingdoms at the Battle of Las Navas de Tolosa. The great Moorish kingdom of Al-Andalus was soon vanquished, and an estimated 300,000 Moors returned to Africa. Alfonso IX (1188–1230) took Cáceres, Mérida and Badajoz. In 1236 and 1248 Córdoba and Seville fell to Ferdinand III (1217–52) and the newly-won territories of the south were incorporated into the kingdom of Castilla y León. Meanwhile, the Kings of Aragón had made strong advances through the east of the Peninsula. Zaragoza had fallen to Alfonso I in 1118 and James I 'The Conqueror' (1213–76) added Valencia, Alicante, Murcia and the Balearic Islands to the Christian reconquest.

By the 14th century, two powerful kingdoms, each with a different focus of attention, had emerged. The rulers of united Aragón and Catalonia expanded eastwards through the Mediterranean, and founded a loose seaborne empire which stretched as far as Sicily. The kingdom of Navarre, meanwhile, looked towards France. Castilian unity, however, was hampered by constant dynastic struggles. Under the Trastamara dynasty, founded by Henry II (1369–79), there were incessant internal quarrels and wars against Portugal and Aragón. But the Peninsula's economic importance grew along with that of northern Europe; in particular the trade in Flanders wool, the best in Europe, progressively made Castile rich.

By the 15th century the Nasrids' hilltop kingdom of Granada, supplied by a few ports along the Andalusian coast, was all that remained of Moorish Al-Andalus. It was the secret marriage in 1469 between Ferdinand II of Aragón and Isabel I of Castile, *Los Reyes Católicos* (the Catholic Monarchs), that brought together the two largest dynasties of Iberia. They were not at first united politically, but both rulers were content to follow a mutual policy of trying to diminish the power of local governing rights or *fueros*, which had initially been granted to attract settlers; and to create a powerful military nobility and bureaucracy. The establishment in 1480 of the sinister Inquisition brought an end to *convivencia*, when Moors, Jews and heretics were forced to conform to Christianity or face expulsion.

Throughout the Middle Ages, the period of *convivencia*, Spain was populated by substantial communities of Jews, the cultural intermediaries between the Muslim and Christian worlds, and their translators, poets, philosophers, diplomats and physicians contributed much to Iberian civilization, until their expulsion in 1492. In most of the leading medieval cities – Toledo, Girona, Córdoba, Zaragoza and Barcelona – there were Jewish quarters, known as *calls* or *juderías* where the Sephards lived.

The year 1492 was a pivotal one in Spanish history. Granada, the last Moorish stronghold of the Nasrid king Abdullah VIII, was taken after a ten-year siege. Columbus set sail for what he thought would be Japan, but which turned out to be America. The country's fortunes, gained through colonial expansion, would make the Spanish crown the richest in Europe by the 16th century, and finance its wars as defender of the Catholic faith and leader of a crusade against Turks and Protestants. The publication in the same year of the *Gramática Sobre la Lengua Castellana* by the Renaissance scholar and philologist Antonio de Nebrija (1442–1522) marked the beginning of Spanish humanism. The reverse side of the coin was the expulsion of the Jews and the migration of over 150,000 Moors and Jews overseas, which deprived the country of a great many of its outstanding craftsmen and scholars.

Two years after the death of Isabel in 1504, Ferdinand assumed government of both Aragón and Castile. By 1512 he had captured Navarre, leaving only Portugal independent. He was succeeded in 1516 by his grandson, Charles I (1516–56), who, as the Holy Roman Emperor Charles V, also inherited the Low Countries and the Austrian dominions as well as the emerging empire in the Americas. Charles spent only short periods of his reign in Spain, though he used its resources to finance his wars against France, the Protestant states of Germany and the Turks. His preference for his Flemish servants led to the revolt of the Communeros (1520–22), but he managed to preserve Spain from the attacks of the Barbary pirates and the Turks.

In 1556 he abdicated and retired to the monastery of Yuste (Extremadura) where he died in 1558. His son, Philip II (1556–98), had an austere temperament and was devoted to what he perceived as his destiny as champion of Catholic authority. His concerns, like his father's, were imperial, and Spanish resources were stretched under his rule in defence of the country's dominions, but he made his home in Spain and his capital at Madrid in 1561. In 1580, with the merging of the Portuguese and Spanish monarchies, the crown possessions included all Iberia, much of Italy, parts of north-eastern France, Belgium, Central and South America, the Philippines, Madeira, the Azores, Ceylon, Sumatra, the Moluccas and much of the East African and Asiatic seaboard. The Portuguese Empire, however, continued to be governed separately, until the Portuguese regained their independence in 1640.

Philip was concerned not only to stamp out heresy at home, but also to maintain his Catholic empire against the Turks and Protestants abroad. The measures he ordered against the Moriscos, nominally Christians but Muslim in their customs, alienated them even further, and revolts in Aragón accentuated the repression of his reign. The victory of the Holy League (an alliance of Christian powers) over the Turks at the Battle of Lepanto in 1571 ended the Turkish domination of the Mediterranean. Philip's victory here, however, was overshadowed by the revolt of the Protestant Low Countries and the defeat of the Spanish Armada in 1588 by the navy of Elizabeth I of England.

Throughout the 16th century Spanish colonial expansion was the means of financing these policies. After the discovery of America by Columbus, the conquistadors rapidly colonized vast areas of the mainland. In 1517 Cortés defeated the Aztec ruler Monteçuçuma and conquered Mexico, and in 1519 the Spanish reached California. In the same year the Portuguese mariner Ferdinand Magellan, commanding a Spanish fleet, set sail west for Asia and navigated the 'Magellan' strait. He was killed in the Philippines but his Basque pilot Juan Elcano finished the voyage, and the first circumnavigation of the world. The Inca Empire and its silver mines in Peru were conquered by the Pizarro brothers in 1531 with a force of less than 200 men. This brought Spain vast riches, and the viceroyalties of New Spain and Peru were established to administer the lands.

Even the wealth from America failed to sustain Philip's imperial ambitions, and by the beginning of the 17th century Castile was exhausted. The reign of his successor, Philip III (1598–1621), conducted mainly by his *valido* or prime minister, the Duke of Lerma, saw peace with France and England, but the expulsion of the Moriscos in 1609 robbed Spain of a valuable industrious element. In the reign of Philip IV (1621–65) Spain once more took up arms against France and the Protestant powers and entered the European dynastic struggle known as the Thirty Years War (1618–48), which began to break up the Spanish Empire. The attempts of Philip's minister the 'Count-Duke' Olivares to spread the economic burden into other regions of Spain led to the revolt of the Catalans in 1640, the loss of Portugal in 1668 and Spanish impotence in dealing with the increasing power of France.

Nevertheless, the 16th and early 17th centuries were Spain's cultural golden age. Apart from the distinctive architecture of the time, there was a literary renaissance which began with the genius and learning of the Spanish humanists such as Antonio de Nebrija (1442–1522) and Luis Vives (1492–1540), flowered in the plays of Lope de Vega (1562–1635) and Pedro Calderón (1600–81) and the strange baroque poetry of Luis de Gongora (1561–1627), and culminated in the greatest of all picaresque novels, Cervantes' *Don Quixote*, published in 1604. Artists, writers and poets were sustained by the brilliant court of the Habsburg kings from Charles I to Philip IV, and by the wealth and patronage of a cultivated nobility. Titian was employed by Charles I, and the unearthly genius of El Greco enjoyed the patronage of Philip II. The native painters reached their apogee in the next century with Murillo's and Ribera's domestic realism, and above all the luminous and utterly Spanish portraits of Velázquez, court painter to Philip IV.

By the end of the blighted and ineffectual reign of Charles II 'the Impotent' in 1700, every level of Spanish society had been impoverished by depopulation, economic recession and famine. Even the wealth of the Americas was draining away into Dutch, French and British hands. With Charles's death the Habsburg dynasty ended and, following the ensuing European wars over the Spanish succession (which included another Catalan revolt), the dominions of the crown were eventually apportioned by

the Treaty of Utrecht (1713). The Spanish possessions in Belgium and Italy were ceded to Austria; and a younger branch of the French Bourbons – to which King Juan Carlos belongs – ruled in Madrid. Philip V (1700–46), the grandson of Louis XIV of France, inaugurated a new era of co-operation with France that helped to sustain the Spanish–American Empire for another century.

In the 18th century Spain's economic fortunes gradually improved, particularly through a firmer control of its trade and a more effective use of its South American resources. A less ambitious foreign role in Europe increased the wealth of the crown, and many improvements in industry and agriculture were made in the enlightened reign of Charles III (1759–88). His achievements were not sustained by his successor, Charles IV (1788–1808): government was handed over to an ambitious army officer and the Queen's lover, Manuel Godoy, who allied Spain with the French Republic. A combined Franco–Spanish navy was disastrously defeated at the Battle of Trafalgar in 1805, which was followed in 1808 by the invasion of Spain by Napoleon's armies and the establishment of a régime under his brother Joseph.

The effects on Spain of the War of Independence or Peninsular War (1808–14) were devastating. The north-west of the country became a battleground, and irregular forces, to resist the hated French invader, invented guerrilla (literally, 'little war') tactics. The bravery of the Spanish is recorded to this day, but the damage was irreversible – monasteries and churches were robbed, and towns were razed to the ground. By 1812, successive victories of the combined English, Spanish and Portuguese armies forced Napoleon to recall his troops, and the Bourbons, under Ferdinand VII, were restored to the Spanish throne in 1814.

The history of 19th-century Spain is a protracted and rather tedious saga of *pronunciamentos* (*coups d'état*), executions, exiles and a growing hostility between the forces of liberalism in the towns, and of royal protectionism, which was especially strong in the northern and western areas of the country. Early in the century the American colonies were lost and the death of Ferdinand VII in 1833 sparked another war of succession, between his daughter Queen Isabel II and Ferdinand VII's brother, Don Carlos. Don Carlos eventually lost, but the threat of his followers, the Carlists, continued. Isabel's rule (1843–68) ended with her exile by General Prim, but the failure of the republic saw the monarchy restored once again, under Alfonso XII (1874–85).

The movement of people away from the land and gradual industrialization of the cities placed considerable strain on Spanish unity, and brought into being an urban socialist movement and a rural anarchist party, especially in Andalusia. In 1876 a new constitution was declared, which limited the power of the monarchy. For the next 40 years all successive and rapidly changing governments were faced with the problems of growing regional discontent, the spawning of different working-class movements, anarchist uprisings and strikes. In 1898 revolution in Cuba led to the disastrous Spanish–American War, in which Spain lost her remaining Spanish–American possessions. Inflation and disillusionment were further increased by the effects of the First World War, in which Spain was wisely neutral.

One positive side-effect of the Spanish–American War, however, was the intellectual renaissance it provoked in Spain. This was spearheaded by the *Generation of '98*, whose objective was to rediscover and revive the essence of Spain. Writers, historians and philosophers, including Angel Ganivet (1865–98), Menendez y Pelayo (1856–1912), Miguel Unamuno (1846–1936), José Ortega y Gasset (1883–1955) and others revived Spanish pride in the past and a sense of national tradition. This movement encouraged the brilliant literary achievements of Federico García Lorca (1898–1936) and Antonio Machado (1875–1939), and the art of Pablo Picasso, Juan Miró and Salvador Dalí.

In 1923 General Primo de Rivera staged a military *coup* which brought a period of peace until his death in 1930. In 1931 King Alfonso XIII (1902–31) was forced to abdicate after the victory of the anti-monarchist parties in local elections. A second republic was declared, but this collapsed because of the increased separatism in the provinces, the failure of the Government to fulfil its extravagant promises, and the army's failure to accept socialism. The crisis deepened until 1936 when General Franco's attempted *coup* plunged the country into full-scale civil war. In one of the bloodiest episodes in Spanish history, Nationalist and Republican hostilities raged until Madrid and Barcelona finally surrendered to the Nationalist forces in 1939. General Franco did not spare the lives of his opponents in the aftermath.

Franco's dictatorship kept Spain

Key Dates in Spanish History

BC

14,000–10,000 Paleolithic cave art concentrated in the northern Cordillera Cantábrica and along the Valencian coast.

1,300–600 Iberian tribes and last Bronze-Age cultures in Iberia.

1100 Phoenician and Celtiberian settlements, including Cádiz.

600 Greek settlements and gradual orientalizing of Iberia.

450–350 Height of Iberian and Celtiberian civilization.

237 Carthaginian conquest of southern Spain by Hamilcar Barca. Capital at Cartagena. Defeated by Romans in 206 BC after second Punic War (218–201 BC).

200–27 Iberia conquered and incorporated into Roman Republic.

27 BC–AD 406 Roman Spain, one of the empire's wealthiest provinces, fully integrated into political, economic and social life of the Roman world.

AD

410–415 Visigoths, Vandals, Sueves and Alans invade Iberia.

430–456 Suevic dominion in Spain.

490 Visigothic kingdom established, with capital at Toledo.

587 Visigothic king Reccared converts from Arian to Catholic Christianity. Visigothic and Roman populations form a cultured and politically stable kingdom.

711 Arab invasion of Spain, followed by rapid conquest; their effective control of the Peninsula lasts until 1492. Religious tolerance of Christians and Jews; some cultural interchange.

718/22 Battle of Covadonga – Christian resistance to Arab power in the north established in Asturias. Kings of Asturias rule until 910.

731 At Battle of Poitiers, Arab advance north of the Pyrenees halted by Frankish king Charles Martel.

740 Berber revolts in North Africa and Spain.

750 Assassination of Ummayad caliphate in the East and rise of Abbasids.

755 Abd-ah-Raman I arrives in Spain and establishes Ummayad emirate, which lasts until 929.

Dynastic Houses of the 10th–16th centuries:

929–1031	Ummayad Caliphate
905–1035	Kings of Pamplona
910–1037	Kings of León
801–1137	Counts of Barcelona
1035–1504	Kings of Castile and León
1035–1162	Kings of Aragón
1137–1516	Kings of Aragón and Counts of Barcelona

801 Franks conquer Barcelona.

866–910 Christian repopulation of the Duero valley and Castile.

1037 Unification of Castile and León under Ferdinand I.

1085 Reconquest of Toledo followed in 1086 by invasion of Almoravids, fanatical tribesmen from North Africa.

1137 Portugal declares independence from Spain.

1140 First Cistercian foundations in Spain.

1145/7 End of Almoravid rule; Almohads (similar tribes from North Africa) establish dominance (ends 1230).

c. 1160 Toledo translation school established and foundation of military orders.

1212 Christian victory at Battle of Las Navas de Tolosa. Series of cities fall into Christian hands: Córdoba (1236); Valencia (1238); Murcia (1243); Seville (1248); Cádiz (1265). Two powerful kingdoms of Aragón and Navarre dominate events; Castile politically disunited but wealthy.

1238 Nasrids establish rule in Granada.

1369–1469 Dynastic struggles among royals and nobility in Spain, following the murder of Pedro the Cruel by Henry Trastamara.

1469 Marriage of Ferdinand II of Aragón and Isabella of Castile – Los Reyes Católicos ('the Catholic Monarchs').

1492 Columbus discovers America. Fall of Nasrid Granada. Expulsion of Jews and Moors, leading to lasting cultural impoverishment.

1494 Treaty of Tordesillas between Spain and Portugal defines spheres of New World conquest.

1513 Discovery of Pacific Ocean by Vasco Núñez de Balboa; conquest of Mexico (1519); conquest of Peru (1531).

1516 Habsburg Charles I of Spain (Emperor Charles V of the Holy Roman Empire) ascends to the Spanish throne (abdicates 1556, dies 1558). Problems of foreign wars and religious upheavals of the Reformation beset reign.

1556–98 Reign of King Philip II. He saw himself as champion of Catholic authority against Protestant heresy and the Islamic world. Spain's empire expanded to include most of South America, and vast riches flowed back to Spain, to be used in Philip's wars.

1571 Defeat of Turkish sea power at Battle of Lepanto. Spanish Armada defeated by the English in 1588. Beginning of struggle for independence from Spain in the Netherlands.

1581 Philip ascends to Portuguese throne and New World dominions.

1598–1621 Reign of Philip III. Expulsion of Moors

1609. Wars of previous reign had exhausted Spain's vast wealth, leaving her increasingly weak in the face of the growing power of France.

1621–65 Reign of Philip IV. Government maintained by the chief minister, the Count-Duke Olivares.

1640 Portugal regains her independence.

1665–1700 Charles II 'the Bewitched' dies without an heir. End of Habsburg dynasty.

1700–13 War of Spanish Succession; European powers fight over Spanish throne. Treaty of Utrecht divides Spain's European possessions.

1700–46 Reign of Philip V, grandson of Louis XIV of France, begins Bourbon dynasty; Ferdinand VI (1746–59); 'Enlightened reign' of Charles III (1759–83); Charles IV's (1788–1806) policy of alliance with the French Republic under Napoleon led to the disastrous Spanish–French naval defeat at Trafalgar (1805), followed by the French invasion of Spain and the establishment of Joseph Bonaparte on the Spanish throne.

1808–14 War of Independence (Peninsular War). The French eventually defeated, at great cost to Spain.

1812 Constitution of Cádiz.

1814–33 Bourbon restoration under Ferdinand VII.

19th C Great political instability and social upheavals, accompanied by repression.

1833–41 Regency of María Cristina. First Carlist War (1833–40).

1841–3 Regency of Espartero.

1843–68 Isabel II.

1868–70 Republic.

1870–3 Amadeus of Savoy.

1873–4 Republic.

1874–85 Alfonso XII.

1885–1902 Regency of Cristina.

1898 Revolution in Cuba. Following Spanish–American War, Spain lost her remaining South American possessions. At home, defeat led to intellectual renaissance with 'Generation of '98', including Picasso, Dalí, Lorca, Miró, etc.

1902–31 Alfonso XIII.

1931–6 Republic, beset by constant political and social divisions.

1936 Fascist coup led by General Franco.

1936–9 Spanish Civil War.

1939–75 Dictatorship of Franco.

1975 Death of Franco. Third Bourbon restoration under King Juan Carlos I; begins transition to democracy.

1978 New Spanish constitution and devolution into 17 autonomous regions.

1982 Overwhelming victory of Socialists under Felipe Gozález in general elections.

1986 Spain joins European Community.

1992 Barcelona Olympics and Expo '92.

ostensibly neutral in the Second World War, although a certain amount of help reached the Axis forces. Economic disaster and diplomatic isolation were alleviated somewhat in the 1950s by the gradually improving relationship between Franco and the US. The installation of American military airbases in Spain and the political recognition of Franco's régime encouraged foreign economic confidence, though rapid inflation forced many Spaniards, especially those from the remoter provinces, to seek work overseas or in other parts of Europe. At the same time, mass coastal tourism emerged as the country's fastest-expanding industry, and agricultural development projects were set up to improve farming in many of the poorer districts. Franco's long, uneventful rule and his plans for the restoration of the monarchy gradually cooled the passions of the Civil War.

There remained, however, considerable anti-Government sentiment in the illegal Communist Party, in a variety of social democratic parties and among Basque and Catalan nationalists, whose activities were increasing at the time of Franco's death in 1975. His chosen successor, King Juan Carlos I, wisely embarked on a process of constitutional democratization. In 1978 a constitution laid down the guidelines for the devolution of much power to 17 autonomous local governments. Spain was the first country in the post-war world to replace totalitarianism with democracy through peaceful elections, and its integration into Europe was confirmed in the 1980s with entry into the European Community.

Architecture

Apart from the earliest Paleolithic cave dwellings, with their remarkably graphic rock paintings, the *talayots* of Minorca and massive dolmens scattered throughout the mainland, little remains from the earliest colonies beyond the exhibits in archeological museums. Later colonists such as the Carthaginians and Greeks built on Phoenician foundations, and established new cities throughout the Mediterranean. Strong traces of their settlements can be seen clearly at Ibiza and Empúries (Ampurias), while the most persistent testament to Iberian ingenuity are the great unhewn blocks of stone in the walls of Tarragona.

Following the defeat of the Carthaginians by Scipio Africanus towards the end of the third century BC, Rome bequeathed to Spain an enduring knowledge of constructional engineering. The fourth-largest amphitheatre in the Roman world was built in the city of Itálica on the outskirts of Seville. The bridge crossing the Guadiana in the provincial town of Mérida is the longest in existence from classical times, and the town has preserved a Roman theatre, circus, amphitheatre, triumphal arch, two temples, two reservoirs and three aqueducts. Elsewhere in the central tableland lie ruins of luxury villas and towns such as Segobriga, which once lay at the centre of rich farming estates. In La Coruña, the Torre de Hércules, an imposing Roman lighthouse, is still in use, as are the bridge at Alcántara and the great aqueduct at Segovia, which is more than 1 km in length and supported by 118 double-tier arches. Other important remains include the walls of Lugo, Ourense (Orense) and Tarragona, while every archeological museum in the Peninsula holds impressive artistic remains from this age.

The Visigoths, entering Iberia by way of northern Italy and southern France, brought with them an early form of Romanesque that was strongly influenced by the East. The few surviving churches were based on the Greek cross. Windows were filled with marble slabs pierced with geometrical patterns known as *transennae*, and crude ornamentation was generally in the form of cable borders, swastikas, Maltese crosses or more Syrian motifs such as discs, stars, helixes and rosettes. The most lasting contribution of Visigothic architecture was the constructional incorporation of the horseshoe arch into many buildings. Impressive remains are to be seen at the Visigothic capital of Toledo; in the dark crypt of Palencia Cathedral; the royal foundation of San Juan at Baños de Cerrato; in the southern reaches of Ourense at Santa Comba de Bande; and in Quintanilla de las Viñas in Toledo.

After the Arab conquest of Iberia, Visigothic methods of building were maintained by the Asturian princes under the influence of the Carolingian court, and a unique style developed in the remotest reaches of Asturias around Oviedo. The ninth-century Asturian churches – so prodigiously decorated and magnificently preserved – constitute one of the great wonders of early medieval European architecture. The purest examples of this pre-Romanesque form are San Miguel de Lillo and Santa María del Naranco, erected during the reign of Ramiro I (842–50).

With the establishment of an emirate at Córdoba, Islamic architectural details reached Spain from the cultural centres of the Muslim Empire, such as Baghdad. In various forms this style has remained an influential force to the present day. Many of the great city fortifications, such as those at Seville, Almería, Ronda and Málaga, date from this early period, as does the mosque at Córdoba, improved and extended by successive Caliphs. Arabic interior decoration was intense and colourful. Features included walls covered in richly inlaid arabesques; interwoven designs and geometric patterns; iridescent, metallic-coloured tiles; and the use of water and fountains to create architectural cohesion. All these details were introduced by the Arabs but they remained part of Spanish architecture until well after the defeat of the last Moorish enclave at Granada in 1492. Muslim architecture was concerned with private tranquillity and relaxation, and to this end the garden patio became the central core of the dwelling.

Innovative building methods whose origins can be traced to the mosque at Córdoba included ultra-semicircular, multifoil and intersecting arching and vaulting with parallel ribs – all methods which subsequently spread throughout medieval Europe. The other great building of this period, whose destruction marked the end of the Caliphate, was the palace city of Medina az-Zahra on the outskirts of Córdoba (see p. 284).

The hybrid style generally termed Mozarabic is a combination of Christian and Muslim artistic and architectural ingenuity. Only two rather ruined churches built by Christians under Muslim hegemony have survived: Santa María de Melque south of Toledo, and Bobastro north of Alora in the province of Málaga. There are more examples of extant Mozarabic architecture in the north, which date to the centuries following the persecution of Christians under Mohammed I (852–86). Small bands of Christian refugees fled to obscure corners of northern Spain, where they founded diminutive mosque-like chapels in this style. The most impressive examples are San Miguel de Escalada near León; San Baudelio de Berlanga near the River Duero in Soria; Santiago de Peñalba in León; and San Miguel de Celanova in Galicia.

The Romanesque style was introduced with the growing momentum of the Christian reconquest, and was the first great architectural form to be adopted throughout Western Europe. It appeared at the end of the first millennium, as the Carolingian Empire was dissolving and the earliest European nations were taking shape. Propagated by the emerging monastic and religious orders and the spirit of pilgrimage and crusade, it quickly swept from Dalmatia to the British Isles and from Scandinavia to Iberia. It was a blend of architectural traditions of the Roman Empire, updated by Carolingian methods. It lasted in Spain well into the 13th century, and its solid and sober lines characterize all buildings of the age – churches, monasteries, castles, villages and bridges – as well as sculpture and stone carvings.

Romanesque was also bound closely to the growing interest in early Western European philosophy and theology, legal codes, poetry and the emergence of Romance languages deriving from vulgar Latin. The earliest buildings using this style appeared in Catalonia, and their form was strongly influenced by contemporary techniques in Languedoc, Provence and

Lombardy. San Clemente and Santa María de Tahull, tucked away in the obscurity of the Pyrenees, show how far Romanesque penetrated into the region, while the splendour of the Benedictine abbey of Ripoll shows how elaborately the form was interpreted. It developed very differently in Castile and along the Camino to Santiago, where Benedictine monastic traditions from the French regions of Auvergnat, Aquitaine, Burgundy, Poitevin and Angevin prevailed. The pilgrim road to Santiago became the catalyst for the explosion of Romanesque architecture that occurred throughout northern Spain between the 11th and 13th centuries. In general, Romanesque architecture of this region has a more robust appearance, as it had to serve both a religious and defensive role in the community. Groundplans were based on the basilica. Stone rather than timber roofs produced long narrow naves with stone vaulting and domes, while capitals, porticoes and tympana were richly embellished with carvings and sculpture, usually with an apocalyptic theme.

The north of the Peninsula is littered with Romanesque churches, and the finest examples of the style can be seen throughout the Pyrenees at the cathedral of Jaca; at San Martín de Fromista; in the pantheon of San Isidro at León; the magnificent cloister to the monastery of Santo Domingo de Silos; and the great basilica of the cathedral at Santiago. By the 12th century the regional characteristics of Romanesque had developed a style peculiar to a number of different areas of Spain, especially in Galicia, Zamora, Salamanca, Segovia and Avila.

In 1131 the first Cistercian monks arrived in Iberia and over the next 150 years their order founded 60 abbeys and monasteries, including Poblet and Santa Creus in Catalonia, Las Huelgas at Burgos, Veruela in Aragón and La Oliva in Navarre. The sobriety and severity of Cistercian Romanesque architecture and design were enhanced by lineal majesty, and the earliest principles of Gothic architecture can be detected in the innovative forms of vaulting used in many of these constructions.

Spanish Gothic was introduced on the back of Cistercian Romanesque. During the 13th century French master builders and masons travelled to Spain to seek the patronage of bishops, and French Gothic made its appearance in the Peninsula in the inspired shape of the great cathedrals of Burgos, León and Toledo. Apart from other cathedrals, however, little civil Gothic architecture appeared in Castile until the 15th century. Matters were different for the Aragonese–Catalan seaborne empire. The Gothic style was prevalent in this powerful and materialistic region, and was used extensively for both civic and religious buildings. Churches capable of holding congregations of several thousand people were built, and an unobscured view of the altar and a wide columnless vault became the supreme considerations of architects. The great hall-churches and cathedrals at Girona, Barcelona and Palma de Mallorca are all magnificent examples of Catalan Gothic, and the civic architecture like the *lonjas* (exchanges) in Zaragoza and Palma de Mallorca show how the form was adapted for civil use.

With the collapse of the Caliphate in 1031, the Christian offensive pushed gradually south and was stopped only by the intervention of fanatical Berber

The Archbishop's palace at Osuna in Seville is an extravagant example of southern Baroque architecture; a style that spread from Italy to Spain and then to the Americas. Incafo

tribesmen from North Africa. The rule of these Maghribian dynasties – the Almoravids and Almohads – left few buildings, but those that have survived are magnificent. Seville ousted Córdoba as the new capital of Al-Andalus and the minaret there, later christened the Giralda (1184–96) and now joined to the cathedral, is one of the most impressive examples of Maghribian architectural ingenuity to be seen. Also in Seville the Patio de Yeso shows how interior decoration was the preferred medium for the skills of Muslim craftsmen: walls wainscoted with coloured tiles and Cufic inscriptions; *artesonados* (wooden ceilings intricately inlaid with star-patterning); and the use of finely carved stucco all combined to create a luxurious atmosphere perfect for hours of private pleasure, contemplation and repose. The most impressive examples of late Maghribian architecture, comparable to any Muslim building in the Islamic world, are the palaces of the Alhambra and Generalife, on a towering promontory overlooking Granada.

From a further cross-fertilization of Muslim and Christian cultures came the second vernacular architectural style of Spain, Mudéjar, a hybrid form adopting both Christian and Muslim elements. Even after the reconquest of large areas of the country, the character of many towns remained Islamic and Muslims, offering cheap labour and skills in carpentry, bricklaying and ornamental plasterwork, continued to live and work under Christian jurisdiction. Toledo and Teruel possess the most gracious examples of this style, easily identifiable by minaret-like towers, decorated brick- and tilework and carved wooden ceilings, although all the major towns of the central *Meseta* feature examples of the work.

Christian kings and nobles tried to emulate the luxury and comfort of Muslim interiors in their palaces and homes. Pedro 'the Cruel' built the *alcázar* in Seville, using architects from the Alhambra, and the private palaces of the Casa de Pilato and Casa de las Dueñas show how this fusion of Western and Oriental sensibilities continued well into the 16th century.

The constantly changing frontiers in the long crusade against Islam, and the later internecine struggles of the nobility, necessitated the construction of imposing castles and fortifications. The Arabs built *alcázars* and citadels to consolidate their new territories, many of which were subsequently taken over by Christian rulers. The two most magnificent Romanesque examples of defensive architecture are the walls of Avila and the fortress of Loarre in Aragón, but castles from all periods, mixing all styles, are found throughout Spain. In the 14th and 15th centuries powerful noble families exerting local sovereignty built ominous *castillos* to protect their great estates. Later fortifications of a less oppressive appearance were constructed, often strongly influenced by Mudéjar work, such as the brick-built *castillos* of Coca and Medina del Campo. Towards the end of the 15th century, as towns became the new centres of power, the nobility built grandiose town palaces instead, and the *castillos* were abandoned to the elements.

The late Gothic style saw the construction of cathedrals at Salamanca, Seville and Segovia, all of which are remarkable for their soaring structures, massive proportions and restrained decoration. Great spires were added to the cathedrals of Burgos and Toledo by builders from Germany, Holland and Burgundy. Gothic elements continued to be used by Spanish architects until the 18th century, when the movement was carried to the New World by Franciscan, Augustinian and Dominican monks who erected Gothic-influenced churches.

The last period of Gothic saw constructional perfection superseded by ostentatious surface ornamentation. Gothic Plateresque or Isabelline architecture allowed the Spanish to indulge their love of flights of fantasy. Façades were festooned with low-relief ornamentation. The term Plateresque derives from the word *platería* (silversmith), and alludes to the delicate masonry covering the façades of many of the buildings decorated in this style. Architecture was plied with surface sculpture in imitation of retables and altarpieces. The church of San Juan de los Reyes at Toledo, intended to be the last resting place of the Catholic monarchs; the Palacio del Infantado, home to the emergent Mendoza family; and the House of Shells in Salamanca, built for the Master of the Order of Santiago, are all good examples of this architectural style.

Plateresque forms slowly yielded to the influence of the Italian Renaissance, which arrived in Catalonia, Aragón and Valencia before reaching Castile. Early sculptural work imported from Italy – especially tombs carved from Carrara marble – became highly fashionable among the nobility, and the symbolism of Plateresque gave way to more classical and Renaissance designs. Façades maintained their Gothic proportions but were rusticated in a Florentine manner, adopting motifs such as medallions, grotesques,

garlands, fruit and flowers. The seemingly limitless supplies of gold and silver enabled many magnificent later Plateresque buildings to be commissioned: the Palace of the Dukes of Medinaceli at Cogolludo, the front of the Royal Hospital at Santiago de Compostela, and the University of Salamanca are three of the finest examples. Of a more classically Italian inspiration were the Palace of Charles V beside the Alhambra in Granada and the Tavera Hospital on the edge of Toledo.

From the end of the 16th century, it is the colossal monastic palace of El Escorial which typifies an utterly Spanish Renaissance form. Built for Philip II, the palace's severe dimensions inaugurated the final phase of Spanish Renaissance architecture and gave birth to a style generally referred to as Herreran after Juan de Herrera, its founding architect. Buildings were stripped of all unnecessary ornament and came to reflect the more austere and catholic sentiments of counter-Reformation Spain.

Following the death of Philip II in 1598, Italian Mannerism and Baroque architecture gained popularity as a reaction against the formality and austere style (*estilo desornamentado*) of Herrera. Once again flamboyance and ornamentation became popular. Compositions verged on the theatrical: columns were twisted, curves broke the formal line of all buildings and, as Bernard Bevan wrote in his classic account of Spanish architecture, 'Spanish Baroque was certainly emotional, and inspired, and perhaps even intoxicated.' Many of the most extravagant and fantastical of these designs were carried out by the family of José de Churriguera, a carpenter and retablemaker, and the style is generally termed Churrigueresque. The most impressive examples include the Transparente in Toledo cathedral, the university façade at Valladolid, La Cartuja in Granada and the Plaza Mayor in Salamanca. Even more fantastic manifestations exist in Mexico, where the style remained popular well into this century.

The Bourbon kings were naturally influenced by the tastes of the French court, and Baroque architecture quickly fell out of favour after 1700. Instead, the royal palaces of La Granja, Aranjuez and Madrid were built on a scale comparable to the Palace of Versailles. In 1744 the establishment of an academy for architects effectively led to a long period of sterility in the country's architecture. All public buildings were obliged to meet with the approval of the Royal Academy, and thus began a long period of inert neoclassicism that produced only a few great architects, among them Ventura Rodriguez and Juan de Villanueva.

Neoclassicism lasted well into the 19th century, until a small group of mainly Catalan architects, under the patronage of some progressive industrialists, rejected the dictates of Vetruvius. They were guided by contemporary passions for medievalism spread by the work of John Ruskin and Viollet de Duc and under their influence the *Modernismo* movement began (see p. 55). This was arguably the most outrageous of all the *Belle Epoque* movements which included French *Art Nouveau*, Italian *Liberty* and German *Jugendstil*. Lluis Domènech i Mortaner, Joseph Puig i Cadafalch and Antoni Gaudí i Cornet – together with other architects, painters, sculptors and

smiths – adopted industrial-age design and worked towards an utterly original style. The whole architectural heritage of Spain was re-examined and, through the extensive use of tiles, laminated brickwork and colourful exteriors, the Islamic influence was reasserted. Symbolism, which included merlons, shields, angels and gargoyles as well as bicycles, light bulbs, gramophones and cameras, linked the neo-Gothic with the New Age. Modernist architects sought the *obra total* (the total work), a consummation of all art forms – both inside and out – so the building became an organic whole and could be judged by artistic criteria as well as in functional terms. The majority of Modernist buildings are to be seen in Barcelona and Catalonia, although many fine examples can be admired elsewhere along the Levante; in the resort town of Comillas; and in Madrid, Zaragoza and Palma de Mallorca.

Post-Civil-War architecture was often as grandiose as Herreran but even more lacklustre, overbearing and conservative, and the years of Franco's dictatorship produced little of positive consequence; cityscapes were often ruined by sprawling high-rise suburbs and magnificent stretches of the coast were indelibly stained by horrendous concrete conurbations. In the last decade there has been a gradual move towards conservation, while many of the modern buildings in Madrid and Barcelona attest to a new post-Modernist school – as good as any in Europe – that has emerged quickly from Spain's recent conversion to democracy. There are no better examples of this than the new exhibition spaces such as the Joan Miró Foundation in Barcelona, the Museum

The castillo *of Loarre in Aragón is the most steadfast example of early crusader architecture. The castle-church, surrounded by its curtain wall, commands an immense view over the flatlands of the Ebro depression.* Angus Mitchell

of Roman Art in Mérida and many of the new buildings along the Castellana in Madrid.

Spanish architecture has always tended to fluctuate between periods of excessive flamboyance – Mudéjar, Plateresque, Churrigueresque and Modernism – and excessive austerity – Cistercianism, Herreran and neoclassicism. Regional differences prevent any coherent or logical development and you will undoubtedly discover many inconsistencies on your travels, such as 17th-century Gothic and 18th-century Renaissance. But though the country has adopted styles from elsewhere in Europe, this has not prevented a distinctively Spanish form from developing. Strong stylistic differences exist between the regions, especially in the case of Catalonia and Castile, and it should not be forgotten that the medieval architecture of the country was the product of two civilizations: Islamic and Christian. The former's architectural style was bound closely to ideals of pleasure, relaxation and private paradise while the latter's was the result of hostility and reconquest. The amalgamation of these styles is what gives many buildings that exotic Spanish touch.

Climate

Average Monthly Temperatures

	Jan	Feb	Mar	Apr	May	Jun	Jul	Aug	Sep	Oct	Nov	Dec
Galicia	8.3	8.8	11.1	12.7	14.5	17.4	19.4	19.8	17.9	14.6	11.1	8.7
Cantábrica region (Asturias, Cantabria, Vizcaya, Guipúzcoa)	8.8	8.7	11.2	12.1	12.9	16.9	17.8	19.3	18.1	15.0	12.1	9.3
Castile-León	2.9	4.4	7.6	10.0	13.0	17.6	20.6	20.3	17.2	10.6	6.9	3.3
Madrid, Castile-La Mancha	4.5	6.1	9.5	12.0	15.5	20.6	24.3	23.7	19.6	13.9	8.7	5.5
Extremadura	8.1	9.5	12.2	14.8	17.7	22.6	25.9	25.5	22.4	17.3	12.1	8.6
Aragón, Rioja, Navarre, Alava	4.4	5.7	9.2	11.4	14.7	18.6	21.0	20.9	18.4	13.4	8.5	5.4
Catalonia	8.6	9.7	11.7	14.3	17.3	21.2	23.9	24.0	21.6	17.2	12.8	9.6
Levant	10.3	11.0	13.1	14.8	17.8	21.7	24.1	24.6	22.5	18.4	14.3	11.1
Sureste region (Alicante, Murcia)	10.8	11.7	14.1	15.9	19.3	23.1	25.7	26.2	23.7	19.1	14.8	11.9
Cuenca del Guadalquivir (Cádiz, Córdoba, Granada, Jaén, Seville)	9.5	10.9	13.3	15.5	18.4	22.9	26.1	26.0	23.2	18.3	13.8	10.4
Costa Sur (Almería, Huelva, Málaga)	11.8	12.3	14.5	16.9	18.9	22.4	25.0	25.3	23.4	19.5	16.0	12.6
Balearics	10.2	10.5	12.2	14.3	16.4	21.3	24.1	24.4	22.5	18.3	14.3	11.7
Canaries	17.4	17.5	18.2	19.2	20.4	22.4	24.2	24.7	24.1	22.7	20.5	18.4
Ceuta, Melilla	12.0	12.1	13.3	14.9	16.8	19.7	22.1	22.8	21.3	18.6	15.4	13.0

Temperature in °C

Documentation

Passports remain the most widely accepted form of identification, although EC members' passports are no longer stamped as they travel into and out of Spain. Americans do not need visas but Australians and New Zealanders do, and in recent years the authorities have tightened up control on this front. Loss of documents should be reported immediately to the nearest consulate and police station.

Holiday insurance is always worthwhile when travelling in Spain. Medical insurance can be arranged in advance with the NHS for UK citizens (see p. 26).

Currency and Banks

Spain's economic boom years of the late 1980s made the peseta the strongest European currency after the Deutschmark, and consequently prices in the more popular coastal resorts in recent years have risen sharply. In less touristic areas prices are a lot lower, and it is still possible to eat and drink extremely cheaply if you are prepared to sacrifice your creature comforts.

The basic unit of currency is the peseta, and coins are issued in denominations of one, five (often referred to as a *duro*), 25, 50, 100 (sometimes referred to as a *nota*), 200 and 500 pesetas; and in notes in denominations of 1,000, 2,000, 5,000 and 10,000 pesetas.

Banks, large department stores, travel agents and hotels are the usual places to exchange money. This can be a problem at weekends, especially Sundays, but there are 24-hour services at most airports and the larger railway stations. *Bureaux de change* are opening up in the larger and most popular tourist destinations and cities, although their commissions remain exorbitant.

Travellers' cheques are no problem to exchange and Eurocheques are even more efficient. Many UK banks issue a Eurocheque card which co-ordinates with machines to be found in cities and major towns throughout Europe. Leading credit cards are accepted in all the major hotels, restaurants and shops in Spain.

For those who intend to spend some time in Spain or who visit the country frequently, it is perhaps worth opening a pesetas account at any of the leading Spanish banks. You will be issued with a chequebook enabling you to cash a cheque at any branch of your chosen bank in the country. You are not allowed to overdraw and you will receive no credit card facilities.

Banking hours are 8.30/9am–1/2pm Monday to Friday, while many banks in the larger cities are open on Satur-days except during the summer.

Luxury goods generally include six per cent IVA (Value Added Tax) in the price, although in some restaurants and hotels this may not be the case and a surcharge will be added to the bill.

Tipping

Many hotels include *servicio* (service charge) in the bill, but a small tip of between five and ten per cent of the total is always expected if the service has been good. In bars it is customary to leave a token tip of between five and 25 pesetas if you've had a drink and *tapas*.

Taxi drivers should be tipped around ten per cent above the charge shown on the meter, and this percentage can be applied to any situation which you think is appropriate.

When shown into a church or monument by a sacristan or local guide you will be expected to give a small 'show of thanks' for their efforts. About 100 pesetas per person is generally correct, although this can often depend on the enthusiasm and help offered by the guide.

Language

Castellano is the national tongue of Spain, but three other main languages exist: Gallego, Catalá and *Euskera* (Basque), as well as seven associated dialects. With the move towards greater autonomy, there has been a corresponding drive to reassert local languages, which has been most evident in Catalonia and the Basque Country. Both these regions have television stations broadcasting in their own language, and many street-signs and tourist information pamphlets are being changed accordingly.

Every year English is becoming more and more widely spoken. In the Mediterranean resorts, in large urban centres and many restaurants, you will encounter a high percentage of English-speaking Spaniards. Nevertheless, it is appreciated if you try to speak Castellano. Remember the Spanish alphabet is different; in a dictionary, words beginning with a 'ch-' are found after 'C' and those beginning with 'll-' appear after 'L'.

Tourist Information

The Spanish Tourist Board prides itself on the quality of its pamphlets and, though the information they contain can be a little exaggerated, the maps and city plans are generally excellent. Tourist offices will also supply information on local *fiestas* and help you find accommodation when requested. Autonomies have also started to produce their own, more detailed, regional information which is available at the regional or municipal tourist offices in all provincial capitals. Details of main provincial tourist offices are given in the practical information section at the end of each chapter in this book.

National tourist information can be obtained from the Spanish Tourist Board in the UK at: 57–8 St James's Street, London SW1, tel (071) 499 0901. Or in the USA at: 665 Fifth Avenue, New York, NY 100 22, tel 212–759 8822.

Telephones

There is a good public telephone network throughout Spain and, as long as the phone hasn't been vandalized, you can generally make international calls from anywhere in the country. Instructions are normally displayed in English and other languages inside the booth. They function with 25-, 50- and 100-peseta coins. For a local call a 25-peseta coin is normally enough for a short conversation. For international dialling you'll need around 400 pesetas. To make an international STD call, first dial 07 and wait for the international dialling code signal. Dial the code for the country, followed by the regional code and the number.

Most bars have telephones, often linked to meters and, though they save the bother of loose change, they are on the whole more expensive.

Major cities and many resort towns have central exchanges where you give the number to the operator, who then places your call direct to an allocated booth.

Hotel telephones are generally wildly overpriced.

The code for Spain from any other country in the world is 34.

Post

There are more than 6,000 post offices in Spain and those in Madrid, Barcelona and Bilbao and at the major international airports give 24-hour service. Stamps can also be bought at *estancos* (tobacconists). Pillarboxes are yellow. The fastest way of sending a letter is *Registrado/Urgente* (Registered Urgent), which should arrive within three working days to other European countries or within five to the US. Several other services are offered by post offices, including *Poste Restante* and a same-day money delivery. Normal hours are 8am–2pm and 5–7.30pm.

Time

George Orwell said in *Homage to Catalonia*: 'In Spain nothing, from a meal to a battle, ever happens at the appointed time', and certainly part of the mystery of travelling in Spain is to adjust yourself to the Spanish clock. Though banks, international companies and some administrative departments are slowly adapting to the north European way of life, the Spanish attitude remains the norm. Shops generally open in the morning 9am–1/2pm and reopen 4.30/5–7/8pm. Banks are open only 9am–1/2pm.

Mealtimes in Spain are generally much later than in other countries:

8–11am Breakfast – coffee, fruit juice, toast or *churros* (large sticks of deep-fried dough)

1pm Pre-lunch *tapas* and drink (see p. 27)

2–3pm Large three-course lunch followed by *siesta*

5–6pm Tea, coffee, chocolate, and *churros* or pastries

8–10pm Evening *tapas*

10–11pm Dinner

The afternoon *siesta* and the evening pre-dinner drink and *tapas* are highly civilized national habits which will never die, and are as much a part of Spanish culture as unpunctuality. Nocturnal hours are equally flexible: Madrid, the late-night capital of Europe, can have traffic jams in the city centre at 3 or 4am.

Museums are generally open daily except Monday 10am–2pm and 4–7pm. Cathedrals open daily and their museums keep the same hours as above.

Security

As in any other country, negligent tourists are easy prey for the petty criminal. But the reputation Spain has in some foreign countries as a hotbed of small-time crime is exaggerated. Security in the *Costas* during high season has been substantially reinforced in the last few years, and this improvement has been extended to many of the larger cities such as Madrid, Seville and Barcelona. There do, however, remain areas in these cities and others where the old-time pickpockets and thieves continue to make a good living. Bag-snatching on motorbikes is a favourite pastime among delinquents of Andalusia; and expensive-looking necklaces are liable to be ripped from people's necks in broad daylight. When travelling by Metro late at night you should be sure to stay in the company of other passengers. But Spanish criminals are not generally violent unless provoked, and even then they tend to run away. Acts of wanton violence are rare, and it may be of some comfort to know that five crimes are committed in England to every one in Spain. Good hotels have safes where any valuables can be deposited for a nominal sum.

There are three police forces in Spain: the *Policía Nacional*, recognizable by their brown uniforms; the *Policía Municipal*, who deal with urban traffic problems, patrol the streets and are the most likely to handle any problem you may have; and the *Guardia Civil*, who patrol the highways and countryside. The Basques and Navarrese have their own regional police forces, distinguishable by their red berets.

Water and Medical

No inoculations are required for Spain. Spain has free reciprocal medical schemes with all EC countries. The form required is an E111, which you must fill in and return to your local Department of Health office two weeks before your departure. Nevertheless, it is wise to take out a general insurance policy for the duration of your stay to cover yourself against theft and so on.

Farmacias will help with any small medical problems and can supply you with basic drugs for minor ailments. Tourist offices will have addresses of local English-speaking doctors if you need one.

Water can be drunk almost anywhere, although tap water in Barcelona and a few of the coastal resorts can have a strong chemical taste. In late summer, when reservoirs are low, you should buy bottled water to be safe. *No Potable* means do not drink the water. On the whole, however, the water is fine and even Madrid, though landlocked, has possibly the best tap water of any capital city in Europe.

Accommodation

The standard of accommodation at all levels in Spain is generally good. Although what you can expect depends entirely upon the grading of the establishment, everything from a one-star pension to a five-star hotel is rated by a governmental body, thus ensuring a high level of quality and fair prices.

Apart from *fiesta* times, when the situation can be impossible, there is normally no problem finding accommodation in most towns and cities in

Spain at any time of the year. Often it is only amenities such as the state of decoration and the cotton content in the bedclothes that distinguish *hostales* costing 2,500 pesetas from three-star hotels charging 5,000 pesetas.

The official governmental price should be displayed inside every room, and by law must be updated each year. This control has helped maintain a high standard, although now many of the package-tour hotels along the *Costas*, in an attempt to cut costs and keep prices down, are often highly overrated for the standard of service they offer.

Blue plaques beside doorways indicate the kind of accommodation on offer. (H) indicates a hotel. *Hotel Residencias* (HR), mainly found in large cities and normally used by business travellers, offer rooms for prolonged stays. *Hostales* (HS) and *Pensiones* (P) are the best form of budget accommodation. In terms of amenities, they offer a basic but perfectly adequate standard of accommodation for a few nights. Rooms will generally be priced according to whether or not there is a private bathroom. Prices range from about 1,500 pesetas for a basic double room without bathroom, to 3,500 pesetas for a double with bath.

Hostales are often grouped together in specific parts of town, sometimes near the railway station but often in the very centre beside the Plaza Mayor. On the whole, it is best to ask to see a room before you decide whether or not to take it, as this generally forces the management to show you the best they have available.

Double beds are uncommon in Spain and almost nonexistent in *hostales*. Where a *matrimonio* room can be found, the price will again be higher. Prices also vary between the high and low seasons. In general, the high season includes the summer months, Christmas, Holy Week and the local *fiestas*. High season in mountainous areas catering for winter sports is between November and March.

Paradors

The most elegant way of travelling through Spain is to stay at the state-owned network of 86 hotels, the paradors, which offer one of the best luxury accommodation bargains to be found in Europe. Many are located in historic buildings, and offer different amenities according to their star rating. Every room has a private bathroom, and the standard of service is generally very high. The restaurant meals are often not as good as the breakfasts, when no expense is spared and an early-morning banquet is provided.

You are required to arrive before 8pm on the day of your reservation, or to ring if you intend to arrive later. Receptionists often speak English and will be happy to make subsequent reservations to fit in with your personal itinerary. Alternatively, there is a central booking office in Madrid at Velázquez 18, tel (91) 435 97 00/435 97 44.

All accommodation in the practical information sections has been rated as follows:

Category A: 15,000–20,000 pesetas
B: 10,000–15,000 pesetas
C: 5,000–10,000 pesetas
D: 3,000–5,000 pesetas
E: Under 3,000 pesetas

Food

Few countries in the world can boast of such a wide selection and variety of food products as Spain and, even though the country has never been acclaimed for its cuisine in the way of, say, France or Italy, this attitude is rapidly changing. The emergence in recent years of *tapas* bars in all major world capitals is just one example of how other nations are finally beginning to appreciate Spanish attitudes to food. Regional autonomy has also fuelled something of a revival in local *cocina casera* (home cooking) but, before looking at the different types of regional cookery, it is first worth saying something of Spanish eating habits in general.

The first cafés open for *desayuno* (breakfast) at around 8am and the typical menu might include a large cup of *café con leche* (white coffee) or hot 'chocolate' and *zumo de naranja* (freshly squeezed orange juice), accompanied by a plate of *churros*, a *tostada* (piece of lightly fried toast), or a *pincho de tortilla* (slice of Spanish omelette).

The mid-morning or pre-lunch *tapas* (see p. 30) are taken between midday and 1pm and consist of light snacks of whatever it takes to stem your appetite before lunch (*la comida*). Lunch is generally the major meal of the day, and consists of three courses accompanied by wine. Restaurants are obliged to offer a *menu del día* (daily menu) which is normally the cheapest way to eat. The set price will include *pan* (bread), *postre* (dessert) and *vino* (wine). It is not necessarily the case that money buys quality; quite often, cheap food cooked for a local clientele far outweighs that to be found in overpriced tourist haunts.

The evening *tapas* are intended to whet your appetite before dinner (*la cena*), which is generally but not always lighter than lunch.

In the information at the end of each section, restaurants have been graded as follows:

Category A: 5,000 pesetas and over
B: 4,000–5,000 pesetas
C: 3,000–4,000 pesetas
D: 2,000–3,000 pesetas
E: Under 2,000 pesetas

Regional Cuisine

Spanish cooking is the result of centuries of refinement. The earliest recipes are to be found in the 14th- and 15th-century records of the monastic foundations of the north. Two of the earliest cookery books in Europe were the 14th-century *Llibre de Sent Sovi* written in Catalá and the *Tractado del Arte de Cortar con el Cuchillo* (Treatise on the Art of Carving with a Knife) by Enrique de Villena composed in 1423. The Arab occupation bequeathed a lasting sweet-tooth to the nation, and many of the almond- and honey-based pastries, as well as the rice-based dishes, are directly descended from Moorish recipes. The discovery of the New World introduced several important ingredients to the European table via Spain, including green and red peppers, tomatoes, potatoes, maize and chocolate. Nevertheless, in every region of Spain, cooking has a strong identity of its own. Perhaps what sets Spanish cooking apart from that of other European countries is the lack of 18th-century French influence, which has helped maintain the peasant roots of the Spanish table. These roots derive from the classic Roman basics of

wheat, olives and wine, and these remain the staple diet in many rural regions.

On the most fundamental level, it is said that the people of the north stew, Castilians roast and Andalusians fry, but ingredients and customs differ from region to region, province to province, and even from one village to another. Olive oil and garlic form the basis for a great many Mediterranean recipes; and food tends to be butter- and milk-based and more substantial in the colder Atlantic regions.

There are, of course, dishes which you will find on menus nationwide – gazpacho, tortilla, paella, Serrano ham and the paprika-flavoured *chorizo* sausage are the more obvious examples – but all have strong regional origins. The sheer variety of natural ingredients is the most striking feature of Spanish cooking. A huge choice of fish and seafood is available at any time of year, and butchers sell every last part of a slaughtered animal. Sophisticated market gardening methods and an exceptionally varied climate mean that an abundance of fresh vegetables and fruits are available to restaurants throughout the year.

The Atlantic coast, with its thousands of fishing villages and expanses of mountain pastureland, is best known for its fresh fish, dairy products and meat. Galicia's long association with the sea has made it the seafood capital of the Iberian Peninsula. *Vieras* (scallops), *almejas* (clams), *ostras* (oysters), *percebes* (barnacles), *pulpo* (octopus), *necoras* (baby red crabs), *gambas* (prawns) and *langosta* (lobster) feature on all good menus. Potatoes and *grelos* (greens) form the basis of the humbler diet and the best-known dishes are probably *lacón con grelos* (boiled pork with turnip tops), *pote Gallego* (Gallegan stew) and the crusty pastry *empanada* (pie) filled with meat or fish. *Fabada Asturiana* is the great regional dish of Asturias – a bean stew spiced with smoked black sausage – followed by the strong blue cheese *queso cabrales*, all washed down with the local cider or *sidra*.

The Basque Country is widely considered to be the gastronomic capital of Spain: a reputation no doubt enhanced by the French chefs who migrated to the Basque Country in the 19th century. In the last few decades the Basques have won wide international acclaim for their *nueva cocina*, a genre heavily influenced by recent culinary trends from northern Europe. Basque cooking is praised above all for its fish dishes such as *marmitako* (fish soup), *bacalao* (salt cod), *angulas* (elvers), *kokotxas* (hake cheeks in a lemon, oil and parsley sauce) and *calamares* or *chipirones en su tinta* (baby squid in their black inky sauce), generally cooked in *cazuelas* (earthenware dishes). The Basques have a passion for food that descends from the men-only gastronomic societies which emerged during the industrialization of such cities as San Sebastián and Bilbao in the mid-nineteenth century. These societies encourage members to socialize, drink and cook for each other, preparing traditional dishes and inventing new ones. In the countryside it is a common sight at *fiesta* times to see villagers competing to make the best *calderete* (a rabbit or beef and vegetable stew). **Navarre** is equally proud of its cuisine and the *Roncal* cheese, baked river trout stuffed with ham, and various pigeon- and partridge-based game dishes are the supreme creations of the Navarrese kitchen.

Catalonia has an equally imaginative table, where influences from the Mediterranean and France predominate, although there is a marked difference between the elegant city and resort cooking and the heartier, rural traditions. Herbs (especially oregano and thyme), garlic and oil are the basis of many of the dishes and sauces such as *allioli* (mayonnaise and garlic), *romesco* (hot red pepper and almond sauce), *sofrito* (onion and tomato sautéed in oil) and *picada* (a mixture of garlic, parsley and nuts). Fish and meat courses are creatively combined with seasonal fruits or sultanas and pine kernels; *oca con peras* (goose with pears), and lobster and chicken in a hazelnut sauce are two of the great Catalan inventions. The trawling fleets of the Costa Brava supply quantities of excellent seafood daily to the many fine restaurants along the coast. There the traditional speciality is *suquet*, a Mediterranean stew consisting of various types of fish. In the winter, game and poultry are often stuffed with sausages, dried peaches, pine kernels and raisins. The tasty *escuedella i carn d'olla*, native to Barcelona, is a chickpea stew seasoned with the white and black *butifarra* sausage, which is used as a basic flavouring in many other winter dishes.

The cuisine of the **Balearic Islands** is similar to that of Catalonia in that sweet and sour combinations predominate, although the country origins of Balearic cooking are more pronounced. The basic foodstuffs are vegetables and pork, and soups and stews are popular – especially the *sopa mallorqina*, a broth of vegetables and sliced bread, which can vary considerably from the sublime to the inedible depending on the ingredients and the chef's ability. On Menorca lobster forms the basis of many great recipes, such as the *calderete de langosta*, allegedly King Juan Carlos I's favourite dish. Many dishes are accompanied by mayonnaise, which was supposedly invented in the capital, Mahon, by the French governor's chef. *La burida de ratjada* (skate with almonds and lobster) and *tumbet* (potatoes and aubergine with a tomato and pepper sauce) are two of the more popular dishes on Ibiza. The *sobrasada* sausage, which is used to season stews, and the snail-shaped pastries (*ensaimada*) are popular throughout the archipelago.

The **Levant** or Mediterranean coast of Valencia is the largest rice-producing area of western Europe, so it is not surprising that rice forms an intrinsic part of the Valencianos' way of serving food. The cooking of this region reveals an even stronger Moorish influence than Andalusia. Paella, the most universal of the rice-based dishes, can be made with any combination of different ingredients, but chicken, pork, shellfish, snails, artichokes, beans, peppers and saffron are the most common. The popular summer drink of *horchata de chufas* (tigernut milk) also originates from this area. Murcia, where the paddyfields and citrus groves are replaced by vegetable *vegas* (cultivated, irrigated land) and fruit orchards, has a distinctive style of cooking based heavily on sauces made from locally grown tomatoes and sweet peppers. *Pescado a la sal*, the popular way of baking a whole fish by packing it in a thick layer of rough sea salt, originates from Murcia but has now spread to all parts of the country.

Andalusia, the land of vines and olive trees, is also the region of the frying-pan where many dishes, particularly fish, are deep-fried to a crispy golden perfection. The chilled gazpacho soup, a mixture of bread, tomato, peppers, garlic and oil is a summer favourite throughout the Peninsula. Its popularity arose with the discovery of the New World, when it ousted from the table the Moorish *ajo blanco*, a cold white soup of garlic, almonds, oil and grapes or melon. The region's *estofado de rabo de toro* (bull's tail stew) uses the tenderest cuts of fighting bulls, while the most expensive cured hams in Spain come from Trévelez in the Sierra Nevada and Jabugo in the Sierra Morena. A dish typical of Granada and of possible gipsy origin is the *tortilla Sacromonte*, an omelette made with fried lamb's brains and testicles.

Above all, Andalusia is the kingdom of the *tapa*, which, when accompanied by a glass of sherry, is an exciting and congenial way to eat. The tradition of the *tapa* – which means 'cover' or 'lid' in Castellano – supposedly derives from the habit of the barmen in Almería of placing a small plate on top of a glass to protect it from the wind and sand. In the south and the larger cities, it is very much an art form, where the reputation of a bar can rest on just one speciality. *Tapas* come in three sizes: a *pincho*, the smallest; a *tapa*; and the largest, a *ración*. In some bars they are provided free as an accompaniment to your drink; elsewhere, you will have to order separately.

The cooking of the **Meseta**, including Castile–La Mancha and Extremadura, seems in many ways to have remained unchanged since the 16th century. Castilians fluctuate, like the extremes of their weather, between banquet-like feasts and humble bowls of *sopa castellana* (meat stock soup), but, whatever the size of the meal, it is always accompanied by generous amounts of the best wine and bread in Spain. Roasting in large *hornos de asar* (wood-burning ovens) is the regional speciality. *Cordero* (lamb), *lechazo* (baby lamb fed only on its mother's milk) and *cochinillo* (baby pig) are to be found on most restaurant menus and are renowned for their tenderness. On a more humble level, *garbanzos* (chickpeas), *lentejas* (lentils) and *judias pintas* (white beans) form the basis of the everyday diet, especially in winter. These pulses are used in many different types of broth made from braised beef, pork, chicken or *chorizo* sausage. Game, particularly *perdiz* (partridge), is the speciality of Castile–La Mancha, although this region is better known for its dry and matured *manchego* cheese and the *pisto manchego*, a mixture of vegetables similar to French *ratatouille*. When driving through Castile–La Mancha, it is worth stopping at the roadside *ventas*, where cured cheeses, hams, wine and honey can be bought cheaply and at their freshest.

The restaurants of **Madrid** are the most regionally diverse and, with the possible exception of Catalonia, many of the country's best chefs work in the capital. Fish and seafood are exceptional considering how far the city is from the sea, and sea produce is flown in daily from the Mediterranean and Atlantic ports. There is, however, really only one dish that is typically Madrileña: the *cocido Madrileño*, a chickpea stew of beef, marrow bones, bacon, *chorizo*, black pudding, potato, cabbage and turnips. A popular local *tapa* is the *Callos a la Madrileña* (tripe stewed with ham, sausages, onion, garlic, paprika and spices).

La Rioja, with its fertile river valleys running into the Ebro, is the market garden of Castile and produces excellent red peppers, asparagus, garlic, onions and potatoes. *Chilindrón*, a red pepper stew of pigeon, quail, meat or poultry, is the most typical dish of the region. The roast lamb of **Aragón**, with an almost sweet-tasting flesh, is considered the most succulent in the Peninsula. Other familiar Aragonese recipes include *sopa Aragonesa* (a soup with liver, cheese and bread), *migas* (fried breadcrumbs), *menestra de verduras* (steamed fresh vegetables) and *escabeche* (an overall term describing the method, originally Arabic, of preserving fish and fowl in vinegar and lemon juice).

Wine and Drink

Wine is an integral part of a Spanish meal, and generally accompanies both lunch and dinner as well as any in-between *tapas*. If you spend time in Spain it will not be long before you are invited into a private *bodega* to taste the proud owner's particular brew. Local wine culture exists in thousands of *pueblos* throughout the Iberian Peninsula, but watch out if you are offered a glass of locally made *aguadiente* (literally, fire water), for this can have the alcohol content of meths and a worse taste.

The first vines were introduced by the Phoenicians and Carthaginians over 2,500 years ago, but it was the Romans who really developed the art of viniculture. Today, Spain has more acres of vineyard than any other country in the world, although the arid nature of the soil puts it behind France, Italy and the Soviet Union in terms of

The Spanish Costas

Back in the 1950s tourists were attracted by Spain's reputation for golden sand beaches, clear blue waters and beautiful uncluttered coastline. Forty years on, the picture is very different. Quiet little fishing villages such as Torremolinos, Calpe and Nerja, along with substantial stretches of the Mediterranean coastline, have been exposed to the worst excesses of holiday urbanization. The concrete plague has infected hundreds of miles of beaches elsewhere, and the natural, unspoilt stretches grow ever scarcer – although they are by no means extinct. The *Costas* have become synonymous with mass tourism and a recent law now protects what undeveloped coast remains, but in too many places the damage has been done and the coast is indelibly scarred. There are, however, over 2,000km of beaches in Spain and, while some of them are polluted and in a deplorable state, others are clean, uncrowded and washed with clear water.

In 1989, 133 Spanish beaches exceeded the levels of contamination permitted by the EC. The figure may appear high but is in fact not excessive when the extent of the coastline is considered. The Costa del Sol of Andalusia, the Costa Blanca of Valencia and the Costa Vasca or Basque coastline were the worst affected areas, and the Spanish have become increasingly aware of the standards expected of their beaches. Below is a short and general outline of where and where not to go.

The level of cleanliness along the 597km of coastline and 334 beaches of Catalonia have been vastly improved, and standards are generally high considering the industrial nature of the region. Beaches in and around Barcelona and Tarragona contain the worst affected areas, and this applies to all the major cities with populations of around 100,000 anywhere on either the Atlantic or the Mediterranean coasts. In Catalonia the cleanest and quietest beaches lie east and north of Girona. Trouble spots in the Balearics, with 1,340km of coastline, are centred around the main areas of tourism such as Puerto de Sóller, San Telmo, Andratx and Palma Nova.

Along the Valencian and Murcian coast the situation deteriorates still further, and some stretches suffer the worst contamination in Europe. The image wars between the resorts have led in recent years to the stealing of offshore sand by local *ayuntamientos* (town councils) in a bid to improve the appearance of their beaches. In Andalusia and the Costa del Sol, matters are not much better and, in a report published by the Servicio Andaluz de Salud (SAS) in 1990, only four beaches out of a total of 325 were given the maximum hygiene rating. The worst stretches of coastline were earmarked in the provinces of Granada and Málaga, and the cleanest in Almería and north of Tarifa in Cádiz.

The Atlantic coast, although generally cleaner, still has its trouble spots. Contamination levels are high around the larger industrial ports, and pollution is particularly concentrated along the Basque coast and in the Rías Bajas between Vigo and Pontevedra. The north-west coast has the cleanest stretches of seashore, especially the Rías Altas, Asturias and Cantábria.

The Spanish government and regional autonomies came under increasing foreign environmentalist pressure in 1990 to protect and clean their beaches. Attention was drawn especially to the important wetlands such as the Coto Doñana National Park, La Albufera and the Ebro delta, all of which are vital stops for millions of migratory birds travelling between Africa and northern Europe. At present the ecology movement is less prominent in Spain than in other European countries, notably at a political level, but there are signs that more and more Spaniards are genuinely concerned with environmental issues. Even hotels in Benidorm are beginning to promote a 'green' image.

The correct management of the Spanish coastline is important not only for ecologists, however. Coastal life is part of both contemporary Spanish culture and its history. The great seaports, such as Barcelona, Tarragona, Valencia, Cartagena, Cádiz, Huelva, Vigo and Bilbao, are all places whose long maritime tradition, whether Mediterranean or Atlantic, has both absorbed and spread influences from abroad and been paramount in the moulding of the country.

Whatever views you may hold about the *Costas*, they are geared in the end to what is possibly an even greater asset to the country than the sun: the Spaniard's natural enjoyment of life. If you visit them in winter, you cannot escape the feeling that the party's over until next summer.

---

production. The 30 most important wines of quality status are covered by the *Denominación de Origen* or DO, while the rest of the crop is made into *Vinos de la Tierra* or distilled into brandy. The quality of the product has improved enormously in the last two decades through the introduction of new grape varieties such as Cabernet Sauvignon, and many wine-growers have changed the character of their wines to suit modern tastes.

The best-known reds for export are made from Tempranillo and Garnacha grapes and are produced mainly in the *bodegas* of La Rioja, along the central Ebro basin, stretching into the province of Alava in the Basque Country. They have a typically succulent oak and vanilla taste created by the wooden barrels in which the wine is aged. The best vintages carry the labels of the Marqués de Murrieta, La Rioja Alta, CVNE, Muga and Marqués de Cáceres. The region also produces pink and white wines of a similarly high standard.

The River Duero (Ribera del Duero) generally produces much heavier reds, as well as Spain's most notoriously expensive wine: Vega Sicilia. This will rarely be found on any wine list for less than 5,000 pesetas, but cheaper Duero wines can have a similarly rich taste and are a particularly good accompaniment to roast meat. The main white from the area, the Marqués de Griñon, is made exclusively from the Verdejo grape and is dry, fresh and aromatic.

Castile–La Mancha produces almost three-quarters of all Spain's wine and is the largest vineyard in the world. Much of the ordinary table wine comes from this area, and is generally served chilled. The rosé or *clarete*, made from a mixture of 85 per cent white grapes

Fiestas

The *fiesta* is the living testament of the longstanding cultural traditions of Spain, and the enormous variety and number of festivals derive from each region's determination to hold on to the deep folkloric, pagan and religious identity of its past. Every year there are over 200 *fiestas* in Spain considered of 'touristic interest' and thousands of village fairs and pilgrimages (*romerías*) that do not fall within this category. Local tourist offices should be able to advise you on all important events in the region. Whatever time of year you happen to be in Spain, something is bound to be happening.

January: 1 – New Year's Day celebration in Granada for the city's capture in 1492. 6 – Children's parade in Madrid. 19–20 – Tamborrada in San Sebastián.

February: 7–17* – Carnival in Cádiz – parades, music, fireworks.

March: 12–19 – *La Fallas* in Valencia – huge spectacle of bonfires, *gigantes* (gigantic papier mâché models) and fireworks.

Semana Santa: Holy/Easter Week* processions throughout Spain. Most spectacular are the processions and *saetas* (laments) in Seville, Zamora and Cuenca; the drums of Calanda in Aragón; Dance of Death in Verges, Girona on Holy Thursday. Regattas and fairs in the north.

April: 16–21* – Seville's April *Feria*, a horse fair that is now one of the country's most important social events. Costume, flamenco, Sevillanas, bullfights, and so on.

May: 5–12* – Jerez de la Frontera's version of the above. 12–30 – San Isidro in Madrid – concerts, jazz and the best bullfights of the year.

Seventh Sunday after Easter: El Rocío. The biggest three-day pilgrimage in Spain, setting out from Seville and ending at the tiny *pueblo* of El Rocío in the Coto Doñana National Park. Flower-festooned wagons, and a strong pagan influence.

Corpus Christi: Thursday following Trinity Sunday, celebrated extravagantly in Toledo, Sitges and Cáceres.

June/July/August: Fiestas throughout Spain, most importantly:

23–24 June – *Paso del Fuego de San Pedro Manrique* in Soria.

14 June–2 July* – Festival of dance and music in Granada.

6–14 July – *San Fermín* in Pamplona.

25–28 July – *Moros y Cristianos de Villajoyosa* in Alicante region.

Regattas along the coast of northern Spain and *vendimias* (food and wine festivals).

15 August – *La Verbena* in Madrid for La Paloma.

August: International festival (of music, dance and theatre) in Santander, and theatre festival in Mérida.

September: Bullfight* in Ronda in 18th-century costume. 24 – Virgen de la Merced in Barcelona. End of September* – International Film Festival in San Sebastián.

October: 8–16 – Virgin of El Pilar in Zaragoza. 27 – Fiesta de la Rosa del Azafran de Consuegra in Consuegra.

* Date changes each year.

and 15 per cent red, is a light and refreshing hot-weather wine. Unfortunately, however, EC regulations have outlawed this wine and its heady days are numbered.

Catalonia is well known for its delicate whites, such as Torres' Gran Viña Sol, and for its full-bodied reds and sparkling *cavas* of Penedés produced by the champagne method. *Cavas* are generally underestimated because they're cheaper, although in terms of methods of production they are far more advanced than their idolized competitor from France. The main wine-growing districts of Catalonia are Ampurdán on the Costa Brava, and Priorato, west of Tarragona, although there are other DOs produced in Alella, Conca de Barberá and Tarragona. Aragón's red Cariñena wine, made from the grape of the same name, is another excellent accompaniment to meat and stews.

Galicia produces some of the most original wines in the country from two native grapes, Loureiro and Treixadura. Galician wines are generally raw, green and zesty and wonderful with seafood. Unfortunately, the consumption of wine in Galicia far outweighs the production, and little wine finds its way into other parts of Spain. Albariño is arguably the most outstanding wine produced in the region, and it compares well with any good young white wine in Europe.

Spain is best known for its sherry or Jerez, which thrives in the *albariza* (chalky soil) in and around the lower Guadalquivir basin of south-western Andalusia. Its particular taste is created by the *flor*: the yeast that grows naturally on the wine in the warm, slightly humid climate. There are four variations on the wine generally termed

sherry. The most popular pre-dinner aperitif is the dry, straw-coloured fino and, in its slightly watered-down state, this is the preferred drink of every Andalusian *fiesta*. Manzanilla is a more aromatic wine, produced exclusively in the coastal town of Sanlúcar de Barrameda and, at its freshest, this tastes faintly of the salt breeze of the Atlantic. Amontillados have more body, a deep amber colour and a nuttier taste; they start life as finos but are then fermented for longer. The deep brown Olorosos in their pure state are again dry, but are better known in their exported form, whereby they are blended with sweeter grapes to give them a creamier edge. Jerez is a wine that does not keep or travel well, and for this reason it tastes in Andalusia as you've never tasted it before.

Other Drinks

Agua mineral (con/sin gas): Mineral water (still or aerated)

Cerveza Beer Caña: Small measure of beer

Chocolate: Hot chocolate

Vino tinto/rosado/blanco: Red wine/rosé/white wine

Horchata: Tiger-nut milk (a healthy and refreshing summer drink)

Café con hielo: Iced coffee

Sangría: Red wine and fruit punch

Cremat: Catalan hot coffee and brandy

Motoring in Spain

Getting to Spain

There are frequent daily ferry connections between the Continent and the UK, and efficient motor-rail services run through France to the Spanish border. The only connection by boat with Spain is the Plymouth–Santander ferry: Brittany Ferries, Millbay Docks, Plymouth PL1 3EW, tel (0752) 221321. The journey takes 24 hours and in good weather is extremely comfortable. From Santander there is an excellent motor-rail service with Málaga, which departs at 7.50pm and arrives in the south at 10.30am. The price is 8,750 pesetas for the car and 3,930 pesetas per passenger, plus a supplement of 1,590 pesetas for a couchette. All major cities in Spain are connected by a similar motor-rail service.

Routes through France

There are several alternative routes you can follow when driving through France. The most direct to the western side of the Pyrenees is Calais – Paris – Orléans – Tours – Poitiers – Bordeaux – Irún. The Camino de Santiago has four main routes through France, following the itinerary as above, but turning inland from Biarritz to St-Jean-Pied-de-Port; alternatively, from Vézelay via Limoges and Perigueux and Mont de Marsan; from Le Puy via Cahors; or from Arles via Montpellier and Toulouse, crossing the Pyrenees into Aragón at Somport. To reach the Mediterranean coast, travel via Paris – Orléans – Bourges – Clermont-Ferrand – Montpellier – Perpignan.

Fly-Drive

Some excellent fly-drive deals with personalized itineraries can be obtained through Mundi Color Holidays, 276 Vauxhall Bridge Road, London SW1V 1BE, tel (071) 834 3492.

Car Hire

Hiring a car in Spain is easy; all the major companies operate out of the large network of international airports in Spain. In terms of quality of cars and service, Avis give the best deals. Cars can be picked up and left at the offices of your choice and prices for a week, with unlimited mileage, begin around £110.

Documentation

A Green Card is no longer required, but the following documents must be produced on demand: passport, driving licence, car registration documents, and an insurance policy valid for all EC countries from the car's country of origin.

Traffic Signs and Traffic Offences

Traffic signs in Spain are to be made bilingual in those autonomies with their own language.

Car fines for 'non-residents' in Spain are divided into three categories: light, serious and very serious. A light fine is up to 15,000 pesetas; a serious one up to 50,000 pesetas; and very serious up to 100,000 pesetas. If you are unable to pay, the car will be impounded and kept in the nearest *ayuntamiento* (town hall) pound until sufficient funds have been raised. Credit cards or travellers' cheques are not accepted.

It is worth knowing that if cars continuously flash as they pass, more often than not it is to alert oncoming motorists that they are about to enter a speed trap.

The castellets *(human castles) of Valls in Tarragona are one of many different ways the people of Spain like to* fiesta. Fiestas *are most easily chanced upon during Easter week, in high summer and during autumn when the harvest celebrations take place.*   Incafo

The Cult of St James

The legend surrounding the cult of St James is one that has been rooted deeply for centuries in both Spanish and European culture. After James was beheaded in Jerusalem in AD 44 on the orders of Herod Agrippa, his disciples rescued his body and sailed in a stone boat to Iria Flavia (Padrón), where they asked the Celtic Queen Lupa for a place to bury his body. Lupa referred them to the King, who threw them in jail, but they were miraculously set free. He pursued them with his army, only to perish with all his men when a bridge he was crossing collapsed. Once again, the disciples sought the help of Lupa, who set them a task of taming two wild bulls, which they successfully managed. Lupa was converted to Christianity and the body of St James was buried in her palace.

On 25 July 813 Bishop Theodomiro of Iria Flavia discovered the remains, and a church was erected by Alfonso II on the site in a place known as Compostela: from *campus stellae* (field of the star) or possibly *compositum* (cemetery). In 1095 the episcopal see was moved from Iria Flavia to Compostela and in 1120 was created a bishopric. St James became the patron of all Spain, and the adopted symbol of reconquest or *matamoros* (the Moor-slayer). He was reported to have helped the Christians in many of their crusades, such as the Battle of Clavijo in 834 where, it was claimed, he personally slew 60,000 infidels. Consequently, King Ramiro I granted a royal tax *in perpetuum*, but the whole story and battle were later discovered to have been contrived. The legend is surrounded with similar fables. Nevertheless, to this day thousands of pilgrims from throughout Europe make the pilgrimage each year from as far away as Scandinavia and Hungary.

The *Liber Sancti Jacobi* – also known as the *Codex Calixtinus* – was written in about 1130 by a French monk called Aymeric Picaud, and may be considered the first guidebook in Europe. This warned pilgrims of the perils they were likely to encounter on the way to Santiago, as well as giving more practical information such as where to expect hospitality, food and accommodation. The symbolism of the cult was carefully thought out by Bishop Diego Gelmirez and it was during his episcopacy that the scallopshell was adopted as the symbol of pilgrimage. The hat and staff were attributes bestowed upon St James as a pilgrim in the 13th century.

For Spain the importance of the Camino de Santiago can hardly be exaggerated. Throughout the Middle Ages it acted as a cultural highway, bringing north European culture into the deepest recesses of the Peninsula and encouraging people from the rest of Europe to resettle the reconquered territories.

Note: In this guide the Camino has been divided into three parts: through Navarre and La Rioja (see p. 151); through Castile and León (see p. 181); and through Galicia (see p. 103).

Roads in Spain

The general standard of roads in Spain has been improved enormously in the last few years, although many more heavy goods vehicles are using them. Even so, lorry drivers are more considerate in Spain than in most countries, and will indicate to the right if the road is clear to overtake. However, a few roads remain hazardous, such as the coastal roads in the south, where the main danger is from pedestrians walking along the side of the road.

Peajes (toll motorways) are the fastest way of moving through the country. The charge varies from region to region but works out at between 8.73 pesetas and 10.19 pesetas per kilometre.

Mountain and coast roads generally have the slowest-moving traffic, while the small routes through the *Meseta* can often turn out to be faster than the main routes if the traffic is particularly bad.

Petrol

'Super' is the basic three- or four-star 96-octane obtained in other European countries. Unleaded petrol pumps are fairly widespread throughout the country, although in more remote districts such as Extremadura, Castile–La Mancha and Aragón you should be sure to stop at the big-name garages such as CAMPSA or REPSOL.

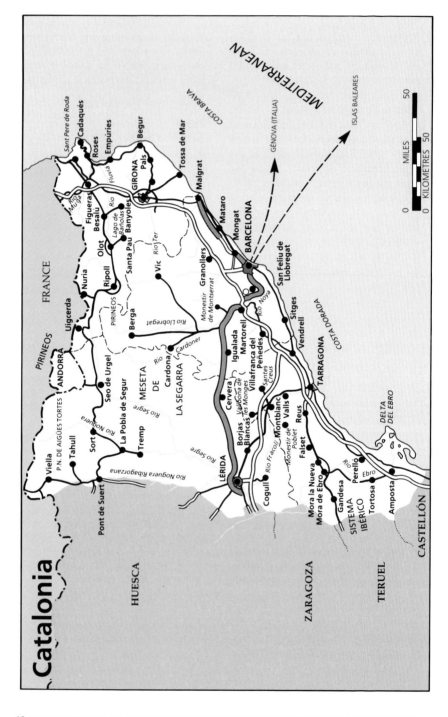

CHAPTER TWO

Catalonia

(Catalunya)

PROTECTED BY THE PYRENEES, the Mediterranean and the empty expanses surrounding the Ebro crescent, Catalunya, or Catalonia, forms a neat wedge of land in the north-eastern corner of the Iberian Peninsula. Between the mountains, valleys, plains and sea you can move through volcanic sierras, idyllic Romanesque villages, great Gothic hall-churches and primeval forests to a coast which, although popularized by tourism, has retained its long sandy beaches and quiet rugged coves. Catalunya's geographical isolation, together with its proximity to France, has made the region almost as much a part of northern Europe as the Mediterranean. The Catalans are a proud, independent and extroverted people, whose desire for independence from Madrid is symbolized by the everyday use of their language, Català. This is a Latin-derived language closely related to the medieval romance tongue Provençal, and during the Middle Ages it became a language of empire as well of courtly poetry. Today dialects are still spoken in most of Valencia, parts of Aragón, in southern France, the Balearic Islands and Sardinia.

A fter the decline of the Catalan–Aragonese Empire and the shift in the balance of power away from the Mediterranean and towards the Atlantic and Madrid, Català fell gradually out of use as the nation was centralized. The language was maintained in only the most isolated rural communities. Not until the 19th century did it find favour again under the Catalan '*Renaixença*' (see p. 43) and was adopted by intellectuals and the romantic literati, in association with Catalanism – the concept of Catalan separateness. After the Civil War, it was heavily suppressed, books in Català were burnt and place-names Castilianized. The language became confined to the *Monasterio de Montserrat*, the spiritual centre of Catalunya. Not until 1975 did a renewed drive to preserve and promote the language begin. It is now taught in all Catalan schools and there is an independent regional television channel broadcasting only in Català. Tourist information is also printed in Català and, if your French is better than your Castilian, then you may find it easier to read.

Language is just one area in which the Catalans have displayed their individuality. Economically, Catalunya is the most advanced region of Spain. A firm industrial base was formed in the last century and has continued to this day, with the region's chemical, paper manufacturing, mineral and hydro-electrical industries. The Catalans' search for influence looks north to Europe rather than south to Madrid. They lead Spain in the fields of publishing and design; their business acumen and common sense (*seny*) is generally envied; and it is these qualities, combined with their skill as traders, that have been most powerful in the formation of their history.

The foundation of a Phocaean Greek colony at Empúries around 550 BC served as a fortified commercial port for the Roman invasion of Spain at the end of the third century BC. From there Tarraco (Tarragona) was founded, which became the capital of Hispania Citerior and later Tarraconensis. The Visigothic impression on Catalunya was slight. After the Arabs were halted by Charles Martel, Charlemagne made the Pyrenees into a natural intermediate zone between Islamic Spain and Christendom. In AD 878, Wifredo 'El Velloso' (the Hairy) (878–897), the Count of Barcelona, was granted a charter of liberties by King Charles 'the Bald' of France for his loyalty and courage: Legend relates how after the successful siege of Paris against the Normans, Charles dipped his finger in the blood running from the wounds of Wifredo and traced four bars across his shield – hence the crimson stripes on the Catalan flag, the *senyera*. What seems more likely is that the name

Catalunya came into use at this time as a derivative of the French word *châtelain*.

The dynastic Counts of Barcelona, established by Wifredo, lasted for over half a millennium and awakened something of a golden age for Catalunya. Great trails of Romanesque architecture spread south and west from the Pyrenees. Monasteries were founded, the first European feudal laws were compiled and a navy was built in 1114, thus marking the beginning of a seaborne empire. In 1137 the marriage between Berenguer IV (1137–62) and Petronila de Aragón forged the union between the two territories and 'Greater Catalunya' was born. In 1179, following the Treaty of Cazorla, the Aragonese–Catalan Empire gave Murcia to Castile and subsequently concentrated its attention on Mediterranean expansion.

Catalunya's landed influence in France diminished as its foreign possessions grew. Commerce with the East ensured Barcelona's wealth kept pace with that of Venice and Genova. The Treaty of Corbeil in 1258 released Catalunya from nominal French control, but in return most of the lands north of the Pyrenees were relinquished except for Roussillon and Cerdagne. James I 'El Conquistador' (the Conqueror) (1213–76) captured the Balearic archipelago and much of Valencia, creating a firm landed base for the development of a maritime empire for the Counts of Barcelona. Pedro III (1276–85) added Sicily in a protracted war. From there the legendary corsairs Roger de Llúria and Roger de Flor terrorized the Mediterranean, with their mercenary sailors gaining Malta, the French Duchy of Athens, including parts of the

Peloponnesian peninsula, Corsica and Sardinia. These events were mirrored by equally dynamic developments in the fields of literature, architecture and painting.

The decline began in 1348 with the bubonic plague, which is said to have accounted for the death of half the population of Catalunya by the end of the century. After the death of Martín 'El Humano' (the Humane) in 1410, a branch of the Castilian ruling house was installed and, under Alfonso V 'El Magnífico' (the Magnificent) (1416–58), Catalunya conquered Naples (1435–42). Following the marriage of Ferdinand of Aragón to Isabel of Castile, the balance of power shifted away from Catalunya and its influence decreased further with the discovery of the New World. From then on, the history of the Catalans became one with the history of a unified Spain, although separatist tendencies continued to assert themselves in the revolt of the 1640s and the Succession Wars of 1700–13.

Industrialization in the 19th century once again opened up Catalunya to common European trends, although the countryside suffered heavily as a result of the Carlist Wars and there was a significant exodus of families from the land into the new industrial centres. These eventually became hotbeds of anarchist and socialist feeling and anti-monarchist sentiment. In positive terms, it helped inaugurate the 'Renaixença' – a movement whose roots spread from the writers and poets who began once again to use Catalá. The feeling spread and permeated all creative media as renewed financial prosperity among the mercantile classes, and the rise of a philanthropic bourgeoisie, patronized progressive

ideas in music, theatre, art and architecture. From this the Spanish Modernist movement developed.

The region is one of contrasts, from the bustle of Barcelona to the isolation of villages buried between the mighty folds of the Pyrenees. Catalunya contains national and natural parks and dramatic stretches of coastline, as well as the sprawling mass-tourism conurbations along the Costa Brava and Costa Dorada and the dust-blown industrial strongholds that account for 25 per cent of Spain's production and foreign trade. The region as a whole possesses a unique pace and history, yet each of the four provinces – Girona, Barcelona, Tarragona and Lérida – remains unmistakably different. However hard a Castilian may try and tell you otherwise, the Catalans are their own people, the most self-contained and advanced autonomous community in Spain.

Girona, Barcelona and the Costa Brava

Crossing the French–Spanish border from Perpignan, there are two alternative routes south to Barcelona – the fast A7 autoroute via Figueras–Girona–Granollers, or the winding coastal road along the Costa Brava and Costa del Maresme.

Figuerás (pop. 30,000), capital of the Alt Empordà region, is a busy commercial town, birthplace of Salvador Dalí (1904–89) and Narcís Monturiol, inventor of the U-boat. It's worth stopping here if only to see the Teatro Museo Dalí where the maverick Surrealist held his first exhibition at the age of 14. The building is easy to distinguish by gargantuan eggs lining the rooftops. Inside are hung some of the artist's most inventive compositions such as *The Raining Taxi* or *El Gran Masturbador*, as well as his more orthodox private collection. When the 'Dalinization' of the theatre began in 1974 under Dalí's direction, he termed it the 'spiritual centre of Europe' and, judging by the thousands who visit this dusty shrine each year (this is the most popular museum in Spain after the Prado), his statement for once had a vestige of basis in reality. Among the more bizarre exhibits are a dolphin bed, a hologram of Velázquez's *Las Meninas* and a life-sized dummy orchestra accompanying something called *The Greatest Show on Earth*. In all,

this is Dalí at his most absurd and preposterous.

The town is laid out in a typically Catalan way. Most of the other main attractions such as the austere Gothic church of **San Pedro**, Toy Museum and Parc Bosc are situated within easy walking distance of the central *rambla*. Further out of town is the 18th-century Castillo de San Fernando, with a massive perimeter wall 5km in circumference. During the Civil War it was used as a camp by the International Brigade, and later as a depository to safeguard works belonging to the Prado Museum. Today, it serves as a military base and prison.

Back on the autoroute, continuing south for 45km beside the vineyards of

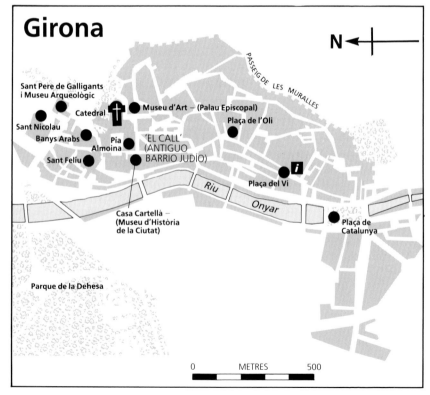

Castellfullit de la Roca in Girona province is a typical medieval stone-built Catalan village, where the landscape was originally used as a natural defence. Sleepy Romanesque villages of this kind can be found throughout northern Spain. Incafo

Ampurdán, you arrive in the provincial capital **GIRONA** (pop. 70,000). Built where the Galligants, Güell and Onyar rivers flow into the Ter, this is one of Catalunya's most legendary cities. Once the industrial suburbs have been navigated, you arrive at the edge of the old town, which is enclosed by walls to the north and the Onyar to the south. Inside lie a maze of steep cobbled streets, a Gothic cathedral with the widest nave in Christendom, and El Call, one of the most lovingly preserved medieval Jewish quarters in Europe. If you spend time in old Girona you're sure to be rewarded.

Medieval Girona was built upon Iberian, Roman and Moorish foundations, and by the 11th century it had become an important diocesan town due to its strategic position at the base of the Pyrenees. Too often it was actively involved in the struggles between the two bordering nations, earning the name *Ciudad de los Sitios* (City of Sieges). In 1809 the city's residents, under the leadership of General Álvarez de Castro, resisted attacks from the Napoleonic armies for over seven months. In recognition of its inhabitants' courage, the city was awarded the title *'Muy noble, excelentísima, fidelísima, muy leal y tres veces inmortal ciudad'* (Most noble, excellent, faithful, loyal and three times immortal city).

Your tour of Girona should begin in the **Plaça de Catalunya**, which spans the river, and where there's good parking. Head north into the old town via the Plaça del Vi and Carrer dels Ciutadans, eventually arriving in the Plaça de l'Oli. From there the Carrer de la Força leads up into the medieval heart of the city, the streets grow narrow, and steep-stepped alleyways climb into dark, enclosed *plaças*. The tall, looming houses and their intricately latticed windows have for much of this century made it an area popular with artists and writers. The Spanish refer to this medieval Jewish area as 'Galdosian' after the 19th-century Madrid novelist, Don Benito Pérez Galdós, who set many of his stories in dark, mysterious urban ghettos. Leaving the Call, continue along Carrer de la Força and you pass the **Casa Cartellà**, an 18th-century Capuchin monastery that now houses the *Museu d'Història de la Ciutat* (Museum of City History). Just beyond it and lining the right side of the 86 stairs ascending to the cathedral is the **Pía Almoina**, a beautiful but austere Gothic building, formerly a charitable institution. On the left side is a gate in the medieval wall known as *Sobreportas*, flanked by two perfectly cylindrical towers through which heretics were led to execution.

The mighty **Catedral de Santa María** warrants the spectacular ascent to the western Baroque façade, which depicts faith, hope and charity beneath a beautiful rosetta window. The main Gothic structure was built over an earlier Carolingian one. The central nave is 50m long, 23m wide and 34m high; it caused consternation in the city council of Girona when Guillem Bofill put forward his plans to build such a massive, unsupported nave in 1417. This is the most magnificent example of the Catalan Gothic hall-church, in which an uninterrupted view of the altar was required for all the congregation; the feeling of space is extraordinary. The alabaster high altar depicts scenes from the gospels, and is crowned by a silver and enamelled *baldacchino* (canopy). Another exceptional five-levelled altarpiece stands on the north wall beside the door leading out into the 12th-century trapezoidal cloister, with 112 carved capitals depicting Biblical themes such as the stories of Adam and Eve and Noah's Ark, as well as abstract animal and vegetable motifs. From the cloister there is a good view of *la Torre de Carlomagno* (the Tower of Charlemagne): a five-storeyed Romanesque structure; the upper four with twin-light windows.

In the church treasury some exceptional illuminated manuscripts include the Beatos de Girona (see p. 124), and the famous Tapiz de la Creación, one of the finest surviving fragments of Romanesque tapestry. In colourful detail it depicts the Creation, with Eve emerging from the side of Adam, strange sea creatures with razor teeth, unicorns and other imaginary beasts, surrounded by the months, seasons and signs of the zodiac. Also of interest is the *Silla de Carlomagno* (Charlemagne's Seat), carved from a single piece of alabaster; and the sepulchres of Queen Mahalda and Count Ramón Berenguer II, Count of Barcelona.

Back outside, walk around to the south side of the cathedral and take a look at the terracotta Door of the Apostles. Even though all but two of the figures were destroyed when the

Monestir de Montserrat

The spiritual heart of Catalunya and one of the most important pilgrimage shrines in Spain is the Benedictine monastery of Montserrat. This is situated high up in the jagged and eroded Sierra de Montserrat, an extraordinary karstic *massif* whose serrated jaw-like summits alchemize under the effects of different lights between slate blue and bright gold. Since the monastery's foundation in 1025, it has played a vital role in the spiritual and cultural life of Catalunya. Most of the buildings were erected in the last century after Napoleon's troops sacked and looted the shrine, and it suffers from the worst excesses of the pilgrimage industry, but its dramatic setting and magnificent views more than compensate for these minor setbacks.

The stories and history surrounding the monastery are numerous. Julius II was abbot here before becoming Pope and commissioning Michelangelo to paint the Sistine Chapel. Wagner was inspired to write his overture to *Parsifal* after visiting the shrine. The 12th-century Black Madonna or *Mare de Déu* (Mother of God) above the high altar, holding the world in the palm of her hand, is said to have been carved by St Luke.

Of particular note within the monastic grounds are the remains of the Gothic cloister, the library and the picture gallery with works by El Greco, Zurbarán and Caravaggio. In the garden stands the Romanesque chapel of Sant Iscle and the Holy Grotto, a Modernist creation by Gaudí and Puig i Cadafalch, which was erected after a vision of the Virgin appeared on that site in 1880.

There are even more beautiful walks in the surrounding mountains: to the chapel of San Miguel, the grotto of San Juan Garín (connected by funicular) and the chapel of Santa Cecilia. At the summit, the chapel of San Jerónimo (1,238m) offers views on a clear day north to the Pyrenees and east across the Llobregat valley and Barcelona to the Balearic Islands.

(Montserrat is reached by car from Barcelona on the N-II Barcelona–Lérida highway, turning off on to either the C1411 to Monistrol or along a smaller road via Guardiola. Be warned that buses thunder at perilous angles around the last few twisting kilometres of the ascent.)

cathedral was sacked in 1936, it is still impressive. Directly opposite is the **Bishop's Palace**, now the Art Museum, where you can wander around cabinets full of fine medieval church art, or just sit quietly in the patio admiring the rich engravings surrounding the Renaissance windows. In the museum, the 11th-century copy of Bede, the 14th-century Madonnas and the painted retables by Lluís Borrassà and

Bernat Martorell reveal the high level of expertise of the Catalan illuminators, Gothic sculptors and painters.

Sant Feliú, instantly recognizable by its truncated Gothic spire destroyed by lightning in 1581, can be reached by walking down the steps and passing through the Sobreportas. Before this ex-collegiate church was built there was a paleo-Christian cemetery on the site where Sant Narcis, the patron saint of Girona, was reputedly martyred and buried. In the walls of the mainly Romanesque interior you can still see a series of beautiful Roman and paleo-Christian sarcophagi depicting scenes of the rape of Persephone and a lion hunt.

Crossing the Río Galligants (literally, cock-crow), you come to the ancient Benedictine abbey of **Sant Pere de Galligants**, an exceptionally well preserved example of Catalan–Lombard architecture. Grooved and spiralled columns are crowned with zoomorphic and botanical motifs, some of which were quite obviously influenced by Visigothic patterns. In the adjoining monastery is the **Archeological Museum**, covering the spectrum of early Iberian history; it includes artefacts found at Empúries and Hebrew steles removed from the Jewish cemetery on Montjuïc (Mountain of the Jews). A walkway, signposted *Paseo Arqueològic* beneath the city walls, is worth a leisurely stroll for the view of the exquisite octagonal dome of the church of Sant Nicholás.

Cross the river again into the Plaça dels Jurats, where you should visit the **Banys Arabs** (Arab Baths), reached through a door in the Capuchin monastery. Cool, luxuriant rooms are dimly illuminated to reveal the most spectacular Mudéjar bathtub in the Iberian Peninsula. Its eight supporting columns, each with a delicately carved capital, are a gracious reminder of Girona's medieval prosperity.

You can return to the Plaça Catalunya beside the river, crossing back and forth over the bridges to see the brightly painted houses along the waterfront from different angles, or you can double back behind the cathedral and follow the path along the city walls, turning at will into the sidestreets for a drink and *tapas* in one of the small bars. The modern town, built on the west side of the Onyar, has little of interest to offer except a few buildings by Girona's Modernist architect, Rafael Masó, and the outdoor cafés in the **Parc de la Dehesa**.

It's a fast 100km from Girona to Barcelona with the motorway cutting alongside the Cordillera Prelitoral. Halfway down you pass the Sierra de Montseny (literally, 'the mountains of common sense'), a peculiarly volcanic limb of the Pyrenees, with one of the great natural arboreta in Europe, and the muse for many 19th-century Catalan poets. If you take time to explore the countryside here, you'll inevitably chance upon some quiet lake, a Romanesque ruin, or perhaps even a raw amethyst.

As Barcelona approaches, ignore signposts for Granollers, Sabadell and Terrassa: a trio of bland, industrial satellite cities surrounding the regional capital, which owe their prosperity to textiles, agriculture and chemicals.

Barcelona

BARCELONA (pop. 3,100,000) burns life and energy like nowhere else in Spain. It is a dynamic European catalyst for progress, creativity, industry, art, design and finance, and overflows with the boisterousness you would expect from a busy Mediterranean port. The ease with which you can absorb its lasting and temporary pleasures at your own pace is the essential reason for the city's endless popularity with travellers, artists and posers. Like Naples and Marseille, this is a great western Mediterranean seaport. Yet

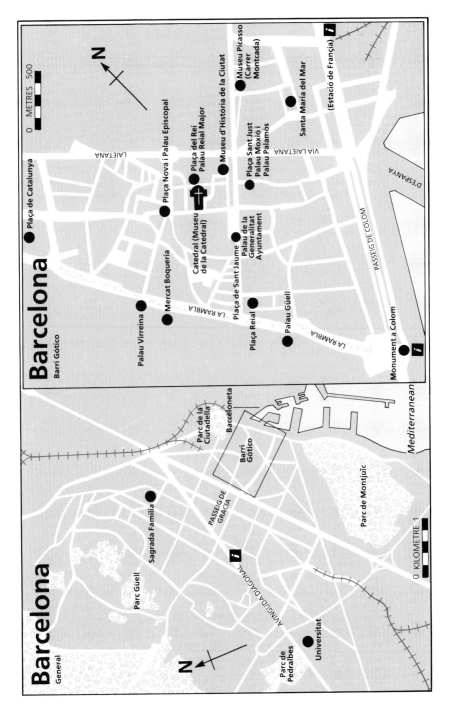

Barcelona
General

Barcelona
Barri Gótic

N

Plaça de Catalunya

Palau Virreina

Mercat Boqueria

Plaça Reial

Palau Güell

Plaça de Sant Jaume
Palau de la
Generalitat
Ayuntament

LA RAMBLA

Catedral (Museu
de la Catedral)

Plaça Nova i Palau Episcopal

Plaça del Rei
Palau Reial Major

Museu d'Història de la Ciutat

Plaça Sant Just
Palau Moxió i
Palau Palamós

Museu Picasso
(Carrer
Montcada)

Santa Maria del Mar

(Estació de França)

LAIETANA

VIA LAIETANA

D'ESPANYA

PASSEIG DE COLOM

Monument a Colom

0   METRES   500

Parc Güell

Sagrada Familia

PASSEIG DE
GRACIA

Parc de la
Ciutadella

Barceloneta

Barri
Gótico

AVINGUDA DIAGONAL

Parc de Montjuïc

Mediterranean

Parc de
Pedralbes

Universitat

0 KILOMETRE 1

N

Principal Museums of Barcelona

Museo Arqueológico, Passeig de Santa Madrona s/n, Parc de Montjuïc. Prehistoric collection from the Levant regions and Balearic Islands, with a good section on the Greek settlement at Empúries. Tues–Sat 9.30am–1pm & 4–7pm. Sun & holidays 9.30–2pm. Cl Mon.

Museo de Arte de Catalunya, Palau Nacional s/n, Parc de Montjuïc. The most important collection of Romanesque and Gothic art in the world. Of exceptional merit are the Christ Pantocrators, Gothic statuettes and 12th-century carving.

Pueblo Español, Avinguda del Marqués de Comillas s/n, Parc de Montjuïc. An open-air model village showing the distinctive features of Spanish vernacular architecture and how it varies between each region. Tues–Sun 9am–2pm. Cl Mon.

Museo de Arte Moderno, Plaça de les Armes, Parc de la Ciutadella. Paintings, sculpture and drawings from the 19th century to the first decade of the 20th century, including work by Sert, Sorolla, Noñell, Miró, Tápies. Tues–Sat 9am–7.30pm. Sun & holidays 9am–2pm. Mon 3–7.30pm.

Museo de la Catedral, Plaça de la Seu s/n, cathedral cloister. Interesting religious art. Daily 11am–1pm.

Museo Etnológico, Passeig de Santa Madrona s/n, Parc de Montjuïc. A good collection of ethnic art from around the world. Tues–Sat 9am–8.30pm. Sun & holidays 9am–2pm. Cl Mon.

Museo Federico Marés, Plaça Sant Iu. The private collection of the sculptor Federico Marés, including 400 polychrome sculptures collected during the Civil War. In other rooms there are odd collections of matchboxes, pipes, cameras and old photographs. Tues–Sat 9am–2pm & 4–7pm. Sun and holidays 9am–2pm. Cl Mon.

Casa-Museo Gaudí, Olot s/n, Parc Güell. Private home of Gaudí from 1906–26. Contains personal objects, drawings and projects from the architect's life. Daily 10am–2pm & 4–7pm. Cl Dec to Feb.

Museo de História de la Ciudad, Plaça del Rei. A visual history of Barcelona including urban archeological finds, maps, plans, etc. Housed in the late-Gothic palace of Clariana-Padellás. Tues–Sat 9am–8.30pm. Sun & holidays 9am–1.30pm. Cl Mon.

Botanical Gardens, Avenida Montanyans s/n, Parc de Montjuïc. Superb collection of Mediterranean plant life, flowers, cacti, etc. Mon–Sat 9am–2pm & 4–7pm. Cl Sun & holidays.

Museo Maritimo, Plaça Portal de la Pau. An old Gothic shipyard converted into a fascinating maritime museum. Tues–Sat 10am–2pm & 4–7 pm. Sun & holidays 10am–2pm. Cl Mon.

Museo Militar, Castillo de Montjuïc. Collection of firearms and military uniforms. Tues–Sat 10am–2pm & 4–7pm. Sun & holidays 10am–7pm. Cl Mon.

Fundació Joan Miró, Plaça Neptú s/n, Parc de Montjuïc. Permanent exhibition of the artist's work. Tues–Sat 11am–8pm, Sun & holidays 11am–2.30pm. Cl Mon.

Museo de la Música, Avenida Diagonal 373. Collection of musical instruments from around the world, housed in a Modernist building by Puig i Cadafalch. Open Tues–Sun 9am–2pm. Cl Mon.

Museo Monasterio de Pedralbes, Bajada del Monasterio 9. A building of great artistic and architectural interest, especially the Gothic cloister. Public rooms contain an important collection of sculpture and painting. Tues–Fri 10am–1pm & 4–7pm. Sat, Sun & holidays 10am–1.30pm. Cl Mon.

Museo Picasso, Montcada 15–19. Paintings, drawings and graphics, showing the progression of the artist's work 1881–1957. Housed in the 13th-century palaces of Berenguer Aguilar and Bará de Castellet. Tues–Sat 10am–7pm, Sun & holidays 9am–2pm. Cl Mon.

Museo de Textil y de Indumentaria, Montcada 12–14. Another converted Gothic palace containing a fine collection of textiles. Tues–Sat 9am–2pm & 4.30–7pm. Cl Sun, Mon & holidays.

Museo de la Sagrada Familia, on the cathedral site at Carrer Mallorca 401. History of the construction, plans, projects and models. Daily 9am–7pm.

Museo de Zoología, Avenida Picasso s/n, Parc de la Ciutadella. Albino gorilla and an aquarium. Daily 9am–2pm. Cl Mon.

even though the sea is a fundamental part of life in Barcelona, you can easily forget its presence when out of sight of the waterfront.

With its delicate Gothic cloisters, the picaresque intensity of Las Ramblas, its endless streets without vanishing points, the sleaze of downtown Barrio Chino and the views from Montjuïc broken by the curvilineal and naturalistic forms of Modernist architecture, the city reveals its richly layered soul to anyone prepared to search. Fast, self-conscious and capricious, Barcelona is the centre for Catalunyan culture both ancient and modern, as well as for chic bar life, cafés, buskers and poseurs.

It's worth scrutinizing a map quite closely before you start to explore the city, particularly the maze-like streets of the Gothic quarter. (The tourist office gives away excellent free street plans with interesting itineraries that will be more than adequate for your needs.) Nevertheless, the city is made for walking, with most of the main museums, plazas, churches, palaces and parks contained in a relatively compact area. The Metro system is also

efficient. Cars can be a heavy responsibility – the congestion in the centre can waste valuable hours, while parking and one-way systems can take years to understand. If you do have a car, park it somewhere safe, preferably in an underground garage, for the duration of your stay and use taxis and public transport.

The Plaça de Catalunya is Barcelona's natural centre. From there, the gentle graduation of Las Ramblas descends to the harbour. On the left is the Barrio Gótico with the Via Laietana and the Parc de la Ciutadella beyond it to the north. On the southern side of the harbour is the Parc de Montjuïc, whose summit can be reached by cable car from the colourful residential neighbourhood of La Barceloneta.

On the far side of Plaça Catalunya from Las Ramblas is the Modernist area known as El Ensanche, divided from east to west by the Rambla de Catalunya and from north to south by the Avinguda Diagonal. This is a chic residential and shopping area enlivened by some of the best Modernist architecture, including part of Gaudí's extraordinary Sagrada Familia cathedral. At the western extremity is the Parc Güell and Mount Tibidabo, with spectacular views across the cityscape – the summit can be reached by a funicular. According to Catalan folklore, it was here that the Devil tempted Christ with all earthly delights.

Your tour of Barcelona should begin with a leisurely stroll along the former riverbed area of **Las Ramblas**, where you will quickly get the feel of the city, walking in the shade of towering plane trees and on crazy-paving designed by Joan Miró. This is Mediterranean metropolitan life at its most colourful and outrageous; a bizarre collection of open-air stalls interrupted by a continuous parade of buskers, fire-eaters, mendicant gurus, flower ladies, *kioskos*, bookstalls, charlatans, gipsies, aviaries, weirdos and performance artists. Barcelona's flamboyant streetlife is of a kind found only in Spain.

It may not be obvious at first, but there are in fact five Ramblas, all of them slight variations on the same general theme. From the Plaça Catalunya you pass into the Rambla de Canletas, followed by the Rambla dels Estudis or 'Rambla dels Ocells', so named because of the stalls selling canaries, chickens and racing pigeons. Beside the Rambla de San Josep or 'de les Flors' you find the Palau Virreina and the Boquería market, which should be visited if only to admire the aesthetic arrangements of fresh fruit and fish. The Rambla dels Caputxins was once the centre of Barcelona's theatreland, but only the Teatro Principal has survived for stage performances and the Gran Teatre de Liceu for opera.

If this interests you, visit the *Museu de les Arts de l'Espectacle* (Theatre Museum) situated in Gaudí's Palau Güell just around the corner in Carrer Nou de Rambla 3 – built in 1888 for the architect's greatest patron, Eusebi Güell. It displays many of Gaudí's finest architectural innovations such as *trencadís* work (the use of irregularly shaped pieces of glazed ceramic), sculpted chimney tops, a parabolic cupola in the main room and highly original brickwork in the basement.

Just down from the opera house is the elegant neoclassical **Plaça Reial** with its palm trees, golden ochre façades and Gaudí-designed streetlamps. If you sit here, quite soon you'll get your first taste of the Barrio Chino that lies on either side of the Rambla de Santa Mónica. Travellers are generally warned away from the narrow streets where pickpockets, transvestites and prostitutes inhabit a small universe of sex and drugs, reminiscent of Jean Genet's Barcelona.

At the end of Las Ramblas is a statue of Columbus, standing high on an iron pedestal and globe, with his finger pointing out to sea. Following the success of his first voyage, Columbus travelled to Barcelona to report the discovery of the New World to Ferdinand and Isabel. Though his discovery in 1492 sounded the knell for Barcelona's commerce, it has not prevented Catalans from claiming Columbus as their own. For a different view of Barcelona, you can take an elevator to the top of the monument and look back up the Ramblas.

The heart of medieval Barcelona is the **Barrio Gótico** (Gothic Quarter), which is contained within the parameters of what was once the Roman wall and has been built on by successive civilizations. Miró lived here and the brothels inspired Picasso's Les Demoiselles d'Avignon, his first major

Barcelona, the most European of Spanish cities and seat of the Catalan government, has long been known for its cosmopolitan street life, its energy and its creative art and architecture. Veronica Janssen

Cubist painting. Today the Barrio remains the centre for the local artistic community. Its heyday was in the 12th, 13th and 14th centuries, when the majority of the city's most important buildings were constructed. It is still one of the finest examples of urban Gothic architecture left in Europe.

Enter via the Plaça Nova, through the Portal del Bisbe. To the left is the *Casa de L'Ardiaca* (Archdeacon's House), with a Gothic cloister-courtyard and a towering palm tree rising from its centre. On your right is the *Palacio del Bisbe* (Bishop's Palace), with its large Romanesque gallery. Beyond the palace the Carrer Montjuïch del Bisbe leads to the enchanting little Plaça de Felip Neri.

The cathedral of **Santa Eulalia**, or 'La Seu', is a mainly Gothic construction with a few Romanesque traces such as the San Ivo Gate. It was built over a Visigothic basilica, which was destroyed by the Franks in the ninth century. The structure is divided into three vaulted naves and 29 side-chapels. The crypt contains the alabaster sarcophagus of Santa Eulalia, patron saint of the city, with scenes from her martyrdom engraved in low relief around the sides. You can make out her death sentence imposed by Diocletian, and her soul rising to

---

Catalan Romanesque Painting

Catalunya's substantial heritage of medieval painting developed from the illuminated codices and manuscripts of Mozarabic and pre-Romanesque art and flowered during the 12th century in the widespread frescoing of churches. The county's close proximity to France and its strong connections with Italy enabled the Catalans to develop an original style, more refined than much of the Romanesque found along the Camino de Santiago, but incorporating Islamic decorative details that set it apart from other European schools.

Catalan frescoing was widespread around the millenium and coincided with a phase of growing political cohesion in the independent county. Today there are some 2,500 Romanesque churches in Catalunya, mainly in the northern Pyrenees, though there were probably twice that number in 1300.

Fortunately many of the paintings have been rescued from the more isolated churches and placed in the Museo de Arte de Catalunya in Barcelona – the most important single collection of Romanesque art in the world. On display are examples of the greatest painters of the genre, such as the Masters of Pedret, Tahull, Santa Coloma and Soriguerola.

In theme and iconography Catalan Romanesque derives from Byzantine forms but is distinguished by vivid and profuse background detail, a factor most probably influenced by the Islamic preference for decoration. The bold dark lines of the master of Tahull working at the beginning of the 12th century was to set a precedent for subsequent muralists and went on to influence the work of 20th-century artists such as Picabia, Picasso and Miró.

---

heaven in the form of a dove. Beneath the organ, the head of a Moor once coughed out sweets for children. In the half-light of the Chapel of the Most Holy Sacrament, on the left of the west door, can be seen the Christ of Lepanto, the figurehead on the flagship of Don Juan de Austria at the Battle of Lepanto. The great iron *rejas* (gates protecting the side-altars) are beautifully wrought Gothic examples from an age when the iron forges of Catalunya produced the most intricate ironwork in Europe.

In the cloister a few fat geese laze around the *Font de los Oques* (Fountain of Geese) beneath the vaulted galleries that are surrounded by a garden containing palm and magnolia trees. Beside the *Puerta de la Pietat* (Doorway of Pity) stands a small chapel with a Gothic fountain. From the cloister you enter the Sala Capitular, the chapterhouse that contains the cathedral museum, notable for a 15th-century retable, a Gothic tabernacle, the silver and gilt throne of Martín I and an 18th-century portable organ.

Walking around the back of the cathedral from the cloister and down Boulevarde Santa Clara, you come to the Plaça del Rei, a gracious square, around which are situated several important buildings. The **Palau Reial Major**, royal residence of the Counts of Barcelona, encompasses the huge five-levelled tower of galleries known as the Mirador del Rei Martín, the Palatine chapel of Santa Agata with the altarpiece of the Lord High Constable, and the great Saló de Tinell, where Columbus delivered his news of the

New World to the Catholic Monarchs. This was formerly a ballroom but its most gracious features remain the Romanesque windows.

Access to these rooms is gained through the entrance on C. Llibreteria to the **Museu d'Història de la Ciutat**, in the old Clarian-Padellás Palace. The history of the city is revealed in archeological finds, maps, photographs and city plans. You can learn of the founding of the city by the Carthaginian general Hamilcar Barca (hence Barcelona); of six centuries of Roman occupation; and of the building of the city walls in the fourth century AD as a defence against the raids from the north by the Franks. There are exhibits dating from Visigothic and Moorish times, and from the city's period of greatest prosperity and expansion between the 13th and 15th centuries. In the cellars are remains of the Roman foundations.

Modernismo

In its widest context, Modernism was a movement that affected all Europe in the decades bridging the 1900s. German *Jugendstil*, Italian *Liberty*, French *Art Nouveau* and Spanish *Modernismo* were all ideologically connected. Even though examples of Modernist architecture can be found throughout Spain (Cantabria, Balearic Islands, Madrid, Valencia, Zaragoza and Murcia), the greatest concentration of buildings is to be found in Catalunya, particularly in Barcelona.

The advent of railways and the growth of industrial towns and summer resorts gave artists and writers new sources of material for their inventive expression. Architects and artists, conscious of their Catalan heritage, created a brilliant movement that plundered the past for its symbolism while experimenting with the materials of the modern age.

A long period of economic prosperity coincided with the cultural renaissance that began in Catalunya at the beginning of the 19th century with the revival of the Catalan language. A new educated bourgeoisie and a few rich industrialists vied with each other to patronize the emergent progressive ideas. The effects of *Modernismo* spread into all creative media, from sculpture to jewellery design, but at the forefront of this innovation was a group of architects including Antoni Gaudí i Cornet, Luis Domenèch i Montaner and Josep Puig i Cadafalch.

The general intention of the movement was to revive something of the cultural splendour of the Aragonese–Catalan Empire and to reinterpret the architectural traditions of the past in the context of the industrial age. Gothic and Catalan symbolism (in particular the region's patron saint, St George), Mudéjar brickwork, Islamic tile patterning, ironwork, carpentry and glass were all employed in the search for the *obra total* (the total work). A building had to fulfil two basic functions: not only as a practical piece of architecture, but as a work of art in its own right, down to the smallest details of the interior and the design of the furniture.

Through their imaginative use of naturalistic and fantastic shapes, bold colours and strange surface textures, this group changed general perceptions of architecture. Even though *Modernismo* had a relatively short lifespan (1888–1916), its influence continued well beyond the subsequent generation of artists, which included figures such as Picasso, Miró and Dalí.

Turning back towards the great west door of the cathedral, you pass the entrance to the **Museu Federico Marés**, which contains an interesting collection of sculptures, medieval imagery and stone carvings from the tenth to the 16th centuries. In *Plaça de la Seu* stands the **Casa de la Pía Almoina**, an institution erected in 1009 to feed 100 poor people daily.

Back in the midst of the Gothic Quarter along Carrer Bisbe, you arrive in the Plaça de Sant Jaume, which is dominated on either side by the Palau de la Generalitat and Ayuntament, the two main bodies of autonomous Catalan administration. The late Gothic façade of the **Generalitat Palace** contains a courtyard with an open-air stairway and a first-storey twin-arched gallery. The palace was constructed in the time of James II (1291–1327) when the Catalan parliament first started to meet. Of particular importance are the chapel of Sant Jordi in the flamboyant Gothic style and, at the back of the building, the orangery courtyard, paved in Carrara marble.

On the opposite side of the plaza, in the **Ayuntament** (City Hall), is an equally impressive courtyard and staircase. In the Saló dels Cròniques within, there are superb murals by Josep María Sert depicting the Catalan expedition under Roger de Flor to the Orient in the 14th century. Behind the Generalitat, in the Plazuela de Sant Just are the impressive palaces of Moxió and Palamós and the church of **Sants Just i Pastor**, thought to be the oldest ecclesiastical construction in Barcelona and used as the parish church by the Kings of Aragón.

The rapid expansion of Barcelona between the 11th and 13th centuries encompassed surrounding areas within its urban network. James I 'the Conqueror' (1213–76) erected Barcelona's second city wall, the boundaries of which became Las Ramblas to the south and the Parc de la Ciutadella to the north. Rich merchants had imposing palaces built for themselves and patronized several churches in the area to the north of the Via Laietana. Most important of these is **Santa María del Mar** between Calle Argentera and Calle Montcada, whose foundation stone was laid by Alfonso III 'the Good' (1327–36) after the capture of Sardinia in 1329, in fulfilment of a vow made by James I. The church of Santa María is a perfect example of pure Catalan Gothic, with its vast buttresses crowning a huge hollow space, supported by sheer octagonal pillars and surrounded by beautiful 15th-century stained glass windows depicting scenes from the Last Judgement, Ascension and Last Supper. After the cathedral, it is the most imposing church in Barcelona.

In the surrounding streets you encounter numerous palaces and Gothic mansions, which were noble residences until the 18th century, when they passed into the hands of the bourgeoisie. In general, the façades are austere and the rooms were built around central patios with magnificent staircases and galleries. Several of these along Carrer de Montcada have been converted into museums, the most famous being the **Museu Picasso** at No 15.

Paintings, drawings, sculpture, graphics, lithographs and books are exhibited from every period of Picasso's life (1881–1973). The most important collection is from his early, pre-Parisian days: family portraits, carnival posters and a strong repre-

Cadaqués was once home to a vital body of surrealist artists centred around Salvador Dalí. It is still one of the most active and unspoilt villages of the Costa Brava. Incafo

sentation from the Blue Period. Of his later work the 50-odd variations on Velázquez's great court painting *Las Meninas* stand out for the artist's exploration of colour.

The **Parc de la Ciutadella**, a few streets further north, is an ideal location to spend a quiet afternoon exploring a more subdued corner of Barcelona. At the western end is the neo-Mudéjar triumphal arch, built as an entrance to the International Exhibition of 1888: the year the Modernist architects first attracted widespread European attention. The park contains the Museums of Zoology, Geology, Numismatics and Modern Art, while the dawn of Modernism can be observed in the fantastical cascade built by Josep Fonserè (with rock arrangements by a young Antoni Gaudí). At the seafront end, there is an excellent zoo containing the only albino gorilla in captivity.

In 1714, after an 11-month siege, the Bourbon troops of Philip V finally entered Barcelona. A rambling citadel was built over the park with the sole intention of intimidating the Catalans, and was pulled down at the first opportunity after the area was returned to the city in 1869. There is a memorial statue to the mayor, Ruis i Taulet, who masterminded the exhibition of 1888 and encouraged the progressive mentality of the city's inhabitants.

Beyond the trees, flowerbeds and fountains, the park as a whole is a historic reminder of Barcelona's fortitude and spirit of cultural innovation that rose from its 19th-century renaissance.

Between the park, the Estació de Francia and the sea lies the 18th-century neighbourhood of **Barceloneta**. This was built to house the displaced families who were forced out of the district now occupied by the Parc de la Ciutadella to make way for Philip V's citadel. The area is full of cosy fish restaurants with glassed-in verandahs that come to life at night and Sunday lunchtimes, when the tables spill out along the waterfront. It's interesting just to walk between the busy apartment blocks that are home to families of fishermen and dock workers; observing the bustle of local Barcelona life in its many guises is one of the city's fundamental pleasures.

Along the seafront stand a collection of civic buildings, including the *Aduana Vella* (Old Customs House), *La Lotja* (Stock Exchange) and Barcelona's central post office on the Plaça Antoni López. Continue to the Columbus monument, where you can take a small boat (*Golondrina*) along Barceloneta's harbour front.

Nearby are the *Reales Atarazanas* (Royal Shipyards) or 'Drassens' that house the **Museu Marítim**. It's worth a visit just to see the spectacular Gothic elements of the building, which is similar in many ways to an elongated hall-church. In one of the dozen parallel naves stands a reproduction of the flagship Don Juan of Austria commanded at the Battle of Lepanto. During the 13th and 14th centuries, Barcelona, together with Genoa, was the largest shipbuilder in the Mediterranean. For coastal trade the yard produced small craft about 9m in length and larger ships weighing 500 tonnes for the run to North Africa and the Near East. They were built mostly of wood, powered by both sails and oars, and painted with stripes of red and gold, the colours of the county of Barcelona.

Every city in Spain has a park that reveals something about its citizens and lifestyle. **Montjuïc** is Barcelona's park *par excellence*, built on the site of the old Jewish cemetery for the international exhibition of 1929. From the citadel at the top, which houses the *Museu del Exercit* (Military Museum), you have magnificent views over the city, harbour and Mediterranean. Elsewhere in the park are Greek amphitheatres, a cactus garden, a miniature city, the *Poble Espanyol* (Spanish Town) that comprises all the main architectural features of Spain, rose gardens, a weekend funfair, illuminated fountains (weekends and Thursdays during the summer), and the **Olympic Stadium** built for the 1992 Games. To explore the park properly you will need at least a day.

The main attraction is the **Museu d'Art de Catalunya**, in the Palacio Nacional, which is considered by some to be one of the great museums of the world and justly deserves its sobriquet of the Prado of Romanesque Art. Romanesque and Gothic altarpieces, statues and frescoes from throughout the region are superbly exhibited, and parts of churches have been reconstructed. In the adjoining buildings are the Ethnological and Archeological Museums. From the *mirador* at the front there are panoramic views down the steps leading to the smaller exhibition pavilions and the Plaça Espanya.

The **Fundació Joan Miró** is the other

main exhibition centre. The Foundation was completed in 1975 by the Catalan architect Josep Lluis Sert, and it serves two functions. On the one hand, it is devoted to the study of the work of Joan Miró and to this end the most important collection of his work is on public display here. Secondly, it helps promote contemporary art in general and holds travelling exhibitions from all over the world. The mercury fountain donated by Alexander Calder in 1990 is one of the strangest exhibits.

The Parc de Montjuïc reflects the last stage of innovative city planning that swept through Barcelona in the first half of the 20th century, but on a civic level the most dramatic work is to be seen along the wide boulevards of the great 19th-century urban extension known as the **Eixample**, initiated by Ildefons Cerdà. Here many of the zaniest Modernist houses can still be admired, with the finest examples to be seen along the Passeig de Gràcia, a tree-lined shopping mall.

On the *Manzana de la Discordia* (the Block of Discord – a pun on the word *manzana*, which means apple as well as block) there are three buildings by the three major Modernist architects. On the corner with Carrer de Consell de Cent stands the **Casa Lleó Morera**, by Domènech i Montaner, with stunning flower details by the sculptor Arnau, the glazier Rigalt i Granell and tiling and mosaics by Margaliano and Bru. A few doors down is the **Casa Amatller**, by the master of the Neo-Gothic, Puig i Cadafalch. This is a composed and elegant construction enhanced by iridescent ceramic tiles. On the first floor is an elaborate fireplace designed like a bar of chocolate in celebration of the founder's fortune. The first floor is now a library and may be visited by ringing the first-floor bell. Next to it is Gaudí's **Casa Battló** (open daily 8–10am) with large Elephantine columns planted firmly on the pavement, and a typically organic façade of bizarre forms and motifs, with a bright blue glazed roof shaped like the spine of a dinosaur.

Further up the Passeig is the **Casa Milá** or 'La Pedrera' (The Stone Quarry), so termed because of the façade which undulates like sand caught in a receding tide. This was Gaudí's last work before he deployed all his energies in the Sagrada Familia. It is possibly his most accomplished building, from its chimneys shaped like carved African heads to the parabolic arches leading into the underground car park. (Visits of the roof and underground stable are conducted at 10/11/noon daily.)

A little further on, the Eixample is bisected by the Avinguda Diagonal. At its southern end in the neighbourhoods of Sarrià and Pedralbes lie the Universitat, Gaudí's convent of Santa Clara, the Pedralbes Palace (now a museum) and the exquisite 14th-century monastery of Pedralbes, which was founded by Elisenda de Montcada, the fourth wife of James II (cloister opened to the public every first and third Sunday of the month from 12–2pm). In the other direction lie more important Modernist buildings, including two by Puig i Cadafalch. The **Palau Vidal-Quadras** at No 373 is now a musical instrument museum, and the **Casa de Punxes**, on an island of its own, resembles something out of Grimms' fairy tales. The most important work by Domènech i Montaner is the Casa de Montaner on the corner of Carrer de Mallorca.

However, the great mecca of Modernist architecture is without question the **Sagrada Familia**, reached by veering left from the Diagonal along Carrer Provença. This was Gaudí's *magnum opus*, in which he tried to create a whole new genre of temple. There is no building like it in the history of architecture, whether you consider it an anachronistic folly or the vision of a genius. Gaudí called it his 'mystic hive' and, though more than 100 years have passed since building started, only a fraction is complete. The final edifice was intended to consist of 12 towers representing each of the apostles, four more for the evangelists, another for the Virgin, and the largest – soaring to a height of over 152m – a symbol of the life of Christ. Every bit of the façade was to tell the life of a saint or writhe with allegorical and natural symbolism. A lift ascends into one of the completed towers, and there is a small museum on the site explaining Gaudí's life and work.

North of the Sagrada Familia is the Hospital de Sant Pau, a vast construction by Domènech i Montaner; and beyond it the **Parc Güell**, which gives an indication of the extent of Gaudí's extraordinary imagination. The area was originally intended to be a smart suburban housing estate on a hill overlooking the city, where the architecture would symphonize with the landscape. Only two houses and the garden were ever completed, however, and the site was eventually turned into a municipal park. The great wavy bench finished with colourful broken tile fragments and the hall of 100 columns show Gaudí's inimitable way of harmonizing nature and architecture through colour and line.

COSTA BRAVA An alternative route to Barcelona from the French border takes you down the Costa Brava, marking the beginning of the great coastal urbanization that stretches around the greater part of Spain's Mediterranean coast. In the same way that the Barrio Gótico is a testament to Catalunya's medieval heyday, so the Costa Brava is a reminder of how Spain sold its coastal soul to mass tourism in the 1950s. The prefab conurbations, high-rise hotels and luxury modern villas seem to scab miles of the coast. None the less, in high summer this is still one of the most favoured sun-seekers' playgrounds of Europe, supplying every conceivable recreational activity including yachting, windsurfing, gambling, watersports, cable television, miles of beaches, long days of guaranteed sunshine and endless numbers of bars, restaurants and discos. In the last few years an average of 16 million tourists have visited Catalunya, most of them staying along this thin line of coast. It is particularly popular with young Germans, locally known as *Las Valkiras*, after the angels of Norse mythology.

It was not always thus. Only 40 years ago Rose Macaulay described the Costa Brava as 'Cornwall in the sun'; only a few decades before the property speculators became high-rise happy. There is, however, still evidence of this idyllic, not-so-distant past. The countryside retains a rugged charm, and many of the secluded inland valleys that support the vineyards of Empordá with their cypress avenues and Italianate farmhouses resemble the landscape of Tuscany. Along the coast – especially around the Cabo de Creus – there are still a few deserted rocky coves nestling quietly between pine-clad cliffsides, and the sea is relatively clean. The coastal roads at night are spectacular for their views of the harbour lights, especially around the Gulf of Roses. In many fishing villages you can still see the fishermen returning with the early-morning catch and their conversations are still punctuated with theories about the great coastal winds of Tramontana, Garbi, Levante and Mediodía which still blow at the intended time each year.

From the frontier at **Port Bou**, the sand-strewn beaches of **Llança** protect several interesting dolmens and Romanesque ruins in the area. On a mountainside overlooking the sea loom the ruins of Sant Pere de Rhodes: one of the most impressive medieval monuments in the western Mediterranean. It is reached by taking the inland road from Llança to **Vilajuiga**, turning left into the village, and continuing for another 4km until the road turns into a track.

The monastery is built on the ruins of a pagan temple dedicated to Venus, overlooking the Cabo de Creus peninsula and the Gulf of Lions, and is considered to be one of the earliest and purest examples of Catalan Romanesque. It was allegedly founded by Pope Boniface IV who sent emissaries to the far side of the Mediterranean to hide some valuable relics, including the skull of St Peter, at a time when Rome was threatened with attack. When the threat had passed and the same emissaries returned, they were unable to find what they had hidden and built a monastery instead. One of the earliest treatises on Catalan wine was written by a monk from the monastery.

Cadaqués (pop. 1,800), thanks to its relative inaccessibility, has remained comparatively quiet and unspoilt. From its origins as a small fishing village surrounding the old castle belonging to the Counts of Empúries, it became a resort town for avant-garde painters, artists and intellectuals in the early years of the 20th century. In the small Museum of Graphic Art there are works by Caravaggio, Zurbarán, Goya and Matisse. Dalí had his holiday home a few kilometres north in Port Lligat.

Returning inland you come to **Roses**, whose original colony founded by traders from Rhodes has long been overtaken by the avenues of *apartamentos* that rise blandly along the shore. The old town is dwarfed by gross development and even the fishing fleet, the largest on the Costa Brava, has been computerized. For energetic holidaymakers, entertainment is to be found in the aquatic parks and on the golf courses.

The Golfo de Roses that stretches south to **L'Escala** does not have a coast road but instead can boast the Empordá marshes (Parc Natural dels Aiguamolls de L'Empordá): a saline delta of lagoons, river estuaries, water meadows, lakes and sand dunes. Until 1983 this important ecosystem was threatened with development, but the area is now protected and the marshes continue to support a huge biological empire of colourful water vegetation, floating aquatic plants, painted frogs, stripe-necked terrapin, grebes, kingfishers, and even flamingoes. The park is on the migratory route for nearly 300 different species of birds, many of which nest among the reed beds. The Catalan Tourist Board produces a good pamphlet on the area, with a map of the small roads running among the watercourses. Be warned, though – the marshes are a haven for mosquitoes.

At the southern end of the park, reached by a road from L'Escala, you come to the ancient site of **Empúries** (open daily 10am–2pm & 3–7pm), where umbrella pines and cypress trees shelter extensive ruins. This was once an island settlement, but is now joined to the mainland. The old town (*palaiapolis*) nearest the sea was first colonized by the Phocaean Greeks from Marseille and subsequently fell under Roman control in the third century BC. A new town (*neápolis*) was erected and thrived for almost four centuries, before it eventually succumbed to repeated Barbary raids. The small museum here has attempted to reconstruct parts of Empúries with a series of plans and models. Only part of the site has so far been excavated, but of interest are the two villas on the hill above the town and the temples to Zeus and Aesculapius, the Greek god of healing. The Olympic flame on its way to Barcelona landed at Empúries. A short walk along the beach lies Sant Martí de Empúries, which has a couple of quiet bars near the beach.

From L'Escala the relentless urbanization continues south into the plain of the River Ter. **Torroella de Montgri** has a certain charm, as the old village has receded inland and thus been spared 20th-century desecration. Off the coast, around the *Iles Medes* there is an underwater nature park known as 'The Silent World', where you can hire scuba diving gear and explore the subaquatic caves. Alternatively, you can take a boat to the islands – now turned into a bird sanctuary – and walk among the huge flocks of seagulls who remain unaware that this was once Spain's Devil's Island.

Pals, a few kilometres inland from Begur (pop. 2,500), has a well-preserved old town. To the south lie camping sites, beaches, coves and more concrete. Places to avoid unless you enjoy northern European coastal culture in a Catalan setting are Palafrugell, Palamós, Sant Feliú de Guixols, Tossa de Mar, Lloret de Mar and Blanes. The Costa Brava ends just south of Blanes and you can follow the N11 right down the Costa Maresme to Barcelona.

TOURIST OFFICES

FIGUERAS: Plaza del Sol, tel (972) 50 31 55.

GIRONA: Rambla 1, tel (972) 20 26 79.

BARCELONA: Gran Via de les Corts Catalanes 658, tel (93) 301 74 43; (Municipal Tourist Office) Passeig de Grácia 35, tel (93) 215 44 77.
(Ferry to Baleares) Cia Aucona, Via Laietana 2, tel (93) 319 82 12.

CADAQUES: Cotxe 2A, tel (972) 25 83 15.

Accommodation, Eating and Drinking

FIGUERAS:

(H&R)**Duran**, C/ Lasauca 5, tel (972) 50 12 50. Hotel with restaurant, excellent seafood casseroles. Good *bodega*. C&B.

GIRONA:

(H)**Bellmirall**, C/ Bellmirall 3, tel (972) 20 40 09. D.
Good cheap restaurants and *tapas* bars in El Call.

BARCELONA (tel code 93):

(H)**Ritz**, Gran Via de las Corts Catalanes 668, tel 318 52 00. A.
(H)**Condes de Barcelona**, Passeig de Gracia 75, tel 487 37 37. Elegantly restored with neo-Gothic *ajimez* (twin-arched windows) and balconied rooms. A.
(H)**Oriente**, C/ Ramblas 45–47, tel 302 25 58. Old atmospheric hotel, recently restored. Central. C.
(H)**Peninsular**, C/ San Pablo 34, tel 302 31 38. Elegantly restored rooms overlooking a plant-filled patio. Highly atmospheric. D.
(H)**España**, C/ Sant Pan 9–11, tel 318 17 58. An *Art Nouveau* fantasy. C.
(H)**Gran Vía**, C/ Gran Vía 642, tel 318 19 00. In a 19th-century palace. C.
(H)**Regina**, C/ Vergara 2, tel 301 32 32. Friendly establishment near the Ramblas. C.
(H)**Augustin**, Pl. Sant Augustin, tel 317 28 82. In the heart of the Gothic Quarter, overlooking the Plaza. D–C.
(H)**Colón, Av. Catedral 7**, tel 301 14 04. Popular with tourists. Opposite cathedral plaza. Faded charm but certainly not for people with a fear of ringing bells. C–B.
(H)**Covadonga**, C/ Avda Diagonal 596, tel 209 55 11. Small, exclusive. C.
(H)**Majestic**, Paseo de Gracia 70, tel 215 45 12. Large, impersonal, with pool. B.
(R)**Casa Leopoldo**, San Rafael 24, tel 241 30 14. In the narrow backstreets behind the Ramblas, this elegant but simple restaurant is one of the most popular local haunts in the capital. Excellent seafood. B.
(R)**Siete Puertas**, C/ Paseo de Isabel II 14, tel 319 30 33. Over 150 years old, well-known among locals for its paella. C.
(R)**Los Caracoles**, C/ Escadellers 14, tel 302 31 85. A typical old tavern with barrels and peppers hanging from the ceiling. Good traditional food. C.
(R)**Can Sole**, C/ San Carlos 4, tel 319 50 12. Traditional Barceloneta haunt. Simple but excellent food cooked in original ovens, which date to the restaurant's opening in 1907. Good value. C.
(R)**Network**, C/ Diagonal 66, tel 201 72 38. Open until 2.30am. Combination of Mexican, Spanish and Italian food. C.
(B)**Cambrinus**, C/ Moll de la Fusta, tel 310 55 77. A popular, inexpensive *tapas* bar with an informal atmosphere. D.
(R)**Eldorado Petit**, C/ Dolores Monserda 51, tel 204 51 53. Expensive, modern restaurant situated in an old town house with tables in the garden. The sort of place where five variations of rolls are served. Booking obligatory. A.

(R)**Amaya**, Ramblas 20–24, tel 302 10 37. Bar and restaurant serving excellent Basque food. Informal, reasonably priced and excellent service. C–B.
(B)**Satanassa**, Aribau 27. Good Barcelona ambience. E.
(B)**La Palma**, C/ Espaseria. Classic but well restored. E.
(B)**Velvet**, Balmes 161. 1950s nostalgia. Young clientele. E.
(B)**El Borne**, Paseo del Borne 26. Good drinks. E.

CADAQUES:

(H&R)**La Galiota**, C/ Narcis Monturiol 9, tel (972) 25 81 87. Hotel with good restaurant. An old haunt for local artists and intellectuals. B.

The Catalan Pyrenees

Cutting from west to east through the Pyrenees, this route covers the northern block of Catalunya. Roads twist and turn down quiet valleys through magnificent mountain scenery with idyllic Romanesque villages of stone houses. One of the more obscure routes into Spain is on the N125 through the Val d'Aran, 'the valley of valleys'. This had independent status until the 18th century, and it was not until the tunnel was built in 1948 that the area became easily accessible. Even now the Aranese speak their own form of Catalá, which derives from a Languedoc variant of Gascon and reflects the former isolation of this Pyrenean community. In recent years a ski resort has opened around **Vielha (Viella)** (pop. 3,000), but you can still enjoy magnificent walks in the river valleys, watching butterflies such as the alpine grizzled skipper (*Pyrgus Andromedae*), and the great clouded apollo with a three-inch wingspan. In January an international horserace over snow takes place in the area, the only one of its kind in the world.

The church of San Miguel in Viella has a gracious octagonal tower and,

above the west door, a 13th-century tympanum depicting the Last Judgement. A plaque on the town hall relates how in 1924 Alfonso XIII, King of Spain, was the first monarch to set foot in Arán.

South-west of Viella lies the **Aigües Tortes National Park** and San Mauricio lake. For dramatic mountain scenery this is magnificent, with massive peaks falling steeply into a web of streams, lakes and meadows. The park is divided into two zones: the western side with the great *massifs* is approached via the tunnel, and the other zone comprises the Boi valley, with its sleepy little villages and the magnificent Romanesque church of St Climent de Taüll. The church is one of the most sophisticated examples of 12th-century Catalan Romanesque, and the frescoes within are reproductions of those to be seen in the Museum of Catalan Art in Barcelona. In terms of theme and iconography, they are clearly descended from Byzantine mosaics and were most probably completed around 1123. They are outstanding for their sumptuous and colourful depiction of clothes, and the lifelike, penetrating gaze of the figures, especially the Christ Pantocrator.

The 12th-century church of San Clemente at Taüll is a fine example of Catalan–Lombard Romanesque, with a six-storey bell tower and, inside, copies of the frescoes by the Master of Tahull (the originals are in the Museo de Arte de Catalunya in Barcelona). Incafo

There are also the peculiar abstract bulls of Taüll, whose freehand tortured expressions were the ancestors of those painted by Picasso in his monochrome mural *Guernica* (see p. 225).

The eastern side of the park can be approached through Espot, and a road leads to the edge of the lake of St Mauricio, where the trails and walks begin. These lake beds were carved out by glacial erosion in the late Quaternary Age and the icy waters in some

places reach to a depth of 46m. Otters live in the banks of the lakes, and wild goats, ibex and eagles thrive in the wild parkland.

Continuing along the C147 after the junction for the slate-roofed village of Llavorsi are the obscure Pyrenean valleys of Cardós and Tor, with their notorious smuggling trails leading over the Andorran border. At **Sort** (pop. 1,200) are the remains of a castle and fortification. At **Gerni de la Sal**,

43km further south, salt has been panned from the river for more than 1,500 years. One of the first Benedictine monasteries in the Iberian Peninsula was established here during the reign of Charlemagne. The 12th-century church has an interesting three-storey belfry, typical of the Catalan Romanesque style. Continuing through the Desfiladero de Collegats, the road veers beside the Embalse de Sant Antoni through a spectacular limestone landscape.

Tremp (pop. 5,700) is a relaxed Pyrenean town with an interesting Gothic hall-church. From Tremp the C147 continues down the Noguera valley into the pre-Pyrenean foothills to **LÉRIDA** or LLEIDA (pop. 108,000), a large, sprawling provincial capital with little to stop for except the old cathedral. The route through the central Pyrenees heads south-east to Isona, an old Iberian settlement, and from there along the L511 to Coll de Nargo. Almost all the villages here – in particular **Boixols** and **Valldarqués** – contain some magnificent remnant of early Romanesque expansion. At **Coll de Nargo** the pre-Romanesque church of Sant Climent with its pyramidal tower and double-colonnaded windows is the most imposing example set against the Sierra del Cadí.

Turning north again, you pass **Organya**, first mentioned in the 11th-century Catalan homilies, which were discovered in the archive of the church of Santa María in 1904. The route continues through the Garganta de Oranya, a 610-metre gorge carved out by the River Segre beside the Sierra del Cadí. For those who want to explore the natural park, it is best done from here; otherwise, continue to La Seu d'Urgell.

Seu d'Urgell (pop. 10,000) is the seat of a bishop who, along with the President of France, is the co-prince of Andorra. If you've entered Spain from Andorra, the great duty-free supermarket high in the Pyrenees, this will be your first stop. The one important sight is the Romanesque cathedral of Santa María, founded by San Ermengol. This was presided over during the 13th century by the notorious bishop, Ponce de Planedes, who fathered ten local children. The cathedral has a fine carved doorway with rectangular towers at each corner. In the museum you can see a copy of the Beatus de Liébana. Otherwise there is little of interest in this mainly modern town.

More noteworthy is the **Parc Natural de Cadí Moixeró**, which is best entered south of Seu d'Urgell, but is more easily explored by its northern approaches. This natural park was established by the Generalitat de Catalunya in 1983 and contains the pre-Pyrenean ranges of Cadí and Moixeró. Once again there are many beautiful Romanesque stone villages scattered through the range. These maintain strong local traditions such as sheepdog trials and the ancient nativity festival of *La Fia Faia* when torches and bonfires are lit throughout the mountains. On the higher slopes between alpine meadows there are wild rhododendron bushes. Animals to be found in the area include wild chamois, red and roe deer, pine-martens and birds such as capercaillie, black woodpeckers and golden eagles. Low temperatures and high humidity are responsible for the strange ecosystem that exists in the park. Detailed information and free maps can be obtained at the *ayuntamiento* (town hall) in Bellver de Cerdanya, Tuixén and Le Seu d'Urgell. The main information centre is at Baga.

The C1313 snakes along the northern boundary of the park and the River Sagre through the villages of Martinet, Lles and Bellver de Cerdanya, with a gracious porticoed plaza and castle ruins.

Puigcerdà (pop. 6,500), a winter resort town, remains the capital of the Cerdanya: a district that once stretched into France. The old walled town stands on a hill above a plain encircled by mountains. The damaged church of Santa María and the convent of Santo Domingo preserve only a few Gothic and Romanesque features. A small road connects the town with **Llivia**, a tiny Spanish enclave in France with one of the oldest pharmacies in Europe, which can be visited 10am–1pm & 3–6pm. The road south via the Cadí tunnel follows the River Llobregat to Barcelona. The scenery becomes increasingly industrialized after Berga. The route through the Pyrenees continues by La Molina and the ski resorts of Ribes de Freser to Ripoll.

Ripoll (pop. 12,000) has little to offer beyond its illustrious monastery, through which Arabic numerals were introduced to Europe. In the 11th and 12th centuries Ripoll was one of the lights of its age. It was a centre for art, poetry, astronomy, music and mathematics, and played a leading role in the resettlement of Catalunya and the diffusion of both Christian culture into Spain and Arabic learning into northern Europe. The Benedictine abbey of Santa María was founded by Count Wilfrid 'the Hairy' in 888 but was destroyed by the Arabs, and the present foundation was not consecrated

until 1032 by Abbot Oliva, Bishop of Vic. The most important surviving part is the west door, which survived an earthquake in 1428 and a fire in 1835 and is considered to be the most outstanding extant example of Catalan Romanesque sculpture. The radial arches of the portal are surrounded by seven horizontal carved bands that depict Biblical and allegorical subjects, including the 24 elders of the Apocalypse, the flight from Egypt, David's vision of the end of the world, Cain and Abel, and include symbols of the evangelists and representations of the months of the year. The 12th-century cloister's carved capital heads are examples of the Romanesque style known as the Ripoll school.

Vic (pop. 32,000), 38km south of Ripoll, has an interesting cathedral with a six-storeyed Romanesque tower and a flamboyant Gothic cloister. The frescoes inside are by the Catalan painter Josep María Sert and, in just two colours of sepia and metallic grey, depict scenes from the Old and New Testaments on a huge visionary scale. The Museo Episcopal, in Plaça Bisbe Oliva, has an impressive collection of Catalan Gothic religious painting, Romanesque frescoes, and a winged altar by Lluis Borassa that depicts the life of Saint Dominic.

East of Ripoll you arrive in **Olot** (pop. 27,000) in the centre of the volcanic region of La Garrotxa. This small industrial town has the little Modernist neighbourhood of La Malagrida, and a Crucifixion by El Greco in the 18th-century church of St Esteban. The Museum of Modern Art in the Torre Castany is dedicated mainly to the 19th-century landscape painters, particularly Joaquín Vayreda, who drew their inspiration from the area.

There are two routes through the park. The C150 goes across the upper valley of the Fluvià via the spectacular medieval village of **Castellfullit de la Roca** and the ancient town of **Besalú**. The latter is a hive of narrow porticoed streets that lead to the Romanesque churches of Santa María and San Vicente (with its carvings attributed to the Ripoll school) and the church of San Pedro, where impressive masonry surrounds the windows. At one end of the magnificent two-storeyed bridge with its irregularly shaped arches is a *mikwah*, a bath used by Jewish women and formerly part of a synagogue.

The GE524 crosses the centre of the natural park of La Garrotxa through a fine volcanic landscape of overgrown cones and basaltic lava flows and medicinal springs. The last eruption was 11,500 years ago. By virtue of its climate, it is a transitional zone between the Mediterranean, sub-Mediterranean and Atlantic. In the evergreen and deciduous oak groves live wildcats, genets and badgers, and there are 15 (mainly ruined) Romanesque churches scattered throughout the park. Main information centres where good walking maps of the area can be supplied are Olot Tourist Office, C/ Mulleres s/n, Plaça del Mercat; or Santa Pau: Can Vayreda Tourist Office.

The spa town of **Banyoles** (pop. 13,000), on the banks of a lake, has an interesting arcaded square and an Archeological Museum in the converted Gothic Pía Almoina. The museum is dedicated mainly to exhibits found in La Garrotxa, such as prehistoric implements and a Neanderthal jawbone unearthed in the cave at Serinyà. The short walk around the lake to Porqueres is worth taking for yet one more jewel of a Romanesque church.

TOURIST OFFICES

VIELLA: Calle Sarriulera 6, tel (973) 64 01 10.

SEU D'URGELL: Avda de Valira, tel (973) 35 15 11.

Accommodation, Eating and Drinking

VIELLA (tel code 973):

(H)**Parador Valle de Arán**, Ctra del Tunel s/n, tel 64 01 00. Overlooks village and forested valley. Popular as winter ski resort. Swimming pool. Magnificent views. C.
(R)**Antonio**, Ctra del Tunel s/n, tel 64 08 07. Local Aranese specialities include pig's trotters (*pies de cerdo*). C–B.

AIGUES TORTES (tel code 973):

(H&R)**Saurat**, Plaza San Martín s/n, Espot, tel 63 50 63. Good functional hotel for exploring park. Cl May and 15 Oct–23 Dec. Good restaurant. Specialities include side of goat (*pierna de cabrito*). D.

(H)**Fondevila**, Unica s/n, Barruera, tel 69 60 11. Homely and comfortable *hostal* in the Boi valley. D.

SORT:

(H&R)**Pessets**, Ctra Seo de Urgel s/n, tel (973) 62 00 00. A functional hotel with swimming pool. Good restaurant for river trout (*trucha Palleresa*). C.

SEU D'URGELL:

(H)**Parador Seo de Urgel**, Santo Domingo s/n, tel (973) 35 20 00. In the old convent of Santo Domingo, beside cathedral and medieval quarter, with rooms surrounding a cloister. Essential to book well in advance. C.

ALAS:

(R)**Casa Dolcet**, Avda de J. Zulueta 1, tel (973) 35 20 16. Cl Fri and Nov. Simple Catalan food and wine. B.

CADÍ MOIXERO PARQUE NATURAL:

Large choice of *hostales* in villages around park.
(H)**Can Francisco**, Gósol Ctra de Berga s/n, tel (973) 37 00 75. Perfectly adequate for exploring the park.
(H)**Parador Duques de Cardona**, Castillo de Cardona, tel (93) 86 91 75. Magnificent parador in the castle of the Duques de Cardona on the road between Seu d'Urgell and Barcelona, overlooking the salt mountain. C.

LA CERDANYA:

(H&R)**Boix**, Ctra Nac. 260km 204–25724 Martinet de Cerdanya (between Seu d' Urgell and Puigcerda), tel (973) 51 50 50. Owned by one of the country's leading chefs; the cuisine is of an exceptional standard. One of the most exclusive hotels in Catalunya. B–A.

LLIVIA (tel code 972):

(H)**Llivia**, Ctra de Puigcerdá s/n, tel 89 60 00. All amenities. C.
(R)**Meson Can Ventura**, Plaza Mayor 1, tel 89 61 78. Good for lunch or dinner.

RIPOLL:

(R)**Grill El Gall**, Ctra Barcelona/Puigcerdá km 109, tel (972) 70 24 51. Delicious meats cooked over a charcoal fire. C.

OLOT (tel code 972):

(H)**Montsacopa**, C/ Mulleras, tel 26 07 62. Reasonable, clean hotel. D.
(R)**Font Maixina**, C/ Afueras, tel 26 10 11. Combination of French and Catalan food. C.

SANTA PAU:

(H)**Bellavista**, C/ Crta de Sant Martí, tel (972) 68 01 03. In an excellent location for exploring the park. E.

BANYOLES (tel code 972):

(H)**Victoria**, Dr Hysern 22, tel 57 12 79. Good for a night. D.
(R)**Flora**, Pl Tures 24, tel 57 00 77. Cl Sun and all Jan. Local specialities. C–B.

Tarragona and the Ebro Delta

This route takes you through lower or new Catalunya, the industrial and agricultural basin of the region and the wine districts of Penedés and Priorat. Once again the Costa Dorada has been scarred by box-like hotels and the beaches swarm with millions of holidaymakers in summer, but there are a few areas which remain unchanged, especially around the Ebro delta. The interior roads are flanked by miles of hazel, almond, pine and olive groves that are particularly colourful in the spring.

From Barcelona the A7 autoroute passes **San Sadurni de Noya**, beneath which lie hundreds of miles of wine cellars used for storing the local *cava*. (Penedés produces more wine using the Champagne method than anywhere else in the world.) Here you can visit the Cordorniú winery in a Modernist *bodega* by Puig i Cadafalch.

Sitges (pop. 12,000), on the coast, has long been the most fashionable resort town on the Costa Dorada. Even today, despite the modern suburbs throttling the old town centre, it retains something of its 19th-century charm along the palm-lined promenade. It is certainly one of the liveliest year-round resorts on the Mediterranean; in high summer the population swells to 50,000 and the town turns into a hedonistic paradise best known for its beach and nightlife.

The old heart of Sitges, originally enclosed within fortified walls, was discovered by one of the great gurus of Modernism, Santiago Rusiñol, who arrived in the town in 1888 and converted some old fishermen's cottages into a studio. He was joined by other members of the *Modernista* fraternity, including Enric Granados, the composer, and the writers Emilia Pardo Bazán, Angel Ganivet and Joan Maragall. The studio has now been turned into the Museu Cau Ferrat, with quaint period rooms containing an interesting collection of medieval Catalan ironwork and paintings by Picasso, Ramón Casa, Zuloaga and Joaquín Sunyer.

Next door, the Museu Maricel de Mar – built earlier this century by the architect Miguel Utrillo – has interesting works by Josep María Sert and some Gothic and Romanesque religious art. It is also worth visiting for the magnificent views over the sea. The Museo Romantico is full of good 19th-century paraphernalia, mechanical toys and so on.

TARRAGONA (pop. 110,000), further down the coast, is set on a hilly promontory overlooking the sea, and is the capital of the province. It was one of the thriving Roman Mediterranean ports (Tarraco) founded by Publius Cornelius Scipio in 218 BC at the outset of the Second Punic War, and was used as a stronghold from which to penetrate the Peninsula. Evidence of earlier Iberian defences can be seen in the cyclopean foundations of the old city wall. The town thrived as a Visigothic bishopric and later burgeoned under the auspices of an important Jewish community. The town's decline began with the rise of Barcelona's fortunes, after which Tarragona's history was one of siege and destruction.

A strong Roman flavour still permeates this busy Mediterranean port. To feel it, head towards the *centro ciudad* (town centre) and park along either of the *Ramblas*: the two main promenades leading towards the Balcón del Mediterráneo. From there you can make out the Roman amphitheatre and inside it the ruins of a Romanesque church. Nearby in Calle Pescadería, beside the Praetorium, is the **Museo Nacional Arqueológico**. Here you'll find some impressive Roman statues of emperors, important bronzes, sarcophagi, mosaics and a peculiar ivory effigy, catalogued as a Roman doll.

The Passeig Arqueológic is an openair promenade between the two defence walls, and leads from the northern extreme of the wall to the Puerta del Rosario. The **cathedral**, built over an old temple dedicated to Jupiter, is an exceptional example of the transition from Romanesque to Gothic. It has defensive features (begun in 1171 and completed in the 14th century), a sculpted Gothic doorway, rose windows and a band of deli-

cately carved apostles on the outside. The dim interior is notable for the exquisitely detailed polychromed and gilded alabaster retable. The apse and lower part of the transept are Romanesque; the rest is Gothic. In the **Museu Diocesá** there is a magnificent tapestry of La Bona Vida, and 211 carved capitals in the cloister.

Just over 1.5km from the city centre are the remains of the **Paleo-Christian Cemetery**, where over 2,000 tombs were unearthed when the foundations for a new tobacco factory were laid. There is now a museum on the site, containing a unique collection of sarcophagi that shed great light on the civilization that struggled to survive after the fall of Roman Hispania and the emergence of Muslim Al-Andalus.

On the outskirts of the town stand several other notable monuments of Roman construction, including the Torre dels Escipions that was formerly on the old Via Augusta. If you spend time in Tarragona and want to escape the city for a quiet afternoon on the beach, then you should head for the fine sand beneath the Castillo de Tamarit a few miles to the north.

Leaving Tarragona on the road to Lérida, you pass the **Roman aqueduct** known locally as the Devil's Aqueduct, with its two rows of arches and length of more than 122m. The next important sites of lower Tarragona are the great Cistercian monasteries of Santes Creus, Poblet and Vallbona, which together rank as one of the most important groups of monastic foundations in Europe.

Cistercian monasticism developed as a reaction against the increasingly decadent lifestyle of the Benedictine Order. It stressed austerity, simplicity and the individual poverty of its members. The monasteries became autonomous, self-sufficient communities, and were generally built in isolated areas recently recaptured from the Moors. They quickly became centres of culture and learning and were patronized by royal and noble families.

The Order's main period of expansion coincided with the demise of the Romanesque architectural style and the appearance of proto-Gothic. The trio of Cistercian monasteries in new Catalunya capture the spirit of the movement perfectly, and in the succeeding centuries Poblet and Vallbona were to found sister foundations throughout the Iberian Peninsula and as far away as Altofonte in Sicily. The arrival of Cistercianism in Catalunya coincided with the conquest and re-settlement of new Catalunya during the reigns of Ramon Berenguer III and IV after the conquest of the Moorish Taifas at Tortosa and Lérida in 1148 and 1149.

Poblet – from the Latin *populetum*, meaning poplar grove – nestles in a valley beneath the Sierra de Prades, and was founded in 1151 as part of the resettlement policy instituted by Count Ramon Berenguer IV. By the 14th century the monastery had jurisdiction over a huge surrounding area and owned more than 60 villages. Moreover, it had become the mausoleum of the Kings of Aragón and Catalunya. By the 17th century the increased temporal role of the abbots marked the beginning of the decline of the Cistercian ideal and in 1835, with the *desamortización* (dissolution), the monastery was sacked by locals, the building was pulled apart and the manuscripts and books therein fed to the flames. Restoration work began earlier

this century after the resurgence of interest in Catalunya's Gothic heritage.

The most impressive entrance to the monastery is the Royal Gate flanked by two polygonal towers. Directly ahead is the large cloister: a fine example of the transitional style, with Romanesque columns supporting Gothic tracery. The *lavabo* (wash basin), in a Romanesque pavilion surrounded by the cloister garden, is an Arabic detail frequently adopted in Catalan and Aragonese monsteries of the period. Roman and Moorish irrigation traditions turned this into a rich agricultural area, and the Cistercian monks continued to respect the importance of water held almost sacred by the Arabs.

The quadrangular chapterhouse, with its gracious cross-ribbed vaulting and four octagonal central carved columns, opens onto the east gallery, where you see the tombstones of a few of the abbots of Poblet. Walk via the locutory to the library, which was built as a scriptorium in the 13th century and which produced the first Catalan copy of the chronicle of St James. But it is the Retablo Mayor by Damían Forment, and the royal tombs that are the undisputed treasures of the monastery. The latter rest on two depressed 14th-century arches and were restored in the 1940s by Federico Marés. On the north side are the tombs of James I, Peter III and his three wives (María of Navarre, Elenor of Portugal, Elenor of Sicily), and Ferdinand I, sculpted by Aloi de Montbrai, Jaume Cascalls and Jordi Juan during the 14th century. On the other side lie Alfonso I, John I with his two wives (Mata of Armagnac and Violant of Bar) and John II with his wife Joan Enríquez. Alfonso IV and Martin I 'the Human' are buried in other parts of the church. One of the

The cloister of the Abbots palace in the Monasterio de Santes Creus. Santes Creus became one of the most powerful Cistercian foundations following the resettling of New Catalonia in the 12th century. Incafo

peculiarities of these sepulchres was pointed out by Richard Ford in his *Handbook for Travellers in Spain* (1845):

> The grand objects, however, were the sepulchres which had this remarkable peculiarity: several of the deceased kings having two effigies, one representing the monarch armed or arrayed in royalty, the other, as clad in the garb of a deacon or a monk; this is truly characteristic of the medieval Spaniard, half soldier, half monk, a crusading knight of Santiago; his manhood spent in combating for the cross, his declining years dedicated to religion. No country has ever produced more instances of kings retiring to the cloister, nor of soldiers resigning the sword for the crucifix, and washing off the blood from their hands, making their peace with God, after a life of battle in his cause.

The monastery's museum is situated in the flamboyant Gothic palace of Rei Martín and during your tour you will also be shown the small Romanesque chapel and cloister of St Esteban. Monastic life was restored in 1940 and the abbey today has an active brotherhood of about 30 monks.

Santes Creus lies 25km east of Poblet and is again situated in a beautiful valley beside the River Gaià, surrounded by vineyards, woodlands, olive trees and almond groves. The first community was established here in 1158 and expanded quickly. The scriptorium developed into an important centre of manuscript illumination and historiography under Abbot Gener (1265–93) and played an important part in the foundation of the Order of Montesa in 1319. Like Poblet, the monastery exercised feudal dominion over many surrounding villages and estates.

The decline began after the Napoleonic Wars, when the monastery was sacked. It is now the property of the Catalan government, who have turned it into a cultural centre to promote such activities as Gregorian chant music and organ recitals. Of particular interest are Santa Lucía's chapel; the great Baroque Puerta Real; the church with Romanesque and Gothic features containing the porphyry tomb of Peter II, and the delicate Gothic sarcophagus of James II and his wife Blanche of Anjou; and the Gothic cloister, again with a central pavilion and washbasin by the English sculptor Reinard Fonoll.

The convent of **Santa María de Vallbona**, the third of these Cistercian foundations, has thrived in another wooded and cultivated valley 40km to the north. The history of Vallbona dates back to a small community of anchorites who lived here during the 12th century. In 1201 Pope Innocent III granted the foundation independence from the Bishop of Tarragona, making the abbess answerable only to the Pope. The daughters of many Catalan noble families took the veil here, and their dowries added to the convent's large quota of land and property.

The perimeter wall encircles three precincts, each displaying several important Romanesque and Gothic details. In the church lies the tomb of Violan of Hungary, wife of James I. Each side of the cloister dates from a different architectural period between the 12th and 14th centuries, and in the chapterhouse lie impressive tombstones of former abbesses and a strange terracotta statue of the Virgin.

The most central and enchanting place to stay while visiting these monasteries is the village of **Montblanc** (pop. 6,000), 'the most noble village of Catalunya', enclosed within 14th-century walls on a promontory beside the River Francolí. Something of its former importance can be understood by visiting the hall-church of Santa María la Mayor, which once served as a courtroom for the Aragonese–Catalan court. The elegant Gothic Casa Josa has been turned into a museum and has a good collection of Hispano–Moresque ceramics. There are several other buildings of interest here, including Romanesque San Miguel and the old hospital of Santa Magdalena outside ˙the walls and across the Gothic bridge.

South-west of Montblanc there are two other villages that merit a detour: **Prades**, another impressive walled town, and **Siurana de Prades**, on a scar overlooking the reservoir of the same name. The latter is one of the most romantically sited villages of Spain, and is currently being restored with careful regard to local building materials and forms. It was here that the Moors made their last stand in Catalunya in 1153, and in several other ways it has a magical atmosphere resembling the location of Granada's great fortress, the Alhambra. A dirt track ascends 7km through a towering limestone gorge to the village, where there are a couple of small *hostales* and restaurants used mainly by climbers. On the edge of the village is a simple 12th-century Romanesque church and a monument to the mountaineers who have died while climbing the impressive cliffs surrounding Siurana.

From Siurana de Prades the view south-west extends over the wine region of Priorat – a succession of picturesque valleys and dusty little villages lying beside the streams that flow to the lower Ebro basin. **Falset** is the capital and natural entrance into the area from Tarragona, with a beautiful Modernist *bodega* by César Martinell, a disciple of Gaudí. The first vines were planted by monks of the earliest Carthusian monastery in the Peninsula. It was founded through the patronage of Alfonso of Aragón in 1163, after the exact site for its location had been revealed to the monks in a vision. You can still see the ruins of the Carthusian monastery of Scala Dei, which sadly fell into ruins after the dissolution in 1836. At *bodegas* in almost every village of 'El Priorat', the wines may be tasted – they are generally strong and fruity with a high alcoholic content.

These fertile southern plains are often termed the 'Andalucía de Catalunya'. Here the mighty River Ebro finally disgorges its waters into the sea, having collected the drainage of 222 tributaries that irrigate nearly one-sixth of the surface area of Spain on its 927-kilometre course. The last kilometres of its journey cut through the rugged mountains covered in fruit trees and fertile *vegas* towards the delta which, thanks to a preservation order, is largely unspoilt.

Many of the towns along the Ebro were badly damaged during the Civil War, when this part of the river became the scene of a long entrenched battle in the summer of 1938 between the Nationalists and Republicans. There were more than 150,000 casualties. Nowadays there's considerable heavy industry in the area, and the best landscape is to be seen between the mountain villages around Gandessa, and **Horta de Sant Joan** in particular, where Picasso spent a few peaceful summers painting.

On a promontory above a curve in the river, **Miravet**'s looming Templar fortress presides over a small town of old mills and workhouses that was a centre for pottery until the expulsion of the Moors in 1610. A sporadic ferry connects you with the left bank of the river, where a small road wiggles through the Sierra de Cardo to Tivenys. The monotonous grey limestone sierras of the area are in sharp contrast to the fertile *vegas* of peaches, oranges and olives along the river.

The Templar citadel at **Tortosa** (pop. 30,000) is built on remains of Roman, Visigothic and Saracen foundations. A story reveals that, after Ramon Berenguer IV captured the Moorish stronghold in 1148, the women of the city repelled a counterattack while the men worked in the fields. For this brave stand they were granted the Order of the Battleaxe, and still walk in front of the men during the *fiesta* marking the event. It's an industrial city, humid in the summer, and a place best to bypass. The cathedral is the principal sight worth stopping for, with its impressive Baroque façade and pure Gothic soul.

At Tortosa, cross the Ebro and follow the right bank to Amposta, where the water is 400m wide. This has an interesting town centre, which was formerly the headquarters of the Knights Hospitallers of Aragón but is nowadays the gateway to the Ebro delta.

The Ebro delta is the Peninsula's great Mediterranean river-mouth, a rich agricultural region famous for its artichokes, maize and rice (exported to China!) and still farmed by hand, mule and marsh pony. The wetlands, dunes, paddyfields and irrigation channels present the perfect environment for birds migrating across Europe. Annual visitors include the red-crested pochard, purple heron, Eurasian wigeon and cattle egret. The flat, expansive fields, broken up by neat lines of irrigation channels and sprinkled with Valencian *barracas* (thatched cottages) is reminiscent of both southeast Asia and Holland. Spring is the best time to visit, when the paddyfields are ploughed and flooded and you are woken by a great wave of wing-beating birds.

The river breaks the park into two distinct areas. To the south it is worth trying to see the afternoon fish auction in the small port of **Sant Carlos de la Ràpita**. The town's wide natural harbour was originally planned by Charles III in 1780 to be a new Mediterranean port, but has ever since remained anonymous for most things except its seafood restaurants. The north side of the delta, containing the natural park, can be reached by river ferries from **Sant Jaume d'Enveja**. These connect with the main town of **Deltebre** where it is worth visiting the delta information centre for the good map they provide. (Plaça 20 de Maig, tel [977] 48 95 11.) At the eastern extreme of the park, a passenger ferry connects you with the **Isla de Buda**.

A great deal of speculation surrounds this island and the origins of its name. It is separated from the mainland by the two largest mouths of the Ebro, and its innocuous shores have been the scene of many shipwrecks, though the lighthouse now lies in ruins. Like Tobago, it is the setting for the equivalent Islamic tale of Robinson Crusoe, of a Moorish soldier who spent 11 years as a castaway on this island. In the autumn, the flamingoes gather in groups along its shallow shores, searching the water for shrimps.

TOURIST OFFICES

SITGES: Oasis Bus Terminal, tel (93) 894 47 00.

TARRAGONA: C/ Fortuny 4, tel (977) 23 34 15.

Accommodation, Eating and Drinking

SITGES (tel code 93):

(H)**Romantic**, San Isidro 23, tel 894 06 43. Rooms overlook an inner patio. Atmosphere reminiscent of *La Belle Epoque*. C.

(R)**El Vivero**, Playa San Sebastián, tel 894 21 49. Cl Tues Dec–May. Panoramic

Sitges, one of the busiest resort towns of the Costa Dorada, is popular for its coastal boulevard of palm trees, restaurants and bars.   Angus Mitchell

views over the Mediterranean and old quarter. C.

TARRAGONA (tel code 977):

(H)**Lauria**, Rambla Nova 20, tel 23 67 12. Central with sea views. C.
(R)**La Guingueta**, Coques 9, tel 23 15 68. Beside cathedral. Good Catalan *nouvelle cuisine*. B.
(R)**La Puda**, Muelle de Pescadores 25, tel 21 15 11. Seafood specialities. C–B.

SANTES CREUS:

(H)**Grau**, San Pedro III 3, tel (977) 63 83 11. Simple, in a picturesque situation beside the monastery.

MONTBLANC (tel code 977):

(H)**Ducal**, Diputación 11, tel 86 00 25. Clean and comfortable. E–D.
(H)**El Senglar**, Espluga de Francolí, tel 87 01 21. A functional and efficient *hostal* 2km from Poblet. D.
(R)**Fonda Colom**, Ctra de Civadeira 5, tel 86 01 53. Home cooking. C.

EBRO DELTA (tel code 977):

(H)**Miami Park**, Avda Constitución 33, San Carlos de la Ràpita, tel 74 03 51. Modern but the best and most reasonable available. C.
(R)**Fernandel**, San Isidro s/n (Valencia/Barcelona road), tel 74 03 58. Sea views. Mainly fish dishes. C–D.

Basic Català Vocabulary

Dilluns	Monday	*¿Com es diu aixó*	How do you say that
Dimarts	Tuesday	*en catalá?*	in Catalá?
Dimecres	Wednesday	*¿On és...?*	Where is...?
Dijous	Thursday	*Cerco...*	I am looking for...
Divendres	Friday	*Voldria...*	I should like...
Dissabte	Saturday	*Necessito...*	I need...
Diumenge	Sunday	*¿Com us dieu?*	What is your name?
Ahir	Yesterday	*Em dic...*	My name is...
Avui	Today	*¿Per anar a...?*	How do I get to...?
Dema	Tomorrow	*¿És lluny/a prop?*	Is it far/close?
U, un, una	One	*¿On és la pròxima*	Where is the next
Dos, dues	Two	*gasolinera/*	petrol station/
Tres	Three	*el pròxim taller*	the nearest
Quatre	Four	*de reparacio*	motor mechanic?
Cinc	Five	*¿Quant val?*	How much?
Sis	Six	*És car*	It is expensive
Set	Seven	*¿En té de més*	Do you have a
Vuit	Eight	*bon preu/més*	cheaper/larger/
Nou	Nine	*gran/més petit/*	smaller one/
Deu	Ten	*un altre color?*	another colour?
Si/no	Yes/no	*¿Té alguna*	Do you have a
(Moltes) gracies	(Many) thanks	*habitació*	room?
Bon dia	Good morning/day	*lliure?*	
Bona tarda	Good evening	*Per una nit/per*	For one night/
Bona nit	Good night	*a dues*	for two
¿Parleu	Do you speak	*persones*	people
castellà/	Spanish/	*Adéu/a reveure*	Goodbye, see you
francès/	French/		again
anglès/	English/		
alemany?	German?		

CHAPTER THREE

Balearic Islands

(Islas Baleares)

THE BALEARIC ARCHIPELAGO, comprising the four main islands of Mallorca, Menorca, Ibiza and Formentera along with dozens of smaller uninhabited or private islets, were called the *Gymnasiae* by the Greeks, as it was customary for the islanders to walk around naked as if in a gymnasium. Later the Romans christened them the *Baleares* because the locals could sling stones and projectiles with deadly accuracy, making their soldiers respected mercenaries. Strangely enough, both these practices have continued in variant forms to this day. In summertime, mile upon mile of beach is crowded with sun-seekers in search of an all-over tan, while at many local *fiestas* the *honderos* still wield the bright streamers weighted with a pebble, whirling them through the air like slings.

Yet each island has an individual character, as well as strong cultural and topographical differences and dialectic peculiarities that define their personalities. In recent decades, tourism has changed the social and economic structure drastically in parts. Terraced farming in particular has been affected; but the main towerblock conurbations have fortunately been concentrated in a few easily avoided areas and, whatever preconceived ideas you may have about Mallorca, the island still contains some of the wildest landscape and quietest coves and beaches to be found anywhere in the Mediterranean.

It is perhaps not merely coincidental that Fray Junipero Serra, the first missionary to open up California and establish towns such as San Francisco and San Diego, should have been born in the village of Capdepera in Mallorca, for if there is any place in Europe with a way of life comparable to that of California, it's the Balearics. For this reason it attracts millions of faithful holidaymakers year after year, while remaining a refuge for musicians, writers and painters.

The idyllic climate and the peaceful island life have a lot to do with it. After the mild, windy days of winter end with the *calmos de enero*, the fortnight of placid seas and blue skies in January heralds the start of spring, when the almond trees start to blossom and strong colours define the landscape.

Balearic Islands

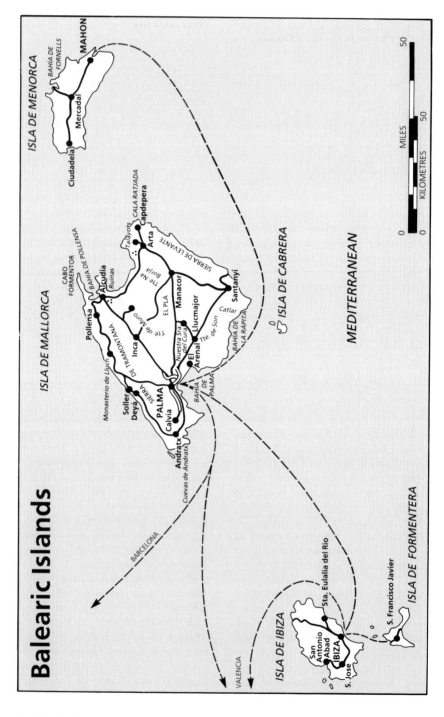

Mallorca

The scorched days of summer arrive towards the end of May, when the yachts and gin palaces start to cruise the coastline.

The history of the islands is long and fascinating, from the period of the mysterious *talayots* and *taulas*, which were part of a highly sophisticated orientalized Bronze Age culture, to the 16th-century *atalayas* (coastal watchtowers) built to warn the islanders of possible pirate attacks. The fortified churches are as much evidence of the islands' strategic importance as the Italianate villas or *sones* are of their long-appreciated restful qualities.

In 123 BC the archipelago was incorporated into the Roman Empire; later, between 430 and 800, it was successively captured by Vandals, the Byzantine General Belisarius, and Moors until its final conquest by James I (1213–76) in 1229. Between 1276 and 1343 it formed a kingdom of its own and included the mainland counties of Montpellier, Roussillon and Cerdagne. This was a period in which the archipelago prospered as a small trading empire, especially with the ports of North Africa. Throughout this period and well into the 18th century the islands became a centre for pirate attacks and smuggling, while the small coves offered perfect cover for the great Catalan corsairs to terrorize marauding Mediterranean shipping. In 1713, after the Treaty of Utrecht ended the War of Spanish Succession, Gibraltar and Menorca passed under British dominion and the latter was not returned permanently to Spain until 1802. In the architecture, food and folklore of the region, the imprint of each of these cultures can be seen.

PALMA DE MALLORCA (pop. 320,000), the capital of the island of tranquillity, is the main city of the Balearics and the natural centre from which to explore the archipelago by boat or the island by car. Even though the city straggles for 24km along the waterfront, the old quarter of whitewashed Moorish streets, señorial palaces, small Gothic churches, modern art galleries and palm-lined boulevards makes this a city worth exploring.

The *seo* (cathedral), built between 1230 and 1600 on the site of a mosque, rises from the wide sweep of the bay like a golden Gothic skyscraper. The carving on the Puerta del Mirador was designed by Guillem Segrera – Palma's greatest Gothic architect – and the Puerta de la Almoina also displays excellent carving. The magnificent proportions of the interior are crowned by El Oculus, the largest rose window in the world, with glass panels built into the structural star of David. In the royal side-chapel containing tombs of the Mallorcan Kings there's a magnificent baldachin over the altar by Antoni Gaudí, and the two Plateresque pulpits on either side of the choir are particularly fine. The chapterhouse and museum contain some impressive Flemish tapestries, as well as a sepulchre of Bishop Gil Sánchez Muñoz, who later became Pope Clement VIII and died in Palma in 1447. Another world heavyweight is the bell known as N'Aloi, forged in 1536 and weighing over 5,760kg.

Several other notable Gothic churches in Palma include those of Santa Eulalia, Santa Cruz and San Jaume. The building of greatest significance is the monastery of

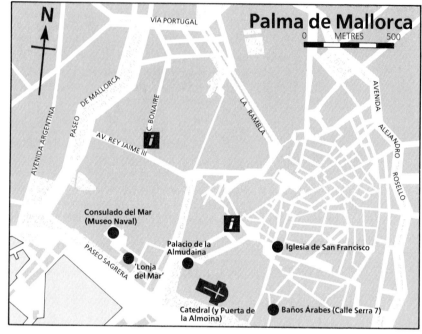

San Francisco, which contains the sepulchre of Ramón Lull and has a magnificent cloister of Gothic arches supported by slender carved columns and crowned by an impressive *artesonado* (inlaid wooden ceiling).

Beside the cathedral is the Palacio de la Almudaina, which was a palace for both the Arab *walis* and later Christian rulers of the island. During the reign of James II (1291–1327) the palace had a roof garden with an exotic menagerie of bears, leopards, lions and monkeys. The courtyard has recently been restored and one wing is still used as a royal audience room by King Juan Carlos I when he holidays in Mallorca each August.

The building that typifies the commercial heyday of medieval Palma is the *lonja* (exchange). This is one of the most perfect examples of civic Gothic architecture to be found and is now used as the city's main exhibition centre. Above the door is the masterpiece of Guillem Sagrera: the smiling face of the custodian angel, patron of Mallorcan merchants, with her face gracefully eroded by years of exposure to the salt breezes. As a medieval institution, the *lonja* helped develop the commercial activities of its merchants throughout the Mediterranean. It commissioned the map by the Jewish cartographers, Abraham and Jafudà Cresques, which showed the compass courses connecting the main ports of Africa with the Mediterranean, thus enabling the Mallorcan mariner Jaime Ribes to explore the west of Africa.

Beside the *lonja* stands the Consulado de Mar, containing a small naval museum on the ground floor. The consulate was established in 1343 following the example of a similar institution set up in Barcelona, in order to administer the *alfondigos* (Mallorcan trading posts) on the north coast of Africa, and as a chamber of commerce to settle any disputes between merchants and ship masters.

The Arabian Baths at Calle Serra 7 are the most impressive remains of Muslim civilization on the island and date from the tenth century. The square room (*caldanium*) with a domed ceiling is supported by 12 columns, each with a different carved capital – evidence of the Muslim penchant for ransacking existing Roman sites for the structural detailing of their own work. The hot baths worked by circulating steam through a narrow space between the stone slabs of the floor.

The Castillo de Bellver, residence of the Kings of Mallorca, is situated on a pine-clad hilltop overlooking the bay of Palma, and is another unique example of civic Gothic architecture with a strong Sicilian feel. The plan of the castle is peculiar in that one of the towers is completely set apart from the main construction: an arrangement that was intended to keep the royal apartments separate from the military headquarters and prison.

Leaving Palma, the main meccas of towerblock tourism that cater annually for around five million sun-seekers are concentrated along the coast stretching west of Palma. So unless that's the holiday you're after, avoid stopping in Cala Mayor, Portals Nous, Palma Nova, Santa Ponça and Camp de Mar.

Andratx, sheltered by the foothills of the Sierra de Transmontana, was moved inland in the 17th century because of repeated attacks by Turkish pirates, though the port, surrounded by *atalayas*, still supports a diehard fraternity of fishermen who spread their nets around the Island of Dragonera.

In the village there's a fine Gothic church and a good view of the surrounding area, with the castle and ruined convent of San Telmo visible on the coast.

From Andratx, the C710 begins its twisting way through the mountains, falling steeply towards the coast. It is unquestionably one of the most spectacular coastal roads in the Mediterranean, with many of the coves you see below accessible only from the sea. In proportion to the size of Mallorca itself, the Transmontanas are a formidable range, stretching across the whole western slant of the island with several peaks (*puig*) more than 1,220m high. Huddling beneath their peaks are small introverted communities that have resisted the onslaught of mass tourism.

All along this road are the main concentration of *sones* (country estates) built by the Mallorcan and Catalan nobility in the Italian style between the 17th and 19th centuries. Some can be seen rising from the fruit orchards and pine groves around **Puigpunent**, while many of the older ones, such as the Alfabia, the ancient seat of the Moorish governors, are located in the steep valleys of the inner foothills.

Estellences, built on a steep slope, has a small port and beach protected by soaring cliffs. Eight kilometres further on, **Banalbufar** is set in a similarly spectacular setting with watchtowers built along the cliff, and restaurants and old fishermen's cottages on the beach. Inland you can visit the fine *sone* of La Granja.

Valldemosa warrants even more attention on account of the great Carthusian monastery, La Cartuja, where Frédéric Chopin lived one winter with the Baroness de Dudevant

By far the best way to reach Palma de Mallorca is by sea. Mallorca's tourism is concentrated in relatively few coastal areas and much of the inner island is unspoilt. Incafo

(better known by her *nom de plume*, George Sand). The affair scandalized European society although it produced the novel *A Winter in Mallorca* and some of Chopin's preludes. Over the years Valldemosa has continued to be a popular retreat for writers, including Jorge Luís Borges and Miguel de Unamuno. During your visit you will be shown around the pharmacy, cloister and library.

Another 19th-century celebrity associated with Valldemosa and the west coast of Mallorca was the Archduke Luís Salvador de Bourbon Habsburg, son of the last Grand Duke of Tuscany, Leopold II, and one of the true spirits of the Romantic age. *L'Arxiduc*, as he was known locally, gathered around him a form of alterna-

tive European court-in-exile of intellects, poets and artists, and set about restoring many old *sones* to accommodate them.

Continuing on the road to **Deyá** you pass the Hotel Madò Pila, the former residence of Catalina Homar, the great love of the Archduke's life. A few kilometres further on is the Miramar estate of Son Morroig, where there's a museum dedicated to the Archduke's memory, and which includes a first edition of his seven-volume *History of the Baleares*. The house has a strong Tuscan air and the small temple in the garden is a replica of that in the Villa Pallavicini in Genoa. If you find yourself here at sunset, it's not difficult to understand why the Archduke never wished to leave the island.

The old smuggling village of Deyá was put on the map this century by the English writer Robert Graves, whose presence here attracted a group of his close friends who still live in several houses in the village. Apart from its magnificent setting, Deyá has several items of interest: a sanctuary dedicated to the moon goddess and an Archeological Museum created by the American philanthropist William Waldren. Graves is buried in the cemetery on a hill above the village.

Sóller is another summer resort that looks magnificent in spring, when the surrounding hills sparkle with wild orchids and the air carries any number of natural herbal aromas. Sóller is connected to Palma by an old narrow-gauge railway, which you should certainly take if you don't have a car, as the route climbs up through the eastern foothills of the range. It travels past two of the most historic *sones*, both of which have superb sub-tropical gardens: the Alfabia, the ancient country house of the Moorish governors of Mallorca, and Raixa.

Above Deyá, the village of **Lluc-Alcari** was the home of the mariner and cartographer Felipe Banzá, who was born in Palma but lived for a great part of his life here. Banzá was the first to map large parts of the South American coastline and Pacific but was exiled from Spain in 1823 and spent the remaining ten years of his life in London. His collection of South American art is now housed in the British Museum, and his body is interred in Westminster Abbey.

Continuing through the mountains, bypassing all the *miradors*, the next major sight is the monastery of Lluc, which was founded in 1239 but was heavily restored by Baroque architects.

It possesses a rare 14th-century black alabaster Madonna. On then to **Pollença**, a village of pink stone set between two summits, with a magnificent flight of steps leading up the Puig del Calvari where you can visit a Churrigueresque cloister in the monastery of Nuestra Señora del Calvario.

The Port de Pollença, 6km further on, is a popular tourist resort. A road leading from the north side of town takes you to **Cabo Formentor**, one of the most imposing headlands in Europe, where the Transmontanas crash into the sea. The soaring cliffside shelters the nests of one of Europe's rarest raptors: Elonora's falcon, which, after wintering in Madagascar, flies across Africa to breed along these precipitous cliffsides. At the extreme northern end beside the lighthouse a sheer rockface plunges 200m into the blue depths.

Returning to Pollença, the road skirts the bay to **Alcudia**, an old medieval port of señorial mansions built on an isthmus separating the bay of Alcudia and Pollença. Nearby are the remains of the Roman city of Pollentia, including an excavated amphitheatre. From Alcudia the C713 returns inland to Palma via the market town of **Inca** – long famous for its shoes and leather – and **Benissalem**, where you can visit the Casa Sureda (open 9.30am–5pm), a typical town mansion house with some impressive period rooms and a *bodega.*

Continuing round the coast beside the lakes and marshland of Albufera, you head towards the mountains of the eastern side of the island and a coast where the coves and beaches have been slightly more developed to cater for tourism. For an authentic view of the island, try to stay on the small inland roads and you will then traverse countryside that has fortunately been affected only slightly.

Near **Arta** are the Talayots de Seis Paisses, the most important Bronze Age monuments on the island. Passing the castillo at Capdepera you arrive at Cala Ratjada where the gardens of the former residence of Bartolomé March, 'Sa Torre Cega', overlook the small fishing village. These are open to the public and merit a visit to see the impressive collection of 20th-century sculpture, including work by Henry Moore, Barbara Hepworth, Eduardo Chillida, a stainless-steel fig tree by Jull Guasp and other work by important Spanish sculptors of this century.

Passenger ferries ply the coast between Cala Ratjada and Cala Millor, where there is a large safari park. Of more interest, especially on a hot day when they are quenchingly cool, are the two great underground caves at **Porto Cristo**: the Cave of Hams and the Cave of Drac. The latter is especially bizarre. A path descends through vast underground caverns to a lake via a succession of spectacular cathedral-like spaces named after themes such as Dante's vision of Hell.

Inland from Porto Cristo, the town of **Manacor** has long been famous for its cultured pearl industry and it con-tains an interesting palace, the former residence of the Kings of Mallorca. In the south-eastern plains of the island there are windmills, salt mines and mainly nudist beaches along the coast. At **San Jordi** or **Puerto Colonia** you can charter a small fishing boat or take the passenger ferry and explore the 17 islets that make up the mini-archipelago surrounding Cabrera. There is environmental pressure on the government at present to close down the military base and turn Cabrera into a national park. Off the coast, whales and dolphins can quite often be seen, while the wild landscape of the island possesses its own indigenous species of lizard and plants. A few breeding pairs of fish eagles as well as the Andouin gull that breeds exclusively on the Isla de Alborán between the Costa del Sol and Africa are also to be found here.

Returning towards Palma between the towns of **Algaida** and **Llucmajor**, and reached by a steep twisting road, stands the 16th-century sanctuary of Nuestra Señora de Cura, offering views over every side of the island. It was here that Ramón Lull had his vision of the Crucifixion and saw the word 'God' written in Kufic script in one of the eyes of Christ, inspiring him to write his strange *Ars Magna*.

TOURIST OFFICE

PALMA: Avda Jaime III 10, tel (971) 71 22 16.

Car Ferries and Inter-island Connections

There are frequent boat trips between the islands and the mainland as well as excursions from most ports. The Barcelona/Valencia–Palma car ferries run once a day throughout the year and more frequently in the summer. Various connections

---

Ramón Lull

No single figure better exemplifies the intellectual spirit of 13th-century Spain than the mystic, theologian and novelist Ramón Lull (1235–1316). His family moved to Mallorca after James I's conquest of the island in 1229, and Lull was educated in the Catalan–Aragonese court. His early life was somewhat profligate, recorded in a few love poems in which Lull speaks of his passion for a beautiful Genoese woman for whom he rode into a church on horseback only to see her reveal a breast eaten away by cancer.

At the age of 30, he had a succession of visions that forced him to renounce his former ways, and from then on he became a passionate missionary set on converting Islam with reason rather than force. To this end he spent nine years during which he studied Arabic, travelled to the great pilgrimage centres of Christendom, founded a missionary school in Mallorca and developed his extraordinary philosophical system, the *Ars Magna*, based partly on Platonist and Cabbalist translations.

In 1280 he embarked on a long European expedition, preaching, lecturing, writing and proselytizing, as well as trying to persuade kings and prelates to finance his missionary schools. During this time he produced some of his most accomplished work written in Catalan, including his novel of love *Blanquerna, The Book of Beasts, The Art of Finding the Truth* and a treatise on astronomy. Lull had a profound and ubiquitous influence that lasted well into the 16th century, and his work had more than a significant effect on Renaissance philosophy and learning. Through his search for method, he effectively laid the foundations of logic, from which the computer was eventually developed.

In 1311 he persuaded the Council of Vienna to establish chairs of Arabic and Syriac at the universities of Paris and Salamanca. Five years later, he was stoned to death at Tunis by an angry mob of Muslims, and his body brought back to Mallorca to be buried in Palma.

---

between Palma and Ibiza/Palma–Mahon. Also with Genoa (Italy), Sète (France) and Canary Islands.

Viajes Interislas: Paseo Mallorca 14, tel (971) 72 61 84.

Transmediterranea, Paseo Muelle Viejo, tel (971) 72 67 40.

Transbalear C/ 16 de Julio, tel (971) 29 60 00.

Accommodation, Eating and Drinking

PALMA (tel code 971):

(H)**Son Vida Sheraton**, Avda Joan Miró 21, tel 23 25 42. Beautifully situated in a reconstructed 13th-century castle. Luxurious and expensive. A.

(H)**Maricel**, 7km from Palma on the road to Andratx, tel 40 27 12. Typical Mallorcan building with a wonderful view of the sea. B–A.

(H)**Bahia de Palma**, C/ Bosque 14, tel 237480. A good pension. E.

(H)**La Paz**, C/ Salas 5, tel 215010. Adequately comfortable rooms for a few days. E.
(R)**Ca's Cotxer**, Carretera Arenal' 31 (Exit 5), Playa de Palma. Cl Wed. Beside the beach, offers fresh traditionally Mallorcan seafood cooking. B.
(R)**Flanigan**, In Puerto Portals, tel 676117. Situated 9km out of town. An informal garden restaurant in the most exclusive marina area on Mallorca, where the smart yachties anchor for the excellent *tapas*. B–A.
(R)**Rififi**, Avda de Joan Miró 186, tel 402035. Good grilled fish. B.

ANDRATX (tel code 971):

(H)**Brismar**, Avda Almirante Riera Alemany s/n, tel 67 16 00. Pleasant hotel with great views. C.
(R)**Miramar**, Avda Mateo Bosch 22, tel 67 16 17. Wonderful terraces. Excellent fresh seafood, prepared in a typical Mallorcan style. C–B.

VALLDEMOSA (tel code 971):

(H)**Vistamar**, C/ Ctra Andratx km 2, tel 612300. Terraces and gardens are the hotel's main features. Also has a popular restaurant famous for its fresh tuna fish salad. C.
(R)**Ca'n Pedro**, Avda Archiduque Luis Salvador, tel 61 21 70. In an old Mallorcan house. Good local cuisine. C–B.

DEYÁ (tel code 971):

(H)**La Residencia**, Son Moragues, tel 63 90 11. Small and highly exclusive. Exquisitely situated in the mountains, surrounded by gardens and swimming pool. B–A.
(R)**Jaime**, C/ Archiduque Luis Salvador 13, tel 63 90 29. Well known for its barbecued fish (*pescados al horno*). B.

SÓLLER:

(R)**Es Canyis**, Paseo de la Playa, Port de Sóller, tel (971) 63 14 06. Cl Mon and from 1 Dec–1 Mar. A beautiful view of the port. Serves excellent fresh seafood. B.
For those without a car Sóller can be reached by an old narrow-gauge railway that chugs its way up and down through the mountain valleys. The FEVE station in Palma is in the Plaza de España.

CABO FORMENTOR:

(H)**Formentor**, C/ Playa de Formentor s/n, tel (971) 53 13 00. A legendary five-star hotel magnificently positioned in the northern end of the island overlooking the dramatic coastline of Cabo de Formentor. Beautiful gardens. Private beach. For those without the necessary credit cards, a drink in the bar on the terrace is worth while for the elegance and the views. A.

Ciudadela, the former capital of Menorca, is a quiet seaside town for most of the year; in summer it is transformed into one of the Mediterranean's yachting meccas, popular with those in search of fresh lobsters and mayonnaise. Incafo

Menorca

Menorca is the most mysterious island of the Balearics – a land of brilliant white dairy farms, windswept pastureland, old freestone walls and Holstein cattle which look strangely out of place when you suddenly arrive in a village which looks as if it has been transported from the agrarian depths of Andalusia. Menorca's geological composition is different from that of the rest of the archipelago, and the presence of the English during the 18th century has left strong traces, particularly in Mahon. Of an earlier age are the 2,000 or so Bronze Age *talayots* and

taulas which at moments make Menorca seem like a vast Mediterranean Stonehenge. It is less tarnished by tourism than the other islands, and along its 230km of coastline some of the emptiest beaches in the western Mediterranean are to be found. The islanders have been keen to hold back the surge of high-rise fever. There are no large rivers and, although the main agricultural produce is typically eastern Levantine, Menorca has long been famous for its cheese, ice-cream and gin.

The two main towns of Mahon and Ciudadela – at either end of the island – are connected by the only main road, along whose course lie the main arterial roads leading to the coastal recesses. The bustling commercial city of **Mahon** (pop. 22,000), known as 'Maó', was created capital in 1722 by the occupying British forces, who realized the strategic importance of the excellent natural deep-water harbour. Even today the strange fenestration of sash cord windows, lace curtains and grand Georgian façades is reminiscent of the century of occupation when Admiral Nelson and Admiral Collingwood spent time on the island.

The two stories that placed Mahon firmly in the geographical vocabulary of educated 18th-century European society began in 1756 when Admiral John Byng decided that the French fleet was too strong for his ships to relieve the garrison at Mahon. He retreated to Gibraltar, where he was arrested, courtmartialled and shot at the insistence of King George II, in order to cover up the inadequacies of the British government. This prompted Voltaire to remark that the English enjoyed shooting an admiral now and again *'pour encourager les autres'*. Shortly afterwards, the head chef of the new French governor of the island, the Duc de Richlieu, discovered a sauce to accompany the local lobster dish; it was later named after Mahon: mayonnaise (*mahonesa*). Never since has Mahon been credited with so much in so short a space of time!

To the right of the harbour is the Golden Farm or San Antonio estate where Nelson stayed – but not, as local history likes to record, in the arms of Lady Hamilton. Other places worth visiting are the neoclassic Palacio de la Casa de Cultura and the church of Santa María, with its magnificent pipe organ by Otter and Kibuz. Alterna-

tively, walk through the narrow backstreets of the old quarter or take a boat ride around the harbour to immerse yourself in the atmosphere of the city.

The Museum of Menorca is situated around the Baroque cloister of the convent of San Francisco, and has an interesting collection of local exhibits as well as a few pre-Columbian Aztec pieces. Joined to Mahon is Villacarlos – formerly Georgetown – where the old neoclassical buildings surrounding the parade ground now form the four sides of the main plaza. You can visit the ancient *talayots* and *taulas* of Trepucó nearby.

The main road west of Mahon to the other main city of Ciudadela passes **Alayor**, which was founded by James II in 1304 and maintains several streets of señorial palaces, calcimined walls and wrought-iron balconies that give it a distinctly Spanish feel. From Alayor you can visit the largest megalithic settlement at Torre d'en Gaumes, with its three giant *talayots*.

Mercadal, standing in a valley beneath the peak of Toro (358m), has a similarly interesting old quarter. A road leads up the hill to the Renaissance sanctuary of Toro, which contains the Virgin of Toro, patron of Menorca, and a monument to the Menorquinas who migrated to San Agustin de la Florida in the 18th century. The views from here over the island are unsurpassed.

Ciudadela (pop. 20,000) is one of the most laid-back and understated resort towns in the Mediterranean. Life goes on at an easy pace within the old city walls, between the noble palaces near the Plaza de España and the bars and restaurants along the Paseo de Puerto. This promenade beside the port is where the big yachts tie up in the summer, and everyone spends long hours over lunch and dinner, picking at great platters of fresh seafood. The former capital of Menorca, Ciudadela remains the seat of the Bishopric, and the neoclassic façade of the cathedral contains an impressive Gothic core. Surrounding Ciudadela are many of Menorca's most important archeological finds, including Stone Age caves in the cliffsides and the Naveta d'es Tudons, a megalithic construction shaped like the overturned hull of a ship.

The great natural attraction of the island is the 120 or so beaches scattered about the coast, interspersed with small fishing hamlets, lighthouses and caves. With a car, you can explore the deeper recesses along the farm tracks that snake around the coast, but beware of getting your vehicle stuck in the sand! The quietest beaches are found on the northern side, known locally as the Tramontana because of the powerful north wind which blows for long periods of the year. On the coast heading north from Mahon, there is a good stretch of sand at Cala Mezquida, and excellent snorkelling in the coves all the way along to Arenal d'en Castell, particularly in the coves and islets around Addaya. Fornells has several restaurants specializing in the local lobster stew, but further west

good roads are scarce and the area has to be explored mainly on foot.

The limestone cliffs and bays of the south coast are sheltered from the wind, and along this coast lie the concentration of troglodyte caves which have yielded large amounts of human remains as well as the strange groups of *talayots* and *taulas*. A great deal of speculation surrounds the origins and purposes of these stone monuments. *Talayots* come in a variety of shapes and sizes but have the general appearance of burial chambers, with a narrow passageway leading into an enclosed central space. *Taulas* are large T-shaped stone tables, with a vertical block supporting a horizontal slab. Three different theories claim these to be sacrificial altars, or symbolic representations of the cross, or the stylized head of a bull. The most important discovery was made at Torre d'en Gaumes, where a bronze statuette of Imhotep, the Egyptian god of medicine, was found among some simple surgical instruments. This seems to indicate that they had some use in religious ritual, but exactly what their true purpose was is impossible to determine. Recent theories suggest that the beating of the stones produces different sounds and that these pitches could be used for ceremonial purposes.

TOURIST OFFICE

MAHON: Pza Esplanada 40, tel (971) 36 37 90.

Accommodation, Eating and Drinking

MAHON (tel code 971):

(H)**del Almirante**, Villa Carlos, tel 36 27 00. Named after Admiral Collingwood. A particularly charming hotel for its price, and a shining exception to the featureless abundance of modern hotels. C.

(R)**Rocamar**, Fonduco 32, Villa Carlos, tel 36 56 01. Excellent seafood with a great view of the sea. Fried lobster (*langosta frita*) is the house speciality. B.

(R)**Pilar**, Forn 61, tel 36 68 17. Cl Mon and in winter. Typical Mallorcan cuisine. Tastefully decorated, with a pleasant atmosphere. C–B.

CIUDADELA (tel code 971):

(R)**Casa Manolo**, Marina 117, tel 38 00 03. Excellent lobster stew and other fresh seafood dishes served on a terrace. B.

(R)**Es Pou**, San Rafael 10, tel 38 42 51. Good seasonal cuisine. B.

Ibiza and Formentera

The Pitusas, or islands of pine as classical authors named them, are the two south-western islands of the Balearics: Ibiza and Formentera. In the last three decades they have become the summer refuge for every alternative form of European society, from hippies to gays and punks, all enticed here by long idyllic summers, the soft Mediterranean landscape, fine white sand, transparently blue seas and the outrageously fashion-conscious and sybaritic nightlife. Though stretches of the Ibizan coast have been horrendously disfigured by ugly hotels and apartments, the interior remains surprisingly beautiful. Out of the burlesque season these islands have much to offer the traveller who seeks more than hedonistic satisfaction.

Early Phoenician and Carthaginian settlers fished for murex shells off the coast and mined salt from the *salinas*. The islands were constantly under threat from pirate raids, and the fortified churches are a reminder of centuries of exposure to these attacks. The town of **Ibiza** (Eivissa) (pop.

33,530) is one of the most magnificent walled towns in Europe. If you approach from the sea, the sight of the vast 16th-century walls surrounding the acropolis is unforgettable.

The old harbour front or *Sa Pena* (downtown) area between the water and the citadel is a labyrinth of narrow, busy streets crammed with shops, bars and restaurants. The oldest quarter is contained within the citadel known as D'Alt Vila (uptown), where there are good walks around the walls and views across the city and bay.

Cars enter the citadel by the Portal de las Tablas leading into the main Plaza Desamparados, full of trinket shops, more bars and excited chaos. Watch where you park – this is one of the few places in Spain where the wheelclamp is in avid use. If you prefer to walk, enter by the pedestrian entrance on the west side through the Portal de San Juan. Apart from the Contemporary Art Museum in Plaza Desamparados, the two main sights are the cathedral, founded in 1235 by James I after he had reconquered the island from the Moors; and the Archeological Museum, where the early history of the island is told through a fascinating series of artefacts.

The Archeological Museum is divided into two parts. The Museo D'Alt Vila occupies an old university building beside the cathedral and exhibits Phoenician, Roman and Moorish items collected from throughout the island, including a fine Romanesque polychrome head of Christ and some good Hispano–Moresque lustreware. The unique part of the collection is housed in a new museum on the Via Romana and contains the exceptional finds excavated from the Punic necropolis of El Puig des Molins lying on the lower slopes close to the modern city.

By the fifth century BC Ibiza was a small city state exporting preserving salt, dyes, wine, oil, wool and fish sauce throughout the Mediterranean. The necropolis provides evidence of the great wealth of this thriving Carthaginian settlement, which possessed its own mint and iron forges. Sanctuaries containing proof of child sacrifices and fertility rites have been found near the city, while the necropolis itself gives a phenomenal insight into the Punic cult surrounding death and the belief in eternal life.

Nudist beaches are to be found on either side of Ibiza at Las Salinas and Es Castellet. To the south there are small *chiringuitos* (beach restaurants), which serve grilled fish and meat for lunch.

Meanwhile, itinerant beauticians can supply sunbathers with almost everything from a haircut or manicure to an all-over psychedelic body paint job. North of Ibiza the coast is scarred quite heavily with coastal development, and **San Antonio Abad** is frankly nothing short of horrendous. To escape this, you're best to head inland along the minor roads skirting the north-eastern side of the island, where you will find among the olive groves and carob trees old whitewashed villages such as **Santa Gertrudis**, **San Juan Bautista** and the fortified village of **Baláfia**.

Alternatively, you might take a trip to the island of **Formentera**. Regular daily boats make the bumpy, one-hour crossing to **La Sabina**. On arrival you can hire a bicycle, moped or car and spend a few hours exploring the flat, barren countryside hemmed in by long white beaches. In Roman times the island was an important wheat-producing area – the name Formentera derives from Latin *frumentaria* (granary). It was deserted from the 15th to the 17th centuries, after the inhabitants were driven away by lack of drinking water and repeated pirate raids. Now the island is inhabited mainly by bright green Ibizan wall lizards that dart between expanses of wild rosemary and pine groves. Bars and beaches are otherwise the other main form of entertainment.

TOURIST OFFICES

IBIZA: Vara del Rey 13, tel (971) 30 10 00.

FORMENTERA: Ayuntamiento, San Francisco Javier, tel (971) 32 20 57.

Accommodation, Eating and Drinking

IBIZA (tel code 971):

(H)**El Corsario**, C/ Ponient 5, tel 30 12 48. In the D'Alt Vila, the best and most atmospheric place to stay in town. Well-converted rooms with magnificent views. D–C.
(R)**Dos Lunas**, on the Ibiza–San Antonio road, 7km, tel 31 40 13. Stunning garden restaurant open only in the evenings. Basic Italian cooking with Ibizan touches. Good late-night bar. B.
(R)**Alfredo**, Paseo Vara del Rey 6, tel 31 42 70. Traditional Ibizan cuisine. C–B.
(R)**Maisa D'en Sord**, on the San Miguel road, 1km. Cl 1 Nov–31 Mar. Set in a traditional Ibizan farmhouse with a lovely terrace. Typical Mediterranean food, fresh fish and grills. B.
Ibiza is home to Europe's most dedicated nightclubbers. **Ku**, 6km from Ibiza in the Urb San Rafael, is the most luxurious and fashionably longstanding club. Others tend to vary in popularity status from year to year.

FORMENTERA (tel code 971):

(H)**La Sabina**, San Fernando and San Francisco Javier all have *hostales*. E.
(R)**El Capri**, Es Pujols. Delicious paella and grilled fish. C.

CHAPTER FOUR

Galicia

OWING TO GALICIA'S geographical isolation in the north-western extreme of the Iberian Peninsula, and the deep-rooted influence of the cult of St James that makes it one of the oldest pilgrimage destinations in Europe, it has an unmistakable feel of poetic melancholy. The people speak their own language – Gallego, which is closely related to Portuguese – and have more in common with their Celtic cousins in Ireland or Brittany than with the Iberians.

A t first it appears a difficult region to penetrate. Along the main roads the country is often overdeveloped, with modern chalet-like buildings and endless hillsides of half-felled pine forests and eucalyptus, and sterile mountains. But if you venture into the interior along the small roads snaking along the river valleys, you will encounter the noble *pazos* (country houses), the sound of *gaitas* (bagpipes), mile upon mile of moss-covered granite walls, hermitage-like *hórreos* (storehouses), a green mantle of vegetation, and proud but impoverished villages. Here small enclosed fields are still ploughed using horses and oxen, and the locals survive on a system of bartering.

Cabo Finisterre – the cape once thought to be at the end of the world – is a windswept headland stretching out into the Atlantic, and the westernmost point of both Galicia and the Spanish mainland. The Gallegans are predominantly Atlantic people and they naturally turn to the sea to seek their fortune, preferring to migrate overseas rather than overland in search of prosperity. The economy of many of the old fishing villages built around the coast along the Rías Bajas, Costa de la Muerte and Rías Altas still depends on harvesting the sea, although an expanding tourist industry is slowly altering this traditional way of life. However, beautiful stretches of sand and rock washed by the Atlantic still remain unspoilt.

The interior is hemmed in to the east and south by the sierras of the western end of the Cordillera Cantábrica and the deep basins and gorges formed by the Sil and Miño . River valleys are the great natural feature of Galicia. Along the courses of the Eo, Foz, Vivero, Barquero, Ortigueira, Betanzos, Ares, El Ferrol, Tambre, Ulla and Lima there

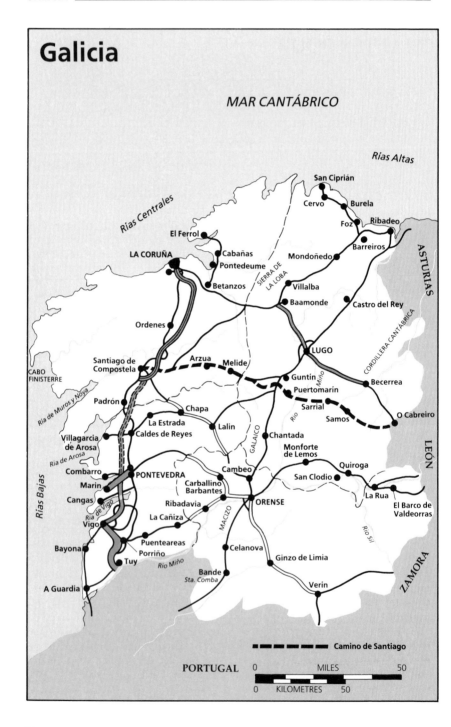

Galicia

MAR CANTÁBRICO

are vineyards, meadows and small agricultural holdings, which typify the landscape of the four provinces of Galicia: Orense, Lugo, Coruña and Pontevedra.

The earliest Bronze Age tribal communities lived in *castros* (fortified hilltop villages), in distinctive elliptical stone houses with *pallozas* (thatched roofs): a style of vernacular architecture still seen in a few impoverished sierra outposts. Many of the place-names have Celtic origins. The Romans, who first referred to these people as Gallaeci, spent more than 100 years and three successive campaigns trying to subjugate the clans. Definitive Romanization was not achieved until the victory of Octavio Augusto in the Cantabrian Wars, but attempts at colonization were not as successful in this area as in other regions of Iberia.

It has been suggested that early Christianity built on strong pagan foundations entered Spain through Galicia with the preachings of St James the Apostle. After the collapse of Rome, the territory was invaded by the Swabians whose ruling dynasty made it an independent kingdom until King Leovigild brought it under Visigothic dominion in 577.

The Moors found Galicia a hostile country to colonize and, though they conquered it in their initial offensive and brought more havoc in an attack on the area by Al-Mansur at the end of the tenth century, it was otherwise left alone for Viking and Norman raiders to terrorize.

In the reign of Alfonso II 'El Casto' (the Chaste) (791–842) the body of St James was discovered at Padrón. The influence of monastic movements, together with a nobility determined to

exert its independence, led to the establishment of Galicia as a kingdom when Alfonso III 'El Grande' (the Great) (866–910) was crowned at Santiago. The Middle Ages were something of a golden age and the *Codex Calixtinus* (1119), the medieval guide for pilgrims journeying to Santiago, describes Galicia as the most culturally developed area of Iberia. The 12th century constituted the height of the Era Compostelana with the building of the great cathedral at Santiago under the energetic bishop, Diego de Gelmirez. In 1128 Galicia declared its independence from Portugal, thereby closely allying itself to León under the Leonese and Castilian kings.

But in the subsequent centuries it suffered variously from civil wars, frontier conflicts with Portugal, and famine. By the 15th century the land was almost exclusively in the hands of five señorial families, who eventually formed an alliance with *Los Reyes Católicos*. As a result, the Galicians came to play a central part in transatlantic expansion, as succeeding generations emigrated to the far-flung corners of the world. There are more Galicians living in Buenos Aires today than in all Galicia. The homeland was left poor and deserted.

Many families return and bequeath their fortunes to ecclesiastical foundations, or engage in private architectural schemes. This partly explains the great Baroque legacy and the beautiful *pazos* (country houses) as well as the modern houses you see in varying states of construction today. Through all this, regionalism has remained strong in Galicia and rural isolation has helped to maintain a strong level of local culture in everything from lace-making to poetry. Nevertheless, it is still a region where many believe that every wave that washes along the miles of rocky coastline contains the soul of a lost sailor.

Southern Galicia and the Rías Bajas

The most direct entry into Galicia from the south-east is on the N525 snaking out of the Sierra de Sanabria in the province of Zamora. It's a good, modern road cutting through isolated mountains before it descends into the fertile Miño basin. If you're heading north to Santiago, take the C533 at La Gudina up the Bibey valley via **Viana del Bollo** on the banks of the Pantano de El Bao beneath the Sierra de Queija. At **Las Hermitas** there's a superb Baroque monastery nestling at the bottom of a ravine. The road continues past the *castillo* ruins at **El Bollo** before emerging onto the N120, the other approach to Orense, which cuts through the Sil basin via Puebla de Trives and Castro-Caldelas. Otherwise the route continues west into the fertile Támega valley.

The first important town is **Verín** (pop. 10,000), sprawled across the Valle de Monterrey. This is an old stronghold of the Counts of Lemos, and large señorial mansions embellished with coats-of-arms are to be found in the old quarter: vestiges of the period of conflict between nobility and church in the 15th and 16th centuries. The mighty Castillo de Monterrey stands guard over the landscape a few kilometres further to the north, built over the ruins of the Celtic Castro of Baronceli. It was here that Pedro 'the Cruel' sought refuge during the war with his brother, Don Enrique

Trastamara. Three rings of walls encircle a 12th-century *castillo*, a 14th-century church, three towers, an arcaded courtyard and hospital – all in various stages of restoration. The Gothic retable in the Chapel of the Counts is a stunning ensemble of stone-carved figures about a Christ Pantocrator.

From Monterrey the road winds through **Xinzo da Lima/Ginzo de Límia** on the banks of the Limia, an old Roman town on the *Via Nova* between Astorga and Braga. The silhouette of the Torre da Pena and other fortified ruins are an architectural reminder of the frontier wars with Portugal. **Allariz**, on a grassy bend in the River Arnoya, was the seat of Alfonso IX's literary court. The three Romanesque churches surrounded by the narrow streets of an old Jewish Quarter have a proud but jaded feel. The Convento de las Clarisas once served as a school for Castilian princes, and now houses some interesting liturgical objects and relics, including a richly embroidered Gothic statuette of the Virgin Abridera.

To the south-west lies the mainly Baroque monastery at **Celanova** – founded in the tenth century by San Rosendo – which later grew into one of the richest and most powerful foundations in Galicia. The monumental complex contains some outrageous Churrigueresque altarpieces set in a basically Renaissance structure but, for all its grandiloquence, it is somehow overpowered by the tiny, Wendy house-size Capilla de San Miguel standing in the shadow of the great monastic walls in the vegetable garden. No bigger than a monk's cell, it is one of the most significant Mozarabic national monuments in Spain, and reflects the influence of Cordoban architecture upon Christian refugees forced to flee Muslim persecution. To see it, you will have to alert the sacristan or call at the small police station between the doors to the monastery and the church.

South of Celanova, in the Valle del Limia, stands **Santa Comba de Bande**, an even older, pre-Romanesque, possibly Suevic church in a tranquil but remote setting overlooking the Embalse de las Conchas. It was probably constructed in the eighth century by fugitive Christians protecting the body of San Torcuato, whose sarcophagus can be seen in the south transept. The finest details left from the original construction are the horseshoe arch into the sanctuary, supported by four crudely carved marble columns, and the pierced *transennae* window, which would originally have been covered with transparent pigskin. Further to the south heading into Portugal lies the Parque Nacional da Peñada-Gerés: a remote sierra rising sharply above the River Limia. The Romans called this the river of forgetfulness, and used its course to navigate their way into Galicia from the south.

ORENSE/OURENSE (pop. 95,000) is a busy transport and commercial hub, whose graceless suburbs hide an interesting monumental centre. Traces of Roman occupation can be seen in the seven ogival arches of the bridge spanning the Miño. The colony grew under Suevic dominion until the Moorish invasion in 716. Repopulated under Sancho II in the 14th century, it remained a prosperous city throughout the Middle Ages and served for a short time (1386–7) as capital to John of Gaunt during his bid for the throne of Castile.

You can still see the steam of the Aquae Urentes rising at a warm 65°C from an old Baroque fountain beside the arcaded Plaza Mayor. Here you'll find the Bishop's Palace, now restored to house the Archeological and Fine Arts Museum. Nearby stands the cathedral, begun at the end of the 12th century and given a rather bland Renaissance facelift. On the outside, the main *Puerta del Paraíso* (Paradise Door) is interesting for the polychrome figures standing on either side of the entrance and in the archivolts. Inside, the columns, buttresses and ribbed vaulting are impressive. About the high altar looms a florid retable by Cornelius de Holanda; in the side-chapels are fine tombs and *rejas* (pierced screens). The most mysterious possession is a wood, hair and cloth Christ, allegedly stitched by Nicodemus and rescued from a church at Finisterre in the 14th century. The Diocesan Museum, off the sacristy, houses other religious curios, including a missal from the first Galician printing press at Monterrey, some rock-crystal chess pieces and a 12th-century travelling altar.

Apart from these sights, Orense has little to offer beyond the practical amenities expected of a provincial capital. A short drive north-east along the Miño takes you to the Sil Gorges, where the two mighty rivers meet and small farms lie scattered among cultivated terraces. On a granite spur sits the monastery of San Esteban de Ribas de Sil, which is worth visiting for the Gothic and Baroque cloisters, though the latter have been ruined recently by insensitive restoration work. Further west is the great grey monastery of **Oseira**, a Cistercian foundation given a magnificent Baroque facelift in 1708, and the scene of the death of

Monsignor Quixote in the novel of the same name by Graham Greene, who described it as follows:

> Almost the only sound during the day is the ring of hammers where half a dozen workmen are struggling to repair the ravages of seven centuries. Sometimes a white-robed figure passes rapidly by on what is apparently a serious errand, and in the dark corners loom the wooden figures of popes and of the knights whose order founded the monastery.

West of Orense you enter the Miño basin and O Ribeiro country of rolling green Galician hills, terraced with vines trained high on stone and wooden pergolas. You will notice that the pergolas are of a soft Mediterranean blue: this is caused by discoloration from the copper sulphate spray used to protect the vines from mildew.

Ribadavia (pop. 8,000) is a noble town of solemn belfries and lichen-covered granite mansions, and was the residence of King García of Galicia (1065–73). With four interesting Romanesque–Gothic churches built about quiet granite streets, and its tranquil *plazuelas* and houses lining the riverbank, this is a peaceful place that is easily explored in a couple of hours on foot. Cylindrical towers and ashlar walls survive from the medieval stronghold of the Counts of Ribadavia. The narrow streets of the ancient Jewish Quarter contain an old bakery and a few run-down bars. The *Fiesta do Viño do Ribeiro*, held annually in the last days of April, brings viniculturists from all over Spain to sample the different denominations of the area and find every excuse to celebrate. The fruity local *viño do Ribeiro* is ideally drunk from porcelain cups to enhance the deep scarlet colour of the wine.

The lower Valle del Miño is divided by two lush glens formed by the Ríos Deva and Tea. The N120 forges on through Melón, where the large Cistercian monastery of Santa María is to be found, to A Caniza, at which point the road starts to climb through the Puerto de Fuentefría to Ponteareas and Porriño, where you join the N550 south to Tuy. An alternative minor route via Salvaterra follows the railway track beside the Miño delimiting the Spanish–Portuguese border. You will also notice *pesqueiras* (lamprey fisheries) on the waterfront and several of the bars will contain a few captive examples of the sucking eel, which, when freshly fried, is remarkably edible and was once a great delicacy at Roman banquets.

Tuy (pop. 16,000) is Galicia's main border town with Portugal. It is an impressive place, built around its fortress cathedral, where a confluence of narrow paved lanes descend to small *hortiños* (garden allotments) colourfully blanketing the riverside. Named Tude by the Iberians, this was the capital of the Suevic kingdom and residence of King Witiza. The Moors destroyed it in 1012 and it was later conquered by the Vikings.

The towers and battlements of the cathedral of San Telmo, covered in luminous lichen with shrubs growing from the crevices between the stones, contain a beautiful 13th-century cloister, with twin columns and intricately engraved capitals. Preserved in the nave are some fine Gothic sepulchres and the remains of San Telmo – the patron saint of seamen.

The iron bridge that crosses to Valença do Minho in Portugal was built in 1884 by the French engineer Alexandre Eiffel, best known for his tower in Paris. In August, a huge canoeing race – *El Descenso del Miño* – finishes beneath the great girdered structure. The old Portuguese town of Valença do Minho is contained within a most impressive walled fortification, which says a great deal about former relations between the two nations.

From Tuy the C550 continues beside the Miño until the estuary meets the sea at **La Guardia**, an old Templar stronghold, which is famous for lobsters, quiet beaches, and the ruins of the Celtic *castro* of Santa Tecla that lies up a steep track south of the town and gives tremendous views over the Atlantic and the Miño basin. Wild horses roam free through these scrubby coastal hills and are rounded up every year by the villagers in a wild *fiesta* known as the *Rapa des Bestas*, when their manes are cut and a few bronco races take place in Galician hill-billy style.

The road then turns north along an expanse of sandy coast to **Bayona**, the first village in the west to hear of the discovery of America on 10 March 1493, when Martín Alonso Pinzón docked in the harbour with the weary crew of the caravel *Pinta*. Set between promontories of pine and eucalyptus trees at the mouth of the Vigo, the town was a consistent point of attack for looting corsairs. The Castillo de Monterreal, now the Parador Nacional Conde de Gondomar, still possesses the cannons used to repel pirates. The views out across the bay towards the Islas Estelas and Islas Cies at sunset should not be missed if the evening is fine.

The Rías Bajas between Vigo, Pontevedra and the mouth of the Ulla contain miles of coastline variously dedicated to the fishing and holiday industries. In mid-November thousands of Galician women of the local fishing fraternity (*cofradía*) wade out into the River Vigo to harvest the clams at the only moment of the year when the tide is low enough. The river is also sprinkled with *bateas* (floating platforms) fixed to the ocean bed, from which are suspended ropes for cultivating mussels.

More tons of fish and transatlantic seaborne traffic pass through **Vigo** (pop. 270,000) than any other port in Spain, which explains its modern industrial character. Apart from the views across the harbour from the fortress-cum-park of San Sebastián, there's not a great deal to detain you, although it is a highly cultured city. The provincial capital, **PONTEVEDRA** (pop. 65,000), has more to offer since the port has silted up and can no longer support large ocean-going vessels. In the señorial old town, several small plazas have interesting *cruceiros* (carved stone crosses). Of particular interest is the sumptuous Plateresque façade of the church of Santa María la Mayor by Cornelius de Holanda, and the shell-shaped chapel of La Peregrina. Interesting stone artefacts are kept in the ruins of the gothic church of Santo Domingo, but the main provincial museum is contained within the two neighbouring palaces of Monteagudo and the Casa García Flóres, where there are good Baroque sculptures by Bernini and paintings attributed to Breughel the Elder, Zurbarán, Tiepolo and Goya.

TOURIST OFFICES

ORENSE: Curros Enríquez 1, tel (988) 234 78 17.

PONTEVEDRA: General Mola 1, tel (986) 85 08 14.

Accommodation, Eating and Drinking

VERIN:

(H)**Parador de Monterrey:** 4km from Verín, tel (988) 41 00 75. Excellent views of the surrounding countryside beneath the Gothic *castillo* of Monterrey. Outdoor swimming pool. Good parador food with dining room overlooking garden. C.

CELANOVA (tel code 988):

(H&R)**Betanzos**, Castor Elices 12, tel 45 10 11; and Celso Emilio Ferreiro 7, tel 45 10 36. Simple rooms near monastery. E. Restaurant specializes in Galician-style fish dishes. C.

TUY:

(H)**Parador San Telmo**, Avda de Portugal s/n, tel (986) 60 03 09. On the banks of the River Miño. Excellent for exploring the inland and southern coastal region. C. (H&R)**Pousada de San Teotanio**, tel (986) 222 42/52, on the other side of the Miño in Portugal at Valença do Minho, in the heart of the old fortified town. Magnificent views over Miño basin. Good restaurant. C.

BAYONA (tel code 986):

(H)**Parador Conde de Gondomar**, Castillo de Monterreal, tel 35 50 00. On a peninsula in the fortress of Monte Real. Large, luxurious rooms overlooking gardens and sea. Pool and yacht club. B. (R)**Los Abetos**, Ctra Vigo-Bayona, tel 36 81 47. In Nigran, 12km from Bayona. Specializing in grilled meats and home-smoked salmon. C–B.

PONTEVEDRA (tel code 986):

(H)**Parador Casa del Barón**, C/ Maceda s/n, tel 85 58 00. In the centre of the Old Quarter, it maintains the elegance of a typical Galician urban *pazo* (country manor). C. (R)**Casa Solla**, Ctra de la Toja (in San Salvador de Poyo), tel 58 26 78. Cl Thurs, Sun evenings and Christmas. In a luxuriously converted *pazo*. Elegantly decorated. Tables overlook the vineyards. B. (R)**Calixto**, Benito Corbal 14, tel 85 62 52. Cl Sun evenings in winter. C–B.

ISLA DE LA TOJA:

(H)**Isla de la Toja**, Pontevedra, tel (986) 86 73 00 25. One of the legendary *Belle Epoque* hotels, famous for its thermal baths and white sand beaches. B.

Camino de Santiago in Galicia

For the last millennium, the bridge at **Piedrafita** has brought sighs of relief from countless pilgrims as they enter Galicia for the final leg of their spiritual odyssey. The last stage of the long pilgrimage road leaves León on the N-VI from **Villafranca del Bierzo** over a vast suspension bridge through the Puerto de Pedrafita do Cabreiro. At **O Cabreiro** stands the oldest church on the road: a pre-Romanesque slate construction founded in the ninth century by Giraldo de Aurillac and still intact. It contains a communion cup considered by some to be the Galician Holy Grail, by others to be a miracle chalice. Nearby lies the Celtic village of *pallozas* (conical houses), where pilgrims can stay; two have been converted into a Museum of Ethnography. From there the Camino climbs along the LU634 between the desolate sierras of Ancares and Caurel, past abandoned villages and mist-enveloped peaks.

At **Triacastela**, according to the medieval customs of the road laid down in the *Codex Calixtinus*, pilgrims pick up a stone and carry it with them to **Castañeda** to 'make lime for the works of the Basilica of the Apostle'. From there you descend to the Benedictine monastery of **Samos** that rises grandly beside the banks of the Sarria. It was founded in the sixth century by the father of Galician monasticism, San Martín Dumiense, who was born in the Balkans and lived among the earliest cenobites and ascetics of Egypt before arriving in Galicia. What you see today is mainly a Baroque edifice built around two fine cloisters.

The road from Samos to Sarria follows the original Camino very closely

beside *vegas* of fruit orchards that line the banks of the river. **Sarria** (pop. 12,000), a former stronghold of the Counts of Lemos, rises from the middle of a fertile plain. Within the modern suburbs lies a medieval heart of small slate-roofed houses surrounding the Romanesque churches of El Salvador, Santa Marina and the hospital of San Antonio. Nearby in **Villaneuva de Sarria** is a former hospice – now the convent of La Magdalena – with an interesting transitional cloister.

The Miño is crossed by a new bridge at **Portomarín**. The construction of the reservoir necessitated the flooding of the village, but the historic buildings were first moved to a neighbouring hill. The fortified church of San Nicolás has a fine rose window. Follow signs to **Palas del Rey** via the N540 northbound and C547. At **Vilar de Doñas** there was once an important residence of *doñas* (noble nuns). In the chancel of the church there, you can still see Romanesque frescoes and tombs of some Knights of Santiago who kept the road open during troubled times. The unobtrusive village of Palas del Rey found great favour with Alfonso IX of Galicia and León, who sponsored the construction of the main Romanesque buildings. The source of the River Ulla is just above the village, and in the surrounding countryside are several 18th-century *pazos*.

From Palas, according to the *Codex Calixtinus*, the 12th and final part of the road begins. The spirit of the pilgrim on foot is kept alive by the slowly diminishing number of kilometres on the road signs leading to Santiago. **Lavacolla** is where the ritual bath was taken and pilgrims were obliged to wash every part of their bodies before entering the holy city, but the old riverbed has been tarmacked over and now supports Santiago's international airport that brings jet-set pilgrims from all over the world.

At Monxoi, the granite spires of **SANTIAGO DE COMPOSTELA** (pop. 85,000), the ancient capital of Galicia, rise into view from the midst of a circle of low mountains. This is one of the great hallowed sites of Catholic Christendom and the most important shrine after Rome's St Peter's and Jerusalem. Pilgrims entered the city through the Porta Francigena (French Gate) into the Barrio Concheiros, which was the haunt of the shell-vendors. Here they bought their cockleshell, wedged it in their hat and headed for the cathedral.

Archeological excavations suggest the **cathedral** was built on the site of a Roman and Suevic necropolis. Alfonso II and his successor, Alfonso III, built and enlarged a basilica but Al-Mansur destroyed it in 997 and took the bells to Córdoba. The earliest parts of the Romanesque shell date to the beginning of the 11th century, but this was subsequently encased in a spectacular Baroque mantle by the local architect Fernando Casa y Novoa. The grandest façade looks out onto the Plaza del Obradoiro (the Square of the Golden Works), and rises like an altarpiece decorated with lines, curves, statues, reliefs and the lichen that spreads wildly over the stone. Between the two 74-metre belfries known as Las Campanas is a central niche containing a statue of St James.

You enter the cathedral through the Pórtico de la Gloria (1168–88), one of the great wonders of Christian art, described by Miguel de Unamuno as 'a poem in stone, expressing all the art and piety of the Middle Ages'. The realism and emotive expressions chiselled by the master mason Maestro Mateo are exceptional. There are three doorways: the central one leads into the nave, and those on either side into the aisles. The bases are finished with grotesque monsters and the symbolic struggle of man against sin.

The central clustered column supports the tree of Jesse, above which, on a capital engraved with figures of the Holy Trinity, sits St James, wearing a crystal-studded nimbus and holding a scroll in his right hand and a staff in his left. On the capital above his head are scenes of the temptation of Christ. The tympanum depicts Christ surrounded by the four Evangelists with their emblematic beasts resting across their laps. Beside them stand angels swinging incense burners and holding the various instruments of the Passion. Above them are the 40 heavenly hosts and the righteous redeemed by Christ; the naked figures signify freedom from sin. Around the circumference of the archivolt sit the 24 elders of the Apocalypse, each playing a different celestial instrument.

The side jambs, supporting figures on a level with that of St James, are: to the left, the Old Testament prophets Moses, Isaiah, Daniel and Jeremiah; to the right, the Apostles Peter, Paul, James and John. Beside each corresponding side door are figures of other prophets and apostles, and facing the portico on the inside of the Obradoiro Job, Judith and Esther gaze at the prophets, while Matthew, Luke and John the Baptist face the Apostles. The archivolts above the side doors depict different scenes of the Apocalypse and Last Judgement. On entering the cathedral, pilgrims traditionally place their hands among the roots of another

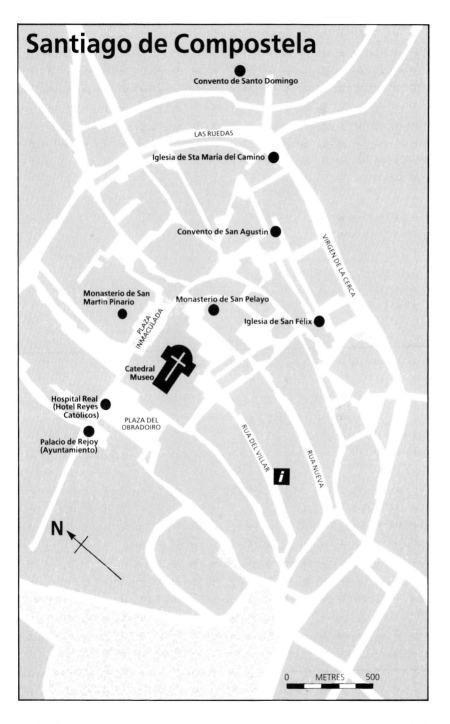

Santiago de Compostela

Convento de Santo Domingo

LAS RUEDAS

Iglesia de Sta María del Camino

Convento de San Agustin

VIRGEN DE LA CERCA

Monasterio de San Martín Pinario

Monasterio de San Pelayo

PLAZA INMACULADA

Iglesia de San Félix

Catedral Museo

Hospital Real (Hotel Reyes Católicos)

PLAZA DEL OBRADOIRO

RUA DEL VILLAR

RUA NUEVA

Palacio de Rejoy (Ayuntamiento)

N

0   METRES   500

tree of Jesse, and touch their forehead onto the head of what may be a self-portrait of Maestro Mateo.

The interior of the cathedral, like most Spanish cathedrals, is built in the shape of a Latin cross. Walking up the tall arched nave between rows of side-chapels crowned by a gallery, you arrive in the transept, where a huge *botafumeiro* (thurible), weighing over 500kg, is swung by the weight of eight men over the congregation during religious festivals, at the same time spitting sparks, blue flame and incense in every direction.

The high altar is a mass of gilt spiralling columns, floating cherubs, candles and carnations, in the most flamboyant and indigestible Churrigueresque style. You can pass behind the altar to kiss the saint's silver robe, which is studded with gems and diamonds. Beneath the altar a crypt has been built into the ninth-century foundations and contains the sepulchre of St James and his disciples, St Theodore and St Athanasius.

A late Gothic–early Renaissance cloister connects the cathedral to the museum, and it is here that pilgrims who have walked, ridden or bicycled along 100km of the Camino receive their *compostela* – a certificate to prove that they have completed the journey. In the library is an early copy of the *Codex Calixtinus* and some interesting illuminated manuscripts. The 16th-century chapterhouse is hung with some rather ordinary tapestries made in the Real Fabrica de Tapíces in Madrid, and from there you pass onto a balcony. In the basement is a museum with fragments and statues by Maestro Mateo.

On the south side of the cathedral is the Plaza de las Platerías, with the Baroque horse fountain. Here you have a good view of the Torre del Reloj, added at the end of the 17th century. The door of Las Platerías, carved in low relief, is another Romanesque masterpiece and depicts scenes of the flagellation, and a peculiar carving of a woman giving birth to a skull.

Climbing up the steps you reach Plaza de la Quintana, with an upper and a lower patio and two more doors that give access to the cathedral, although the Puerta Santa is opened only in jubilee years. One huge wall of the monastery of San Pelaya de Ante-Altares closes off the plaza to the east. Further up the steps you arrive in the Plaze Inmaculada or Plaza de la Azabachería, where jet carvers once sold sacred mementoes to the pilgrims. Opposite looms the monastery of **San Martín Pinario**, founded in 899 but completely redesigned by Ventura Rodríguez in 1770. Here the monks used to give new clothes to the needy and, above the door of the monastery, you can still see a carving of San Martín covering a poor man with his cloak.

Turn left through the vaulted passage beside the Palacio del Arzobispo Gelmirez and you arrive back in the Plaza del Obradoiro. To the north is the old **Hospital Real** – now the Hotel de los Reyes Católicos – with an extraordinary Plateresque façade and medallions of the Catholic monarchs embedded above the arch of the doorway. The interior is built around two austere Herreran courtyards designed by Enrique de Egas. Also worth visiting are the chapel and a royal audience room with frescoes by Arias Varela. Beside this building stands the 18th-century neoclassic Palacio de Rejoy, which is now the town hall and seat of the *ayuntamiento* of Galicia.

Rosalía de Castro

No single figure in the long tradition of Galician poetry captured so profoundly the beauty and desperation of her region as Rosalía de Castro. Born during the first Carlist War on 24 February 1837, she was the child of a liaison between a 39-year-old priest and Doña Teresa de Castro. Her early life was plagued by typhus and the series of famines that plagued Galicia during the 1840s. In 1856 she went to Madrid and in the following year published *La Flor* (The Flower), her first collection of poems. In 1860 she married the Galician historian Manuel Martinez Murguía and soon afterwards published her first novel, *La Hija del Mar* (The Daughter of the Sea). This is a strongly autobiographical story of an illegitimate girl who, after suffering a blighted childhood, forms an obsession with the sea in which she eventually drowns herself.

The spiritual malaise of Rosalía de Castro can be seen in the recurring themes of her book: the strong Celtic fascination with death; the misery of a people forced to emigrate to the other side of the world; the power of myth and religion; the uncertainty of famine; and the overpowering beauty of her native region. She identified closely with the poverty of her people, and with the despair, sorrow and apparent hopelessness of their destinies.

In 1885, after raising six children, Rosalía died of cancer at the age of 48. Her work – especially her *Cantares Gallegas* – has become a central part of folk culture, and her ballads are still sung at *fiestas* and fairs to this day. Above all, she helped rekindle the flame of the Galician language, and stood for a while at the centre of the regional renaissance or *Rexurdimento* in the 1870s and 1880s. The house where she lived for many years beside the Sar at Padrón has been converted into a museum, and her body lies in the pantheon of illustrious Gallegans in the convent of Santo Domingo in Santiago de Compostela.

The commercial end of the town lies south of the cathedral, and it is worth wandering down the arcaded streets of the Rúa del Villar or Rúa Nueva which both emerge in the Plaza Toral. Excellent tourist information can be picked up from the main office at Rúa del Villar 43. The other main sights – including the university, the Romanesque church of San Félix, the Palacio de Mondragón, the convent of San Agustín and the church of Santa María del Camino lie along the Rúa Virgen de la Cerca.

It is worth visiting the convent of **Santo Domingo** situated up the Cuesta de Santo Domingo. It has a unique triple-spiral staircase, each one ascending to a different floor so the monks and nuns never had to come into contact with each other. The late 17th- and early 18th-century building also houses the Pobo Gallego Museum, which contains objects and instruments that explain something of popular Gallegan culture. Of greater importance is the pantheon for famous Galicians, which includes the tomb of the poetess Rosalía de Castro. At **Santa María del Sar**, a mile west of the cathedral, subsidence of the foundations has made the building slant alarmingly. Inside, however, there's a wonderful cloister with intricately carved capitals attributed to Maestro Mateo or his school.

Santiago is a city of emotion, imagination, blind faith and legend and, whether or not you believe the story of St James, you cannot help but be struck by its unique atmosphere.

There is, however, an afterword to the journey. A few strands of the legend have spread further west than Compostela, beginning with the village of Padrón that lies at the mouth of the Ulla. It is better known today as the birthplace of Rosalía de Castro and Camilio José Cela (Nobel Prize for Literature winner in 1989) than for its medieval fame as Iria Flavia, the seat of the bishopric and the place where the body of St James was first discovered. On the Baroque coat-of-arms on several of the señorial mansions in the town, you can see the stone boat crewed by the two disciples who are supposed to have brought the body of St James from Egypt to Spain in seven days. Beneath the altar of the church of Santiago beside the bridge is the stone to which the boat was allegedly moored.

Along the coast road to **Noia** you pass Monte Barbanza, Galicia's Mount Olympus, where Noah's Ark supposedly landed. The Mirador de la Curota, reached by a road from **Puebla de Caramiñal**, has unsurpassed views across the Rías Bajas up to Cabo Finisterre. Continuing around the headland you arrive at Noia, nicknamed 'Little Florence' because of its gracious hive of alleys, churches and 15th-century palaces overlooking the Ría de Muros e Noia. Its name apparently derives from a legend that the white dove sent by Noah to discover whether the great flood was over found its olive branch here.

All the villages along this stretch of coast have something to offer the visitor: the fortified port of **Muros**; the longest *hórreo* (storehouse) in existence at **Carnota**; the extravagant courtyard-palaces of **Corcubión**; and remnants of the oldest settlement in Galicia in the fishing village beside Cabo Finisterre. Until land further west was discovered this was, for all but the last 500 years, considered by most people to be the end of the world.

TOURIST OFFICES

SANTIAGO DE COMPOSTELA: Rúa del Villar 43, tel (981) 22 18 22.

Accommodation, Eating and Drinking

PEDRAFITA DO CEBREIRO:

(H)**San Giraldo de Aurillac**, El Cebreiro. Rooms in old *pallozas* (conical houses). A long-established rendezvous for pilgrims. E–D.

SANTIAGO DE COMPOSTELA (tel code 981):

Accommodation of all types can be found in the city. A few suggestions include:
(H)**Parador de los Reyes Católicos**, Plaza Espana 1, tel 58 22 00. Founded as a hos-

pital by the Catholic Kings. Entrance through a magnificent Plateresque portal. Rooms are built around four austere central courtyards; many with four-poster beds. Humbler pilgrims showing their *compostela* can eat for free in a small dining room off the kitchen. B.

(H)**Suso**, Rúa del Villar 65, tel 58 66 11. Good budget alternative. Centrally situated. Good *tapas* bar. D.

(H)**Hospidaje Rodriguez**, Pisón 4. Tranquil and centrally situated. E.

(R)**Anexo Vilas**, Avda de Villagarcìa 21, tel 59 86 87. Cl Mon. A family-run restaurant founded in 1915. Superb Galician cooking. B.

PADRÓN:

(R)**Casa Ramallo**, in the village of Rois, 3km from Padrón on Carretera de Noya, tel (981) 81 12 10. Good home cooking. C.

FINISTERRE:

(H)**Cabo Finisterre**, C/ Santa Catalina, tel (981) 74 00 00. Good clean rooms. E.

Northern Galicia and the Rías Altas

The north coast of Galicia, including the Costa de la Muerte and the Rías Altas, has a jagged and often forbidding littoral with a network of slow, twisting roads that cut in and out between the coves and creeks beside pine-covered hillsides and ancient fishing hamlets. A local fable claims that certain families in the area are descended from a liaison between a sailor and a mermaid, and if you stay near the coast you cannot fail to become immersed in the whole sea culture. There are the fishermen who risk their lives to pull from the rocks *percebes* (barnacles), which are then immediately transported to the most exclusive fishmongers in Madrid; the quaysides entangled with nets; brightly painted trawlers idling in the waters; and the piping-hot plates of seafood *tapas* in local bars.

The towns of **Muxía** and **Camariñas**, exposed to every climatic extreme on either side of the mouth of the Camariñas, are famous for their intrepid trawling fleets and the local cottage industry of lace-making. On any warm afternoon the *palilleras* congregate with their bobbins on the doorsteps of the narrow streets, to chatter the hours away until the men return with the afternoon catch. Inland at **Vimianzo** there's an impressive *castillo* and the beautiful Renaissance Pazo de Trasariz, which was built by a local family on the proceeds from the gold mines in the district. At **Laxe** there are more señorial mansions, such as the Palacio Moscoso near and around the Plaza del Arco.

From Laxe to **Malpica**, the sea is renowned for its unpredictable ferocity. This is the main stretch of the *Costa de la Muerte* (Coast of Death), so termed because of the shipping lost each year in these tempestuous waters. At Malpica flocks of seagulls fish the shallow waters between the mainland and the Islas Sisargas, and venture out on occasions to the large ocean-going tankers seen cruising along the horizon.

A CORUÑA/LA CORUÑA (pop. 240,000) is the centre of a major canning and fish curing industry. It was founded by the Phoenicians, but the great emblem, the *Torre de Hércules*, on the city's coat-of-arms derives from the lighthouse built by the Romans. Now electrified and restored, it continues to cast its beam across the water and is the oldest functioning lighthouse in Europe. It was from La Coruña that the Spanish Armada set out in 1588, and where the final retreat of Sir John Moore ended in 1809 with his death and the successful evacuation of most of the British forces.

Park along the harbour front in the area known as the *Dársena*, which is easily reached by following the signs for tourist information. Here you will see the distinctive *solanas acristaladas* (glass-fronted houses), designed to keep the wind out but to bring the sun in, which have lent the sobriquet 'city of glass' to Coruña. From here you can explore all the major sights on foot. Of particular interest is the Romanesque church of Santiago, dedicated to pilgrims who journey to Compostela by sea, with a carved relief around one of the doors of St James killing Moors at the non-existent Battle of Clavijo.

Nearby is the Casa de Doña Emilia Pardo Bazán, a great 19th-century Spanish novelist and short-story writer, whose *La Tribuna* and *Los Pazos de Ulloa* are considered the two finest novels describing Galician life. Pass the Baroque palace of the Capitanía General and follow the old sea wall until you arrive at the Jardines de San Carlos, which contain the tomb of Sir John Moore. The gardens are full of typical Galician plants and flowers such as rhododendrons, camellias, azaleas and chrysanthemums.

Overlooking the bay to the south is the 16th-century *castillo* of San Antón, which once stood on its own island but is now connected to the mainland. Inside is the Archeological Museum, with some good exhibits from *castro* and Celtic cultures. The Torre de Hércules is situated at the other end of the headland, to the north. From an inscription in stone at the foot of the lighthouse, it would appear that the original tower was constructed in the second century AD by a Lusitanian architect called Cayo Servio Lupo. You can climb the 242 stairs for a privileged view across the Atlantic.

Leaving La Coruña, the road leads past the sardine port of **Sada** and the Pazo de Meirás, built for Emila Pardo Bazán but now the ancestral home of General Franco's family. At **Betanzos** dreary suburbs surround an interesting town centre with its streets of glass façades, a fine Plaza Mayor with outdoor cafés, and a copy of the fountain of Diana at Versailles. A wild boar – the emblem of the Andrade family, who were the medieval magnates of this area – can be seen on top of the church of San Francisco, and more marble examples inside prop up the tomb of Fernán Perez de Andrade. The ancestral estates once included several señorial mansions in **Pontedeume**, which retains something of its medieval character every market-day when *pulpeiras* set up their makeshift restaurants and boil up fresh octopus to serve with a sprinkling of paprika.

From Pontedeume the road follows the course of the Eume through forested countryside and after 12km reaches a footpath leading to the ruins of the Cistercian monastery of Caaveiro. This was erected at the end of the 12th century and is unique in that the apse of the church is built upon a platform to counteract the uneven lie of the land. Your route continues north to **El Ferrol**, an 18th-century town founded as a naval base and shipbuilding yard during the reign of Charles III which, though it is a good example of urban development of that period, offers little of great interest today.

The coast road north is a rather drab succession of modern houses built among eucalyptus and maritime pine forests. **Cadeira**'s elegant glassed-in houses retain a certain dignity, and anyone who is at all superstitious will have to make the detour along the road to **San Andrés de Teixido** on a bluff overlooking the sea. Here pilgrims can be exorcized of all evil, and the consumption of the local doughnuts will keep you safe from the evil eye. The penalty for not doing so allegedly results in reincarnation as a lizard.

The resort town of **Ortigueira** is renowned throughout the Celtic music world for its annual jamboree, when bagpipers and flautists arrive from Brittany, Ireland and Scotland to jig the week away. **Viveiro/Vivero** (pop. 15,000) has several interesting medieval buildings within the confines of the old town walls, including the Romanesque church of Santa María and the Renaissance *aduana* (customs house). Busy little fishing ports thrive all the way along the coast to **Foz**, where a road branches inland to **Mondoñedo**, the old provincial capital. The town is protected in a quiet wooded valley of chestnut trees and its austere cathedral has suffered somewhat on account of a Baroque facelift. Venture inside, however, for worth seeing are the 16th-century frescoes on either side of the Plateresque choir and, on a plinth in the high altar surrounded by angels, Nuestra Señora de los Ingleses: a Gothic Virgin salvaged from St Paul's cathedral during the English Reformation. In the Diocesan Museum are works by El Greco and Zurbarán and, elsewhere in this city of fewer than 7,000 inhabitants, some other flamboyant Baroque buildings.

From Mondoñedo or **Ribadeo**, beside the River Eo that delimits the border with Asturias, you can reach Lugo via **Meira**. Here one of the most extraordinary doors in Spain gives access to the convent-church of Santa María. From there the road cuts through a series of river valleys to **LUGO** (pop. 63,000). After Lugo was captured from the Celts by Augustus, it became a popular town with its Roman conquerors on account of its plentiful supply of lamprey eels from the River Miño, and its hot medicinal springs that were believed to alleviate rheumatism. To defend their settlement of Lucus Augusti, they built a massive wall, rising to a height of 10–15m and over 2km in circumference, which has remained in a remarkable state of preservation to this day. One of the city's other major attractions is the cathedral, a Romanesque structure based on that at Santiago. This was not finished until the 18th century, when the Baroque cloister was completed by Fernando de las Casas y Novoa. The interior is notable for the Plateresque altarpiece by Cornelius de Holanda, and the sidechapel that contains the polychromed alabaster Romanesque Madonna, Nuestra Señora de los Ojos Grandes (Our Lady of the Big Eyes). Around the

The Pórtico de la Gloria (the Glory Door), leading into the cathedral at Santiago de Compostela, is the work of the master mason Maestro Mateo, considered one of Europe's greatest Romanesque sculptors.   Incafo

cloister of the convent of San Francisco is the Museum of Fine Arts – one of the most important of its type in Spain. It boasts a fine collection of ceramics from Sargadelos and the Celtic gold torque of Burela.

TOURIST OFFICES

LUGO: Plaza de España 27–9, tel (982) 23 13 61.

LA CORUÑA: Dársena de la Marina, tel (981) 22 18 22.

Accommodation, Eating and Drinking:

LA CORUÑA (tel code 981):

(H)**Finisterre**, Paseo del Parrote 22, tel 20 54 00. Central, in the artistic *barrio*. All amenities. Swimming pool. B.

(R)**El Rápido**, La Estrella 7, tel 22 42 21. Aquarium-like façade. Excellent seafood. C–B.

(R)**La Viña**, Puente del Pasaje 5, tel 28 08 54. Typical Galician cuisine complemented by interesting wine cellar. B.

(R)**Mesón de la Cazuela**, Callejón de la Estacada 1, tel 22 24 48. Traditional home cooking, popular among the locals. Basic seafood and meat courses. C–B.

BETANZOS (tel code 981):

(H)**Los Angeles**, C/ Angeles 11, tel 77 15 11. Inexpensive, central and clean. E.

(R)**Casa Edreira**, Linares Rivas 8, tel 77 08 03. Homely restaurant. Traditional Galician food. Good local red wine. Cl Mon except Aug. C.

EL FERROL (tel code 981):

(H)**Parador El Ferrol**, Almirante Vierna s/n, tel 35 67 20. In an old *pazo* in the medieval heart of the city. C.

(R)**Pataquiña**, Dolores 35, tel 35 23 11. Good Galician cuisine. Excellent bean stew (*fabadas*) and different kinds of octopus (*pulpo*). B.

(R)**Casa Paco**, Ctra Jubia, 5km away in Jubia, tel 38 02 30. Stewed octopus, *merluza* (hake) stew. C.

VIVERO:

(R)**Nito**, Playa de Area, tel (982) 56 09 87. Hotel annexe opposite the beach. Outstanding seafood as well as delicious meat dishes. C–B.

RIBADEO:

(H)**Parador de Ribadeo**, C/ Amador Fernàndez s/n, tel (982) 11 08 25. Overlooking the estuary of the Eo (good salmon and trout fishing). Good base for exploring Mondoñedo and Lugo hinterland. B.

VILLALBA:

(H)**Parador Condes de Villalba**, C/ Valeriano Valdesuso s/n, tel (982) 51 00 11/51 00 90. Former stronghold of the Andrade family. Only six double rooms. Good base for exploring Northern Galicia. Cl Wed & 8 Jan–8 Feb. C.

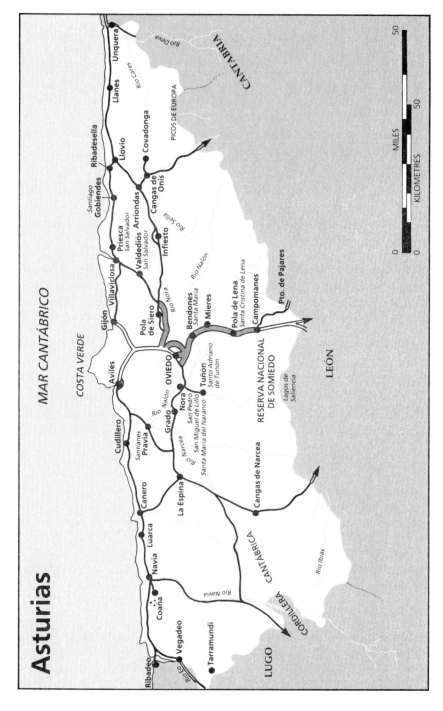

CHAPTER FIVE

Asturias

THE PRINCIPALITY OF ASTURIAS is divided into three distinctive areas. The Costa Verde (Green Coast) is a succession of rugged bays surrounded by cliffs, with numerous broad beaches and secluded coves. It remains one of the few undeveloped *Costas* left in Spain. Behind it rises the mountainous hinterland, which is divided into a series of isolated rural river valleys running out of the peaks of the Cordillera Cantábrica. This area is a refuge for several endangered species, including the European brown bear, the wolf, and several types of eagle and vulture. The third area is the Picos de Europa: mountains whose mighty summits delimit the frontiers of Cantabria and Castile.

Until recently, tourism was the exception rather than the rule in Asturias. When most coastal regions were cashing in on development, Asturias held back. Now, with an increasing interest in the environment, it has started to take advantage of its 'green' image and promote an alternative form of tourism for the environmentally aware.

The early history of Asturias is in many ways the starting-point of the history of Spain. It was from the desolate and impenetrable mountains surrounding Covadonga that the *Reconquista* of Al-Andalus began, and the unique collection of pre-Romanesque churches of the eighth and ninth centuries near the regional capital of Oviedo are a testament to the epoch

when the Kings of Asturias carried the banner for all Christian Spain. The kingdom lasted for almost two centuries from the victory at Covadonga in 718 or 722 until 910, when the capital was moved by King García (910–14) from Oviedo to León.

Little is known of the dynasty beyond a few sketchy facts but it seems clear that Alfonso I 'El Católico' (the Catholic) took advantage of the Arab disorder and made raids into Galicia and as far south as Zamora and Salamanca. With the establishment of the Emirate, the Asturians found themselves on the defensive, but the rule of the last two Kings of Asturias, Ordoño I (850–66) and Alfonso III 'El Grande' (the Great), saw expansion south into the *Meseta* and east into Alava.

With the growing importance of Castile and León, Asturias faded into the background of national history, yet it produced a few notable characters, such as the painter Juan Carreño; and the great Enlightenment figure of Fray Benito Jerónimo Feijóo (1676–1764) – the 'Spanish Voltaire' – who vigorously attacked the superstitious ignorance of Spain in his letters and essays.

Even today, however, local custom and superstition have persisted in this small autonomous region. Its geographical isolation has helped to preserve its folklore and the area's great monuments, which range from the cave art and monuments of Peña Tu, Tito Bustillo and El Pindal to the fortified *castros* (prehistoric villages), the dolmens and small thatched mountain cottages where transhumant shepherds have sought refuge for centuries.

Above all, this is a region that has survived for the last 2,000 years on the products of its forests, its fishing, mining and small farms, and on the determination of its people, descended from the Celtiberian tribe, the *astures*.

OVIEDO (pop. 185,000), the commercial capital of Asturias, rises from a belt of green hills between the coast and the Cantabrian mountains. Over the years, the buildings have turned a leaden grimy-grey due to the coke furnaces and coal-mining towns in the Nalón valley to the south-east. The 19th-century industrial suburbs have little to offer the visitor, and it is best to head straight for the centre of town, parking as near the cathedral as you can.

The flamboyant Gothic cathedral stands on the site of an original church founded by Fruela I in 781. The exterior has some good Gothic detailing, and the Cámara Santa inside, constructed in the time of Alfonso II, is well worth a visit. On permanent exhibition are the great treasures of Asturian art: the early ninth-century Cruz de los Angeles, a masterpiece of gold filigree work inlaid with gems and cameos; the Cruz de la Victoria; and a sumptuous reliquary coffer, the Arca de las Agatas, which once contained a sandal of St Peter, one of the 30 pieces of silver given to Judas Iscariot, and a fragment of the staff of Moses.

The main west door of the cathedral faces out onto the Plaza de Alfonso II, where the church of San Tirso, although heavily restored, has preserved its pre-Romanesque three-light window in the apse. In the surrounding streets are the great señorial palaces of Camposagrado, Valdecarzana and Marqués de Santa Cruz de Mercenado. In the Palace of Velarde you can visit the Museum of Fine Art, which has a portrait of Charles II 'El Hechizado' (the Bewitched) by Carreño, and important work by Asturian artists of the 19th and 20th centuries. The Archeological Museum is housed in the ex-convent of San Vicente and has a collection of artefacts discovered in the principality.

The pre-Romanesque churches of Asturias comprise the most complete complex of ninth-century buildings in Europe, and they stand apart from any contemporary or subsequent architectural style. Their construction coincided with the reigns of the three great Asturian monarchs: Alfonso II, Ramiro I and Alfonso III. The relative isolation of these churches has helped preserve them in an extraordinarily good state and, on the whole, they can still be admired in the surroundings in which they were originally conceived.

Architecture during the rule of Alfonso II (792–842) is characterized by classical, almost Pompeian tendencies: the Holy Chambers in Oviedo cathedral and San Tirso both date from this era. **San Julián de los Prados** at **Santullano** is the largest pre-Romanesque structure, with its monumental red and ochre frescoes that conform to a strong classical tradition. They depict a vision of paradise and scenes from the Apocalypse, presided over by the Maltese Cross of Victory, emblem of the Asturian monarchy. Remains of similar wall paintings and particularly beautiful *transennae* windows can be seen in **Santa María de Bendones**. This church was badly damaged during the Civil War and reconstructed from the ruins. **San Pedro de Nora**, in a wonderful setting beside the River Nora, is attributed to the reign of Alfonso II, though there are several features which are plainly Mozarabic.

It was during the short reign of Ramiro I (842–50) that the most elegant pre-Romanesque buildings were created, identifiable by their verticality and profuse decoration – a style generally referred to as 'Ramirense'. Part of **Santa María del Naranco** originally served as a royal audience hall, and there is a beautiful triple-light loggia at one end. Inside, the outstanding sculptural decoration has strong Byzantine overtones. Nearby, on a hill of the Sierra de Naranco, rises **San Miguel de Lillo**. The internal features, such as the iconostasis and reliefs around the door jambs, are particularly fine.

All the churches above (as well as **San Adriano de Tuñón**) are within 20 minutes' drive of Oviedo. Further afield is **Santa Cristina de Lena**, 40km south of Oviedo off the N630 near **Pola de Lena**. This is the third church attributed to the reign of Ramiro I and is remarkable for the delicate carving of the interior. In the south wall of the sanctuary above a small loophole window is a fluted carving of the Peninsula's earliest known scallopshell: the symbol of the Compostela pilgrimage. Although the Camino does not pass through Asturias, there are a great many cult-related churches and much related symbolism.

During the long reign of Alfonso III (866–910), the introduction of Mozarabic architectural elements by Christian refugees from Al-Andalus caused the pure pre-Romanesque to give way to a more arabized style. The richly decorated capitals, ultrasemicircular horseshoe arches, *ajimez* (twin-arched windows) and floral tracery designs typical of the Mozarabic style can be seen in **San Salvador de Valdediós** (between Villaviciosa and **Nava**); **Santiago de Gobiendes**, south of **Colunga**; **San Adrian de Tuñón** and **San Salvador de Priesca** near Villaviciosa. All these later churches embody the mysterious grace and beauty that emerged from one of the darkest periods of Spanish history.

From Oviedo most of Asturias lies within a day's drive and, unless you can't survive without the five-star luxury of the Hotel de la Reconquista, your best option is to explore the region's rural edges. The coast lies less than 30 minutes' drive away along the national highway towards **Avilés** (pop. 80,000) and **Gijón** (pop. 260,000), the two main industrial ports of Asturias, which have been steadily growing since the establishment in the 19th century of their large iron- and steelworks. On the headland between the two cities lie the fishing villages of

Luanco (pop. 5,000) and nearby **Candás** (pop. 6,500) where every year, at low tide, the sea is blocked off with barriers and a bullfight takes place on the sand inside the harbour walls.

The coast west from Avilés towards Galicia consists of steep cliffs broken by several points and inlets that hide some tranquil expanses of beach. Small fishing hamlets nestle precariously between the ocean and the mountains that rise steeply from the sea. **Cudillero** (pop. 7,000) is particularly charming, with its whitewashed houses clustered around the port and spreading hazardously up the steep hillside. The streets are narrow and you'll find several simple fish restaurants specializing in *merluza* (hake) around the diminutive Plaza Mayor.

In a more sedate setting at the mouth of the River Negro, **Luarca** (pop. 18,000) is an old whaling port and a long-established resort town. It can be enjoyable to explore by weaving back and forth across the seven bridges that straddle the river as it snakes its way beside the boulevard to the port.

These are two of the most characteristic but certainly not the only ports worth visiting along this coast and, if you're planning to spend some time beside the sea, it's also worth exploring **Otur**, **Puerto de Vega**, **Tapia de Casariego** or any of the small, discreetly signposted coves and beaches that normally lie at the end of untarmacked roads. Here there'll be little more than a field in which to park your car, a farmhouse that may moonlight as a summertime bar, plenty of clean sand and sea, and half a dozen *siesta*-bound Asturians.

Ortigueira and **Figueras** are towns whose economy is based on a mixture of resort, industrial and fishing revenues. Both are built around the estuaries of the Rivers Navia and Eo, two good salmon rivers. Roads turn inland up each respective river valley, divided by the Sierra de la Bobia, towards the Cordillera Cantábrica and some of the wildest and most isolated sierras of northern Spain – *terra incognita*. Outside Ortigueira, rather confusing and sporadic directions lead to the *castro* of Coaña, a large Iron Age *castro* settlement, with excavated streets of circular houses on a natural elevation, which gives extensive views across the surrounding hillsides.

Alternatively, turn inland along the Eo, which marks the Asturian–Galician border, and head south. At Vegedeo you will see directions for **Tarramundi**, a village which has been specifically converted to cater for rural tourism in what is otherwise a mountainous wooded wilderness. At Tarramundi a parador-style hotel has been built, from which walks through the local countryside or more adventurous excursions by Land-Rover into the forests can be made. The hotel's information centre will advise you exactly how to get to **Teijos** and **Aguillón**, two old mining villages where drop-forges are still in use.

Philologists have suggested that the original settlers in this area were a group of persecuted Etruscans or Oscans from central Italy, who introduced original methods of forging. More certain is the Romans' presence in the area. They mined the rich mineral deposits on a large scale, and the locals will no doubt tell you that the nails used to build the ships of the Spanish Armada were made here. South of Tarramundi and stretching into León lies the mighty oak forest of Muniellos: 50sq km of unadulterated natural habitat for wolves, bears and capercaillie, which is now a zoological reserve and a wonderful place to walk.

The valleys of the sierras of the Cordillera Cantábrica heading east from Muniellos were farmed by the earliest settlers of the Peninsula. If you spend time searching the area, evidence of their cultures can be seen everywhere: dolmens, tumuli, unexcavated *castros* and derelict gold mines. The area has few monuments apart from the Palacio de Peñalba and a couple of ruined monasteries, but its real attraction lies in its rural culture. Of interest are the local village chapels with occasional Romanesque details; and the *pallozas* and thatched huts used by the *vaqueiros* (transhumant shepherds) on their migration between high mountain pastures in the summer and the coastal plain in winter. The roads leading south from the main N634 between Oviedo and Luarca are the best means of exploring the area, although generally you have to move in a north–south direction, following the river valleys and taking cul-de-sac minor roads up to individual villages.

The most spectacular corner of this range is the Reserva Nacional de Somiedo, reached by taking the N633 and turning left to **Pola de Somiedo** and **Valle de Lagos**. Somiedo and the Lagos de Saliencia were a former stronghold of the *vaqueiros*, and their *brañas* (small mountain hamlets of thatched stone houses) are where they lived with their cattle. The most beautifully preserved of these, **La Pornacal**, is reached along a minor road leading out of **Aguasmestas** towards **Figueña**. After about 8km the road becomes a dirt track, and you finally arrive in the village among the strange primitive community of thatched and stone huts

joined by muddy paths. It is a sight belonging not to another century but another millennium.

The *vaqueiros*, like the gipsies, have always remained on the fringe of society; a migratory clan who move through these mountains with their flocks and with all their earthly possessions stacked on ox-carts, scraping a living where they can. As in some African cultures, cows are more highly valued than women, and there is a refrain in a *vaqueiro* ballad that translates literally as 'It's better to be a cow than a cowgirl!' The place is steeped in legend and folklore; it is said that in the glacial lakes of Saliencia dwell the *xanas* (water nymphs), who guard a great treasure. East of Somiedo lie the Sierra de Pajares and other wooded valleys of the cordillera, today mainly hunting reserves and mining districts.

The coast east of Gijón has far more to offer in the way of monuments, especially around **Villaviciosa** (pop. 15,500): a small señorial town at the centre of an apple-growing region, surrounded by villages containing many interesting medieval towers, mansions and early churches beyond those mentioned in the paragraphs above on pre-Romanesque (see p. 116). They include the 12th-century San Juan de Amandi, just 2km south, with its beamed ceiling and Romanesque apse and door. **Lastres**, on the coast, is a busy little fishing port; you can gain a good view of the harbour and quay from the summit beside the chapel of San Roman.

Leaving Lastres, you join the N632 beside the Sierra del Sueve, where wild Asturian ponies roam free. A magnificent view up and down the coast can be gained from the Mirador del Fito – a detour of 5km worth

The pre-Romanesque church of Santa Cristina de Lena in Asturias was founded by Ramiro I in the ninth century and is a symbol of the earliest resistance to Islamic occupation of Iberia.　Incafo

making up the C637 towards **Arriondas** – before you arrive at **Ribadesella** (pop. 7,000). This is an attractive resort town at the mouth of the Sella. From here you can visit Tito Bustillo, the best of several rupestrian caves in Asturias, where you can see peculiar depictions of what some experts assume to be female genitalia used for fertility rituals as well as red, purple and chiaroscuro outlines of deer and horses.

The coast from Ribadesella east towards Cantabria has several good beaches beside the ports of **Barro**, **Celorio**, with ruins of a Romanesque monastery, and Llanes. **Llanes** (pop. 15,000), the capital of eastern Asturias, is too commercial to warrant much attention, although the streets around the old harbour are full of señorial mansions and glass-fronted houses that point to the town's former importance. Nearby are the Cueva del Pindal and the peculiar Bronze Age standing stone Peña Tú on the road inland towards the Picos de Europa.

TOURIST OFFICES

OVIEDO: Plaza de la Catedral 6, tel (985) 21 33 85.

LUARCA: Plaza Alfonso X 'El Sabio', tel (985) 64 00 83.

Accommodation, Eating and Drinking

OVIEDO (tel code 985):

(H)**de la Reconquista**, Gil de Jaz 16, tel 24 11 00. A former 18th-century hospital, luxuriously furnished with antiques, sauna, etc. Good value. B–A.

(H)**Fruela**, Calle Fruela 2, tel 21 82 78. In an old house, central and clean. E.

(R)**Casa Conrado**, Argüelles 1, tel 22 39 19. Traditional family business. Classic, unpretentious, Asturian cooking. C.

(R)**La Máquina**, 6km along the road to Avilés in Lugones. The best Asturian *fabada* in the country. Cl Sun and 25 June–25 July. C.

LUANCO:

(R)**Casa Nestor**, Conde del Real Agrado 6, tel (985) 88 03 15. Centre of the old fishing town. Excellent seafood straight from the trawlers. C–B.

CUDILLERO (tel code 985):

(H)**Portobello**, El Relayo-Villademar, tel 59 02 92. Small. Good central location near harbour. E–D.

(R)Delicious grilled sardines to be found in bars along the harbour.

LUARCA:

(H)**Cobas**, Pl de los Pachorros s/n, tel (985) 64 00 70. Central; picturesque; with bar. E–D.

TARRAMUNDI:

(H&R)**La Rectoral**, Tarramundi, tel (985) 63 40 60. Parador-like luxury and peace in the middle of nowhere, this is where you have to stay in order to explore the west of Asturias. C. Good restaurant. B.

VILLAVICIOSA (tel code 985):

(H)**Congreso**, Generalísimo 25, tel 89 11 80. Small, simple but good. E.
(R)**La Nansa**, El Muelle, in Tazones, 10km north of Villaviciosa, tel 89 70 38. Good home cooking. Excellent local cider poured from a height. C–B.

RIBADESELLA (tel code 985):

(H)**Gran Hotel del Sella**, Ricardo Cangas 17, La Playa, tel 86 01 50. Old señorial palace. Elegant rooms overlooking the beach. B.
(R)**La Chopera**, 3km away in San Martín de Collera, Ctra Vieja Ribadesella/Llanes, tel 86 04 45. Excellent home cooking. C–B.

The Picos de Europa

The Picos de Europa, incorporating the National Park of Covadonga, are the most spectacular mountains of the Cordillera Cantábrica, comprising the three massifs of Cornión, Urrieles and Andara. In the space of 25km from the Atlantic coast, they rise to majestic heights of over 2,600m, a succession of jagged karst summits plunging into sheer-faced gorges and chasms. On their lower slopes there is a network of sheltered, virescent valleys with small villages stuck like swallows' nests beneath the precipitous slopes. This is a natural paradise for botanists, ornithologists and anyone in search of simple pleasures such as fresh mountain air and open spaces. In the months of high summer, the area can become uncomfortably congested with people escaping the city heat, but for the rest of the year the peaks are virtually deserted except for a few mountaineers and speleologists.

To the Spanish the Picos de Europa remain a point of pilgrimage, a symbolic shrine. It was here that Don Pelayo and a few Christian guerrillas made the first successful stand against the Moorish General Alkama in either 718 or 722, kindling the initial sparks of the Reconquest that culminated in 1492 beneath the highest peak on the Iberian Peninsula, Mount Mulhacén in the Sierra Nevada. But before that, the Astures had used the mountains to harass the Roman legions. This mountain range, united by art, nature and religion, is the place where the Spanish nation was born.

The Picos form the border between Asturias, Cantabria and Castile–León, and can be approached from any of these regions. The Asturian valleys of the north can be explored in the 50km between Cangas de Onís and Panes, reached easily from the coastal towns of Ribadesella or Unquera.

Cangas de Onís, was the first Christian capital of Spain after the Arab invasion, and it was here that the second Asturian King, Favila, founded a church on the site of an old Celtic tumulus. Crossing the Sella by a Romanesque bridge, the road east (C6312) passes the Magdalenian Cave of Buxtu, and after 5km forks to the right along the River Reinazo to **Covadonga**, a small village geared to the pilgrim trade. Of interest are the abbey and collegiate church – with remains of the original tenth-century cloister – and, in an overhanging crag above a waterfall, the Cave of Auseva. Reached by a flight of marble steps, this is where Don Pelayo planned his attack and where he was later buried with his family. A tunnel continues to the neo-Romanesque–Gothic basilica built at the end of the last century on a spur overlooking the wooded valley. The road continues to the Lago Enol and Lago de la Ercina, beneath the *massif* of Peña Santa.

Returning down the valley, the route to Panes continues via **Arenas de Cabrales**, which is the centre of the local cheese-making industry. The cheese is made from ewe's, goat's and cow's milk, and matured in naturally aerated underground caves to give it added piquancy. If you feel like taking the most breathtaking walk of your life, turn right out of the village to **Poncebos**, where a 12-kilometre footpath snakes its way along the Divine Gorge beneath the vertical limestone peak of Naranco de Bulnes to **Caín**. This is a four- to five-hour ascent (the descent from Caín reached from **Posada de Valdeón** takes 30 minutes less), through tunnels, across bridges and along the wall of rock carved out by the River Cares. For long stretches of the route, the world is reduced to a narrow slice of sky above, and in some

places a sheer drop of almost 2km to the icy depths of the thunderous river echoing below. It's certainly not for the faint-hearted, who should attempt easier walks to **Camarmeña** or the bridle path to **Bulnes**, the most remote village in the Picos, below the peak of Naranco. The shepherd hamlets of **Tielva** and **Sotres** can be approached by a road. From Sotres you can trek in a day across the peaks to **Espinama**.

Back at Arenas, continue along the gorge of the Cares or north-west via the villages of **Arangas**, **Rozagas**, **Ruenes**, **Ales** and **Niserias** to Panes. At **Panes** there's a small Mozarabic chapel and here the road cuts south along the N621 through the Liébana valley and into Cantabria. For 22km you travel though another gorge that is covered in chestnut trees growing precariously at irregular angles. At the village of **Lebeña**, surrounded by apple orchards and vineyards, there is an exquisite Mozarabic church with outstanding Corinthian capitals. The church was founded and generously supported in its construction by a local nobleman, Alfonso, Conde de Lebeña, at the end of the tenth century, and is one of the purest and most idyllically situated examples of its style.

Potes (pop. 1,500), at the confluence of three valleys, is the ancient commercial capital for both the eastern side of the range and the whole of the great valley of Liébana. The old centre hums with excitement on market day every Monday – a particularly good opportunity for buying local cheeses. The Old Quarter is situated on either side of the river and is joined by two bridges. The most important monuments are the cubic Torre del Infantado and the 14th-century church.

Above Potes, encircled by mountains

Beato de Liébana

The Mozarabic movement is defined not only by its unique collection of ninth- and tenth-century churches such as San Miguel de Escalada, Santa María de Lebeña and San Baudelio de Berlanga, but equally by its *sui generis* illuminated manuscripts and, most specifically, by the commentary on the Apocalypse known as the *Beato de Liébana* – the great illustrated text of early medieval Spain.

More than 20 versions of this work exist, having been illuminated in different monastic scriptoria between the eighth and 13th centuries, and all of them were copied from the original manuscript written by the monk Beatus de Liébana in about 776. As works of art, they are on a level with the caves of Altamira, the portraits of Velázquez, the black paintings of Goya, or anything by Picasso and Dalí, and are exceptional for their emphatic use of colour.

The idea of the Apocalypse undoubtedly loomed large in the consciousness of the early Asturian courts. St John's fantastic visions of the triumph of the people of God over the false prophets had a direct relevance to the early Christian crusade against the kingdom of Al-Andalus. It is not surprising to find Muslims portrayed as beasts of the ten trumpets and Mohammed as the apocalyptic beast. Nevertheless, the irony is that Mozarabism was a movement inextricably influenced by Córdoban culture – the word itself means 'arabicized' – and in these manuscripts the depictions of architecture, zoomorphic patterning, and even clothing illustrate a clear descent from Arabian forms.

By the 11th century, with the sway of the Cluniac monks, Mozarabism was swallowed up by artistic trends from northern Europe, but these original manuscripts remain as a testament not only to those centuries of uncertainty and the fear of the Asturian kingdom, but also to its grace and brilliance. Copies are on public display at several monasteries throughout the country, including Santo Domingo de Silos, Burgo de Osma, Seo de Urgel, Girona cathedral library and Montserrat.

---

of pine forest, rises the monastery of San Toribio de Liébana. It was founded by Alfonso I in the eighth century and is where Beato wrote the original commentary on the Apocalypse. The monastery's most revered possession is the *Lignum Crucis*, thought to be the largest fragment of the Holy Cross. The whole complex was restored earlier this century, although many of the original Gothic features were preserved. After Covadonga, it is the most sacred site of the Picos.

From Potes the road continues beside the River Deva, along a rich agricultural dale where almonds, oranges and olives grow. It gradually ascends through steep pastureland past old señorial villages such as **Mogrovejo** to **Fuente Dé**. The latter is situated at the head of the valley in an amphitheatre of soaring limestone cliffs, and water cascades from hundreds of metres above. Behind the parador, a cable car ascends 2,000m to the lunar-like plateau, which is pitted with *hoyos* (craters) filled with limestone splinters. The area is drained by underground streams that run beneath the *massifs*, and here serious hikers, mountaineers and speleologists can tackle the colossal snow-capped heights of Torre Cerredo (2,648m), Torre Llambrión (2,641m), Peña Vieja (2,613m), Pico Tesorero (2,570m) and Naranjo de Bulnes (2,519m). The mountains are surprisingly well equipped with overnight refuges.

The road that encircles the southern reaches of the Picos between Cangas and Potes and cuts through the valley of Valdeón is somewhat bleaker but no less spectacular. The town of Posada de Valdeón is the natural centre for exploring these parts, which include *miradores* (look-out points), and the lofty defile of Garganta de los Beyos on the road to Cangas de Onís.

The peaks have long been an important navigational landmark for ships returning to the ports of northern Spain, and the name Picos de Europa derives from the old nautical name for the *massifs*, which for generations of mariners were the first sight they caught of Europe after their transatlantic voyages. In the autumn, when the early morning mist disperses over the peaks, or in the spring when the gentle blue Castilian sky is silhouetted against the snow-line, the Picos remain mountains not easily forgotten.

TOURIST OFFICE

POTES: Casa de Liébana, C/ Independencia s/n, tel (942) 73 08 20.

Jeeps can be hired from Potes and Cangas de Onís. From late spring until late autumn almost all the roads are clear and accessible to any kind of car. The most accurate map if you're planning on walking off the beaten track is that published by the Federación Española de Montañismo. There are not many banks in the area.

Accommodation, Eating and Drinking

CANGAS DE ONÍS:

(R)**El Llagar de Juan**, Avenida de Covadonga 20, tel (985) 84 80 12. Asturian cooking. C.

COVADONGA:

(H)**Pelayo**, tel (985) 84 60 00. Small but intimate. Beside the basilica of Nuestra Señora de las Batallas. Good restaurant serving typical Asturian cuisine. Cl Jan. C.

POTES (tel code 942):

(H)**Valentino**, La Serna, tel 73 04 58. Good, clean and simple. In town centre. D. There are good hotels and *hostales* all the way up the valley in the villages between Potes and Fuente Dé.

FUENTE DÉ:

(H)**Parador de Fuente Dé**, tel (942) 73 00 01. A spectacularly-situated modern parador surrounded by towering cliffs. A cable car ascends to the *massif*.

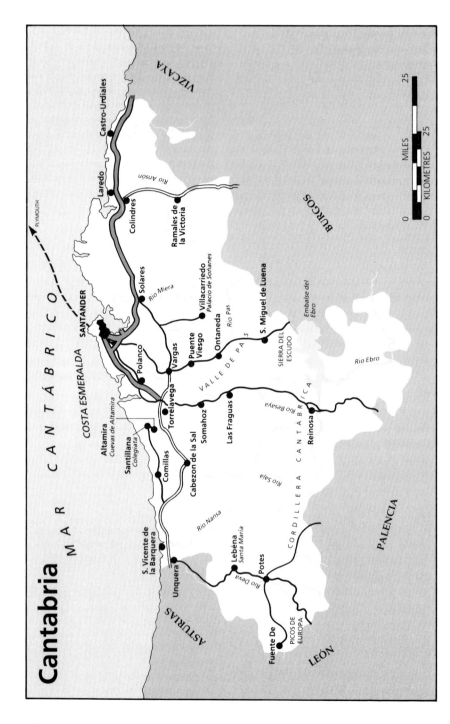

CHAPTER SIX

Cantabria

IN MOST WAYS Cantabria is a topographical continuation of Asturias, but the coast is not quite as rugged and relatively empty stretches of sand-flats washed by the Mar Cantábrico can be found even in August. The coastal resort towns, particularly Santander and Comillas, have been popular since the last century for their mild summers. All along the coast there is a faint air of 19th-century seaside nostalgia interspersed with some dreary industrialization, especially around Torrelavega. But the heart of the region is in its mountains, which flank the coast and rise towards the border with Castile and the *Meseta*.

Although the Spanish rather cynically refer to the villages in these half-forgotten valleys as *pueblos malditos* (damned communities) because of their poverty and medieval-like agrarian existence, the countryside is undeniably breathtaking, and the way of life possessed of a charm all its own. In these colossal sweeps of green hillside, the natural silence is penetrated only by the bells of the cattle and the noise of the strange wooden clogs the old villagers wear to help them along the muddy streets and paths.

SANTANDER (pop. 190,000), the capital of Cantabria, has the best natural harbour on the coast and a heavy mercantile and maritime presence along the waterfront. The university adds a lively student element to an otherwise rather faceless port. The heart of the city, which was badly damaged by a freak fire and hurricane in 1941, lies behind the harbour where the ferries dock. It has a few interesting sights, such as the heavily restored cathedral containing a gracious Gothic crypt and, in the surrounding streets near the Plaza Porticada, a Municipal Museum exhibiting local artists' work. The Biblioteca Menéndez Pelayo next door at Calle Gravina 4 is the former home of this historian and medieval hispanist, and now houses his library.

If you're interested in the prehistoric caves of Cantabria, then you should certainly visit the Museo de Prehistoria at Calle Juan de la Cosa 1, which exhibits many of the finds from the 20 rupestrian or troglodyte caves in the region. Further east the Palacio de la Magdalena can be seen rising from the sandy tongue of land that juts into the sea. This Victorian-looking mansion, built for Alfonso XIII in 1912, imitated the English convention for holidays beside the sea at a time when Santander was highly fashionable among noble Castilian families wishing to escape the great heat of the *Meseta*.

El Sardinero, the seasonal suburb developed to fulfil these needs, can be admired in all its carefully tended *Belle Epoque* grandeur by walking north along the tamarisk- and palm-shaded boulevard, above the two beaches called Primera Playa and Segunda Playa. The great attraction is still the Gran Casino del Sardinero, which, although lacking the international *élan* of Monte Carlo or Deauville, is nevertheless very much an important part of the city. Santander may have been persuaded to finance so lavish a building by the presence in the town in about 1900 of the King of Monaco, who used to make forays in an open-top Rolls-Royce into the Cantabrian hills to explore the caves and their paintings, accompanied by a German archeologist, a French monk and a Spanish priest. The best month to visit is July, when the city hosts an important cultural *fiesta* of music and theatre.

Travelling east from Santander, there are beaches and campsites all the way to the **Isla de Santoña**. Isla has a fine Baroque church and **Laredo** – often referred to as the Torremolinos of northern Spain – has been blighted by high-rise accommodation. **Castro Urdiales** (pop. 13,000), near the border with Vizcaya, is more agreeable, with a harbour dominated by the cathedral-sized Gothic church of Nuestra Señora

de la Asunción. This is still essentially a fishing port, with narrow arcaded streets and glass-fronted houses in the *mediavilla*, guarded by a large pentagonal *castillo* that now contains the lighthouse.

West of Santander, on the coast road towards Asturias, there is more to see. **Santillana del Mar** should be your first main destination and is one of the most genial villages in the north of the country. Each evening the cows are brought in from the surrounding fields and driven into sheds beneath the houses. Although loads of day-trippers are emptied out into the cobblestoned streets at weekends and throughout the summer, the charm has not been too much affected. Along the two main streets there are several important señorial mansions, with beautifully worked *rejas* (grilles) and wrought-iron balconies and grand *escudos* (coats-of-arms) above the doors. The village was the fictional setting for the 18th-century picaresque novel *Gil Blas* by Alain-René le Sage, and was also the home of Iñigo López de Mendoza, Marqués de Santillana (1398–1458), the poet responsible for commissioning the first translation into Castellano of Dante's *Divine Comedy* from his charlatan friend Enrique de Villena.

Santillana's *pièce de résistance* is the Romanesque collegiate church of Santa Juliana, which possesses the remains of the fourth-century martyr. The south door – with slightly damaged Apostles standing on either side of a Christ Pantocrator, supported by four angels – is unique of its kind; and the restored cloister within is even more striking, with capitals supported by twin columns carved with themes such as the baptism and the descent from the cross.

From Santillana the road continues for 18km through soft rolling hillsides to **Comillas** (pop. 2,500), whose personality is split between its medieval centre of noisy seafood *tapas* bars and its folly-like Modernist buildings. The character of Comillas was modified in the space of a decade in the latter half of the 19th century, when it became a testing ground for aspiring Modernist architects. The change was brought about by the vision of a rich transatlantic shipping magnate, Antonio López y López, later the first Marqués de Comillas, who decided to make this town his home. He founded the vast neo-Gothic seminary or university on a hill overlooking the town, which was built to plans drawn up by Juan Martorell, with ornamental details such as the bronze doors and staircase by Domènech i Muntaner. López commissioned the Palacio de Sobrellana for his family home and, beside it, the private chapel and pantheon, resembling a miniature Gothic cathedral.

Nearby stands one of Gaudí's earliest houses, *El Capricho* (The Whim), a bizarre hybridization of Gothic and neo-Mudéjar fantasy richly embellished with yellow and green sunflower tiles, which blends in ingeniously with the surrounding landscape. The building has recently been converted into a restaurant.

The last coastal resort of importance is **San Vicente de la Barquera** (pop. 4,000), another quiet little fishing port, well sited around the estuary of the Escudo, with arcaded streets, a ruined castle and dilapidated mansions, which is transformed for three months of the year into a busy holiday haunt. The town's one artistic treasure is the white marble sepulchre of the Inquisi-tor Antonio del Coro in the church of Santa María. The tranquil pose of the reclining subject, reminiscent in many ways of the late-Gothic tomb of El Doncel at Sigüenza, is a particularly elegant example of Renaissance funerary carving, attributed to Juan Bautista Vázquez.

The interior of Cantabria, the heartland of the Cordillera Cantábrica, is very different to its coastal *alter ego*. Beautiful yet impenetrable mountains are dotted with small stone villages sheltered in the cleft of lush vales inhabited in the east by a cattle-herding people known as *pasiegos*, whose origins are even more obscure than the *vaqueiros* of Asturias. In the seven main river valleys that divide the sierras – the Nansa, Saja, Besaya, Pas, Pisueña, Miera and Asón – there are 15 Paleolithic Caves, one of the highest concentrations of Romanesque churches in Spain, and thousands of cows wandering nonchalantly along the high roads in a zone where agriculture is still dependent upon ox- and horse-power. You need a detailed map, a strong sense of adventure and a steady nerve on the high mountain roads, which at times can become alarmingly narrow, especially when you are faced with an oncoming milk lorry.

The most dramatic entrance to Cantabria is from the Valle de Liébana along the C6314, 12km south of Panes. The road cuts east across the Rivers Nansa and Saja, through the valley of Cabuérniga. At the small village of **Carmona** there is a small regional parador in a converted palace, which is ideally situated for exploring the caves of Micolón and Cufín. Here the drawings are on the outside of the caves: the only example in Cantabria of an open-air sanctuary. The village of **Barcena**

Mayor, situated in a dead-end valley, is one of the purest examples of a Cantabrian mountain community.

Further south, **Reinosa** (pop. 14,000), rising from a plain surrounded by mountains, is the commercial capital of southern Cantabria. Almost every village in the Campoo valley has a crumbling Romanesque church; of particular interest are the erotic corbels supporting the roof of San Pedro at **Cervatos**, which are intended to discourage members of the congregation from sins of the flesh. Also worth seeing are the peculiar rupestrian cave churches, the ruined Roman city of **Juliobriga** near **Retorillo**, and the vivid Romanesque frescoes at the church of San Martín de Elines. The River Ebro rises at the foot of Peña Labra, some 5km west of Reinosa, its waters being collected first in the Embalse del Ebro before beginning the 918-kilometre course that drains the southern slopes of the Pyrenees and meets the Mediterranean at its delta south of Tarragona.

From Reinosa the C611 follows the course of the River Besaya to **Torrelavega** (pop. 60,000), a rather dusty industrial town just inland from the river mouth. The neighbouring valleys to the east above the Pas and Pisueña contain the caves at **Puente Viesgo** and the most impressive examples of Cro-Magnon cave art after Altamira, including hand negatives and dot patterns or 'tectiforms' which, like the aborigine art of Australia, were blown onto the wall through a pipe and might be described as prehistoric abstract expressionism. South of Puente Viesgo, pass the monastery church at **Iruz** and follow the River Pas to **Vega de Pas**, before turning north into the valley of the Pisueña. At **Selaya** and **Villacarriedo** there are some magnificent country palaces, built during the 18th century when subsidies from the New World enabled the nobility to indulge their extravagant tastes.

At the eastern end of the cordillera, along the valleys carved out by the Rivers Miera and Asón, are the more isolated group of caves of Covalanas and La Raza. You can find a guide at the nearest village of **Ramales** by asking at a bar or in the plaza and, with enough persuasion, someone will show you the way if you're prepared to drive. The last part of the ascent is 1.5km up an almost sheer mountain, which you may prefer to climb on foot. From the small mouth of the caves you will be led by the light of a paraffin lamp into the pitch black to look at the strong ochre outlines and narrow incisions chiselled into the rock. Whatever sense they make to you, the trip will have been worthwhile just for the view across the border into Vizcaya.

TOURIST OFFICES

SANTANDER: Plaza Velarde 1, tel (942) 31 07 08. Also Brittany Ferries, Estación Marítima, tel (942) 21 45 00.

Accommodation, Eating and Drinking

SANTANDER (tel code 942):

(H)**Real**, C/ Pérez Galdós 28, tel 27 25 50. Luxurious *Belle Epoque* hotel that has maintained the décor of that age. B–A.
(H)**El Sardinero**, Plaza de Italia 1, tel 27 11 00. A cheaper alternative to the Real. Overlooking the El Sardinero beach and beside the Casino. C–B.
(R)**Zacarias**, on the corner of C/ Hernan Cortés and General Mola, tel 21 06 88. Tables amusingly installed in 19th-century coaches, around a beautiful glassed-in patio. Bar and *tapas* served here too. Inventive cuisine. B.
(R)**El Café de Cándido**, C/ Perines 24, tel 37 13 87. In the heart of old Santander. Garden terrace, *tapas* bar and plush dining room. Grilled meats and cocktails are the speciality. C–B.

SANTILLANA DEL MAR (tel code 942):

(H)**Parador Gil Blas**, Plaza Ramón Pelayo 11, tel 81 80 00. A classic luxury parador in an old señorial mansion. C.
(H&R)**Altamira**, C/ Cantón 1, tel 81 80 25. A 17th-century mansion, quiet rooms. Restaurant specializes in roast meats. C.

COMILLAS (tel code 942):

(H)**Casal del Castro**, San Jerónimo s/n, tel 72 00 36. Central. Picturesque old mansion-house. C.
(R)**El Capricho de Gaudí**, Barrio de Sobrellano s/n, tel 72 03 65. After lying empty for many years, this remarkable early resort palace by Gaudí was turned into a restaurant in 1989. Small dining rooms with glasses, etc, in keeping with the Modernist style. Cocktail bar upstairs. C–B.

SAN VICENTE DE LA BARQUERA (tel code 942):

(H)**La Barquera**, Paseo de la Barquera s/n. Simple and in the centre of the old town. E.
(H&R)**Miramar**, Paseo de la Barquera, tel 71 00 75. Family-run. Overlooking estuary. Creative home cooking. C&B.

CARMONA:

(H)**Venta de Carmona**, Barrio del Palacio, tel (942) 72 80 57. Idyllically situated in the tiny mountain hamlet of Carmona, in the highlands of the Cordillera Cantábrica and perfect for exploring the west of the region and the Picos de Europa. In an old village palace. C.

A view of Santoña in Cantabria; a region of rolling coastal hills that rise steeply to the heights of the Cordillera Cantábrica – the ridge of mountains that run parallel to the north Atlantic coast. Incafo

REINOSA:

(H&R) **Vejo**, Avenida Cantabria 83, tel (942) 75 17 00. Good regional cooking in the restaurant. C.

PUENTE VIESGO:

(H&R)**Puente Viesgo**, Barrio de la Iglesia, tel (942) 59 80 11. A good base for exploring the caves in the region and the eastern Cantabrian valleys. Good river trout (*trucha*). D&C.

Altamira

The cave of Altamira is situated on a limestone hill about 2.5km inland from Santillana del Mar. Since its discovery in 1879, it has become one of the great monuments of prehistoric art: a masterpiece of man's earliest artistic brilliance.

Above the entrance to the cave stands a small memorial to Marcelino de Sautola who, with his young daughter María, was the first person to explore the cave and draw the world's attention to its magnificent prehistoric murals. He was to dedicate most of his life to proving the authenticity of the paintings in the face of strong scepticism – a battle which eventually led to his premature death. Many thought it a grand hoax and attributed the work to a mute French painter called Ratier.

The dark chamber called the Hall of Bisons, popularly referred to as the 'Sistine Chapel of Quaternary Art', is an extraordinary depiction of bison in a variety of positions – running, sleeping, stationary – and is almost academic in its execution. The work is exceptional for the quality of the painting, the strong lines, the movement of light and shadow, and the use of the natural relief and swell of the rock to define shape.

Carbon-14 dating has placed the paintings in the lower Magdalenian period (around 13,500 BC). The effects of the thousands of people visiting the shrine each year have forced the closure of the cave, unless prior permission is obtained months in advance. Beside Altamira there is, however, a small museum that graphically explains the work.

The Great Hall of Bisons in the cave of Altamira near Santillana del Mar is known as the 'Sistine Chapel of Quaternary Art'. Prehistoric caves are scattered throughout the mountains of the north. Incafo

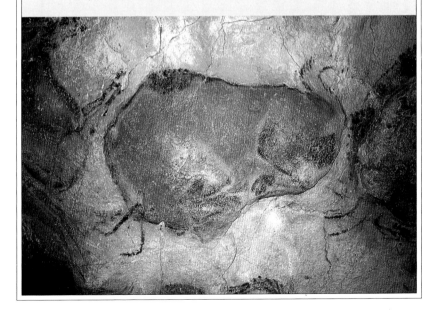

CHAPTER SEVEN

Basque Country
(Pais Vasco)

THE BASQUE COUNTRY or *las Provincias Vascongadas*, consisting of the three united provinces of Alava, Vizcaya and Guipúzcoa, forms the most densely populated area of Spain. It is a land of colourful fishing ports, heavy industrial suburbs, and serene stretches of country and mountainside scattered with *caseríos* (wood and stone farmhouses). No people have a more proud and self-contained nature than the Basques, whose history has always been a long struggle for independence.

Basque nationalists claim to have inhabited the same territory since Neolithic times, believing themselves to be the oldest pre-Indo-European people in Europe, with a unique physical identity, a blood type (O rh+) that supposedly proves the purity of their racial lineage, and an inscrutable language with no definite source, which philologists have variously tried to connect with Berber, Georgian and Pictish. The problem with proving the authenticity of any of these theories is that there are few early written records of the language, and little archeological evidence to throw light on the Basques' early history, which has made some historians doubt whether their origins are as pure as the nationalists believe.

By retreating into the remote crannies of the western Pyrenees, they managed to resist conquests by Romans, Visigoths and Moors, and they maintain a strong cultural identity. This can clearly be seen in regional games such as *pelota* and *cesta punta*, known as *Jai Alai* (literally, happy celebration) in Reno and Las Vegas: two cities with large migrant Basque populations. Their cultural identity is strongly maintained through their idiosyncratic games held at *fiesta* times: shearing sheep and chopping wood; hair-raising tobogganing races through the cobbled streets; pulling giant stones with teams of oxen; and the annual regattas, when the local fishing villages vie to win rowing races along the coast. Cooking is another art in which the Basques are widely acclaimed masters, and one of the great attractions of visiting the region is the standard of the food.

Throughout the 18th century the Basques grew rich, along with much of

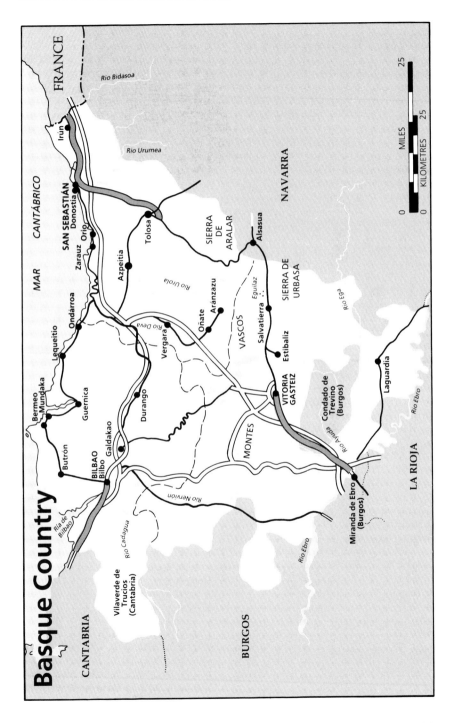

Basque Country

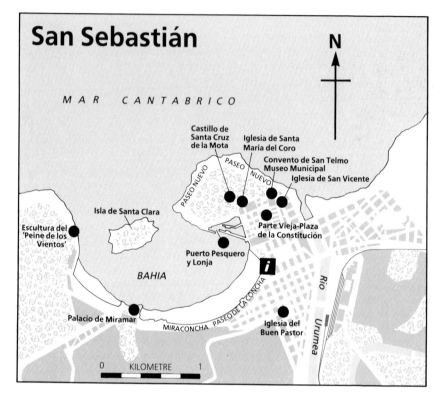

San Sebastián

N

MAR CANTABRICO

Castillo de Santa Cruz de la Mota
Iglesia de Santa María del Coro
Convento de San Telmo
Museo Municipal
Iglesia de San Vicente

PASEO NUEVO
PASEO NUEVO

Isla de Santa Clara

Escultura del 'Peine de los Vientos'

Parte Vieja-Plaza de la Constitución

Puerto Pesquero y Lonja

i

BAHIA

Río Urumea

Palacio de Miramar

MIRACONCHA   PASEO DE LA CONCHA

Iglesia del Buen Pastor

0   KILOMETRE   1

northern Spain, by exporting to the Americas the iron ore to be found in the local hills. In the 19th century, when Europe became fiercely nationalistic, the Basque determination to assert autonomous control grew apace. But their struggle to maintain their early *fueros* (governing rights) and local identity has not been easy. Under Franco, Basque rebelliousness was subdued with a state of martial law and local cultural identity was suppressed without mercy. It nurtured a generation of activists, the group known as ETA (*Euskadi Ta Azkatasuna* – literally, Freedom for the Basque Country). In recent years, though they have become less active politically and seem motivated more by ecological

issues, the assassinations and terrorist acts have continued, although targets are mainly high-ranking officers in the *Guardía Civil*, as well as politicians, judges and generals who reside in cities outside the region. Their objective remains the reunification and independence of all Basque lands, including the three provinces of southwestern France and Nafaroa (Navarre).

With the advent of regional government the Basques have been quick to re-establish their cultural identity. Their language, *euskera*, is taught in all local schools. Place-names have been changed from the Castellano: now Fuenterrabía, San Sebastián and Pamplona are called Ondarribia, Donostia and Iruña respectively. A regional police force, the *ertzaintxa*, has been established. The local television channel dubs American soap operas into *euskera*. Economically, the region remains one of the strongest in the country and many of the most important businesses and banks are run by Basques. Regional pride, evident in the widespread fluttering of the *Ikurriña* – the red, green and white flag, the pattern of which was copied from the Union Jack, and which flies from every flagpole in the region – remains as strong as ever.

From the frontier at **Irún** (pop. 55,000) and the colourful fishing port of **Ondarribia/Fuenterrabía** (pop. 14,000), with painted houses adorned with potted plants climbing up the whitewashed walls in the streets in and around La Marina, it is 30 minutes' drive along the autoroute to the most elegant and cosmopolitan city on the Atlantic seaboard: **DONOSTIA/SAN SEBASTIÁN** (pop. 180,000), capital of the province of Guipúzcoa. Though it was first granted *fueros* in 1180, San Sebastián was frequently burnt down and what remains today dates mainly from the 19th century. In 1886 it achieved fashionable status following visits by the Queen Regent, María Cristina (1833–41), and since then it has remained a popular and chic holiday retreat, with a temperate summer climate liable to sudden bouts of *sirimiri* (soft rain).

The city is built along a wide sweeping bay around the mouth of the canalized River Urumea, which is spanned by a series of rather imaginative bridges. It is widely considered to be the most unspoilt and beautiful city of northern Spain; accordingly, property prices are higher than in even the smartest neighbourhoods of Madrid.

There are excellent shops along Avenida de la Libertad, some fine restaurants, and a fast-paced urban streetlife that becomes even busier in the summer months and during the jazz festivals in July, *Semana Grande* in mid-August and the International Film Festival in September.

The **Parte Vieja** (Old Quarter) stands beneath the wooded eastern promontory of Monte Urgull. It is a hive of busy streets, which are crowded before lunchtime and dinner with Guipúzcoans in search of seafood *tapas* that may be washed down with a glass of the local light white wine, *txakoli*, or with red wine – a ritual known as *poteo* in the Basque Country. The centre of this area is the grand arcaded Plaza de la Constitución: nearby are the main monuments, including the churches of **Santa María del Coro** and the Gothic **San Vicente**.

An early morning visit to **La Lonja**, the fish market, will quickly bring home to you the importance of fish in the lives of the local people. Each day, gourmets and members of the gastronomic societies come here to buy the freshest of the morning catch, a spectacle that partly explains why food is an intrinsic part of Basque culture. The exclusively male gastronomic societies, *txokos* (see p. 29), developed in the 19th century, when the men were forced to leave the family *caseríos* to find work in the burgeoning industrial centres. Missing home cooking, they founded dining societies, where members would take it in turns to cook, and the inbred competitive spirit of the Basques produced an exceptional standard of cuisine. Nowadays, some attempts have been made to introduce women to the societies, but the idea has found little support.

Nearby, in the former Dominican convent of San Telmo is the **Municipal Museum**. There are some works by El Greco and Goya but the museum is mainly concerned with the Basque people and their history. Of particular interest are the peculiar discoidal funerary steles engraved with the *lauburu* (literally, four heads, each one of which represents a Basque province) and different geometrical patterns, which are still copied for headstones. In the adjoining church are bright golden murals by the Catalan painter Josep María Sert, depicting different scenes from Basque life.

The most enchanting aspects of Donostia are discovered simply by ambling along the tamarisk-shaded promenades. The River Urumea divides the Old Quarter from the rather run-down fishermen's neighbourhood of Gros, which is packed with cheap bars and restaurants where old men play the card games *mus* and *julepe* for hours every afternoon.

Leaving the fishing harbour near the great *ayuntamiento* (town hall) and climbing up the tree-covered slopes of Monte Urgull, you arrive at the 16th-century *castillo* of **Santa Cruz de la Mota**; there are magnificent views over the bay and the hills that rise behind the city, which explain why Donostia, surrounded by the ocean in an amphitheatre of hills, cannot easily expand beyond the limits of the city you see today. Take the ferry or hire a rowing boat if you're feeling fit, and cross the bay from the harbour to the Isla de Santa Clara.

Alternatively, walk above the beach along the Paseo de la Concha beyond the mock-Elizabethan Palacio de Miramar to the Playa de Ondarreta, with its distinctive blue-and-white striped bathing tents. Beyond it rises Monte Igueldo; you can take a funicular to the top, or walk along the twisting road in less than 20 minutes to obtain more dramatic views from the summit. Below, on a platform facing the ocean, is the work of art by the Basque sculptor, Eduardo Chillida, which is known as *El Peine de los Vientos* (The Comb of the Winds). It is a contorted iron structure that leans towards the Atlantic and, when the sea rushes in, water spurts out of holes drilled into the rock. Looking west, you can see the small coastal road wending its way towards the small fishing port of **Orio** (pop. 4,500).

From Donostia the N-I autoroute continues west, but it is worth turning off for the old fishing ports of Zarautz and Getaria. The former shipbuilding port of **Zarautz/Zarauz** (pop. 17,000) is a popular summer resort, with an interesting Old Quarter and two good beaches. The best of these is Playa Zuloaga, named after the Basque painter Ignacio Zuloaga who so vividly captured in his work the fishermen and Basque rural life at the turn of the century. His house behind the beach has been turned into a museum and contains many examples of his work. Beside the house is the 12th-century chapel of Santiago Etxea with its fine Romanesque cloister.

Getaria/Guetaria (pop. 2,300) is an idyllic little fishing port, perfect for a leisurely lunch near the harbour, which is dominated by the beautiful Gothic church of San Salvador. The port was the birthplace of Juan Sebastián Elcano, who took over the captaincy of the caravel *Vitoria* after the death of Magellan in the Philippines during the first circumnavigation of the world (1519–22) (see p. 9).

A short detour south takes you to **Azpeitia** (pop. 13,000) and the monastery of Loyola, birthplace of Iñigo López Recalde (1491–1556), better known as San Ignacio of Loyola, the founder of the Jesuit Order. The church commemorating his life is a highly decorated Baroque affair. Further south and situated at the end of the rolling fertile Aránzazu valley is **Oñate** (pop. 11,000), ruled by the Counts of Oñate until 1845. Here you can find the Renaissance university with several fine Plateresque buildings and, in the church of San Miguel, the exquisite alabaster tomb of the university's founder, Bishop Zuázola of Avila. From Oñate a road climbs 9km further up the mountain to the Sanctuary of Aránzazu, a peculiar Modernist church guarding a 14th-century Virgin in an otherwise isolated setting beneath the peak of Aitzgorri. In many ways the Sanctuary typifies the strong Catholicism of the Basques, who are perhaps the most devout people in all Spain.

Returning to the coast, continue into the province of Vizcaya, along the beautiful stretch of Basque coast between San Sebastián and Bilbao. Any of the three colourful fishing villages of **Mutriku/Motriko** (pop. 5,500), **Ondarroa** (pop. 12,500) and **Lekeitio/Lequeitio** (pop. 7,000) are worth stopping for, if only to understand the strong seafaring traditions of the Basques. Each village is beautifully positioned about the folds of green, pine-covered hills, and a morning or afternoon can easily be spent exploring the tall, narrow streets around the harbour, where the fishermen and their families live and where hole-in-the-wall bars sell delicious seafood *tapas*.

Gernika/Guernica (pop. 18,000) is the spiritual capital of the Basquelands, and is the proud possessor of the *Gernikako Arbola*: the enshrined petrified tree trunk around which the Basque parliament traditionally meet in the nearby Casa de Juntas. The tree symbolizes the permanence of the roots of the Basque people, and even the King of Spain has to swear the *fueros* beside it to become sovereign of the Basques. The sculptor Eduardo Chillida recently installed a granite window 100m away. Otherwise the rest of the town is modern, rebuilt after its destruction by German bombers during the Civil War. Driving towards the fishing harbour at **Bermio/Bermeo** (pop. 18,000) you travel past **Mundaka/Mundaca**, a resort well known for its surfing. From the road, after driving through the small town of **Pedernales**, there is a magnificent view of the Ría de Kanala, on the other side of which you will find the wonderful beaches of Laga and Laida.

BILBO/BILBAO (pop. 385,000) is the polluted but prosperous industrial heartland of the Basque Country, with its factories and iron- and steelworks built along the navigable estuary of the River Nervión. Understandably, the town is not noted for its charms, although in recent years there has been a concerted effort to tidy up the city with such innovations as a Metro designed by Norman Foster. But, apart from the Casco Viejo (old neighbourhood) situated at a loop in the river and containing the cathedral of Santiago, arcaded Plaza Mayor and the Museo de Bellas Artes – which contains one of the best collections of Old Masters in Spain – there is less to see here than in most Spanish cities of comparable size. If you don't have much time, it's better

The finely carved doorway into the church of Santa María in Laguardia, Alava is a well restored Gothic example of the tradition of religious wood carving that is normally associated with church interiors.   Incafo

to leave Bilbao out of your itinerary, but if you do happen to find yourself here at the end of August, the city throws one of the wildest *fiestas* in the whole country: an uninterrupted week-long bacchanalia.

From Bilbao a motorway heads south to Vitoria, but the more scenic route is along the Alto de Barázar through the Sierra de Gorbea or on the smaller roads that bypass the lakes of Alava on the way to the capital of the province, **GASTEIZ/VITORIA** (pop. 212,000). This is another city of sprawling industrial suburbs thrown up in the last 40 years, which hide a well-preserved medieval and neoclassic core. The plain surrounding the city was the site in 1813 of a battle between Wellington's army and the retreating French forces of Joseph Bonaparte in the last year of the War of Independence.

Try to park as near as you can to the Plaza de la Virgen; from here you can explore on foot most of the main sights in and around the old Jewish Quarter of narrow cobbled streets that are joined by steps. The Gothic cathedral of Santa María has a beautifully carved triple tympanum above the west door; and the church of San Miguel contains some fine tombs, as well as the axe of Vitoria, where the custodians of the city swore, on penalty of being beheaded, to maintain the interests of the city.

In the surrounding streets several important palaces are to be found. These include the Bishop's Palace, built by Hortuñi Ibáñez de Aguirre, a counsellor to Isabel la Católica and Charles I; and the Escoriaza-Esquibel Palace, built by Fernán López de Escoriaza, the private physician to Henry VIII and Catherine of Aragón. The Museo de Ciencias Naturales y Arqueología is situated in a beautiful half-timbered house on Calle Correría. The Museo de Bellas Artes on Paseo Fray Francisco de Vitoria, near the railway station, contains work by several Spanish masters, from Ribera and Morales to Picasso and Miró, as well as some good Gothic sculpture.

South of Vitoria lies the area known as the Rioja Alavesa, a series of wide, well-farmed valleys dotted with copses of pine, beech and oak, where cattle graze or vines are cultivated and where you can see the wide sloping rooftops of the *caseríos* so typical of the Basque Country. This area is more like Castilla, with its señorial villages and grand palaces, its Romanesque architecture and magnificently neglected altarpieces. It is best approached on the small road that snakes south from Vitoria through the Puerto de Vitoria, where you have a dramatic view south across the Condado de Treviño, a small enclave of Burgos in Alava. At **Peñacerrada** there are some excellent tombs of local nobles in the church, but don't miss the walled town of **Laguardia**, founded by Sancho 'the Wise' of Navarre in the 12th century, and the centre of the Alavesa wine co-operatives. The Gothic church of Santa María de los Reyes has a peculiar late 14th-century portal of polychromed sculpture, and no less strange is the 18th-century Churrigueresque chapel of El Pilar beside the Romanesque chapel of San Juan.

TOURIST OFFICES

IRÚN: Puente de Santiago, tel (943) 62 22 39; or Estación del Norte, tel (943) 61 15 24.

DONOSTIA/SAN SEBASTIÁN: Reina Regente s/n, tel (943) 42 10 02.

BILBO/BILBAO: Alameda Mazarredo, tel (94) 424 48 19.

GASTEIZ/VITORIA: Parque de la Florida, tel (945) 13 13 21.

Accommodation, Eating and Drinking

ONDARRIBIA/FUENTERRABÍA (tel code 943):

(H)**Parador El Emperador**, Plaza de Armas, tel 64 21 40. Small but luxurious parador in a huge castle dominating the Bidasoa bay. Founded by Sancho Abarca and later reinforced by Charles V. Within easy walking distance of the bright life of the old fishing quarter. C–B.

(R)**Alameda**, Barrio Alameda, tel 64 27 89. An old travellers' inn once used by the muletrains passing between Spain and France. Plain but excellent home cooking. D.

(R)**Ainere**, Mayor 31, tel 64 01 46. Another renovated tavern. Grilled meats and fish. C.

(R)**Arraunlari**, Paseo Butrón, Casa Etxe-Alai, tel 64 15 81. With a summer terrace overlooking the sea. Fish recommended. C.

DONOSTIA/SAN SEBASTIÁN (tel code 943):

(H)**María Cristina**, Plaza República Argentina 4, tel 42 49 00. Opened in 1912. Another *Belle Epoque* classic, overlooking the River Urumea. A.

(H)**Londres e Inglaterra**, Zubieta 2, tel 42 69 89. Rooms with beautiful views across the bay. Casino. B–A.

(R)**Akelarre**, Paseo Padre Orcolaga 56, tel 21 20 52. Magnificently positioned on Monte Igueldo with superb views over the Atlantic and bay. Pedro Subijana, the head chef and owner, is something of a local celebrity. The menu takes traditional Basque cooking and turns it on its *nueva cocina* head. The downstairs bar is worth a visit for the views alone, and there's no obligation to eat. A.

(R)**Arzak**, Alto del Miracruz 21, tel 28 55 93. The owner, Juan Mari Arzak, was one of the founders of *nueva cocina* in Spain. The food is more egg- and cream-based than at Akelarre. A.

(R)**Casa Nicolasa**, Aldemar 4, tel 42 17 62. On the edge of the Old Quarter. Another gourmet shrine. A.

(R)**Lanziego**, Triunfo 3, tel 46 23 84. Menu combines traditional Basque cooking with more experimental courses. B–A.

(B)For *tapas* there are dozens of cheap bars around the Old Quarter and fishing harbour.

GETARIA/GUETARIA (tel code 943):

(H)**San Prudencio**, Barrio San Prudencio, tel 83 24 11. Intimate and central. E.
(R)**Elkano**, Herrerieta 2, tel 83 16 14. In step with the atmosphere of the fishing port. Beautiful summer terrace. Expensive but worth it. Typical Basque cooking. A.
(R)**Masoparri**, Sagartzaga 1, tel 83 57 07. Terrace in front of the monument to the navigator Elcano. Good local cooking. B.

MUTRIKU/MOTRICO:

Unfortunately there is no accommodation in Motrico or Ondarroa but the restaurants are good.
(R)**Jarri Toki**, Ctra Deva-Motrico, tel (943) 60 32 39. In an old villa with panoramic views from dining room. B.

BILBO/BILBAO (tel code 94):

(H)Hotels are generally expensive and geared towards executive/business travellers. If you've got a car stay 20 minutes' drive north of the city at **Torrea Hotel**, José M Cirarda 4, Basigo de Baquio, tel 687 37 25. In an old resort house overlooking the bay. D–C.
(R)**Lasa**, Av de Zumalacárregui 123, tel 446 48 30. Tables overlook the basilica of Begoña. Good service. Traditional Basque cooking. A.

GASTEIZ/VITORIA (tel code 945):

(H)**Parador de Argomañiz**, Ctra Madrid–Irún km363, tel 28 22 00. Just 12km from Vitoria but very much in the countryside, in an old Basque palace and former home of the Larrea family. Well-decorated, with antiques from the region. C.
(R)**Zabala**, Mateo Moraza 9, tel 23 00 09. Popular local restaurant. Good value for the standard of food. C.

LAGUARDIA:

(H)**Pachico-Martínez**, Sancho Abarca 3, tel (941) 10 00 09. Perfectly adequate for the night. Central, with views of the old town. E.

CHAPTER EIGHT

Navarre

(Navarra)

BOTH CULTURALLY AND HISTORICALLY, Navarre is closely linked with the Basque Country. In the valleys of the north, dialects of *euskera* are still spoken, and the strong similarities in the folklore of the two regions arose when the two areas were united for long periods. Even so, since the founding of the kingdom of Navarre in 842 by Iñigo Arista, the Navarrese have always been fiercely independent and have carefully guarded their privileges and *fueros* (local governing rights) against the ambitions of Castile and Aragón. Today, though Basque nationalists would like to consolidate Pamplona and much of the north of the region with the Pais Vasco, the Navarrese, in general, are not interested.

Navarre was the last kingdom to be incorporated into the united Spanish monarchy in 1512, but it still maintained its privileges – including the minting of its own currency – until the 19th century. The determination to maintain the Navarrese *fueros* has been the guiding principle of local politics, and explains the people's traditional loyalty to the Carlist cause, even though in the 20th century Navarre has been industrialized and now less than 15 per cent of the population work in agriculture.

Navarre possesses a distinct topographic character. The Pyrenees have a gentler disposition than their counterparts further south, caused by the cooler and damper Atlantic climate. The bucolic river valleys of the north – Roncal, Salazar and Baztán – are covered with beech, oak and chestnut forests, and dotted with farmhouses surrounded by small fields of vegetable crops and cattle pastureland. Each autumn the farmers gather to net the vast coveys of pigeons that migrate among the woodlands, and the strong traditions of each village are apparent throughout the spring and summer in some of the most colourful *fiestas* in the country. By contrast, the south grows more Mediterranean the closer it gets to the Ebro basin; the land, in turns, is fertile and arid, with abundantly productive plains covered with fruit trees and vegetable crops in the more irrigated areas interspersed by the peculiar wind-beaten desert of Bardenas Reales that lies south of Tafalla and

Navarre

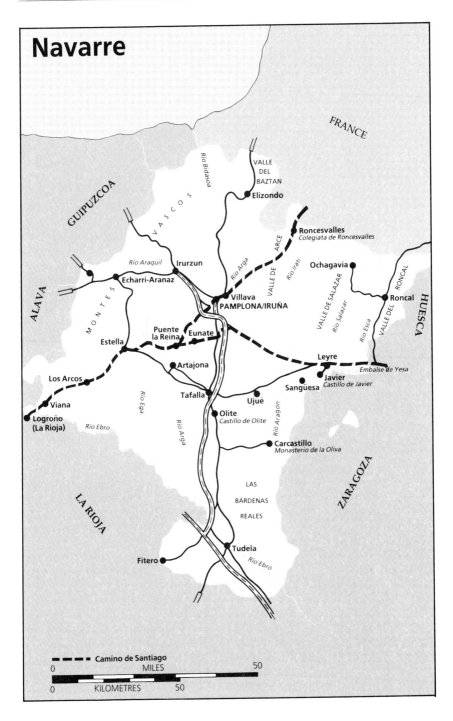

FRANCE

GUIPUZCOA

VALLE DEL BAZTAN

Elizondo

Río Bidasoa

VASCOS

Roncesvalles
Colegiata de Roncesvalles

Río Araquil

Irurzun

Echarri-Aranaz

Río Arga

VALLE DE ARCE

Río Irati

Ochagavia

RONCAL

ALAVA

MONTES

Villava
PAMPLONA/IRUÑA

VALLE DE SALAZAR

Río Salazar

Roncal

HUESCA

VALLE DEL

Río Esca

Puente
la Reina

Eunate

Estella

Leyre

Embalse de Yesa

Artajona

Los Arcos

Javier
Castillo de Javier

Sangüesa

Viana

Tafalla

Ujué

Río Ega

Logroño
(La Rioja)

Olite
Castillo de Olite

Río Ebro

Río Arga

Río Aragón

Carcastillo
Monasterio de la Oliva

ZARAGOZA

LA RIOJA

LAS

BÁRDENAS

REALES

Tudela

Fitero

Río Ebro

Camino de Santiago

0   MILES   50

0   KILOMETRES   50

forms the border with Aragón to the east.

A great number of prehistoric dolmens like those on Monte Aralar surround the Sanctuary of San Miguel and important churches and monasteries along the road to Santiago. This cuts through the heart of the region and was the single most important factor in the creation of the medieval kingdom, which once included Basse-Navarra, now in France. The ancient connection between these two regions is celebrated every year on 13 July with the tribute of three cows. Summer is in many ways the best time to visit the region, when there are countless carnivals and pilgrimages as well as more amusing local competitions, such as *harrijasotzailes* (stone-lifting) and *aizkolaris* (wood-chopping). But the *fiesta* most often associated with Navarre is the running of the bulls at San Fermin in Pamplona between 6–14 July. At this time, the population of the city triples, accommodation is booked years in advance and each day revolves around the few short minutes when the bulls run through the streets, and stab with their horns at the hundreds of sprinting figures wearing white shirts, trousers and the distinctive blood-red sash. There are few years when there is not at least one fatality.

For the rest of the year, **IRUÑA/ PAMPLONA** (pop. 183,000) adopts a more subdued face as capital of both the Foral region and the ancient kingdom of Navarre. Founded by the Roman general Pompey, from whom the city derives its name, Pamplona is a busy commercial centre, with the *Casco Antiguo* (Old Quarter) well sited on a promontory overlooking the River Aga. Its position as the geographic focus of Navarre makes it a good place from which to explore the region. Park as close to the arcaded Plaza del Castillo as you can.

Here you can see the Baroque façade of the **Palacio de Navarra** or Diputación Foral, which contains the sumptuous throne room of the Kings of Navarre, and fine paintings of former rulers, including a portrait of Ferdinand VII by Goya. In the royal archive, beside it, there is a collection of medieval documents, including the *fueros* by which the Navarrese Kings swore to uphold the rights of the people; and nearby, in the Paseo de Sarasate, a large romanticized bronze statue (1903) of a female figure holds out the scroll of foral laws. In her other hand hang the chains won by Sancho VII at the Battle of Navas de Tolosa in 1212, which overthrew Moorish power in the Peninsula.

The rather staid neoclassic façade of the cathedral rises on the north side of the Plaza. The interior is Gothic and within lie the exquisite alabaster tombs of Charles III and Queen Leonor of Castile and a magnificent 14th-century cloister. The museum housed in the old kitchen and former dining room for pilgrims on the road to Santiago contains the French Gothic reliquary of Santo Sepulcro, some good Gothic retables, and a small painting attributed to Van Dyck.

The other museum of interest is the **Museo de Navarra** in the old hospital of Nuestra Señora de la Misericordia, with its fine Plateresque doorway. Its interesting regional finds include Roman mosaics; coins from the Navarrese mints; a magnificent 11th-century Cordoban (Hispano–Arabic) casket carved in ivory; and a portrait by Goya of the Marqués de San Adrián.

There are good parks to explore here, as well as the walls of the *ciudadela* or old citadel, and fine palaces dating mainly from the 18th century. The smart restaurants, the Opus Dei university, and the prosperous-looking people in the *paseos* and the square at night reflect the new Navarre.

To the north of Pamplona lie the dramatic Pyrenean valleys, which can be explored easily from the capital. The most eastern of these, the Roncal valley, has the most dramatic landscape. You enter from the south through **Burgui**, with a beautiful Roman bridge over the River Esca. **Roncal**, at the centre of the valley, is famous for its local cheese, and for a 19th-century

Romantic memorial by the Modernist sculptor, Benillure, in remembrance of the world-famous tenor, Julián Gayarre (1844–89). **Isaba**, at the confluence of the Ustarroz and Bellagua, is an important winter resort for skiing in the Belagua valley.

From Isaba a road leads via **Uztarroz** to **Ochagavia** and the Valle de Salazar. The *agotes*, whose former territory stretched into Basse-Navarra in France, are, like the *vaqueiros* of Asturias and *pasiegos* of Cantabria, another group of semi-outcasts whose origins are obscure. Some claim they are descended from Goths who took refuge from the Moors in these mountains; others claim, unconvincingly,

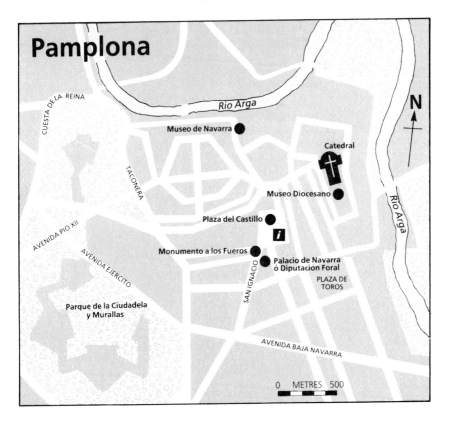

Pamplona

Rio Arga

N

Museo de Navarra

Catedral

Museo Diocesano

Plaza del Castillo

i

Monumento a los Fueros

Palacio de Navarra ó Diputacion Foral

PLAZA DE TOROS

Parque de la Ciudadela y Murallas

AVENIDA BAJA NAVARRA

0   METRES   500

CUESTA DE LA REINA

TACONERA

AVENIDA PIO XII

AVENIDA EJERCITO

SAN IGNACIO

Rio Arga

The castillo *of Olite, built by the Navarrese King Charles III 'the Noble' (1387–1425), was originally designed to have a hanging garden, a lion's den and an aviary for the royal falcons.* Incafo

that they were originally lepers banished to this valley. Certainly, they earned their living as masons and healers and were heavily persecuted during the Inquisition, and many of the women were burnt for witchcraft in *autos-de-fé* of the 16th century.

The two most northern valleys, Baztán and Bidasoa, are not quite as dramatic as the others in the region, but the villages found among their terraced fields contain impressive streets of palaces, stamped with stone escudos and shields to remind you of the long-standing importance of the powerful rural families who once ruled these valleys. Among the more peculiar

fiestas held in these remote northern corners of Spain is *zikiro-yate*, a vast banquet at which sides of meat are roasted on spits in the shelter of a cave at Zugarramundi, famous for the ancient celebration of *akelarres* held by the Basque *lamiak* (witches).

South of Pamplona, **Tafalla** (pop. 11,000) is the commercial and administrative centre of a rich agricultural *huerta* producing olives, wheat, wine and asparagus. The town has a few rambling señorial palaces, but otherwise not a great deal to offer its visitors, although there is a lot more to see in the surrounding area. **Olite** (pop. 3,000) contains one of the most imposing *castillos* in Spain and, although over-zealous restoration work has given it a slightly unreal appearance, there is no building in Navarre that evokes so well the kingdom's medieval magnificence. It was built during the reign of Charles III 'the Noble' (1387–1425) as a refuge from rioting townspeople in the capital of Pamplona. The mighty walls and towers contain a succession of great vaulted halls and, according to local tradition, as many rooms as there are days of the year. The interior was decorated by Mudéjar craftsmen in gold, silver and enamel, and copper discs were suspended from the ceiling to create 'pleasant harmonies' when they moved in the wind. Underground passageways (closed to the public) lead to subterranean rooms and to the vast hall beneath the Plaza Mayor. Gothic masons from France were commissioned to finish the two chapels and the exquisite cloistered portal of the church of Santa María. An exotic touch for Charles III was provided by his roof-garden, which housed his menagerie of buffaloes, lions, bears and giraffes, caged among fountains, fruit trees and vines growing from Gothic vaults. It is claimed that the orange tree was introduced to France from here.

Another less pampered town northwest of Tafalla is **Artajona**, surrounded by a 12th-century wall. The hilltop village of **Ujue**, a short distance into the pre-Pyrenees to the east, is better still and particularly impressive on a warm summer evening when thousands of swallows arc and dive through the air. The views from the Romanesque and Gothic fortified church of Santa María are unparalleled anywhere in Navarre. You look north to the Pyrenees and south across the empty windswept and deserted expanses of Bardenas Reales to the Ebro basin. Ujue has a wonderfully unspoilt atmosphere, and an excellent restaurant in the plaza below the church steps. Also worth a visit is the Cistercian monastery of La Oliva, which has a fine Gothic cloister but a rather over-restored church façade. Here you can buy excellent cheese, wine and honey made by the monks.

Tudela (pop. 25,000), the second largest city of Navarre, lies in a fertile plain that borders the River Ebro, and is in many ways one of the forgotten monumental cities of the river, even though it stands at the confluence of both road and water systems. It has several buildings of interest and a Jewish Quarter, which provided a refuge for several Sephardic notables including the poet and Talmudic scholar Meir ben Ezra. Under Moorish dominion from the ninth to the 12th centuries and then later under the Christians, Tudela was a centre for the *convivencia* of different religions (see p. 6). It was the last town to surrender to the troops of the Duke of Alba, which marked the end of Navarrese autonomy in 1512.

The early Gothic cathedral was built on the site of a mosque and is easily recognizable from miles around by its looming 18th-century octagonal belltower. It has an exceptional tympanum showing scenes from medieval Navarrese life, as well as some gruesome-looking scenes of the Last Judgement. The 12th-century cloister and Mudéjar chapel is considered by some to be an old synagogue and is equally impressive. Tudela, of all Navarrese cities, has the strongest Mudéjar feel, possibly because of its proximity to the River Ebro and the influences of Aragón.

TOURIST OFFICE

PAMPLONA: Duque de Ahumada 3, tel (948) 22 07 41.

Accommodation, Eating and Drinking

PAMPLONA (tel code 948):

During San Fermín in the first week of July, hotels generally triple their high-season price. They should be booked well in advance.

(H)**La Perla**, Plaza del Castillo 1, tel 22 77 06. Central. Rooms overlooking the central plaza. D–C.

(H)**Casa García**, San Gregorio 12, tel 22 38 93. Spartan and cheap but situated in the atmospheric heart of the Old Quarter. E.

(R)**La Olla**, Avenida de Roncesvalles 2, tel 22 95 58. Young, chic and popular. Barbecued meats are the speciality. B–A.

(R)**Las Pocholas**, Paseo de Sarasate 6, tel 22 22 14. An old Pamplona classic. Specialities include stuffed bull's tails (*rabo estofado*) A.

(R)**Shanti**, Castillo de Mayo 39, tel 23 10 04. Home cooking and frequented by locals. C.

(R)**Café Iruña**, Plaza del Castillo, is the most historic of Pamplona's several wonderful old *Belle Epoque* cafés.

NAVARRESE PYRENEES:

(H)**Isaba**, Ctra de Roncal, Isaba, tel (948) 89 30 00. Organizes horse-riding and various other outdoor activities. C.

(R)**Venta de Juan Pito**, Puerto de Belagua, Isaba, tel (948) 89 30 80. Typical Navarrese cooking. C.

CENTRAL NAVARRA:

(H)**Parador Principe de Viana**, in the *castillo*, Olite, tel (948) 74 00 00. Luxurious. Former palace of the Kings of Navarra. C.

(H&R)**Mesón Las Torres**, Ujue tel (948) 73 81 05. Magnificently situated beneath the collegiate walls. A few simple rooms and delicious farmhouse restaurant. E–D.

TUDELA:

(R)**El Arco**, Cortadores 1, tel (948) 82 25 95. In an old *bodega*. D.

Camino de Santiago in Navarre and La Rioja

The rise of the kingdom of Navarre went hand in hand with the early development of the Camino de Santiago, spurred on by the work of the Benedictine monks. It is no wonder, therefore, that the cult is highly developed in the region. Around the millennium Sancho 'el Grande' (the Great) used the Camino to encourage repopulation in his kingdom, and offered favourable *fueros* to those who settled. He commissioned the building of churches and hospitals all along the route, which encouraged not only pilgrims – some of them royal – to take to the road, but also merchants and artists. Navarre is full of the relics of this early colonization, with its gracious arched bridges, Romanesque churches, monasteries and sanctuaries.

Of the four alternative Caminos that arrive at the Spanish border through France, three of them converge at Sant-Jean-Pied-de-Port to meet the frontier above the Valle de Roncesvalles: the route known as the Camino Navarro. The fourth enters Navarre from Aragón and continues to Puente de la Reina via Leyre and Sangüesa and Eunate. The first main building on this secondary route is the monstery of **San Salvador de Leyre**, in the foothills of the Roncal valley. This is one of the great monastic complexes of Spain, and was well endowed by the Kings of Navarre, several of whom are buried in the mausoleum. The crypt, with its peculiar stunted capitals, is the earliest part and dates from the 11th century, but recently it has been restored after lying neglected for many decades following the *desamortización* (dissolution).

Javier, on the road towards Leyre, has a 13th-century fortified castle-church. It is the birthplace of San Francisco Javier, the great apostle of America and Japan, who is credited with having converted over a million Indians. The building is now a Jesuit college but you can still visit to see the exceptional 13th-century polychrome crucifix and a haunting mural depicting the dance of death.

The next main stop on this Camino, in the foothills of the Pyrenees beside the River Aragón, is the monumental town of **Sangüesa**. It has several extraordinary features, including the main portal of the church of Santa María. This is another dramatically sculptured Romanesque door, divided into three parts – the tympanum, the arcade and a stone gallery – and depicts soldiers, mathematicians, and imaginary beasts as well as more familiar Biblical allegories. The church of Santiago is mainly 12th-century with traces of Gothic; and the other churches of San Salvador and Carmen are also worth visiting, the latter for its plain 13th-century cloister. Of the civil buildings, there are several interesting palaces such as the Palacio de Vallesantoro, the Palacio del Príncipe de Viana and the Renaissanace Casa Consistorial.

Before the Caminos join at Puente la Reina, another important church stands alone amid fields beside the road. This is the Templar church of **Eunate**, an extraordinary 12th-century octagonal structure enclosed by a circle of arches. Several conflicting opinions contest the origins of this church: some believe it is based upon the church of the Holy Sepulchre in Jerusalem, while others claim it is a cemetery church, possibly founded in memory of an important but unnamed person who died here while making the pilgrimage to Santiago.

For those pilgrims following the Camino through the Roncesvalles valley, the last village of France was Sant-Jean-Pied-de-Port, the capital of Basse-Navarra and part of the medieval kingdom. This was the setting for one of the great epics of medieval poetry, the *Song of Roland*, which is the story of the slaughter of Charlemagne's rearguard by vindictive Basques. It relates how Charlemagne laid waste Pamplona on a campaign against the Moors and how, while retreating through the Pass of Roncesvalles, he was suddenly set upon and several of his most chivalrous knights, including Roland, were slain.

These days **Roncesvalles** is a comparatively tranquil enclave of the western Pyrenees, with a beautiful collegiate church that contains the Virgin of Roncesvalles, one of the great symbols of the road, as well as a beautiful gothic cloister and the tomb of Sancho VII. Beside the collegiate stands the *Templum Sancti Spiritus*: a shrine to pilgrims who died on this inhospitable part of the road, and a museum with the exquisite silver-and-enamel reliquary known as the Chessboard of Charlemagne. South of Roncesvalles in the Valle de Aezcoa is the vast beech forest of Irati.

The Camino descends through picturesque villages and winds out of the valley via **Burguete**, **Erro** and **Arre** to Pamplona (see p. 146). Pamplona owed its prosperity to the Camino in the Middle Ages, when it was one of the most vital cities in Christendom. Several monuments, in particular the Puente de la Magdalena and the cathedral, were meeting points for pilgrims.

Puente La Reina is where the Camino Navarro and Camino Aragonés converged. It is an idyllic village that straddles the River Arga with a beautiful six-arched Romanesque cobblestone bridge, built at the command of Queen Doña Mayor, the queen of Sancho 'el Grande'. The church of Santiago retains the original Romanesque portal, although the main structure is 15th-century Gothic. Here you can see a 14th-century statue of Santiago (St James) as a pilgrim. The church of the Crucifijo originally belonged to the Knights Templar, and beside it a hospice for pilgrims once stood: one of the arches above the door is shaped like a scallopshell. Puente la Reina is a quiet but attractive village of straight, tall streets, which are shrouded in richly patterned fabrics for the Corpus Christi celebrations, when a large procession marches through the streets to the accompaniment of a brass band.

The next main stop, **Estella**, built about a meander in the River Ega, was founded by Sancho Ramírez, who granted the people a *fuero* in 1090 to consolidate this part of the route. The town remained a residence of the Navarre court throughout the Middle Ages, and was a Carlist stronghold in the last century. It is now a busy local town, with some exceptional monuments in the narrow alleyways on either side of the riverbank and around the Judería. San Pedro de la Rúa is entered through a magnificent radial doorway, the influences for which were clearly Cistercian and Mudéjar designs. The cloister – half of which was destroyed when the neighbouring *castillo* was pulled down in 1572 – is remarkable for its carved capitals and the peculiar twisted columns like those at Santo Domingo de Silos. Other fine Romanesque sculpture can be seen at the churches of San Miguel and Santo Sepulcro and the convent of Santo Domingo.

The Palacio de los Reyes in the Plaza de San Martín, built for the Dukes of Granada de Ega, is a magnificent example of civic Romanesque. It contains a library and houses a museum with a permanent exhibition by local Navarrese painters. On one of the capitals on the outside the figure of Roland jousts with the giant Ferrugut.

West of Estella stands the monastery of Irache, formerly a university. At **Los Arcos** there's an impressive parochial church with a fine Renaissance cloister. In **Viana**, the last town in Navarre on the Camino, there are rambling mansions, broken walls and the vandalized tomb of Caesar Borgia in the impressive Baroque church of Santa María.

From here the La Rioja region begins, where you cross the mighty Ebro by the Puente de Piedra into the regional capital of **LOGROÑO** (pop. 120,000). The agricultural prosperity of La Rioja has seen this city expand at an alarming rate in the last 20 years, and it is now swamped by large industrial suburbs. The centre has a few interesting old features, in particular the hall-cathedral of Santa María la Redonda, recognizable by its two great Baroque towers. Also worth seeking out is the 18th-century statue of the Apostle Santiago in his role as *Matamoros* (Moor-slayer), next to the church of Santiago el Real. A short detour south of Logroño takes you to the impressively sited *castillo* of Clavijo where, according to legend, St James spent one of his most successful afternoons as a Christian crusader, killing

more than 60,000 infidels!

At **Navarrete** the former hospital run by the Order of St John has disappeared, but a beautiful portal leads into the cemetery, and the carved capitals depict scenes from the Camino. At **Nájera**, the historical capital of La Rioja, is the mighty red-stone monastery of Santa María la Real, a former pantheon of the Kings of Navarre, where Ferdinand III 'the Saint' was crowned. The late Gothic cloister has particularly fine tracery, as does the sepulchre containing the bones of Sancho III's queen, Blanca. But the town is somewhat rundown and warrants little attention beyond this one sight.

From Nájera, many pilgrims took a winding detour through the rolling potato fields and pine-covered slopes of the Sierra de Demanda to the monastery of **San Millán de la Cogolla**, a vast Benedictine abbey referred to as the El Escorial of La Rioja. This singularly impressive building was founded in 1053 by King Garcia Sánchez, and it was given a severe Herreran facelift in the 16th century. Unfortunately, the treasures it once contained, including paintings, miniatures and codices, have mainly been dispersed, or were stolen by the French in the War of Independence; what remains is not as good as might be expected of such a formidable building. The most important relics are the manuscripts of Gonzalo de Berceo (c. 1190–c. 1264), the first man to write in Castellano and whose *Lives of the Saints* did much to promote the cause of the Camino.

Berceo wrote a life of San Millán, a shepherd who spent his life praying in a cave and later miraculously appeared in battles to fight the Moors. He lived on the site of the Mozarabic monastery of Suso, a short walk up the hill above the great abbey. Though a humbler building than the San Millán monastery it is in most ways more interesting and certainly more endearing, with part of the church buried in the hillside and caves that serve as side-chapels. There are good walks through the forest behind the monastery.

Return to the main Camino via the impressive Cistercian Hall-church and convent of Santa María de Cañas, with its beautiful Romanesque sepulchre of Doña Urraca López de Haro (c. 1262) in a small relics room and museum just off the cloister. The Camino is rejoined at **Santo Domingo de la Calzada**, a peaceful, unspoilt town and a good place to stop overnight. Santo Domingo is another saint with a reputation for helping pilgrims and, beside his tomb in the 12th-century cathedral, you can still see the sickle used for cutting back the undergrowth so pilgrims could pass through forests more easily. The strangest testament to the miracles he performed are the cock and hen kept in the cathedral. The traditional legend surrounding these strange feathered members of the congregation relates how a family of pilgrims were staying at the hospice beside the cathedral on their way to Santiago. Working there was a maid who was enamoured of the son, who refused her advances. In revenge, she planted some silver in his luggage and reported him as a thief to the authorities. The boy was promptly arrested, sentenced and hanged, and his parents continued their grief-stricken way to Compostela. On their way back, they passed through Santo Domingo again and saw their son alive and well. So they explained their story to the judge, who remarked that there was as much chance of their son being alive as the roast chicken on his plate. At this point the chicken miraculously started crowing, since when the two birds have been kept in the church to remind the world of the miraculous ways of Santo Domingo. Pilgrims traditionally pluck a feather and tuck it in the rim of their hat for good fortune as they leave Navarre and begin their journey across the mountains to Castile. (See p. 181.)

TOURIST OFFICE

ESTELLA: Palacio de los Reyes de Granada.

Accommodation, Eating and Drinking

RONCESVALLES:

(H)**La Posada**, tel (948) 76 02 25. Simple, austere accommodation for pilgrims. E.

SANGÜESA (tel code 948):

(H)**Yamaguchi**, Ctra de Javier, tel 87 01 27. One of the two hotels in town. D.
(H)**Las Navas**, Alfonso El Batallador 7, tel 87 00 77. The alternative to the Yamaguchi. E.

(R)**Asador Mediavilla**, Alfonso El Batallador, 87 02 12. Simple, well-prepared food. C.

PUENTE LA REINA:

(H)**Mesón del Peregrino**, Ctra Pamplona–Logroño km23, tel (948) 34 00 75. An upmarket pilgrim pit-stop. C.

ESTELLA:

(R)**La Cepa**, Pl de los Fueros 18, tel (948) 55 00 32. Good local home cooking. C.

NÁJERA (tel code 941):

(H)**San Fernando**, Paseo San Julián 1, tel 36 37 00. The only option but good for a night. E–D.
(R)**Mesón Duque Forte**, Paseo de San Julián 15, tel 36 35 20. D.

SANTO DOMINGO DE LA CALZADA (tel code 941):

(H)**Parador Santo Domingo de la Calzada**, Plaza del Santo 3, tel 34 03 00. In the former hospital for pilgrims founded by Santo Domingo beside the cathedral. Recently restored. An ideal place for exploring all of the La Rioja region. B.
(R)**El Rincón de Emilio**, Plaza de Bonifacio Gil 7, tel 34 09 90. Traditional Riojan cooking, including *cochinillo* (suckling pig). C.

CHAPTER NINE

La Rioja

LA RIOJA, THE SMALLEST of the mainland regions, is renowned above all for its viniculture. Much of its land is irrigated by the River Ebro and eight main tributaries that meander through eroded limestone escarpments out of the sierras of the Sistema Ibérico to the south. The strong farming tradition of the region originated with the network of powerful monasteries that were founded in La Rioja in the tenth century.

Historically, La Rioja has always been bound closely to Castile and the Camino de Santiago, and has played the part of a sort of market garden for the great *Meseta* towns. Every autumn the grape harvest is followed by one of the most inebriated *fiestas* in the Peninsula, the *fiestas de la vendimia*, when wine battles among the local Riojanos sees thousands of litres of young wine thrown about with wild abandon.

The eastern zone, the Rioja Baja, is in many respects the remotest area of the region, especially in the sierras of the southern border with Soria and Aragón. The area is best approached from **Calahorra** (pop. 19,000), the next main town after Logroño. This was an ancient Iberian settlement, known as *Calagoricos*, that underwent a long siege against the Romans in 71 BC. The inhabitants preferred to resort to tribal cannibalism rather than surrender and

a local story relates how, when the city was eventually captured, there was only one survivor: a lone woman found chewing on a human arm and stoking fires in the streets to convince her enemies that there were more survivors. Under Roman occupation the town produced writers such as Quintilian and Prudentius; and it was the site where Henry of Trastamara was later proclaimed king. On arrival, park your car in the Calle Grande and walk down towards the *Casco Antiguo* (Old Quarter). The Gothic cathedral with a neoclassical façade is the most important building here, and contains a beautiful Plateresque alabaster altar in the chapel of San Pedro and good paintings by Zurbarán, Ribera and Titian in the chapterhouse. Scattered elsewhere are other interesting palaces and foundations.

Leave Calahorra and follow the rich *vega* beside the River Cidacos to **Autol,**

A Romanesque church amidst vines in La Rioja; a sight common throughout the regions of the north. Incafo

known for its two strange karstic towers, El Picuezo and La Picueza. At **Arnedo**, a busy industrial town beneath a crumbling *castillo*, turn south across the river to the monastery of Vico, which is set on a small spur in the middle of a great fertile expanse. At **Arnedillo** there are ancient thermal baths that form the basis of the town's conversion into a modern spa resort dealing specifically with rheumatism and sciatica. Ferdinand VI used to have this water specially bottled to treat the melancholia of his queen, Barbara de

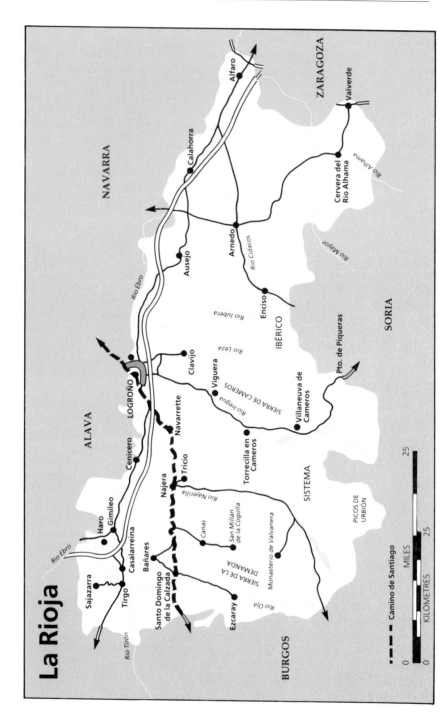

La Rioja

Braganza. In the deserted villages near **Enciso** there are several dinosaur footprints embedded in the limestone rock in the Gully of Valdecepillo. During the Mesozoic era this area was popular with Tyrannosaurus and Triceritops. The Ebro formed a shallow sea that stretched across the great cultivated limestone plains you see today, and dinosaurs wandered between the forested heights and marshy flatlands.

In the neighbouring Alhama valley, the landscape is even more barren, with hills covered in rosemary and thyme and a large pyrite mine, which explains the sound of thunder you hear in the distance. To complete the circuit back to the Ebro at Alfaro, travel via the great cylindrically turreted castle at **Cornago** and the village of **Cervera del Rio Alhama**, which remained a stronghold of Moorish culture even after their expulsion in 1609.

Alfaro is the centre of an important artichoke industry and has all the qualities of an old Castilian town. Its zenith came in the 17th and 18th centuries, when powerful rural families built palaces here to enhance their prestige. Its proximity to Aragón lends the architecture a certain Mudéjar quality, as can be seen by the twin brick Baroque towers of the church of San Miguel, and the important ceramics and tilemaking industry, which has continued here since Moorish times.

The Rivers Irequa and Leza, winding out of the Sierra de Cameros, water the central zone of La Rioja and the great agricultural plain around Logroño. The Iregua carves out a magnificent limestone valley of soaring gorges, scattered with small wine-growing *pueblos* with their family-run *bodegas* built into underground caverns in the surrounding hills. One of the strangest *fiestas* occurs on the third Sunday of May in the village of **Sorzano**, with the procession of *Las Doncellas*, when young girls dressed in white parade through the streets carrying bunches of flowers and stems of holly to commemorate the refusal by Ramiro I in the ninth century to pay Abd-ah-Rahman II a tribute of 100 damsels.

La Rioja Alta, the most north-westerly area of the region, is in many ways the most interesting. **Haro** (pop. 9,000), between the Rivers Tirón and Ebro, is the centre of the wine industry. It is a busy, seldom-visited town, where the only building worth stopping for is Santo Tomás with its Plateresque façade. To the east, **San Vicente de la Sonsierra** is the headquarters of the Guild of Flagellants who, three times a year, walk through the village streets, bare-backed and hooded, flagellating themselves before an image of the virgin. La Rioja is otherwise remarkable for its sierras and, in particular, the upper river valleys of the Oja and Najerilla that flow out of the Sierra de la Demanda.

TOURIST OFFICE

LOGROÑO: C/ Miguel Villanueva 10, tel (941) 25 54 97.

Accommodation, Eating and Drinking

LOGROÑO (tel code 941):

(R)**La Merced**, Marqués de San Nicolás 109, tel 22 11 66. In an old Riojan palace. Expensive but superb local Riojan cuisine. B–A.

CALAHORRA (tel code 941):

(H)**Parador Marco Favio Quintiliano**, Paseo Mercadal, Calahorra, tel 13 03 58. A purpose-built parador, well situated for exploring the south-east of the region. C. (H)There is an extensive *hostal* and pension network in the villages along the river valleys running south from the Ebro.

(H)**Balneario**, Los Baños, Arnedillo, 39 40 00. Medicinal spring baths in a magnificent setting beneath a sheer *massif*. A place long acknowledged for the curative powers of its air and water. With good walks, gardens, tennis, etc. C–B.

CHAPTER TEN

Aragón

GRAFFITI ON A SLUM wall in a Zaragoza suburb reads: '*Agotados de esperar el fin*' (Exhausted from waiting for the end). The words are as harsh and down-to-earth as the cruel north wind, *el cierzo*, which for two-thirds of the year blows relentlessly out of the Pyrenean peaks in the province of Huesca, across the arid dust-basin carved out by the River Ebro, and finally dissolves into the mountainous uplands of Teruel.

But the urban elegy speaks only of the modern plight of the Aragonese as a people. It says nothing of the landscape – the Pyrenean *massifs* sprinkled with jewels of Romanesque architecture; the formidable Cistercian monasteries; and the patchwork *huertas* furrowed beside lonely river courses. Here, too, are to be found unsullied Mudéjar villages in the south and endless stretches of flat open road, fragmented by medieval shanty villages where the inhabitants seem to be outnumbered by scavenging dogs.

If you spend time in Aragón, be prepared for the emptiness of the landscape, and your patience will be rewarded when you chance upon villages where you'll be the only traveller seen in days and the locals will treat you with enormous hospitality. Though Spaniards may consider the Aragonese stubborn, they are always open and friendly to strangers.

The kingdom of Aragón arose simultaneously with the increasing territorial gains of the *Reconquista* at the beginning of the 11th century; and its rulers, through a series of adroit marriage settlements and native business sense, began with the Counts of Barcelona to co-govern a large section of the Mediterranean. The reign of James I (1213–76) marked the height of the united kingdom's power, with the integration of Murcia, Mallorca and Valencia into the 'empire'.

But the power of the nobility and the crusading orders, particularly the Knights Templar, was gradually checked and the strong local *fueros* (privileges) were limited. With the unification of the crowns of Castile and Aragón through the marriage of Ferdinand and Isabel, provincial Aragonese prerogatives became an increasing stumbling-block to the royal plan for a united Spain. When disturbances

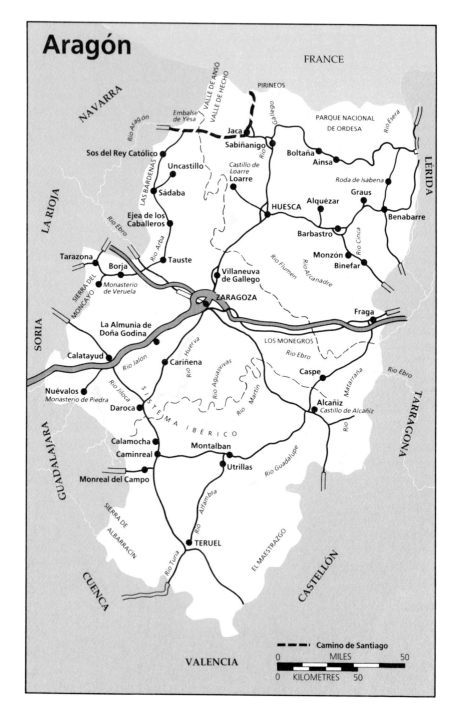

Aragón

FRANCE

NAVARRA

PIRINEOS

Río Aragón

Embalse
de Yesa

VALLE DE ANSÓ

VALLE DE HECHO

Gallego

Río

PARQUE NACIONAL
DE ORDESA

Río Ésera

LÉRIDA

Jaca

Sabiñanigo

Boltaña

Ainsa

Sos del Rey Católico

Uncastillo

Castillo de
Loarre

Loarre

Roda de Isábena

Graus

Benabarre

Sádaba

Alquézar

HUESCA

Barbastro

Río Cinca

LA RIOJA

LAS BARDENAS

Ejea de los
Caballeros

Río Ebro

Río Arba

Monzón

Río Flumen

Río Alcanadre

Binefar

Tarazona

Borja

Tauste

Villanueva
de Gallego

SIERRA DEL MONCAYO

Monasterio
de Veruela

ZARAGOZA

Fraga

SORIA

La Almunia de
Doña Godina

LOS MONEGROS

Río Ebro

Calatayud

Río Jalón

Río Huerva

Cariñena

Río Aguasvivas

Caspe

Río Ebro

Nuévalos

Río Jiloca

SISTEMA IBÉRICO

Río Martín

Alcañiz

Castillo de Alcañiz

Monasterio de Piedra

Daroca

Matarraña

Río

TARRAGONA

GUADALAJARA

Calamocha

Montalban

Caminreal

Utrillas

Río Guadalupe

Monreal del Campo

SIERRA DE ALBARRACÍN

Río Alfambra

EL MAESTRAZGO

CASTELLÓN

CUENCA

Río Turia

TERUEL

VALENCIA

- - - - Camino de Santiago

0   MILES   50

0   KILOMETRES   50

broke out in 1591 between the two realms Philip II marched an army into Zaragoza, executed the troublemakers and choked the power of the *fueros* so far as he was capable.

In 1610 the Aragonese economy was devastated as a result of the expulsion of more than 61,000 Moriscos. The fertile land and villages south of the Ebro became deserted almost overnight, and a valuable source of labour was lost. Many of the medieval villages to be found there today have remained virtually unchanged for the last 400 years.

The film-maker Luis Buñuel, born in the small town of Calanda on the edge of Aragón's desert, records in his memoirs how the Middle Ages did not end in his village until the outbreak of the First World War. He vividly describes the close-knit community struggling to survive, apparently unaware of the events and innovations in Modernist Zaragoza less than 100km away: 'Progress, a word no one seemed to have heard, passed Calanda by, just like the rain clouds.'

The Civil War put an abrupt end to rural tranquillity. Aragón witnessed several of the bloodiest and bitterest conflicts of the war, and since then the region seems to have gradually faded in importance. Teruel and Huesca are two of the most underpopulated provinces in the land, and almost three-quarters of the area's population lives in Zaragoza. Certainly this is a far cry from the time four centuries earlier when Aragonese princesses were among the hottest marriage properties in Europe.

In recent years the autonomous economy and provincial road system have improved, yet Aragón remains the least known of any Spanish region,

even by Spaniards, and the area is generally dismissed by guidebooks as a place to pass through quickly, on the road between Castile and Catalunya, admiring its odd Mudéjar architecture and its inaccessible Pyrenean Romanesque as you hurtle past. Yet in many ways Aragón has as much to offer as both of these regions; and far fewer tourists. At moments, the silhouette of a Mudéjar tower in the distance makes it look more Oriental than European, while the great *castillos* of Loarre, Monzón, Alcañiz, Alquézar and the Maestrazgo testify to the long magnificent era when its Kings and its crusading orders ruled over the reconquered eastern territories.

Alto Aragón and the Pyrenean River Valleys

The Aragonese Pyrenees comprise the most isolated valleys and forbidding peaks of the range. This is an area of outstanding beauty, whose scanty population is concentrated in a few towns and stone-built, slate-roofed villages. To the east, the three highest Pyrenean mountains – Aneto in the Maladeta ridge, Posets and Monte Perdido – are surrounded by deep limestone gorges and towering rock walls. Though Huesca is now one of the most underpopulated provinces in Spain it was not always thus, and its exceptionally high concentrations of Romanesque architecture are remnants of an age when it was the stronghold for the second great offensive of the Christian Reconquest. From the north, one of the oldest roads into Spain is the second route of the

Camino de Santiago through the Puerto de Somport to Jaca, the most central town for exploring the high Pyrenees.

Jaca (pop. 14,000) was the first capital of the kingdom of Aragón; an ancient frontier citadel that possessed some of the earliest *fueros* in Spain. Its privileged situation at the crossroads between the Camino de Santiago and the ancient Arab trade route along the Via de Bearn between France and Zaragoza has invested it with an ancient, prosperous air. The cathedral is undoubtedly its greatest monument, erected during the first half of the 11th century to consolidate the small Christian kingdom that had started to develop on the periphery of the kingdom of Al-Andalus. There are clear Byzantine influences to be seen in the carved capitals. In the Diocesan Museum in and around the cloisters there is a stunning collection of Romanesque frescoes rescued from the province, including those found at **Ruesta** in the church of San Juan. Jaca's other main monuments, such as the large pentagonal citadel and the *ayuntamiento* (town hall), are of 16th-century origin. In the Benedictine monastery is the exceptional Romanesque sarcophagus of the Infanta Doña Sancha (d. 1096), daughter of Ramiro I of Aragón.

West of Jaca, the monstery of **San Juan de la Peña** is another early spiritual centre of Spain, where the Aragonese flame of reconquest was kindled. It retains its Romanesque church and cloister in a magnificent, naturally defended position hidden in the cleft of an overhanging limestone cliff. In 1770, on the orders of Charles III, it was designated the official burial ground of the Kings of Aragón. At first

sight, it is not difficult to understand why the shrine is steeped in numerous legends, including that of the Holy Grail. Many have tried to trace the *Munsalvaesche*, mentioned in European Grail songs of the 12th century, at San Juan, and indeed the monks did possess a jewel-studded chalice, which can now be seen in the cathedral of Valencia.

North of San Juan, reached by roads from **Puente la Reina de Jaca** and **Berdún** respectively, are the two most sequestered valleys of Aragón – the Valle de Hecho and Valle de Ansó – divided by the jagged peaks and sculpted limestone forms of the Sierra de Dos Ríos. Preserved here are some of the strongest elements of the Aragonese dialect, *cheso*, and in several of the villages the locals still wear traditional dress each day. **Hecho**, where Alfonso I 'El Batallador' (the Soldier) was born, has narrow winding streets and diminutive plazas with old wood-burning bakery shops. In July and August, the village hosts a symposium of modern sculpture and painting. Further up the valley at **Siresa** looms the ancient Augustinian monastery of San Pedro, founded in the ninth century and largely rebuilt in the 11th.

Ansó can be reached via a small forest road from Hecho, and here the interesting sights include a Gothic church, a 13th-century tower and an Ethnography Museum containing examples of local costumes. Several of the houses are carved with strange, indecipherable symbols, possibly left by the *cagote* population in the neighbouring Navarrese valleys. North of Ansó in the Zauriza valley there are several spectacular walks and riding excursions into the high valleys.

East of Jaca lie the highest *massifs*

Torla, sheltered among the heights of the Ordesa National Park in Huesca, Aragón, is a well preserved example of a stone-built Pyrenean village. Incafo

of the range, and the dramatic Ordesa National Park, situated beneath the mighty peak of Monte Perdido (3,350m): the highest in this range known as Las Tres Sorores (the Three Sisters). Waterfalls spill down the sheer limestone cliffsides into isolated canyons, while raptors glide above curious geological rock formations. On the lower slopes there are good walks through the forests of beech and silver fir, but more serious walkers must obtain a map at the park information centre at Jaca or in the village of **Torla**. The great *fajas* (natural limestone balconies) should be visited, from where the views across the green valley and the cascades are unsurpassed.

The eastern side of the park can be approached from **Ainsa** (pop. 1,400), the ancient capital of the kingdom of Sobrarbe, dominated by the ruins of an Arab *castillo*. Continue up the steep karstic Cinca valley to **Bielsa**, where the French come to buy cheap Spanish foodstuffs from the three main supermarkets. A road climbs from the back of the village through the Pineta valley to the Monte Perdido Parador, imposingly situated beneath the towering range in a looming amphitheatre of snow-capped mountains, the Circo de Pineta. The wildlife in Ordesa is magnificent, and includes Pyrenean chamois and ibex on the higher slopes, bearded vultures or lammergeier drifting between the peaks, and foxes, jabali and otters on the lower ground.

Further east of Ordesa are the highest peaks in the Pyrenees: Pico de Aneto (3,404m) and Pico de Poset (3,371m), which loom above the señorial village of **Benasque**. Sadly, the timeless tranquillity of this valley has been scarred by skiing facilities, but it is nevertheless a breathtakingly beautiful area, and there are several subsidiary valleys that remain peaceful refuges for the alpine flora that thrives in the climate here.

The Pyrenean valleys of Alto Aragón, especially in this eastern sector, are littered with Romanesque monuments; every village almost without exception contains some crumbling church or hermitage to recall the history of this early Reconquest buffer zone. The monument that perhaps typifies the age above any other is the miniature cathedral at **Roda de Isábena**, a village of fewer than 200 inhabitants that is lost in the Valle de Isábena between Benasque and Benabarre, and surrounded by pastureland. The church was consecrated in 957, and it is a miracle that the cloister and its delicate masonry have survived. In the crypt lies the exquisite sepulchre of San Ramón, overlooked by a fine 13th-century mural of Christ Pantocrator.

Commanding this eastern sector of the foothills of the Pyrenees in the midst of a wide agricultural plain is **Barbastro**. This is a busy market town remarkable for little except its early 16th-century cathedral with an altarpiece by Damián Forment, unequalled among Renaissance sculptors, whose great alabaster retables are one of the lasting treasures of Aragonese art. It was also the birthplace of José María Escrivá de Balaguer, who founded the ultra-conservative Catholic group, the *Opus Dei*. To the north and south of Barbastro lie two impressive *castillos*.

To the south the grandiose silhouette of the *castillo* of Monzón looks out across the agricultural plain beside the banks of the River Cinco. It is built upon the site of a former Roman *castro* (fortified hilltop village), which was reconstructed by the Arabs, conquered by Pedro I and subsequently passed in the will of Alfonso 'El Batallador' to the Knights Templar. The line of Aragonese kings was continued through Alfonso's brother, Ramiro II 'the Monk', who renounced his vows, sired a daughter and married her off in infancy to Count Ramón Berenguer IV of Barcelona, thus forming an alliance between Aragón and Catalunya. From the 14th to the 16th centuries Monzón was the seat of several meetings of the Aragonese court, and was finally destroyed by the French general, Mina, in 1814 after a six-month siege.

North-west of Barbastro rises **Alquézar** (from the Arabic Al-Kasr, meaning fortress), a village boasting a magnificent mixture of architectural styles. It is a typically Moorish collection of narrow streets connected by arches and tunnels, whose balconied houses are calcimined with white and cobalt wash. The *castillo* is an extraordinary combination of military, civil and ecclesiastical architectural elements. The beautiful vaulted chapel is in the best-conserved part of the structure, but just as impressive are the Gothic cloister and colonnaded loggia overlooking the tiled rooftops of the village.

West of Alquézar, the intense network of run-down villages are once again strewn with Romanesque monuments all the way to **HUESCA** (pop. 45,000), the capital of Alto Aragón. This small city is generally considered to be bland and uninviting because of its slow provincial ambience, but it has taken big steps to improve its image in the last few years and is a pleasant enough place to stay overnight.

The town was known as *Urbs Victrix Osca* to the Romans, and the first university in the Peninsula was founded here by Sertorius in 75 BC. The town has always played an important role in the defence of the central Pyrenees. Of the 90 towers that once surrounded the Muslim stronghold, only one – adjoining the church of San Miguel – survives. The four Arabian heads on the city's coat-of-arms signify the four Saracen princes killed when it was successfully reconquered by Pedro I in 1096, whereupon it became the capital of Aragón until the capture of Zaragoza.

Work began on the cathedral during the reign of James I, and original Mudéjar elements such as the brick gallery can still be seen. Inside is another alabaster altarpiece by Damián Forment, considered by many to be his great masterpiece, and containing the sculptor's self-portrait in a medallion built into the work. The Episcopal Museum and chapterhouse contain several Romanesque and Gothic murals rescued from churches in the region, as well as retables and beautiful 13th-century painted miniatures.

The Archeological Museum is housed in the old university, and contains objects of prehistoric and classical interest and paintings by numerous Spanish artists. In the Palacio de los Reyes de Aragón is the infamous Sala de la Campana where Ramiro II rallied his rebellious nobles, supposedly to consult them about the casting of a new church bell that he wished to be heard throughout Aragón. But the meeting was a ploy to rid his court of unsavoury elements, and he ordered his guards to behead all the nobles as they assembled at the palace. The goriest ending relates how the 15 heads were laid out in the shape of a bell and the last one was used as the hammer. The other important sight is the church of San Pedro el Viejo, containing the tombs of Ramiro II (d. 1157) lying beside his brother Alfonso I 'El Batallador'. The Romanesque cloister (1140) is particularly fine, with double colonnades supporting carved capitals that depict Old Testament scenes.

The last great sight of northern Aragón is the *castillo* of Loarre; if there is any structure that illustrates the dream-like qualities of a castle in Spain, then this is it. It is one of the most majestic examples of Romanesque architecture. Built over a Moorish fortress by King Sancho Ramirez of Aragón at the end of the 11th century, the castle sits disguised on a mountainside of shale and pine trees, 3km above the village of **Loarre**. The main body of the *castillo* itself is surrounded by a half-ruined curtain wall; the original structure was intended to contain the royal household, soldiers and Augustinian monks. You can visit the old courtrooms of the Kings of Aragón, the chapel and crypt, the triple-storeyed Torre de Homenaje and climb up on to the roof, from which on a clear morning or evening you can see south across the great farmed plains of Aragón and the Ebro basin to Zaragoza.

TOURIST OFFICES

JACA: Plaza Calvo Sotelo s/n, tel (974) 36 00 98.

AINSA: Avda de Pineta 1, tel (974) 50 07 67.

HUESCA: Coso Alto 23, tel (974) 22 57 78.

Accommodation, eating and drinking

JACA:

(H)**Conde de Aznar**, General Franco 3, tel (974) 36 10 50. The right mountainous atmosphere. (R)La Cocina Aragonesa serves local specialities, such as *Lentejas con lengua de cerdo* (lentils with pig's tongue). B.

HECHO:

(H) **Casa Blasquico**, Pl Palacio 1, tel (974) 37 50 07. A central *hostal* D.

ANSO:

(H)**La Posada Magoria**, Valle de Anso, tel (974) 37 00 49. A humble pension in a 19th-century house. Vegetarian restaurant. E.

ORDESA NATIONAL PARK:

(H&R)**Ordesa**, Ctra Torla/Ordesa, tel (974) 48 61 25. The most comfortable place to stay on the western side of the park. Telephones in all rooms. Popular in the summer. Cl mid-Oct–Easter. C.

(R)**Bodegas del Sobrarbe**, Plaza Mayor 2, tel (974) 50 02 37. One of the best restaurants in the Pyrenees, to be found in an old underground cellar. Specialities include: *Cabrito y ternasco al horno de leña* (goat and steaks cooked in a wood-burning oven). C.

BIELSA:

(H)**Parador Monte Perdido**, 11km up the Valle de Pineta s/n, tel (974) 50 10 11. Almost buried beneath sheer mountainsides. Cross the stream and within ten minutes you're surrounded by waterfalls and lazing cattle. Very out of the way. Good for a few days' deep relaxation.

BENASQUE:

(H)**El Puente**, San Pedro s/n, tel (974) 55 12 11. A good mountain hotel. E–D.

RODA DE ISABENA:

(R)**Hospedería La Catedral**, Plaza Pons Sorolla 2, tel (974) 54 00 26. The original Cistercian *hospedería* beside the Romanesque cloister maintains a tradition of offering food. Simple cooking but a good menu for 1,000 pesetas. E.

BARBASTRO:

(H)**Rey Sancho Ramírez**, on the main N240, tel (974) 31 00 50. All amenities. B.
Cheaper *hostales* in the centre of town.

HUESCA (tel code 974):

(H)**Pedro I de Aragón**, el Parque 34, tel 22 03 00. Top of the range. A.
(H)There are plenty of cheaper alternatives in Paseo Ramón y Cajal.
(R)**Venta del Sotón**, halfway along the fast straight road to the Castillo de Loarre,
Esquedas(14km), tel 27 02 41. One of Aragón's most atmospheric restaurants. The
chorizos are dried in the darkness of a huge bell. Popular with the French, who are
often claimed to know the Aragonese Pyrenees better than the Spanish. Excellent
wine list. C.

Western Aragón and the Ebro Depression

From the pre-Pyrenees the land falls
sharply away into the flatlands surrounding the depression on either side
of the River Ebro. These wide agricultural plains are interspersed by empty
arid deserts and escarpments, and
dusty, bedraggled brick villages lie
along the routes. Dogs bask in the
middle of the road, moving with casual
indifference out of the way of oncoming traffic.

Forming a natural defensive line
with Navarre along the western border
are the Cinco Villas, five medieval villages raised to the status of towns by
Philip V for their loyalty in the War of
Succession (1700–13). For the most
part, they have remained quiet, rarely
visited enclaves, but they are surprisingly well endowed artistically. They
are divided in the north by bleak
mountains, scattered with ruined
farmhouses and narrow, furrowed
fields meandering beside the line of
the thin watercourses.

The most northern of the villages,
the walled **Sos del Rey Católico**,
perches on a hilltop beneath the pre-
Pyrenees, and was the birthplace of
Fernando el Católico (1452–1516).
The Palacio de los Sada where he was
born has been converted into a cultural
centre and small museum. In the hive
of narrow cobbled streets there are
other equally grand señorial mansions
in varying states of restoration, with
typical architectural details of the age,
such as window *rejas* (grilles) and large
armorial stones above the arched
doorways. The church of San Esteban
is worth a visit for its Romanesque
crypt, frescoes and font and the small
adjoining museum. For a specatcular
view, climb up to the *castillo*, which was
built on tenth-century foundations but
greatly enlarged by Ramiro II.

The road south-east to **Uncastillo**
cuts through a barren wilderness. The
village rises like a stone oasis beside
the River Riquel, sheltering beneath
the one remaining military tower of
the castle, which gave its name to the
pueblo. The main monuments are well-
signposted from the outskirts of the

The Monastery of Piedra

Cistercian monasticism crossed the Pyrenees at a time when the gathering momentum of the Reconquest demanded the opening up, settlement and defence of large areas of previously unoccupied territory. From the great foundations in New Catalonia small parties of monks were despatched to establish sister monasteries in lower Aragón. They founded the monastery of Rueda, now a ruin beside the Ebro east of Zaragoza; Veruela, in a fertile valley south of Tarazona; and Piedra, the most dislocated of the three, on the south-western perimeter of the region between Molina de Aragón and Calatayud, an area described in medieval chronicles as 'an oasis amidst interminable desert'.

The monastery of Piedra crouches on a promontory overlooking an almost sheer limestone fault in the middle of wild and arid uncultivatable *Meseta*. Its extensive perimeter walls contain what must have appeared to the founding party of monks like a miniature garden of Eden in the midst of earthly oblivion. The first abbot, Don Gaufrido de Rocaberti, erected a church on the site and, in the years 1195–1218, under the royal patronage of Alfonso II and James I, the monastery grew to include a cloister, chapel, Mudéjar tower, abbot's palace, torre del Homenaje, farm and outhouses.

The natural beauty of its location, however, is owing to the dramatic early course of the River Piedra that cascades through the valley immediately below the monastery. A place long loved by tranquillity-seekers, the monastery has now been converted into a simple but comfortable parador-like hotel (tel [976] 84 90 11), and the river valley into a natural park. (C).

---

village. Narrow alleyways ascend to Santa María la Mayor, with its magnificent carved portal, fortified Gothic belltower and Plateresque cloister. The other important church, that of San Juan, is built over a paleo-Christian cemetery and contains impressive 13th-century wall paintings. Wander through the streets beside the arcaded Plaza Mayor and soak up a way of life that has changed only marginally in hundreds of years.

Between **Sádaba** and **Layana** lie the remains of a second-century Roman mausoleum of the Atilia family, and the excavations of the Roman settlement of *Clavina* including a temple, aqueduct and baths. Locals will give you exact directions on how to get there. Sádaba is in another impressive

setting beneath a looming square-towered *castillo*, and the 14th-century Gothic church is also interesting.

Surrounded by a rich agricultural *huerta*, **Ejea de los Caballeros** is the largest of the quintet of border towns, and was the scene of some very smart manoeuvring in 1808 during the War of Independence. About 150 French troops managed to break through the barricades and walls of the city, whereupon the villagers let loose a herd of bulls, which stampeded and killed the aggressors. This was an age-old Iberian tactic used by Hannibal's Iberian troops against the Romans, who unleashed into the enemy camp 2,000 bulls with lighted torches strapped to their horns. The fortified Romanesque church of El Salvador is impressive, with gracious exterior carvings depicting the Last Supper. Equally interesting is the church of Santa María, formerly connected to Alfonso I's fortress at Ejea, which has since disappeared. Inside stands a unique alabaster pulpit carved with Mudéjar motifs.

Tauste, the last and most southerly of the *Cinco Villas*, is recognizable from afar by its 73-metre, 13th-century octagonal Mudéjar tower. Crossing the sluggish Ebro at **Gallur**, the architecture changes abruptly from Romanesque to Mudéjar. To the west lies **Borja**, the medieval stronghold of the Borja family before they moved in the 14th century to Jàtiva, and from there to Italy as the Borgias.

Tarazona (pop. 11,500), a former episcopal see and residence of the Aragonese court, has an impressive cathedral with a Mudéjar tower and a peculiar brick cloister (currently undergoing restoration). Straddling the banks of the River Gueiles, Tarazona is the most northerly of the Mudéjar cities and, although run-down and dusty, it has several monuments of interest. These include the Tower of La Magdalena, the Gothic Bishop's Palace, the 16th-century church of San Miguel, and the *ayuntamiento* (town hall) with a Plateresque façade depicting the final capture of Granada. Its bullring has been bricked up and turned into apartments.

Between Borja and Tarazona the Cistercian monastery of **Veruela** rises from a wide fertile plain; it was founded following a vision by the Lord of Borja, Don Pedro de Atarés, around 1146. A tall turreted wall surrounds the monastic grounds that contain the abbot's palace, a church and cloister.

The whole complex has recently been restored and turned into a Museum of Contemporary Art. The church's radial masonry and the ironwork details of the west door are original. The cloister is a beautiful combination of proto-Gothic, with tracery windows filled in with locally mined alabaster and a small *lavabo* (pavilion) at one side. The upper gallery – richly decorated with medallions and zoomorphic high reliefs – is a later Plateresque addition.

Returning to the Ebro, the Logroño–Zaragoza autoroute forges east to connect the Atlantic to the Mediterranean. **ZARAGOZA** (pop. 572,000) is the spiritual, economic and demographic centre of Aragón; the former royal residence of the Kings of Aragón; a university town; and the seat of an archbishopric. The Roman settlement of *Caesar Augusta* was built over the Iberian settlement of *Salduba* and became the most important administrative centre of Tarraconensis after Tarragona. In 716 the Saracen general, Musa Ibn Nusair, stormed the city and it remained under Moorish rule until 1118, whereupon it became the capital of the Aragonese–Catalan empire after the amalgamation of the two kingdoms. In 1808 it was granted an honourable surrender from the French after a long and costly siege, during which half the population of 100,000 died. In the 19th century Zaragoza was endowed with some impressive Modernist buildings, but since the city's rapid expansion in the 1950s the old Mudéjar Quarter is now surrounded by extensive industrial suburbs.

The heart of the city and the main area worth exploring lies on the south bank, reached by following the signs to *centro ciudad*. Go first to the Plaza del Pilar and the mighty silhouette of the basilica of **Nuestra Señora del Pilar** – a mixture of Baroque and neoclassic grandiloquence. The basilica was built by the two greatest architectural dynasties of their respective periods, Francisco Herrera (son of Juan de Herrera) and the neoclassicist Ventura Rodriguez. Along with Santiago de Compostela and Montserrat, this is one of the great pilgrimage shrines of Spain. According to legend, the first church on this site was built following a vision of St James, who was preaching in *Caesar Augusta* in AD 40. The Virgin appeared on a marble column surrounded by angels and ordered a church to be constructed in her honour, though one wonders whether she intended such an extraordinarily sumptuous building!

On the roof, the main dome is surrounded by 12 cupolas and tiled with iridescent yellow and blue *azulejo* tiles. The four brick towers rising from each of the corners are a Baroque addition. Inside, there is an imposing collection of frescoes, paintings and relics that require their own guidebook for a full explanation. Of particular note are the frescoes by Goya above the choir vault and the alabaster high altar by Damián Forment that depicts scenes from the life of the Virgin. Alabaster is one of the great architectural subtleties of Aragonese architecture, and can be no better appreciated than at el Pilar. The white-and-maroon streaked translucent stone came from mines between Gelsa and the ruined Cistercian monastery of Rueda. They were opened by the Romans and have been used extensively ever since for filtering the burning sun. Light through a window of alabaster is one of the unforgettable sensations of Aragonese interiors.

The Virgin is a 14th-century sculpture and wears a halo of jewels – one of the richest single settings of precious stones in the world – which includes several thousand diamonds, gems and rubies. The treasury is entered via the sacristy of the Virgin.

At the other end of the Plaza del Pilar is the **cathedral**, which incorporates part of an earlier mosque and has a spectacular Mudéjar exterior of patterned bricks and tiles. Inside, you can see another fine alabaster retable, and some paintings by Goya, Zurbarán and Ribera in the chapterhouse, together with an important tapestry collection that includes two early 15th-century hangings based on cartoons by Giotto. The last main building on the plaza, between the two cathedrals, is the Renaissance *lonja* (exchange), a large rectangular hall with a Gothic structure and vaulting, finished with Plateresque decoration. (While in the Plaza del Pilar, visit the tourist office, located in the Torre de La Zuda – the only surviving tower from the palace of the Arab governors.)

A short walk from the cathedral, in Calle Espoz y Mina, is the **Museo Camón Aznar** with one of the most engaging collections of Spanish paintings put together by one individual, with work by most major Spanish painters. In the surrounding brick-walled streets are impressive Mudéjar churches, particularly Santa María Magdalena, San Gil, San Miguel de los Navarros and San Pablo Apóstol, the last two with retables by Damián Forment. The Museo de Bellas Artes at Plaza los Sitios 6 is situated in the south-western quarter of the city and contains a wide cross-section of artefacts, which include early archeological discoveries, primitive Aragonese art from the tenth century, and ceramics and lustreware from the 15th- and 16th-century factories at Teruel and Muel.

The strangest monument in Zaragoza is perhaps the **Aljafería**, originally an Arabian pleasure-palace founded in 864 but extended under the Tojibids (1019–39) and the Hudids (1039–1118): the last two ruling houses of Zaragoza. Through the 14th and 15th centuries the city became the residence of the Kings of Aragón and later of the Inquisition. The interior of the Aljafería is a succession of lavishly decorated courtrooms, pavilions, pools and porticos, richly ornamented with stucco and *artesonados* (inlaid wooden ceilings). The Sala de Santa Isabel is where St Isabel, Queen of Portugal (1271–1336), was born. It is claimed that the gilt leaf adorning the ceiling was from the first cargo of gold brought back by Columbus from the New World.

East of Zaragoza, the Ebro continues its sluggish way through a landscape that changes dramatically between the windblown desert of Los Milagros, to the olive groves and vineyards that stretch beyond the Embalse de Mequinenza into southern Catalunya.

TOURIST OFFICE

ZARAGOZA: Plaza de Santiago Sas 7, tel (976) 23 00 27.

Accommodation, Eating and Drinking

SOS DEL REY CATOLICO (tel code 948):

(H&R)**Fernando de Aragón**, tel 88 80 11. A parador built into the medieval walls. Rooms with balconies overlooking the town, plains and sierras. C–B.

EJEA DE LOS CABALLEROS:

(H)**Cinco Villas**, Paseo del Muro 10, tel (976) 66 03 00. Adequate. D–C.

ZARAGOZA (tel code 976):

(H)**Gran Hotel**, Joaquin Costa 5, tel 22 19 01. Zaragoza's attempt at *Belle Epoque* hotel elegance. Recently restored after its royal opening by Alfonso XIII in 1929. A.
(H)**Avenida**, Avda César Augusto 55, tel 43 93 00. A cheaper central alternative to the Gran Hotel. D.
(R)**Gurrea**, San Ignacio de Loyola 15 tel 23 31 62. Local produce, imaginatively cooked. Menu changes daily. B–A.
(R)**Mesón del Carmen**, Avda Hernan Cortés 4, tel 21 11 51. Heart of the Old Quarter. Regional cooking. D–C.

Teruel and the Maestrazgo

Teruel and lower Aragón has always been the link between the central Ebro basin and the coast of Valencia. It is an area of spectacular beauty: forgotten sierra villages; vast, red-clay plains of olive groves where centuries of Moorish rule still linger in forgotten brick-built *pueblos* and bleak rock-covered mountainsides. The capital of the province is **TERUEL** (pop. 28,000), on the banks of the Turia. It was the centre of a close-knit Iberian tribe known as the Turboletas, and contains the most important examples of Mudéjar architecture of any city in Spain. Under the Moors, Teruel became a thriving part of the kingdom of Al-Andalus and, even after the recapture of the city in 1171 by Alfonso II of Aragón, the rights and freedom of the large Morisco population were guaranteed by *fueros* (privileges) granted in 1176.

For the next two centuries Teruel became one of the most progressive strongholds of *convivencia* in the Peninsula: Morisco artisans continued to ply their skills as builders, carpenters and ceramicists, and a vital Jewish community thrived in the city. In 1502 the last mosque was closed by royal decree, and the city settled into a long period of decline after the expulsion of the Moors in 1610, although many of them remained in the area, migrating to the depths of the surrounding sierras. Fortunately, much of the great patronage of this era endured the freezing winter of 1937–38 when Teruel was the scene of a bitter siege between the Nationalists and Republicans during the Civil War, which left 25,000 dead.

The five surviving Mudéjar towers rise above the bland modern suburbs of Teruel. All the important monuments are concentrated in a relatively small core of central streets; try to park near the Plaza Carlos Castell, recognizable by the bronze bull fountain at its centre, the emblem of the city. A short street away soars the tower of the cathedral, a magnificent mixture of Romanesque features and Moorish decorative detail, which uses patterned friezes of bricks and olive-green and purple lustrous columns to define the twin-light windows. Inside, there's a dazzling polychromed *artesonado* (inlaid ceiling) in the nave, and an impressive Plateresque retable by Gabriel Joli (1536) over the high altar, but otherwise the interior is mainly Baroque.

The Torre de San Pedro beside the church of the same name has more defined Gothic elements adorning its 13th-century minaret. The church itself, however, is generally put in the shade by the gracious sarcophagi to be seen in a small pantheon beside the tower: for Spanish couples this has long been a shrine of romantic pilgrimage. The two horizontal marble figures with their hands gracefully touching are Diego de Marcilla and Isabel de Segura, the 'Lovers of Teruel' – Spain's Abelard and Heloïse. The story is told of how in the 13th century the pair pledged their everlasting love on the night that Diego left on a five-year crusade against the Saracens. On the day of his appointed return, when he failed to appear, Isabel's parents married her off to another local *señorito*. When Diego rode into Teruel the following day and heard the news, he died of grief and was soon followed to the grave by a remorseful Isabel. Their mummified bodies have lain on this site since 1708.

The other two great Mudéjar towers – of San Martín and San Salvador – belong to a later period of tower-building defined by the use of green-and-white octagonal stars of Islam built into the masonry. Teruel is also exceptional for its 16th-century aqueduct and two museums: the Diocesan Museum in the Renaissance Bishop's Palace with good medieval paintings, and the Archeological Museum in the Casa de la Cultura (Plaza Fray Anselmo Polanco) with its unique collection of local Hispano–Moresque ceramics and lustreware.

West of Teruel lie the desolately imposing Montes Universales and the Sierra de Albarracín, an isolated sheep-farming district that has preserved almost intact its medieval Moorish character. The village of **Albarracín** is a mass of huddled rooftops on a ridge above a bow in the River Guadalaviar. On the hills surrounding the village lies a semi-ruined, towered and crenellated curtain wall, a testament to the strategic importance of the area during the *Reconquista*. At that time it was a small independent *taifa* kingdom ruled over by the Aben Racin dynasty, who were originally vassals to the Caliphate of Córdoba but later paid their dues to the Kings of Aragón and El Cid. Cobbled lanes run between half-timbered houses and lead to the cathedral, where you will find a fine collection of Flemish tapestries, and the originally Mozarabic church of Santa María.

Elsewhere the landscape of the sierra is decidedly rugged: dramatically eroded ravines, virgin pine forests, lonely stone farmhouses situated in the most improbably precari-

ous positions, transhumant flocks of goats and sheep, and isolated peasant communities make this one of the most enrapturing sierra landscapes south of the Ebro. The main route, however, continues first south-east then north from Teruel into the lands of El Maestrazgo on the borders of the province of Castellón in Valencia. This is the *Meseta* at its most extreme: summers scorch the earth brown and winters freeze the landscape with a mantle of ice and snow. The villages here have the most potent Moorish quality north of Andalusia and there is an abundance of massive *castillo* ruins, many of them former strongholds of the religious military orders.

Mora de Rubielos crouches beneath the solid, impenetrable façade of a 15th-century *castillo* that hides an elegantly austere courtyard. On another ridge there is a Gothic collegiate church, which is worth a visit for the brightly decorated side-chapels walled with patterned *azulejos* (glazed tiles) from the former pottery workshops at Manises near Valencia. You enter the walled village through the tall oblong Portal de los Olmos and walk along the narrow whitewashed streets to the arcaded central plaza.

From Mora a beautiful stretch of road snakes north through the Sierra de Gúdar via the Baroque Sanctuary of the Virgen de la Vega to **Alcalá de la Selva**, site of a former Muslim *castillo* donated by Alfonso II to the French abbey of Selva Mayor. After 15km the road turns east over the bare limestone *massifs* to **Cantavieja**, a typical walled village with a pretentiously large Baroque church and sleepy, arcaded plaza.

In the surrounding mountains are several equally imposing but dusty *pueblos*, each one like a small museum of late medieval civil architecture. For its size, **La Iglesuela del Cid** has several fine señorial mansions; as does **Mirambel**, which still nestles within the safety of its old perimeter wall. At **Villarluengo** whitewashed houses tumble down the crag beneath the twin-towered Renaissance belfries. The entire area remains one of the great refuges of traditional rural life, with each village specializing in a craft such as wickerwork, iron-forging or pottery for which it is locally renowned. Though most villages have suffered heavy depopulation since the Carlist Wars of the last century, many are currently undergoing renovation and enjoying at least a slight economic recovery due to a steady stream of tourists who visit these villages from the Valencian coast in the summer.

Returning north, the landscape spreads into vast plains of olive groves on either side of the River Guadalope. **Alcañiz** (pop. 12,500) is dominated by a stately palace-*castillo*, built by the Order of Calatrava towards the end of the 12th century on the site of a Moorish *fortaleza*. It has been turned into an elegant parador, but even if you don't intend to stay here, the inner cloister-courtyard and early Gothic frescoes in the chapel should not be missed. It was from here that James I and his captains Nuño, Folalquer and Blasco planned and set out on the conquest of Valencia. In the chapel, entered through a finely carved door, is the Plateresque alabaster sepulchre of a former viceroy of Aragón, Don Juan de Lanuza, a work attributed to Damián Forment.

In the town's Plaza España is a beautiful Gothic *lonja* (exchange) in the Italian *Quattrocento* style, with a fine first-floor loggia. Beside it stands the early neoclassic *ayuntamiento* (town hall) with gabled windows and a large stone *emblasonado* of the town's coat-of-arms. Walking a few yards up the slope, you come to the colossal Baroque façade that leads into the collegiate church of Santa María la Mayor – its size would put many cathedrals in the shade – where San Vicente Ferrer often used to preach. Several monasteries were founded under his influence in the surrounding streets between the 15th and 18th centuries.

East of Alcañiz the road traverses a great limestone *minimeseta* surrounded by great folds of mountains. Above the agricultural *pueblo* of **Calaceite**, reached via a bumpy farmtrack, lie the ruins of an Iberian village where wild thyme grows in between the neat streets of circular houses. From the summit the views across the neatly farmed hinterland appear endless: east to Catalunya and south across the Maestrazgo to Valencia.

The tower of San Martín in Teruel is one of the finest examples of Mudéjar architecture, a hybrid style that combined Moorish and Romanesque building techniques. Incafo

TOURIST OFFICE

TERUEL: Tomás Nougués 1, tel (974) 60 22 79.

Accommodation, Eating and Drinking

TERUEL (tel code 974):

(H)**Parador de Teruel**, Ctra de Zaragoza s/n, tel 60 18 00. Ideal for exploring the city and the surrounding sierras. C.
(R)**Civera**, Avda de Sagunto 37, tel 60 23 00. Regional cuisine. C.
(R)**Mesón Rufino**, Ronda de Andeles 36, tel 60 55 26. Regional cuisine. C.

ALBARRACÍN (Tel code 974):

(H)**Albarracín**, Azagra s/n, tel 71 00 11. Thoughtfully laid out in an old building in a central location, with a good restaurant. C–B.
(H)**Arabia**, Bernardo Zaparter 2, tel 71 02 12. In an old building, with a restaurant, but slightly cheaper than above. C.
(R)**Mesón del Gallo**, Los Puentes 1, tel 71 00 32. Local Teruelense cooking. D.

MORA DE RUBIELOS:

(H)**Jaime I**, Pl de la villa s/n, tel (974) 80 00 92. Good for a few nights if you want a rural atmosphere. C–B.

ALCAÑIZ (tel code 974):

(H)**Parador de Alcañiz**, Castillo Calatravos, tel 83 04 00. Dramatically located in the *castillo* overlooking the city. Worth visiting even if you don't stay there. C.
(H&R)**Meseguer**, Avda Maestrazgo 9, tel 83 10 02. A cheaper alternative to the parador, with the best restaurant in town. Comfortable, air-conditioned rooms. D–C.

CHAPTER ELEVEN

Castile and León

(Castilla y León)

ON THE STRENGTH of a banner depicting two castles, two lions and a coronet, Castile–León became the axis of Hispanic unity. Out of the dry, relentless terrain, scattered with *castillos* dating from the Reconquest, sprang the soul of Spanish nationhood. From this region of windswept plains and earth-coloured panoramas the native language, *castellano*, disseminated throughout the world.

Today, Castile is a place where the grazing lands of the *toros bravos* (fighting bulls) co-exist with mountain *pueblos* where life appears hardly altered by centuries and villagers live in adobe houses and pray each Sunday before a worm-eaten, gilt altarpiece. *Ancha es Castilla* (Wide is Castile) runs the proverb.

The 94,000sq km of Castile–León makes it the largest single region of Europe: a little bigger than Portugal, and three times the size of Holland. The undulating plateau of the central *Meseta* is surrounded on all sides by mountains. In the north a line of river valleys drain the snowy slopes of the Cordillera Cantábrica; at their western extreme are the Montes de León and El Bierzo, where isolated villagers still live in fear of wolves and witches. To the south, the mighty *massifs* of Gredos and Guadarrama form a natural frontier with Castile–La Mancha and Extremadura. The Sistema Ibérico, running through Soria in the east, is a desolate chain of sierras embracing crystal-clear lakes and impenetrable

pine forests, where the dark hills mask the source of the River Duero.

The mighty Duero, 936km long and collecting the water of 60 major tributaries, is Spain's third-largest river after the Ebro and Tajo. It irrigates more than 405,000ha of farmland, and generates almost a sixth of the country's hydro-electric power before disgorging itself into the Atlantic at Oporto in Portugal. Without it, you imagine the central basin as a desert.

Early Iberian settlements and small farming communities flourished along the fertile banks until the Romans conquered Spain, when the united *Meseta* tribes were virtually wiped out after the siege of Numancia. Two opulent villas recently excavated in southern

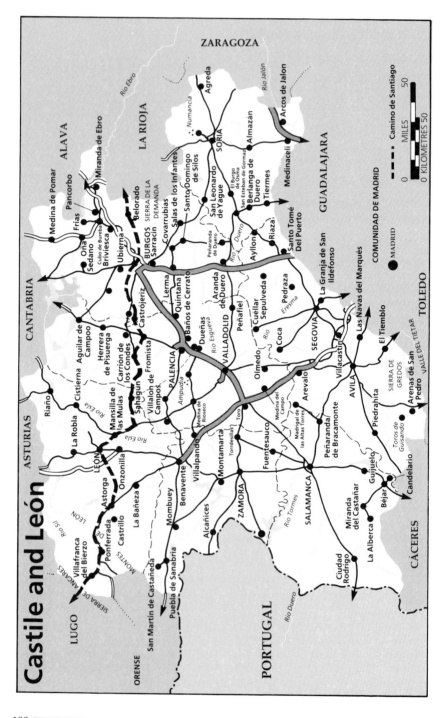

Castile and León

ZARAGOZA

ALAVA

LA RIOJA

CANTABRIA

ASTURIAS

LUGO

ORENSE

PORTUGAL

SALAMANCA

ZAMORA

CÁCERES

TOLEDO

GUADALAJARA

COMUNIDAD DE MADRID

MADRID

AVILA

SEGOVIA

VALLADOLID

PALENCIA

BURGOS

SORIA

Camino de Santiago

MILES 50

KILOMETRES 50

Palencia, at Quintanilla de la Cueza and Pedrosa de la Vega, attest to the powerful families who colonized the area, while the aqueduct at Segovia confirms the *Meseta*'s development under the Roman Empire. The Visigoths, though few in number, also derived benefit from the land, but the Arab invasion forced widespread depopulation that lasted until the gradual emergence in the tenth century of the Kingdom both of León in the western marches and of Castile across the central *Meseta*.

With the Reconquest came the consolidation of Christian kingdoms, which gradually expanded southwards into Muslim-occupied territory. By the end of the reign of Alfonso III (866–910), a new Christian buffer state had developed in the fertile lands of the Duero plain, which was christened *Castilla* because of the network of large fortified castles erected as bulwarks against constant Moorish attacks. The people and powerful warlords of this land came to dominate the Reconquest, and the epic hero El Cid (c. 1043–99) embodies Castilian characteristics as well as frontier virtues of the 11th century.

As the front line moved south, a pastoral and ranching economy developed in the *Meseta*, based on the transhumant movement of merino sheep along the migratory grazing routes known as *cañadas*. The area's increased prosperity led to the subsequent development of great lordships, monastic foundations and military orders, which took an even stronger political hold. The crown-controlled co-operative of sheep farmers, the *Mesta*, gave Castile a prosperous commercial base, while the wool and textile fairs of Medina del Campo became

centres for international trade.

Castile became increasingly concerned with imperial issues after its union with the kingdom of Aragón. Under the Habsburgs, Spain was effectively 'Castilianized' and, throughout the 16th century, both the land and the people were bled dry to maintain the sprawling empire. The present population of Castile–León is a third of what it was in 1500. The forest that once covered vast areas of the region is all but extinct and the soil eroded. The nine provinces – Valladolid, Burgos, Palencia, León, Zamora, Salamanca, Avila, Segovia and Soria – make up the modern autonomous region. Fortunately, geographical fragmentation has preserved proud and strong local identities.

Camino de Santiago in Castile and León

The Camino de Santiago (N120) continues out of La Rioja over the pine-forested Montes de Oca onto one of the most beautiful sections of the road leading to Burgos. Redecilla del Camino and Castildelgado are typically run-down villages, which, though prosperous in the 16th century, have been in decline ever since. The first town of note is **Belorado**, with its Renaissance buildings surrounding a medieval plaza. At **Villafranca Montes de Oca** there is a late 12th-century church and monastery at San Juan de Ortega, named after a saint who dedicated his life (1080–1163) to helping pilgrims. He is buried in a 15th-century sarcophagus in the church. From there the road descends along the poplar-fringed River Vena into the plain of Burgos.

BURGOS (pop. 157,000) is protected by an old restored fortress, which has served in its time as the seat of the Castilian court, as well as a royal prison and gunpowder factory. Napoleon fortified the citadel on his initial offensive into the Peninsula, but blew it up on his retreat to France. The strong military presence established by the Nationalists during the Civil War continues in Burgos to this day.

The main entrance to the medieval city is through the **Arco de Santa María** whose 16th-century façade was erected to appease Charles V after Burgos's involvement in the revolt of the Communeros. The figure of the Habsburg emperor stands in the central niche of the upper panel of the arch, next to Fernán González, the first Count of Castile and its historical founder. Beside him stands El Cid, the 11th-century soldier of fortune, and finally the figure of Count Diego Porcelo, who founded Burgos in 884 on the orders of Alfonso III.

With its topiary hedges and wide riverside *paseos*, the city has something of a genteel French atmosphere in its narrow streets lined with old-fashioned provincial shops and smart delicatessens. The pigeon-filled Plaza Mayor and the surrounding streets have been the heart of the city since the Middle Ages, when Burgos was the centre of the wool trade and commercial hub of northern Castile.

Try to park in the Plaza del Rey San Fernando in front of the **cathedral**, whose unmistakable open-stone tracery towers can be seen for miles around. The exterior is a 'Gothic filigree fantasy' carved from the local lead-grey stone, and bursting with gargoyles, turrets, radial buttresses, geometric articulations, external galleries and roseton windows. In 1221 Fernando III (1217–52) blessed the foundations on the occasion of his marriage to Beatrice of Swabia, and the building is remarkably harmonious, considering it was constructed over a period of more than 300 years.

Of the four doors leading into the cathedral, the most distinguished – the Puerta de Sarmental – is on the south side at the top of a grand flight of steps. The figure of Bishop Mauricio stands on the central column between Moses and Aaron, Peter and Paul. Above their heads the 12 Apostles sit in a line, casually chatting while Christ dictates to the evangelists, and angels and musicians arch overhead. Entrance to the cathedral is through the main west door from the elegant little Plaza de Santa María. Much of the finest carving for the cathedral was carried out by Gil and Diego de Siloé, the master masons of medieval Burgos and two of the finest sculptors of the Gothic age.

The sombre yet extravagant interior is the combined effort of over 120 architects and masons. On entering look out for 'Papamoscas' (above and to the left), the Germanic-looking manikin who opens and closes his mouth as the hour strikes. On the wall of the first side-chapel, the Capilla del Santísimo, hangs a large crucifix, the 'Cristo de Burgos', which has attracted suitably Gothic legends that bridge the absurd and the sublime. Some claim this to be the petrified body of Christ, washed up on the coast of Galicia; others say the image was carved by St Nicodemus and the hair and nails still grow in the night. Whatever the story, there is a group of dedicated widows who keep a near-constant vigil over what has been clinically diagnosed as a piece of bullhide.

On a more down-to-earth level it is possible here to trace the development of Castilian ecclesiastical architecture through 700 years of history. This begins with the proto-Gothic capitals depicting the marriage of Ferdinand III and his Swabian queen in the cloister, and ends with the slab of inscribed marble marking the tomb of El Cid and his wife, Doña Jimena, finally brought to rest beneath Burgos's star-vaulted lantern in 1921.

The grilled-in choir, normally kept locked (the sacristan has a key), is remarkable for the intricate fence of wrought-iron work and the 103 walnut stalls engraved with stories from the New Testament and other, more licen- tious scenes after the influence of Rodrigo Alemán. This is the work of Felipe Vigarni, the master mason also responsible for the stone carvings in the ambulatory and the Capilla de la Presentación. The limousin-enamel and copper effigy at the centre of the choir is another representation of the co-founder, Bishop Mauricio.

The main structure of the cathedral was completed by three generations of the Colonia family, and their Germanic origins are most obviously apparent in the Condestable Chapel behind the high altar with its fine octagonal dome accentuating the light and height. More imposing than the Plateresque retables – joint endeavours by Vigarni

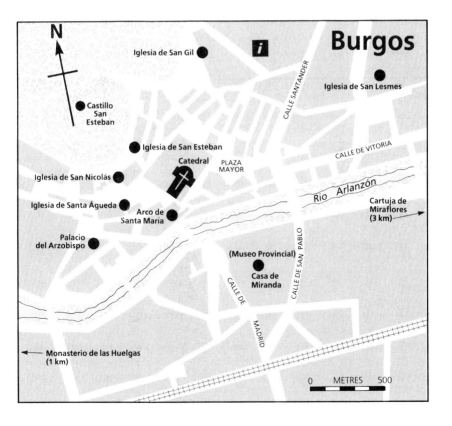

N

Burgos

Iglesia de San Gil

Iglesia de San Lesmes

Castillo San Esteban

Iglesia de San Esteban

Catedral PLAZA MAYOR

CALLE DE VITORIA

Iglesia de San Nicolás

Río Arlanzón

Iglesia de Santa Águeda

Arco de Santa Maria

Cartuja de Miraflores (3 km)

Palacio del Arzobispo

(Museo Provincial)

Casa de Miranda

CALLE SANTANDER

CALLE DE SAN PABLO

CALLE DE MADRID

Monasterio de las Huelgas (1 km)

0 METRES 500

and the Siloés – are the serene marble sepulchres of the Condestables with their rich adornments and patient lap-dogs. Other side-chapels of impor-tance include the Capilla de la Presentación, again the work of Vigarni (1519–21), and the Capilla de la Visitación that contains the tomb of Bishop Alonso de Cartagena by Gil de Siloé.

The cloister (1290–1324) has been turned into a small museum, and the treasury displays various cathedral rel-ics, such as vestments, tapestries and ecclesiastical portraits. Of passing interest are the marriage agreement between El Cid and Jimena, and the large chest known as *El Cofre Del Cid*, which the Cid is supposed to have filled with sand to bribe the Jewish money-lenders before he was forced into exile. The cult of the Cid is strong in Burgos.

Though the cathedral is Burgos's main attraction and, with Toledo cathedral, the most richly endowed in Castile, there are several other areas of interest that help to explain the great Gothic prosperity of the city. Foremost is the **Real Monasterio de las Huelgas** on the urban periphery, reached by turning right along the south bank of the River Arlanzon, after which it is well signposted.

Las Huelgas was founded in 1187 by Alfonso VIII (1158–1214) and Queen Eleanor of England, the daughter of Henry II, as a place of retirement for noble ladies and as a pantheon for the Kings of Castile once the city was securely established as the regional capital. The abbess was invested with enormous power, including the death penalty, and the landed riches of the foundation grew quickly from endow-ments.

As a piece of architecture it is a pure, austere and composed example of the Cistercian style, with patterned carv-ing and strong lines. Inside, the guided tour will more than fill you in on the history of the two cloisters, Mudéjar chapel and royal tombs. You will also be shown some fascinating and unique exhibits of Gothic textiles and bro-cades saved from the royal tombs after their desecration by French troops rampaging through Burgos in the early 19th century. They include the castle-and-lion embroidered coat and cap of Prince Fernando de la Cerdà, and the Moorish standard won by the united Christian armies at the decisive Battle of Las Navas de Tolosa in 1212. In the Capilla de Santiago is the strangest exhibit, and the one most associated with the Camino: a small mechanical statuette of St James holding a sword in a counterpoised arm – used, so you're told, for the knighting of kings.

The other great monastery located on the south-eastern side of Burgos is **La Cartuja de Miraflores**. Originally this was the royal palace of Henry III (1390–1406), but it was subsequently extended by John II between 1441 and 1451 and bequeathed to the Carthusians on his death in 1454. Inside, the most remarkable works of sculpture are all by Diego de Siloé. They include the tombs of John II (1406–54) and Isabella of Portugal (the parents of Isabel La Católica), and the Infante Don Alfonso: Isabella's brother whose death at the age of 17 made her the natural successor to the throne of Castile.

The last of the trio of monasteries surrounding Burgos has a less regal appeal and is of interest to those intrigued by the life of El Cid. The early Benedictine **monastery of San Pedro**

El Cid

Rodrigo Díaz de Vivar, known by his Christian chroniclers as 'El Campeador' and by the Muslims as 'El Cid', was most probably born in the village of Vivar just north of Burgos in about 1043. As was expected of a young nobleman, he learnt in his youth to ride, hawk and hunt.

Following the death of Ferdinand I of Castile in 1065 and the division of the Christian kingdoms, Rodrigo was sent to the court of Sancho II of Castile, where he became constable of the royal bodyguard. In 1072, after successfully wresting Galicia and León from his cousins, Sancho was treacherously murdered beneath the walls of Zamora and was succeeded by Alfonso VI. Rodrigo was replaced as commander of the royal bodyguard, and in 1079 was sent to exact a tribute from Al-Mutamid, Governor of Seville.

A battle ensued at Cabra, during which Rodrigo captured several dignitaries of the Castilian court, including Count García Ordoñez. He stripped them of their knightly possessions and released them, but this incident subsequently caused Rodrigo's expulsion and exile from the court in 1081. He found refuge as a mercenary with the Banu Hud rulers of Zaragoza, and by 1084 had become a major figure at the Arab court. The following year Alfonso VI captured Toledo and demanded the surrender of Seville: a Christian victory that resounded through the Islamic world. Consequently, a vast army from North Africa, led by the Almoravides, entered the Peninsula and King Alfonso was heavily defeated at the Battle of Zalaga near Badajoz later that year.

Alfonso VI paid Rodrigo handsomely to return to his ranks and, to repay his loyalty, gave him large estates, which included the *castillo* of Gormaz and lands of the eastern Duero as well as territories further north. The Cid immediately embarked on a campaign along the Mediterranean coast near Valencia, and in 1090 gained a brilliant victory at the Battle of Tévar against a combined Muslim and Catalan army. In 1092 he took revenge on Count García Ordoñez and laid waste his estates in the central Ebro depression. Two years later, following a two-year siege, he captured Valencia, which he successfully defended and governed until his death in 1099.

Throughout his life he never lost a battle, and in the centuries following his death he became revered as a crusading hero and the object of a great reliquary cult that has continued to this day. An extensive mythology still surrounds his life, due largely to the *Poema de Mío Cid* which, although historically unsound, is Spain's greatest medieval epic poem. It is irrefutable, however, that El Cid was a soldier of fortune who fought in the pay of both Christian and Muslim rulers, but who above all exemplified the knightly virtues of his age.

de Cardeña is located 6km from La Cartuja and is reached by taking a left turn after the village of Cardeñajimeno. This was where the Cid's wife lived while her husband was in exile, but only a few Romanesque traces of the original structure remain after the extensive restoration work that was carried out in the 17th century.

A strange story surrounds the death of El Cid that hints at both the near-mythical reputation he achieved in Castile during his own lifetime, and

---

The River Esla

Though the River Duero relates in architectural terms to the 11th and 12th centuries and the growing importance of Castile as a military power, the structures along the Esla valley derive from an earlier period. The minor road that follows the river's 285-kilometre course from the southern slopes of the Picos de Europa to its confluence with the Duero, a short way west of Zamora, is one of the most culturally rewarding routes cutting north–south through the region.

In many ways it may be considered as an artistic tributary of the Camino de Santiago, which it meets at the walled village of **Mansilla de las Mulas**, and was surely the natural route for the movement of the ninth-century Asturian court south to León. Along the Esla stand two Mozarabic churches: San Miguel de Escalada (**Gradefes**) and San Pedro de la Nave (**El Campillo**), the latter with earlier Visigothic details.

During the 12th century the Esla was just as vital for the southward diffusion of monastic culture. The imposing ruins of the monastery of Moreruela (1131) was the first Cistercian house in Spain, and there are foundations in varying states of ruin at Gradefes and **Sandoval**.

The area also has its share of *castillos*, the most spectacular of which is Valencia de Don Juan, a striking crenellated and towered ruin on the banks of the Esla. It was erected in the 14th century as a fortification commanding this beautiful road along the river valley between Zamora and León.

---

the extraordinary influence Islamic teaching had on his life. It is said that in his last week he sought advice from Muslim doctors, stopped eating, and drank myrrh and balsam to preserve his body after death. The corpse was removed from Valencia to San Pedro and, in accordance with the Cid's own instructions, was seated on a throne of ivory, swathed in silk and wearing his sword. After almost 15 years, when his body had disintegrated to a virtual skeleton, he was buried beside his wife Jimena until their bones were removed to Burgos cathedral earlier this century.

In Burgos several other monuments worth seeing include the Gothic churches of San Nicolás, San Gil, San Lesmes and Santa Agueda; and the **Archeological Museum**, in a former palace, with a gracious central courtyard. Here you can see more work by the Siloés, such as the magnificent enamel altar front originally in the monastery of Santo Domingo de Silos, and good Gothic and Renaissance Castilian paintings.

The province of Burgos is culturally one of the most heavily endowed areas of the Peninsula, and is best explored from the capital. To the north lie the great señorial towns like **Sedana** and **Briviesca**, at the centre of an extensive wheat-growing district. **Oña** is one of the most sacred shrines of Castile, and the early capital of the kingdom before Alfonso VI (1072–1109) moved the episcopal seat to Burgos in 1075.

Of most interest is the **monastery of San Salvador**, founded in 1011 by Sancho García, Count of Castile, and containing another pantheon of the founding Kings of Castile, including Sancho 'the Great' of Navarre (d. 1035). His death saw the division of the northern Christian territories between his three sons, with Aragón bequeathed to Ramiro I (1035–63); Castile (1035–72) and León (1037–72) to Ferdinand I; and Navarre to García III (1035–59).

Nearby **Frías** is the most spectacularly situated of these señorial towns, with palace-lined streets leading from the precipitous ruins of an early Christian frontier castle. The Ebro runs through one of its loneliest stretches here, carving out a great canyon over 1km deep in parts that is home to breeding pairs of vultures and eagles, whose high-pitched calls are the only sound that pierces the desolate silence.

Many of the most breathtaking views of the *Meseta*'s uninhabitable expanse can be appreciated by following the small roads, often no more than tracks, that follow the course of the river. Limestone *massifs* rise abruptly to the south before flattening out into isolated moorlands. The villages that lie along the Ebro's course, surrounded by hand-cultivated orchards and *vegas*, are generally blessed with a half-ruined Romanesque church. A few on-shore oil wells are lost in the northern recesses. In late autumn, when the terrain is frosted with snow and ice, and fogs move in without warning from the north, it is a landscape that defines the extremes of the word *meseta* perfectly.

South of Burgos, the country is gentler. Horizonless agricultural plains, so typical of northern Castile, are broken up by sheer limestone ridges, and the villages and towns are of an equally imposing and proud dis-

position. **Palenzuela** is an unruffled medieval *pueblo* on the banks of the River Arlanza, with wood and adobe houses leaning over a narrow hive of streets. At **Lerma** (pop. 2,500) you can see the formidable silhouette of the palace built, with lavish amounts of public funds, for the Duke of Lerma, Philip III's prime minister and favourite, in the first decades of the 17th century.

Covarrubias (pop. 800) is a popular weekend resort, long loved for its good restaurants and peaceful ambience. The village lies among the fertile orchards that flank the streams of the Sierra de Covarrubias, and is entered through a 16th-century gatehouse. The two main monuments are the Torre de Doña Urraca, with what appears to be a Visigothic window in its austere façade; and the Colegiata dating from the 14th to 16th centuries.

The impressive interior contains over 40 tombs of illustrious Castilians, including Count Fernán González (931–70). The other distinguished sepulchre contains Princess Cristina of Norway (d. 1262), wife for just four years of Philip, the son of Ferdinand III 'the Saint' (1217–52) and León (1230–52). In the Capilla de los Reyes is a magnificent triptych by Gil de Siloé depicting, in the central panel, the Adoration of the Magi. The cloister and museum are also worth visiting, the latter for its paintings by Berruguete, El Greco, Zurbarán and the medieval painter, Alonso de Sedano, from Burgos.

Covarrubias is also a good point of departure for exploring the ruined monastery of San Pedro de Arlanza, the Mozarabic church at **Quintanilla de las Viñas**, or the spectacular foundation of Santo Domingo de Silos, one of

The chapel of the Constables in the cathedral at Burgos contains the tombs of the hereditary Constable of Castile, Pedro Hernández de Velasco (d. 1492), beside his wife Mencia de Mendoza, carved in Carrara marble by an Italian sculptor. Incafo

the richest and most imposing monasteries in Europe.

Of the many monastic foundations of Old Castile, which include San Millán de la Cogolla and Santo Domingo de la Calzada, none better illustrates the flowering of artistic brilliance in 11th- and 12th-century Spain than **Santo Domingo de Silos**. Tours of the monastery, pharmacy and museum are conducted by a Benedictine monk, who first shows you into the restored two-levelled cloister. The quality of the carved capital heads is comparable to that of the Puerta de la Gloria at Santiago de Compostela, one

of the great miracles of Romanesque sculpture. The cloister ceiling has an equally beautiful polychromed *artesonado* (inlaid ceiling), which would seem to confirm that Moorish craftsmen were used extensively when the monastery was built. The museum is just as richly endowed and contains good enamels from Santo Domingo's 12th-century workshop, ivory caskets, a Mozarabic chalice and another copy of the *Beato de Liébana*.

Returning to Burgos and continuing on the Camino de Santiago along the N120, you pass the pilgrimage churches at **Sasamón** and beneath the castle ruins of **Olmillos de Sasamón** before you enter the straggling Burguensian village of **Castrojériz**. Here, beneath the crumbling fortifications, are several dilapidated churches that merit attention. The best of them is San Juan, easily recognized by the fish-scale tiles capping its fortified tower, and remarkable for its spoilt proto-Gothic cloister crowned by a peeling *artesonado* ceiling. In the collegiate church of Santa María, near the gate as you enter the village, is a solemn-faced Madonna lost within a typically ramshackle Baroque altarpiece.

From there the road crosses the River Pisuerga, delimiting the border between Palencia and Burgos. Palencia has for most of its recent history been a bridge between the kingdoms of Castile and León: the *Tierra de Campos*, a land of expansive wheat plains, of nomadic shepherds and lonely predatory eagles. To the north, in the foothills of the Cantabrian mountains, lies another heavy concentration of popular Romanesque architecture. In fact, Palencia has more Romanesque churches than any other single province and they can easily be explored from the old señorial town of **Aguilar de Campoo** (pop. 5,500), which today is the sweet-smelling home of a biscuit factory.

The discovery of several Roman villas in the plains north of the capital at **Quintanilla de la Cueza** and **Pedrosa de la Vega** has proved that this was one of the most prosperous farming districts of Roman Hispania. Likewise, the Mozarabic church at **San Juan de Baños** – the foundations of which have been dated to 661 and the reign of King Recceswinth (649–72) – is an architecturally important monument for understanding the sequential history and development of Christian church decoration during the end of Visigothic rule and the rise of the kingdom of Asturias between the eighth and tenth centuries. The capital of the province, **PALENCIA** (pop. 78,000), is somewhat faceless, but does contain a few good medieval buildings, three of which are well worth visiting: the cathedral built on a seventh-century Visigothic crypt; the Gothic church of San Pablo; and a richly endowed Archeological Museum containing mainly local discoveries.

Fromista (pop. 1,500) is the first main town on the Camino in Palencia. Its most distinctive monument is the church of San Martín, founded between 1035 and 1066 by the widow of Sancho 'the Great' to commemorate the death of her husband. Its carving is exceptional, but sadly the church no longer functions in a religious capacity and has been converted into a simple museum. Two other churches of note in the *pueblo* include San Pedro, with its good Mudéjar brick details; and Santa María, with a sumptuous retable of 29 painted Gothic Flemish panels.

From Fromista the road cuts through flat prairieland via ramshackle agricultural villages that are famous for little but the crumbling silhouettes of their circular dovecotes, now forsaken by all except a few sparrows and the occasional stork's nest. Not so long ago, however, these played an important part in the rural ecosystem, when bird droppings fertilized the fields and the pigeons were killed for the pot.

It's worth stopping at **Villalcázar de Sirga** (pop. 3,000) for the Romanesque church of Santa María la Blanca, which contains the stone and polychromed sepulchres of Ferdinand III's son, Philip, and his second wife, Leonor

Ruiz de Castro. In terms of the intricacy of the carving and state of preservation, these are two of the most beautifully preserved royal tombs in all Castile.

Carrión de los Condes is the next important town, a former seat of the court of Castile and fief of the infamous Condes de Carrión who, in the historically unreliable *Poema Del Mío Cid*, married Doña Elvira and Doña Sol, the daughters of El Cid, only to squander their dowries and leave their young wives 'for dead in the oak forest of Corpes'. Fortunately, the Cid suspected something and sent his servant, Félez Muñoz, to keep watch over his precious progeny. Muñoz returned safely with the women, and the Cid finally won back his family honour at a royal court hearing in Toledo, stripping the Condes de Carrión of all they possessed and marrying his daughters to the far more eligible Princes of Navarre and Aragón. According to romantic notion, the bodies of the two disgraced brothers are supposed to rest in two Romanesque sarcophagi in a side-chapel of the convent of San Zoilo.

The church of Santiago near the Plaza Mayor is the main attraction in Carrión, defined by the horizontal frieze of figures above the portal and in the archivolts. Though much of the sculpture has deteriorated badly, the Christ in majesty and amusing depictions of secular life such as cooks and farm workers give it a lighter touch than the standard Apocalyptic visions and bands of Apostles that are generally to be found.

From Carrión, you carry on west through flat and bleak expanses with few signs of life except for the occasional wandering flock of grazing sheep and the silhouette of the Cordillera Cantábrica that runs parallel to the road in the north before crossing the border into León. Soon you arrive in **Sahagún**, where you can see what some experts consider to be the two earliest brick Mudéjar churches in the Peninsula: San Tirso and San Lorenzo. Following the repopulation of the reconquered territories in the tenth century, Sahagún was the centre of a thriving civil and ecclesiastical community. The monastery of San Benito, now in ruins, was one of the most powerful Benedictine foundations in Spain and an early pantheon for the Kings of León, but now only the tomb of Alfonso VI (1065–1109) and his Saracen queen, Zaida, remain. The town was irreparably sacked during the War of Independence, and has remained woebegone ever since.

With a small huddle of houses built around a central arcaded plaza and protected by crumbling freestone walls, **Mansilla de las Mulas** is the last stop before the former capital of the kingdom of León is entered. Here the Camino crosses one of Castile's great tributaries, the Esla (see page 186).

LEÓN (pop. 130,000) lies on a pale green plain surrounded on every side except the south-east by mountains. It has always been of vital strategic importance for the movement of people, commerce and armies between the *Meseta* and west Atlantic ports, and today it is a busy industrial centre of wide, tree-lined *paseos* leading into large plazas with well-tended flowerbeds and over-efficient traffic police.

Compared to other *Meseta* cities, it has a sombre, Atlantic atmosphere, especially on wintry days when overshadowed by the tall, dun-coloured apartment blocks that were erected towards the end of the 19th century. However, the city possesses three of the most stirring examples of Romanesque, Gothic and Plateresque architecture in the land, and for this reason alone it is worth staying the night.

León became the capital of the kingdom of Asturias under Ordoño II (913–23), but its sacking during Al-Mansur's foray through the north in 988 meant that the old parts of the city date to the early 11th century. In 1037 Ferdinando I of Castile was crowned King of León and, for the next three centuries, the city prospered as the capital of a kingdom that came to include Galicia and most of the territories of the present-day provinces of Zamora, Salamanca, Cáceres and Badajoz. For some people the ancient lands of the crown of León – the western marches with Portugal – are the most beautiful and mysterious area of the whole Peninsula.

The best place to park your car, even if you're not staying there, is in front of the magnificent Plateresque Hostal San Marcos (now a parador), beside the River Bernesga. Founded in 1168 by the Knights of Santiago, it was richly endowed by *Los Reyes Católicos* at the beginning of the 16th century, supposedly in gratitude for the Order's help during the conquest of Granada. Yet this was, in fact, wily diplomacy on the part of Queen Isabel in order to check the power of the knights. This she successfully achieved by having her husband elected Grand Master and merging the vast estates of the Order with those of the crown.

No structure until Santiago de Compostela better exemplifies the Plateresque style than the Hostal San Marcos. The decoration includes scallopshells, the emblem of the Order, and rows of medallion-busts of emperors, kings and mythological heroes, separated by columns and pilasters. In the chapterhouse and 16th-century cloister is the Archeological Museum, which includes some priceless works of various faiths: a sacrificial altar to Diana, an 11th-century ivory Christ and a tenth-century Mozarabic cross from the church at Santiago de Peñalba. The receptionists at the front desk will be happy to let you visit the *hostal* if you ask.

From there, walk into the city centre along Avenida de José Antonio, continuing directly through the Plaza de Calvo Sotelo to the Plaza Santo Domingo – the nerve centre of the city, and on the edge of the *Casco Antiguo* (Old Quarter). Gaudí's neo-Gothic Casa de Botines is found on one corner and should be noticed in passing, though it is certainly one of his less inventive works and was recently bought by a building society.

Sequentially, the first place to visit is the Romanesque **Collegiate of San Isidoro el Real**. The original ninth-century church was destroyed by the Arabs and rebuilt by Ferdinand I (1037–65), who ordered the relics of San Isidro to be moved here from Seville. Ferdinand died on the site a few days after its consecration in 1065, and extensive alterations were made during the 12th and 16th centuries. The quality of the carving both inside and out is exceptional. But the unquestioned highlight, and one of the masterpieces of European Romanesque art, is the great western narthex, or the Panteón de los Reyes.

The crypt is supported by substantial columns and finely sculpted capitals. In between the vaulting are the radiant colours of the exalted 12th-century frescoes. They represent Christ Pantocrator surrounded by familiar Biblical scenes: the Massacre of the Innocents, lives of the Apostles and allegorical portraits of the Evangelists, interspersed by signs of the zodiac, pastoral scenes, farm animals and imaginative decorated friezes.

The cloister and treasury are reached from the pantheon. The treasury contains some elaborately worked chalices, processional crosses and the great Bible of 960 illustrated by a scribe called Florentius. This is one of several manuscripts produced by the Leonese school of illumination, which followed the court of Ordoño II to León from Asturias and flourished from the early tenth to late 11th centuries. It produced a style of book painting unique for its colour and line, other examples of which can be seen in the cathedral.

León's **cathedral of Santa María de Regla**, sometimes referred to as the 'crystal house', is an example of French Gothic at its purest. As you enter through the tripartite west door, the grime-encrusted sandstone exterior gives little indication of what awaits inside. It takes a few moments for your eyes to adjust to the gloomy twilit interior and the strange sensations of light but, when they do, the initial impact of the stained glass has understandably been termed 'divine'.

The glass, decorated with much medieval Biblical symbolism, dates from the 13th to the 20th centuries – some of the oldest can be admired in the rose window above the door as you enter – and if possible should be appreciated at different moments of the day, as the colours alchemize under changing lighting conditions

depending on the position of the sun. The ochre reds, bright 'Seville' oranges and saffron golds are hues particular to Spain; so too is the strange black glass seen in a few of the compositions. The cathedral's museum and chapterhouse are worth visiting for more Leonese manuscripts, Visigothic legal codes, the Romanesque polychrome sculptures and rare pieces of Mudéjar furniture.

The Plaza Mayor and the old medieval heart of León lie south of the cathedral. Here the true spirit of the city can be discovered in small hole-in-the-wall bars and busy little cobbled shopping malls that run between unrestored Gothic churches and forsaken señorial palaces with balconies looking out over crooked plazas.

West of León the mountains grow dense as the road winds its way towards **Astorga** (pop. 13,000), an ancient Roman walled stronghold. The imposing, mainly 15th-century cathedral is notable for the richly carved Baroque doorway and the high altar (1562) by Gaspar Becerra, who studied in Italy under Michelangelo and was well patronized by Philip II to adorn the churches of Castile. The large Cathedral Museum is also worth a look, not only for the large quantity of sculpture collected from different churches in the surrounding villages, but also for the jewel-studded casket dating from the rule of Alfonso III (866–910).

Just down from the cathedral is another rather misplaced Gaudí building: the white-stone, neo-Gothic Bishop's Palace. No edifice ever involved the Astorgan diocese in so much controversy. Gaudí had known the bishop, Juan Bautista Gran i Vallespinos, during his time at

The Panteón de Los Reyes in the church of San Isidro in León is decorated with some exceptional Romanesque frescoes and was the burial chamber for the early medieval kings of León. Incafo

Tarragona, when they had become close personal friends, and he was commissioned to draw up plans for a new palace after the old one was destroyed by fire in 1887. His designs met with stiff opposition, and Gaudí at one point threatened to burn his drawings, swearing never to set foot in Astorga again or even fly over it in a hot-air balloon. In 1964 the building was finally converted into a museum dedicated to the history of the Camino de Santiago; in other rooms some archeological finds and local ethnography can be seen.

Astorga is a centre of local ethnography as it is the capital of a desolate mountainous area known as the *Maragatería*, home of the displaced tribe of *Los Maragatos*. Several theories surround the origins of these people, who for centuries were prized for their honesty as traders and muleteers. Some claim they are of Bedouin descent and arrived in the Peninsula in 711 with the first Arab and Berber armies, and that their name derives from King Mauregatus, who was forced to pay a yearly tribute of 100 virgins to the Moors. Others trace the name to *moros gotos* (Moorish Goths): displaced Christians living under Muslim law. Another more recent theory, based on local archeological evidence, particularly Punic funerary discoveries, concludes that they were Phoenicians, enslaved by the Romans to work in the local gold and iron mines.

For the Romans, this area was as lucrative in terms of its minerals as were the mines of Rio Tinto in western Andalusia. Undoubtedly a considerable social infrastructure far greater than the one you see today must have existed. The main body of mines was in the sierras of El Bierzo further to the west, and it is into these inhospitable highlands that pilgrims on the Camino must brace themselves when they leave behind the neo-Gothic turrets and pinnacles of Astorga. After a few kilometres the Camino branches off the main N-IV and climbs up through the Montes de León via sleepy little villages such as **Castrillo de los Polvazares**, **Rabanal del Camino** and **Acebo** through the Manjarín Pass into the Ponferrada valley and the heart of the Sil basin.

Ponferrada (pop. 55,000) is the commercial hub of El Bierzo and an industrial and mining centre rising from a plateau dominated on every side by snow-capped mountains in the winter. The former Templar fortification above the town was built to protect the faithful, and has recently been restored. But this is an ugly, run-down town, with a neglected soul of streets around the Plaza Mayor.

To give you a taste of El Bierzo, a worthwhile detour takes you 20km south of Ponferrada up the Valdueza valley to the village of **Peñalba de Santiago**, beneath the towering peak of Cabeza de la Yegua. The heart of the community is still the Mozarabic church, founded by monks fleeing persecution from the Caliphate at

Córdoba towards the end of the tenth century.

The sierras of El Bierzo that stretch across the north-western frontier of León are steeped in myth and ancient folklore, described by Richard Ford in 1845 as 'the Switzerland of León . . . a district of alpine passes, trout streams, pleasant meadows, and groves of chestnuts and walnuts'. Since that was written, life has changed only marginally, although once again depopulation has left many of the *pueblos* semi-ruined, and the average age of the villagers appears abnormally high.

El Bierzo includes the Sierra de Ancares, one of the last important habitats of the European wolf and El Bosque de Muniellos, a vast oak forest that covers more than 3,000ha stretching into Asturias. Yet the most haunting elements in this landscape are the man-made ridges of Las Médulas, reached from the village of **Carucedo**, south-west of Ponferrada.

In the first century AD, following the subjugation of the northern marches by the Romans, gold was discovered in these inhospitable chestnut-covered hills. To extract the ore, canals were built to divert the waters of the River Cabrera, 30km to the south. It has been estimated that almost 240 million cubic metres of earth were shifted in the following 200 years to extract 960,000kg of gold. The surreal pinnacles and peaks are the enduring scars of that labour.

The Camino continues to ascend from Ponferrada over the highlands to **Villafranca del Bierzo** (pop. 6,500) – literally, the village of the French – a town buried in a funnel of mountains. Once again the place is interesting for a smattering of Romanesque churches such as San Juan opposite the imposing palace of the Marqués de Villafranca and Santiago, with good carvings around the door. In the convent of San Francisco is a stunning 15th-century *artesonado* Mudéjar ceiling.

Villafranca is a good place to stay overnight, and in the evening it is worth taking a walk through the dim backstreets with their overhanging wooden balconies. Alternatively, you could drive into one of the surrounding villages, in particular **Corcullón**, where there are magnificent views across the depression scoured out by the River Sil. This wide fertile gorge, generally referred to as the Sil basin, marks the transition between the Cantabrian mountains and the granitic tableland of north-western Iberia.

From Villafranca the road winds up the steep-sided Valcarce valley over the suspension bridge straddling the Puerto Piedrafita and into Galicia.

TOURIST OFFICES

LEÓN: Plaza de la Catédral 4, tel (987) 21 10 83.

BURGOS: Pl Alonso Martínez 7, tel (947) 20 31 25.

Accommodation, Eating and Drinking

BURGOS (tel code 947):

(H&R)**Mesón del Cid**, Plaza Santa María 8–10, tel 20 87 15. Beautifully situated overlooking the cathedral. Modernized rooms and excellent value. Garage. The adjoining restaurant serves typical Burgos food. D&C.

(H&R)**Fernán Gozález**, Calera 17, tel 20 94 41. Well situated, with comfortable rooms. Restaurant serves *nueva cocina* dishes. C & C–B.

(R)**Casa Ojeda**, Vitoria 5, tel 20 90 52. Beside the Plaza Cordón, a classic Burgos restaurant with a good *tapas* bar. C–B.

COVARRUBIAS:

(H)**Arlanza**, Plaza Mayor 11, tel (947) 40 30 25. Occupying one side of the Plaza Mayor, this is an ideal base for exploring the south of the province. C.

(R)There are several good cheap restaurants in and around the plaza, all of a similar quality and serving good Castilian food.

FROMISTA (tel code 988):

(H)**San Telmo**, Martín Veña 8, tel 81 01 02. Cheap and central. E–D.

(R)**Hostería de los Palmeros**, Pl San Telmo 4, tel 81 00 67. A restored hostel for pilgrims, furnished with antiques. Specialities: *menestra de verduras* (vegetable casserole), *revueltos* (scrambled eggs). C.

VILLALCAZAR DE SIRGA:

(R)**Mesón Villasirga**, Plaza Mayor, tel (988) 88 80 22. In an old house. Homely touches like ceramic plates and glasses give it an antiquated feel. Specialities: *sopa Castellana* (soup with bread and an egg) and good local cakes. C.

LEÓN (tel code 987):

(P)**Parador de San Marcos**, Plaza de San Marcos, tel 23 73 00. One of the great Plateresque buildings of Spain. Luxuriously furnished. Pool. Sauna. Tennis. A–B.

(H)**Quindos**, Av José Antonio 24, tel 23 62 00. An adequate and cheaper central alternative. C–D.

(R)**Mesón Leonés del Racimo de Oro**, Caño Vadillo 2, tel 25 75 75. A traditional 17th-century inn with one of the best atmospheres in León and a summer patio for outside dining. In the heart of the *barrio antiguo*. Specialities: *ancas de rana* (frogs' legs), *lenguado con piñones y pasa* (sole with pine nuts and raisins), *asados* (roast meats). C–D.

ASTORGA:

(H&R)**La Peseta**, Pl de San Bartolomé 3, tel (987) 61 72 75. Excellent restaurant with Galician influenced cooking. Good comfortable rooms. Ideal for an overnight stay. D & D–C.

VILLAFRANCA DEL BIERZO (tel code 987):

(H)**Parador**, Avenida Calvo Sotelo, tel 54 01 75. Small and unpretentious parador on the edge of town just off the main road. Eat at the modern restaurant opposite. C.

(R)**La Charola**. This must be one of the great motorway cafés of Europe. Typical Leonese cooking with a Galician touch. Excellent value. D–C.

The River Duero

The 936km of the Duero drains the sierras of the northern *Meseta* that comprises the southern slopes of the Cordillera Cantábrica and the western valleys of the Sistema Central. Of the five great rivers of the Peninsula, this is the least polluted and, though it lacks the might of the Ebro, the splendour of the Guadalquivir, or the drama of the Tajo, it irrigates more lands than any of them. Culturally and materially, it is the heart of Castile.

The river rises among the great pine forests of Monte Urbión, bordering northern Soria and La Rioja. For the first kilometres of its course it zigzags through rock-strewn highlands past stone-built villages such as **Molinos de Duero** and **Vinuesa** into the icy, glacial waters of the Laguna Negra. The landscape is bleak. Logging trucks chunter up the steep, twisting slopes, eagles hang in the cold air currents, and snow completely blankets the earth through the long winters. The villages smell of wood-smoke well into May.

Though Soria is the most underpopulated province of Iberia with fewer than ten people per square kilometre, it has a peculiar isolated beauty. Nowhere is this more dramatically apparent than at **Numancia**, the first great heath-clad promontory overlooking the Duero plain. The place is encircled by dark, shadowy hillsides, which appear to have been left bare by centuries of incessant grazing. Below, across the plain, runs the meandering course of the Duero.

Numancia is another of those mythical places rooted deep in Spain's historical psyche. Today, it is simply an archeological curiosity, where a few travellers come to look at the monument, the weed-infested excavations and immovable, circular millstones. But this was once a thriving Celtiberian city of 10,000 inhabitants that became the great thorn in the side of the Roman occupation of Hispania. After years of siege, the city was finally taken by the legions of Scipio in 133 BC, though the Numancians preferred cannibalism and mass suicide to surrender, and few survivors were taken. The impressive artefacts of this civilization are to be seen in the Museo Numantino, or in the Archeological Museum in the provincial capital of Soria a few kilometres away. Of particular interest is the polychromed pottery incised with patterns of different animals and human figures.

SORIA (pop. 32,000) may once have been Castile's most inspiring provincial capital, but this is certainly no longer the case. Gone are the centuries of isolation that lent it the air of a living Romanesque city at the beginning of this century, and encouraged several of the greatest poets and writers of the Generation of '98, which included Unamuno, Bécquer and Antonio Machado, to immortalize it in verse. The gracious golden sandstone towers and plazas have been swamped in the last 30 years by urbanization of the worst kind. Nevertheless, Soria still possesses some of the most beautiful 11th- and 12th-century churches in Castile, and for those alone it merits a short visit; it is also a good base for those who wish to explore the province.

The city is built between two hills – Castillo and Mirón – rising above a curve in the Duero. Its naturally defended position gave it great strategic importance in the Middle Ages as a junction between the kingdoms of Castile, Aragón and Navarre. Of the Romanesque buildings, the most interesting are the two cloisters of the co-cathedral of San Pedro and San Juan de Duero, both near the river. Though roofless and semi-ruined, the latter shows evidence of strong Mudéjar decorative influences and appears notably strange in contrast to the pure simplicity of the church (now a museum). In the town the interior of San Juan de Rebanera is one of the most balanced examples of pure Castilian Romanesque to be found in the region. Santo Domingo is more notable for its west façade, which shows a stronger French or Poitevin influence.

Though the capital is a slight disappointment when compared to other great Castilian cities, the province of Soria certainly makes up for it. Beyond the culture that spread along the Duero there are several stunning Sorian villages. One such place is **Medinaceli** (pop. 1,000), set in an exalted position on a lonely limestone mountain, from where it commands breathtaking views over the *Meseta* and the province of Guadalajara. The place was an important Celtiberian, Roman and Moorish settlement and it was here in 1002 that Al-Mansur died after his campaigns against the Christian kingdoms of the north. Later that century the lands were given to El Cid. But the town's present name – meaning 'city of the sky' – derives from more recent times, when the surrounding areas formed the estates of the Dukes of Medinaceli, whose 18th-century palace occupies one complete side of the Plaza Mayor.

Of a different beauty is the monastery of **Santa María de Huerta**, east of Medinaceli on the border with Aragón. Founded in 1162 and generously endowed by Alfonso VIII, a king responsible for patronizing a great deal of Sorian Romanesque architecture, this is arguably the greatest Cistercian monastery in Castile. A short drive to the north leads to an equally compelling example of military architecture at **Monteagudo de los Vicarias**.

Returning to the Duero, the next town of prominence is **Almazán** (pop. 6,000), whose name hints at its importance as an Arab stronghold, though it remained influential after it was reconquered by Alfonso I of Aragón in 1128. Park in the Plaza Mayor opposite the Hurtado de Mendoza Palace beside the Romanesque church of San Miguel. On the outside, this is remarkable for its strong Mudéjar details and brick belfry. Inside, the star-vaulted cupola and stone carvings depicting the murder of St Thomas à Becket are both exceptional. The town is also interesting for its walls, gates and peaceful position beside the river.

After Almazán the wheat prairies and agricultural basin of the Duero begins in earnest and you enter one of the most sublime stretches of open road in Soria. Continue to **Berlanga de Duero** (pop. 1,500), whose humble village is guarded over by one of the most robust and spectacular *castillos* in this land of castles. The impressive line of cylindrical-towered curtain walls protect a majestic structure, which is the former palace of the Marquises of Berlanga.

On entering the village it is equally astonishing to find a massive Gothic–Renaissance collegiate church dwarfing the humble farmhouses and narrow streets radiating from the Plaza Mayor. It was constructed in 1526 by an architect from Burgos, Juan de Racines, and in terms of scale and its collection of Baroque altarpieces, it is one of the great hall-churches of the 16th century.

A few kilometres south-east from Berlanga, reached by a road just outside **Casillas de Berlanga**, is another church that in terms of size and age could not provide a more curious contrast. **San Baudelio de Berlanga** is one of the great beauties of Mozarabic culture – a tiny *ermita* with the artistic significance of a cathedral. On entering, you are immediately struck by the large central column, like a palm tree, from the middle of which radiate eight broad vaulting ribs. To the Muslims the palm was a symbol of reason overcoming doubt; it stood at the centre of almost every Cordoban patio during the height of the Caliphate, and one cannot help but feel that the small party of refugee monks who constructed San Baudelio at the end of the tenth or beginning of the 11th century had the same considerations in mind.

At the west end of the church is a

gallery supported by 18 miniature columns forming horseshoe arches. Theories differ as to the use of the gallery and the minute oratory pierced by two windows, but it was most probably intended to segregate the monks from the congregation. Another peculiar feature is the anchorites' cave, which was inhabited by the founding fathers of San Baudelio before the church was built and later used as a hiding place in times of danger.

But the frescoes that once completely covered the interior are the most extraordinary feature of the church. Many were stolen in 1922 and sold to American dealers, though they have since been restored and now lie in the vaults of the Prado in Madrid. Once again, several conflicting theories exist as to the significance and symbolism of these paintings. One possible explanation – the one the guardian likes to give about those that remain – is that the profuse number of animals, including dogs, camels, rabbits, elephants, bulls, bears, deer, horses and falcons, were intended to give the feeling that this was a spiritual fort, a kind of landlocked Noah's Ark.

The **Castillo de Gormaz** lies about 30km to the west of San Baudelio and was constructed at about the same time, but it is in complete contrast to that humble, struggling community and its diminutive church. This massive Arabian fortress demonstrates the strength and splendour of the Caliphate at its zenith. The ruins of its mighty walls and towers sit on a naturally disguised crown of rock. A road leads from the village lying in its shadow, to just below the main *castillo* entrance. On a clear day, looking through the great horseshoe gateways, the views are unprecedented – to the north across the lonely expanses of Soria as far as the Sierra de la Demanda, and to the south-west over the invisible 'black' or slate villages of the northern Guadarrama towards Madrid.

The Baroque towers of **El Burgo de Osma** (pop. 5,000), just 15km to the north as the raven flies from Gormaz, are obscured by another castellated peak; nonetheless, this is one of the Duero's most enchanting towns. Park in the wooden porticoed plaza in front of the beautifully carved, late 13th-century south door that gives access to the **cathedral**. From here you will be given an hour-long conducted tour of the cathedral and its numerous treasures by the sacristan and a covey of local children who switch the lights on and off as you enter and leave each room. Artistically, the cathedral offers an almost indigestible succession of side-chapels and chapterhouse/museum rooms of various dates from 1100 to 1900. It contains several treasures, including the 11th-century *Beato de Liébana* and 15th-century *Book of Devotions*.

The core of the cathedral and vaulting is essentially Gothic (1232–1300), although strong Romanesque influences are noticeable in several window details and capital heads. The high altar (1550–54) is a fine Renaissance work by Juan de Juni, Juan Picardo and Pedro Andrés. On Easter Thursday, Friday and Saturday it is covered with the Veil of the Passion, a vast painted altar shroud attributed to Alonso Berruguete although it is more likely to have been done by one of his pupils. The wrought-iron *reja* (screen) guarding the high altar is no less magnificent, and is the work of Joan Francés, better known for his work in Toledo cathedral. The white marble pulpit beside it is attributed to the school of Gil de Siloé at the end of the 15th century.

The side-chapels are equally imposing, particularly the neoclassic Capilla del Venerable Palafox, a rich combination of jasper and bronze by Juan de Villanueva and Francesco Sabatini (1772–81), erected in honour of the former bishop and viceroy of Peru, Juan de Palafox. The Capilla del Santo Cristo del Milagro shows how Baroque extravagance can swamp an exceptional Romanesque Christ.

On the way through to the museum, you pass the 13th-century carved and polychromed sepulchre of San Pedro de Osma, supported on the backs of peculiarly human-looking lions. Like an animated cartoon in limestone, it tells the story of the saint's life, depicting in low relief those people he cured and the pilgrimages he undertook, as well as more menial activities such as eating and drinking.

The museum continues through the remaining rooms with a good collection of manuscripts, reliquary boxes, enamels, chalices, carvings and retables. From the late Gothic cloister there is an ant's-eye view of the Baroque tower by Domingo Ondategui, which was added between 1739 and 1744. The sacristan will make sure that you leave the cathedral culturally exhausted, and some sort of restorative will be required before you explore El Burgo de Osma's other main sight, the hospital of San Agustin. This plain Herreran building is to be found in the Plaza Mayor, and is a sober respite after the extravagance of the cathedral.

The Duero is rejoined at **San Esteban de Gormaz**, site of another *castillo* but better known for its two Romanesque churches, San Miguel

and Rivero. Both of them are worth visiting to see the internal galleries and atrium supported by carved capitals inspired by Mudéjar motifs. About 38km south of San Esteban, across empty highlands, stands a similar porticoed church at **Tiermes**. But the village really warrants the detour for the peculiar excavations of a rupestrian or troglodyte city, dug out by the central Iberian people, the *Arevacoes*, more than 2,500 years ago. These tribesmen were not conquered by the Romans until 98 BC, and the subterranean houses were used by their descendants as a final refuge. An Archeological Museum tracing the various cultures that have occupied the place since then has been built on the site.

Leaving San Esteban, the road skirts the north bank of the Duero and bypasses the ruined *castillo* at **Langa de Duero**, before crossing the provincial border from Soria into Burgos. Here you enter the first main wine-growing district. Leave the river and turn off for **Peñaranda de Duero**. This is guarded by the crenellated silhouette of another *castillo* on a karstic spur dominating a fertile valley of vineyards.

The dusty, broken-down, half-timbered village is seen at its best in the late afternoon when the bars are half-filled with old men playing *mus*, and the sun seems to gloss over the cracked walls and piles of rubble with a deep golden light. Peñaranda has three features worth stopping for: a lovingly preserved 17th-century pharmacy and, facing each other in the Plaza Mayor, a large collegiate church and the Renaissance palace of the Duques de Avellaneda. The last of these three is a school, but it can be visited if you ask the caretaker discreetly. The palace was designed by Francis of Cologne

A view across the wild karstic landscape of Castile and León. Incafo

and built in 1520 for Don Luis de Zúñiga, Count of Miranda, later becoming the property of the Empress Eugénie, wife of Napoleon III.

You enter through a boldly carved doorway into a magnificent Plateresque patio with an arcaded gallery running around the four sides of the first floor. The high-relief medallions of Roman emperors in between the columns are a flamboyant detail matched by an elegant marble staircase. The great interior feature of the rooms are the carved ceilings; in fact, this is the most important single collection of *artesonado* ceilings in the Peninsula.

From Peñaranda the road follows the poplar-shaded river Arandilla to **Aranda de Duero** (pop. 29,000), the capital of southern Burgos and a good place for a glass of wine and a quick look at the Isabelline Plateresque door of the church of Santa María. There is little else to detain you here, and it is best to continue along the north bank of the river to **Roa de Duero**. Again, this is a rather colourless place, where Cardinal Cisneros, the great archbishop of Toledo, died on his way to meet Charles I in 1517. For their views across the Duero, the Gothic hall-church and the placid, arcaded Plaza Mayor are worth a fleeting visit.

Peñafiel (pop. 6,000) has much more to offer its visitors. The *castillo* seems to float across the flat horizons of the Duero like a ship without sails. It was constructed towards the end of the 15th century on the site of older fortifications, and is a perfect example of a ridge castle built on a crest of rock, referred to in early chronicles as 'the most faithful rock of Castilla'. Peñafiel's peculiarity is that, apart from the Torre de Homenaje, it is uninhabitable and useful only as an impregnable position overlooking the river. Its dimensions alone are indicative of this: 212m by 32m at its widest point.

The village, too, has a suitably eccentric appearance. The Plaza Mayor is covered in sand, reminding everyone that this is one of the oldest bullfighting venues in Spain. All the houses surrounding the square are shuttered against the heat and cold until the appointed day of the fight, when the blinds are lifted and Peñafiel celebrates in a style perfected over a period of 500 years. The main church of San Pablo is notable for its Mudéjar details.

As Peñafiel retreats in the rear-view mirror, the road cuts along the southern bank of the Duero before turning north towards **VALLADOLID** (pop. 325,000) which, although not technically on the Duero, is large enough for its industrial presence to be felt. This is the regional capital of Castile–León, the administrative and commercial mecca of the central *Meseta* and seat of an archbishopric and university. But, apart from a few good monuments and a Museum of Medieval Art, this busy and confusing metropolis is of interest mainly to historically-minded travellers as a 16th-century capital, about which a few words should be said.

Before Madrid was made capital in 1561, Valladolid had become the principal city of Castile; Columbus died there in 1506 and it was the birthplace of Philip II (1527) and Anne of Austria (1601). The years from 1460 to 1530 were the city's great epoch, when it was the primary seat of royal power. Two of its greatest buildings, both of them Plateresque, date from that time: the sculpted façade of the church of **San Pablo** (1463) and the **Colegio de San Gregorio**, now containing the Museo Nacional de Escultura Religiosa. The museum was established after the *desamortización* (dissolution) in 1836 as a sanctuary for some of the best medieval religious polychrome sculpture. Work by most of the great Castilian carvers can be seen here, and Alonso Berruguete, Diego de Siloé, Gregorio Fernández and Juan de Juni are all well represented.

The Plaza Mayor, a favourite location with the Inquisition for their *autos-da-fé*, is the centre of the old town. In the surrounding streets you will find the extraordinary church of **San Benito** by Gil de Hontañón; the **cathedral** (worked on by the unlikely combination of Juan de Herrera and Alberto Churriguera, but never finished); and several imposing Renaissance and Baroque palaces. The problem with Valladolid, though, is that it does not cater readily to the traveller. Churches are too often closed, parking can be tiresomely difficult, and even the tourist office staff seem reluctant to impart the most basic information. But if you find yourself with time on your hands, you may consider visiting the three small museums dedicated to Cervantes, Columbus and the Romantic poet Zorrilla, as well as the peculiar Museo Oriental, with its very disoriented mixture of pottery and art from China, the Philippines, Peru and Colombia, collected mainly by Jesuit missionaries.

If you bypass Valladolid then **Simancas** is a quieter and less hectic alternative as a place to stop. This is an anonymous-looking village with an impressive *castillo* that guards the lion's share of the national archive – over 33 million documents. Admittance can be gained to look at a few of the more sensational primary sources of Spanish history, such as marriage certificates and the autographs of illustrious rulers. From Simancas, the road enters the *Tierra del Vino* to Tordesillas.

Tordesillas (pop. 7,000), rising above its arched bridge over the Duero, has been of great significance since classical times, when it was known as *Turris Sillae*. Park your car in or close to the whitewashed and porticoed Plaza Mayor and explore from there on foot. The town's most notable historical date was 7 June 1494, when a treaty between the Spanish and Portuguese fixed the Meridian of Tordesillas and settled the boundaries of discovery and colonization in the New World between the two maritime powers. Castile was effectively given all lands west of Brazil, even though the whole of South America was yet to be discovered.

The most historic monument in the city is the Real Convento de Santa Clara, originally a Mudéjar palace founded in 1340 by Alfonso XI (1312–50) to celebrate his victory at the Battle of Salado. Moorish masons and carpenters from Seville and Toledo were commissioned to carry out the work. The decoration of the Mudéjar state rooms and the Arab patio typify the influence of the conquerors upon the Spanish monarchs, who wished to emulate the luxurious manners and lifestyles of the sultans. During the reign of Pedro I (1350–69) the building was given to Alfonso's illegitimate daughters as a convent, which it has effectively remained ever since.

It was here that Juana 'la Loca' (the Mad), the daughter of *Los Reyes Católicos* and mother of Charles I, went into self-imposed seclusion for almost half a century (1506–55) after the death of her husband. Sad rather than mad, however, would be a better sobriquet than the one history has designated to her memory, for her problem was not insanity but rather manic depression. The monastery can be visited under the guidance of the Patrimonio Nacional, who give a highly detailed tour of the main state rooms and works of art.

It is also worth visiting the Gothic brick church of San Antolín near the monastery, which is now a Museum of Sacred Art and Sculpture. Of passing interest is the Virgin known as Nuestra Señora de la Guía, who supposedly guided Francisco Pizarro on his conquest of Peru and is honoured every September with the most important local *fiesta*.

After Tordesillas, the Duero winds south and then north, crossing the provincial border between Valladolid and Zamora, before rejoining the road at **Toro** (pop. 10,000). The country is given over to wide irrigated fields and vineyards whose Tempranillo grape produces the dark, full-bodied red wine Rivera de Duero, which can be drunk in any bar in town for around 30 pesetas a glass and is a delicious accompaniment to all roast meats.

Toro is another of those half-forgotten *Meseta* towns endowed with magnificent but run-down buildings, each one a testament to its former greatness. It was here in 1476 that the decisive battle took place between the faction of La Beltraneja, backed by the Portuguese army, and Los Reyes Católicos, whose victory placed the crown of Castile firmly on the head of Isabel. In 1645 the Count Duke Olivares, the great minister of Philip IV, died here, haunted by his part in the financial and military downfall of the country and empire he had essentially ruled over from 1622.

Park beside the Colegiata de Santa María la Mayor; this superb building, along with the cathedrals at old Salamanca and Zamora, is of a school of Romanesque architecture unique to the 13th-century kingdom of León. The style is remarkable for exquisite sculpted details and peculiar lantern towers. Inside, the dome above the crossing, surrounded by columns, allows a constant stream of light to illuminate several important Gothic tombs of the Fonseca and Ulloa dynasties and a portrait known as the *Virgen de la Mosca* (Virgin of the Fly), whose face is supposedly that of Queen Isabel.

If asked, the sacristan of the colegiata will show you the other Romanesque church of San Lorenzo, which is interesting for the friezes of Mudéjar patterns and a Gothic retable by Fernando Gallego. Toro has two other good Mudéjar churches – San Salvador and Santo Sepulcro – and a good Baroque clocktower, the Torre del Reloj, rising on the opposite side of the old town from the colegiata.

Overall, Toro is a place that should not be rushed through in a long afternoon but should be peacefully enjoyed overnight, when the bars around the crooked porticoes of the Plaza Mayor fill with local life, and the dim alleys of the old *converso* quarter and the view from the *Mirador* beside Santa María make for atmospheric after-dinner ambles.

ZAMORA (pop. 60,000) is one of the most prosperous cities of Castile, made rich by the surrounding seas of wheat and vines. Its name romantically derives from the Arabic word for turquoise – *samurah* – though the Romanesque heart of the ancient city you see today dates mainly from 1065 and the reign of Ferdinand I. The strong defensive walls and the town's naturally safeguarded position on a spur above the Duero are a reminder that for many centuries this was a highly contested city near the frontier between Spain and Portugal.

Follow the signs through the modern suburbs to the *centro ciudad* (town centre) and the *Parador Nacional,* then park in front of the parador or as near to it as you can. Like Toro, Zamora will need at least a day to be appreciated to the full, and you will need longer if you find Romanesque architecture particularly interesting. The cathedral lies at the western end of the city near the garden containing the castle and traitors' gate. It was founded and endowed by Alfonso VII in 1135, completed in 1171 and, although a featureless Renaissance façade was built around the north door, the original oriental-looking structure is still apparent.

The unique composition of the tower, *cimborio* (turreted lantern), graceful colonnaded windows and the rooftops tiled with slabs of stone in a fish-scale pattern give Zamora a unique position in Spain's complex cathedral history. Most experts agree that the architect was influenced by the construction of the church of the Holy

Sepulchre in Jerusalem, built a few years prior to the construction of the cathedral in Zamora. The interior is equally impressive for the massive piers, the *media naranja* cupola, choir-stalls in the style of Rodrigo Alemán, and the delicate ironwork of the *rejas* and pulpit. Upstairs in the museum are an exceptional series of 15th-century Flemish tapestries, recognizable from their use of black thread and the Gothic-style interpretation of classical themes such as the history of Tarquin and the Siege of Troy.

Zamora's other Romanesque churches are too numerous to describe in detail and are generally quite difficult to gain access to unless a service is taking place. It may be said that the whole of the city centre is a 'museum of Romanesque'. The most enjoyable way to discover them is to walk through the streets joined by sleepy little plazas, and hope you will stumble upon one that is open. But even if they are closed, their exterior carving and proportional purity are generally distinguished enough to make the search worth-while.

The recent prosperity of Zamora has meant that the city is currently under-going a serious programme of restora-tion, and modern gallery spaces are being created in several old señorial palaces. The Museo de la Semana Santa, in a rather ugly building in Plaza Santa María la Nueva, contains a col-lection of *pasos* (processional sculp-tures) that are used during Holy Week. The general Museo de Zamora still awaits inauguration. There are, how-ever, generally quite good travelling exhibitions to be seen; and the elegant provincial shops in the new part of town provide a fascinating contrast, especially at night, to the rather austere historic centre.

After passing between the delicate arches of the bridge at Zamora, the waters of the Duero course more dra-matically towards Portugal, cutting a deep canyon through granite outcrops. For 136km the river forms the frontier between the two nations, in an area important as a nesting ground for sev-eral magnificent species of raptor that nest in the inhospitable cliffs and hunt across the bleak escarpments of the Sierra de Sanabria to the north. Vil-lages are scarce. In Portugal the river becomes known as the Douro, passing beneath hilltop communities that sur-vive by fishing, and by farming the famous port-wine grapes. Its waters are finally disgorged into the Atlantic beyond Oporto.

TOURIST OFFICES

SORIA: Pl Ramón y Cajal, tel (975) 21 20 52.

VALLADOLID: Plaza de Zorrilla 3, tel (983) 35 18 01.

ZAMORA: Santa Clara 20, tel (988) 51 18 45.

Accommodation, Eating and Drinking

SORIA (tel code 975):

(H)**Parador Antonio Machado**, Parque del Castillo, tel 21 34 45. A modern and comfortable parador overlooking the city and river. C.
(R)**Casa Garrido**, Vicente Tutor 8, tel 22 20 68. Near the bullring, with a good *tapas* bar and restaurant serving typical Sorian cuisine. C–B.

MEDINACELI:

(H&R)**Duque de Medinaceli**, Ctra N11 km150, tel (975) 32 61 11. Adequate overnight stop for travellers. Good restaurant decorated with antique clocks. D–C.

EL BURGO DE OSMA:

(H&R)**Virrey Palafox**, Universidad 7, tel (975) 34 02 22. Adequate rooms. Restaurant is one of the best in Castile. Specialities: all game and fish dishes. Excellent *bodega*. D&B.

PEÑAFIEL (tel code 983):

(H)**Infante Don Juan Manuel**, Ctra Valladolid/Soria km56, tel 88 03 61. Good atmosphere and relaxed Castilian bar. E–D.
(R)**Asador Mauro**, Atarazanas, tel 88 04 98. Castilian food. C.

VALLADOLID:

(H)**Imperial**, Peso 4, tel (983) 33 03 00. In a 16th-century palace. C.

TORDESILLAS (tel code 983):

(H)**Parador de Tordesillas**, Ctra N620 km155, tel 77 00 51. A favourite stop for people travelling between Madrid and the north. Good views. C.
(H&R)**Hostal Juan Manuel**, N620 Ctra Burgos–Portugal, km 151, tel 77 04 11. Basic accommodation. Good restaurant. D–C.

TORO:

(H)**Juan II**, Plaza del Espolón 1, tel (988) 69 03 00. Magnificent views over the Duero basin. Typical Castilian food. Excellent local wine. D&C.

ZAMORA (tel code 988):

(H)**Parador Condes de Alba y Aliste**, Plaza Viriato 5, tel 51 44 97. Magnificent 15th-century palace in the centre of city, with suits of armour and antiques around the glassed-in Renaissance patio. C–B.
(H)**Pensión Balborraz**, Balborraz 25, tel 51 55 20. Very much a downtown pension above a bar and restaurant, but what it lacks in luxury it makes up for with atmosphere. E.
(R)**Pizarro**, Cuesta Pizarro 7, tel 53 43 66. Beside the Duero. Traditional Zamoran

cooking served by waiters in local costume. Beautiful courtyard around medieval well. B.

(R)**Paris**, Av de Portugal 14, tel 51 43 25. Popular local haunt. Typical local cooking. B.

PUEBLA DE SANABRIA:

(H)**Parador de Puebla de Sanabria**, Ctra del Lago 18, tel (988) 62 00 01. This parador, and the one below, are excellent for exploring the north-west of the region and the River Esla. C–B.

BENAVENTE:

(H)**Parador Rey Fernando II de León**, Paseo Ramón y Cajal, tel (988) 63 03 04. An ancient seat of the Castilian court, beautifully restored. Good views over the Esla valley. C–B.

Southern Sierras and Cathedral Cities

The Sierra de Guadarrama and Sierra de Gredos, comprising the central and southern *massifs* of the Sistema Central, creates the natural south-eastern boundary of Castile–León. This route is most easily approached from Madrid. **SEGOVIA** (pop. 52,000) lies an hour away from the capital, and is reached by taking the first exit after the tunnel through the mountains on the N-IV La Coruña–Madrid autoroute. To do the city justice, you will need at least one night and two full days to explore its many important monuments; more time if the nearby palaces of La Granja and Riofrío are to be visited.

This is undoubtedly one of the most pleasant small cities of the *Meseta*, impressively set beneath the sierra, richly endowed architecturally and with an easy pace of life. Most roads enter by way of the roundabout in the shadow of the aqueduct. From there it is best to carry on up the hill to the

Plaza Mayor in the town centre. From here everything can be quite easily explored: the main Romanesque churches and Renaissance urban palaces, the narrow alleyways of the Jewish Quarter and the local Museo de Bellas Artes.

The **cathedral** occupies a corner of the Plaza Mayor. This is a late Gothic edifice, started in 1525 under the direction of Juan Gil de Hontañón. The impressive interior reflects the elegance and austerity of the outside, and contains several important works by Castilian carvers, including a good retable by Juan de Juni in the Capilla del Santo Entierro. The museum and Sala Capitular are reached through the rather jaded cloister by Juan Guas, though from here there is a dramatic view of the cathedral tower.

A short walk down the hill from the cathedral is the *Alcázar*, perched on the edge of a steep spur of rock at one end of the old town. This fantastical, Xanadu-like building was once a royal residence, used in particular by the

Trastamaran kings during the 15th century, and it was restored rather too enthusiastically after a fire in 1862. You enter across a drawbridge that spans a moat cut into the rock. A few interior rooms have been turned into a Museum of Armour and Weapons; of the state rooms, several good Gothic–Mudéjar details remain. The *artesonados* (inlaid wooden ceilings) in themselves are worth the visit.

Looking from the battlements of the Plaza del Alcázar north over the valley of the River Eresma, there are several buildings of interest outside the old city walls. In the convent of Carmelitas Descalzas are the remains of the poet and mystic, San Juan de la Cruz, whose simple tomb was replaced earlier this century by the monstrous marble monument seen today. Next door, the dodecagonal Templar church of La Vera Cruz (1208) is interesting above all for its shape and the views from its tower. The Casa de la Moneda minted all the national money until 1730, but is now abandoned. The Hieronymite monastery of Parral, once set in a legendary Castilian garden, is now maintained by a handful of monks; a fine Plateresque retable can be seen in the chapel. All these buildings make an enjoyable half-day extramural walk.

The third great monument of Segovia besides the cathedral and *alcázar* is the **Roman aqueduct**, dating from the first and second centuries AD. This is one of the great testaments to Roman engineering extant in the Iberian Peninsula, and would be considered a remarkable construction in any age. It is built from undressed granite ashlars, which hang together with no binding agent except gravitational precision, and is over 762m long and 29m high in parts. When Segovia was an important military outpost of Hispania, the aqueduct was constructed to channel the waters of the River Riofrío into the city from 16km away, and remained in use almost without interruption for the next 1,800 years. Though it still functions today, its workload has been substituted by modern sanitation methods. At the eastern end of the aqueduct is the monastery of **San Antonio El Real**, occupied by Franciscan nuns, who will show you around if you ring the bell and wait. This was originally a private palace of the Trastamaran kings, and contains several superb 14th- and 15th-century *artesonado* ceilings off a very beautiful cloister.

A grand flight of steps rises to the western end of the aqueduct, and from here you can explore the several smaller features of interest in the old inner city. The Romanesque churches are worth seeking out, particularly **San Martín** and **San Esteban**. Segovian Romanesque dates mainly from the 12th and 13th centuries, and is characterized by the atria (colonnaded lateral porticoes), which were probably used as covered market places and general civic meeting places before the advent of the *ayuntamiento* (town hall). Other defining characteristics of the style include the gargoyle-like corbels; Mudéjar-inspired timber ceilings; and a preference for frescoes. In all, there are 18 Romanesque churches in and around the city; the extramural churches worth the detour are **San Justo** for its frescoes, and **San Millán**.

Calle Real, Segovia's main shopping mall, contains the **Casa de los Picos**, with a strange Plateresque façade of pyramid-shaped stones. This is the most extreme example of exterior wall decoration that adorns so much

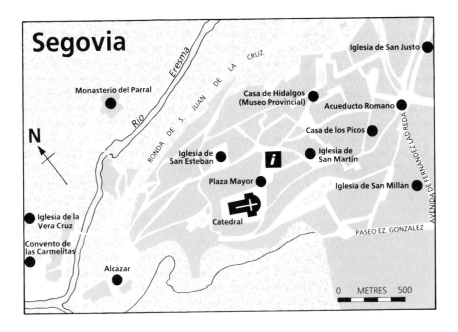

Segovian architecture. The more typical patterning is two- rather than three-dimensional, and is known as *esgrafiado* – once again possibly a Mudéjar invention, whereby the cement and plaster used to cover a building is skilfully worked into repetitive patterns.

The main museum is the **Museo de Segovia**, whose collection is split between the Casa del Sol in the Paseo Juan II, and the section of Bellas Artes in the Casa del Hidalgo in Calle San Agustín. The latter contains some fine painting and glass from the former glass factory at La Granja.

La Granja de San Ildefonso (pop. 5,000) lies 11km south-east of Segovia, above the village of San Ildefonso, and makes an enjoyable half-day – preferably afternoon – excursion from the city. The original hunting palace was erected for Henry IV (1454–74), but it was not until the reign of Philip V

(1700–46) that the present edifice was begun in what can clearly be seen as a strongly French style. There can be no doubt that the first Bourbon King of Spain, influenced by his education at Versailles, had a definite predilection for the high court tastes of Louis XIV. The palace can be visited, and incorporates a few rather overpoweringly overdecorated rooms that are interesting for a few pieces of furniture and glass. In the chapel lie the tombs of Philip V and his wife, Isabel Farnese. It is in the gardens, however, that more of your time should be spent.

The grounds stretch over 145ha and are planted mainly with avenues of elm and chestnut; they were designed by the French landscapers Carlier and Boutelou in the 18th century and are remarkable above all for their Baroque bronze fountains depicting familiar allegorical and classical scenes such as the Dance of the Three Graces. Sadly, their consumption of water is so great that they are seen to function on only a few afternoons and evenings in the year and even then at the convenience of the Patrimonio Nacional. However, ask at the tourist office in Segovia or Madrid to find out whether they will be in operation on your visit, as the spectacle of them in full flow should on no account be missed.

Segovia's other local royal palace of **Riofrío** rises above a deer park 10km south of the city. This is less formal and was built by Italian architects for Isabel Farnese after the death of Philip V. Its pink and peeling green façade and stable yard have a faded elegance. Inside, there is a museum dedicated to hunting prints and associated paraphernalia.

From Segovia the route continues north along the N110, turning off after 25km to **Pedraza** (pop. 500), a beautiful medieval walled village that has been thoughtfully restored. It is a popular weekend resort for Madrileños seeking good Castilian cooking and fresh country air. The old Plaza Mayor, surrounded by houses supported by stone and wooden pillars, still serves as a bullring at the *fiesta* held each year in the second week of September. From the *castillo*, the former residence of the painter Ignacio Zuloaga, dramatic views extend over the surrounding *Meseta*.

The road north bypasses Castilnovo, whose towers rise from a forest of pines and birch trees, and leads to **Sepúlveda** (pop. 1,500), a superbly sited Romanesque town on a precipitous spur above the River Duratón. Sepúlveda's fortunes peaked during the 12th century due to its favourable *fueros* (governing rights), granted by

Alfonso VI in 1076, which gave the village virtual autonomy. The three main churches of El Salvador, San Bartolomé and San Justo all date from that period and are fine examples of the provincial Romanesque style. From Sepúlveda, the round trip to Segovia can be completed by way of **Turégano** (pop. 1,300) with its impressive ruins of a *castillo* and church.

Another worthwhile local detour takes you a few kilometres north-west of Sepúlveda to the anonymous-looking village of **Villaseca**, where a dirt road traverses the isolated *Meseta* to the church of San Frutos del Duratón. Few buildings can boast of a more precarious situation, perching as it does on the summit of the mighty canyon carved out by the Duratón, whose green waters wind their way slowly towards the Duero. Though the church is usually locked, it has good exterior sculptures, and some strange body-shaped graves carved into the rock. Above all, the bumpy ride is worthwhile for the views of the natural rock-strewn wastelands of the *Meseta* disappearing into infinite horizons.

Continuing west through the wheatlands and sleepy stone villages of Segovia, you pass through a succession of towns presided over by massive *castillos* that formerly defended the western marches of the provinces and were seats of important local families in the 14th and 15th centuries. To the south of the province the great umbrella pine trees are sporadically tapped and the sap used in the manufacture of paraffin.

Cuéllar (pop. 9,500) is distinguished by its mass of Mudéjar belfries, and the 15th-century *castillo* with a Renaissance courtyard, which was the former residence of the Dukes of Albur-

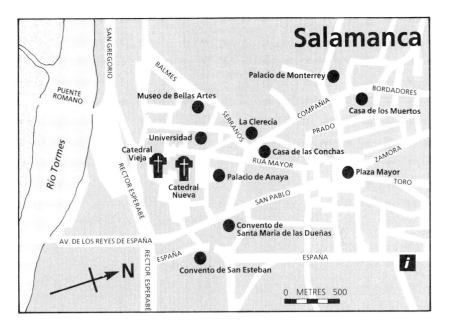

querque. **Coca** (pop. 2,200) has a pretentiously oversized brick *castillo* in an essentially Gothic form, although the decorative details and construction were obviously undertaken by Moorish craftsmen. The village's Gothic church of Santa María contains tombs of the Fonseca family. **Arévalo** (pop. 7,000), the southernmost of the towns, is another centre of Mudéjar architecture, with several important brick churches in varying states of restoration; a few crumbling señorial palaces and more than a handful of *antiguedades* (antique shops). **Olmedo** (pop. 4,000) has a similar collection of Mudéjar edifices.

The 14th- and 15th-century economy that financed these now dust-blown and forlorn towns was based on the sheep trade centred at **Medina del Campo** (pop. 20,000). From its present state, it is hard to imagine that this community once hosted the most important trade fairs and markets in Europe, which attracted Genoese bankers and Hungarian and Polish merchants. The brick-faced *castillo*, like that at Coca, dominates the town, and is another fine example of Spain's very individual interpretation of Gothic military architecture.

South of Medina rises the walled *pueblo* of **Madrigal de las Altas Torres** (pop. 2,000), one of Castile's most illustrious royal *pueblos* and a place certainly worth a few hours of your time. The perimeter wall – 2,300m in circumference – contains another Mudéjar core. But this otherwise rather dislocated Castilian village is better known as the birthplace of Isabel le Católica in 1451 and the home town of Gabriel Espinosa, the pretender to the Portuguese throne who was beheaded for treason by Philip II. The most interesting feature is the convent of Monjas Agustinas, the former palace of Juan II, Isabel's father.

You enter the convent through an old urban farmyard, complete with dozing dogs and nervous hens, and washing pegged onto the overhanging wooden balconies. The immaculately whitewashed cloister could not be in greater contrast. A nun then escorts you to the various royal chambers, into the chapel and upstairs to the bedroom where Isabel was born. There are several important antiques and relics, including a remarkable ivory Christ and the usual assortment of 16th-century objects, such as inlaid coffers, missionary chairs and heavy oak tables.

From the convent, walk to San Nicolás de Bari: the grand brick-built Gothic church in the smaller plaza on the other side of town. The sacristan lives next door. It is worth the effort for the *artesonado* ceiling that covers almost three-quarters of the roof's length, and for the various medieval objects arranged rather haphazardly in a side-chapel, including the font where Isabel was christened.

From Madrigal, the dry, horizonless wheatplains continue from the province of Avila to **SALAMANCA** (pop. 160,000), where the imposing silhouette of the cathedral rising above the River Tormes has been slightly throttled by the growth of modern urbanization. But, that apart, this is one of the great cities of Iberia and worth a visit above all for its unique examples of Plateresque and Baroque architecture. A few pleasurable days can be spent exploring Salamanca's sights as well as the province as a whole, including **Alba de Tormes** (pop. 4,000), the Sierra de Francia and the bull-breeding ranches around **Vitigudino**.

The centre of life in Salamanca is the grandiloquent **Plaza Mayor** (1733), where students and Salamantines gather in the afternoon to drink in the open-air cafés and watch the stone alchemize to a deep golden brown in the mellowing light. The plaza is generally acknowledged to be a Churrigueresque masterpiece and, though its main architects – Alberto Churriguera and Andrés García de Quiñones – were both great disciples of the form, the decoration is generally more restrained than the outlandish flights of fancy normally apparent in this style. The prevailing feeling given by the high-relief medallions of illustrious kings of Spain staring from between the arches of the arcade is essentially high Renaissance.

From the plaza, the Rua Mayor leads beside the Plateresque façade of the **Casa de las Conchas** (1483), founded by Rodrigo Maldonado, a Master of the Order of Santiago. There is no finer example of urban palace-building than this to show the development of Plateresque design, from the eccentric exterior carvings of scallopshells to the Renaissance decoration around the *rejas* (wrought-iron grilles) covering the Gothic *ajimez* (twin-arched windows). The interior twin-storeyed arcades of the courtyard are equally majestic, and complemented by a superb staircase and *artesonado* ceiling.

A few steps further on, you enter the Plaza de Anaya, where the neoclassic Palacio de Anaya on one side looks across the shaded square to the elevated mass of the new and old cathedrals. From the outside it is worth looking at the sumptuous carving around the Isabeline Plateresque west door (1513–33), with its retable-like masonry. Adjacent to this is the mighty belfry, containing the towers of both the original Romanesque and Gothic cathedrals. It was encased in stone in the mid-18th century to strengthen the structure after the Lisbon earthquake. The south side of the cathedral – best admired from the Plaza Chico – comprises the bulk of the older Romanesque church and features another example of a Romanesque lantern, known as the Torre del Gallo, with corner turrets and fish-scale tiles like those at Toro and Zamora. This was built in the Romanesque style unique to western Castile and the southern cities of the medieval kingdom of León.

Returning to the Plaza de Anaya you enter the **New Cathedral**, which is impressive above all for its star-vaulting: the work of the cathedral's main architect, Juan Gil de Hontañón. The basic style is late Gothic – 'the last Gothic breath in Spain' – but the choir and lantern are the work of the Baroque partnership of Joaquín Churriguera and Andrés García de Quiñones (1705–33). In the side-chapels are some more bombastic examples of their work, particularly the Capilla del Carmen, with its Byzantine crucifix that is entirely lost within the extravagant spirals of a retable by Joaquín Churriguera.

The **Old Cathedral** – 'where the air is solemn and more beautiful' – is reached down a short flight of steps from its new counterpart. This is a shrine to the Romanesque style (1102–60), which here reaches an artistic zenith in the carving of the capitals and the elevated simplicity of the space. It is a reflection upon the 16th-century bishops of Salamanca that they could ever have wished to replace this cathedral with their overbearing new one.

The retable (1445), consisting of 55 painted panels, is a masterpiece by Nicolás Florentino, who is also responsible for the fresco of the Last Judgement in the half-cupola above. A Romanesque mural on the same theme can be admired in the Capilla de San Martín. Elsewhere, you should be sure to see the sepulchre of Bishop Diego de Anaya, protected by an intricate wrought-iron *verja* (grating); and the cloister and museum that contains several works by the Salamantine retable painter, Fernando Gallego.

Make your way next to the **university**, which backs on to the west of the cathedral and is reached by turning left at the end of Calle Libreros. The entrance is another Plateresque masterpiece (1516–29) of Renaissance motifs, with a central medallion depicting *Los Reyes Católicos*, with coats-of-arms of Charles V and various 16th-century popes and cardinals woven together by a delicate mass of chiselled detailing. It is the *magnum opus* of the Plateresque movement.

The university of Salamanca was founded in 1218 by a charter granted by Alfonso IX and subsequently endowed by Alfonso X 'El Sabio' (the Learned). Originally it was housed in the old cathedral, but was extended towards the end of the 15th century to accommodate the expanding requirements of the schools. Surrounding the central courtyard are the main lecture rooms, some of which retain their original desks, benches and tables. The most notorious is the hall of Fray Luis de León, where the poet and mystic Luis de León was arrested by the Inquisition for translating the *Song of Songs*. After five years of imprisonment, he began his reinauguration lecture with the throwaway line: 'As we were discussing yesterday . . .' This century the hall was the setting for more unpleasant scenes concerning the poet and essayist Miguel de Unamuno, whose virulent attacks on the Nationalist party in 1936 led to his dismissal as Rector. There followed a long period of intellectual decline for the university, from which it is still recovering. A carved staircase leads up to the first floor and the gallery composed of mixtilinear arches, from which a Gothic door leads into the manuscripts library.

Outside again, in the small Patio de las Escuelas, presided over by a bronze statue of Fray Luis de León, you should proceed to the Escuelas Menores, reached via a short passage in the far left-hand corner of the plaza. It leads into a beautiful arched cloister and the **Museo de Bellas Artes**. This contains local archeological finds and some good examples of Gothic and Renaissance sculpture and painting, but the visit is worth making for the fresco *The Sky of Salamanca* by Fernando Gallego, depicting the constellations and signs of the zodiac. The university chaired one of the most important schools of astronomy during the 15th century.

Returning to the Plaza Mayor, you pass Le Clerecía, a heavy and overbearing Baroque seminary school with a massive domed roof and severe cloister. This is a favourite nesting place for the many white storks that glide nonchalantly between the towers of the cathedrals and churches.

Salamanca's two other great Plateresque masterpieces lie at the southern confluence of its two main shopping streets, Calle San Pablo and the Gran Via. The convent of **San Esteban** is distinguished by another remarkably detailed carved stone façade depicting the martyrdom of St Stephen. The cloister is by Juan de Badajoz, and the church by Juan de Alava, complete with a voluptuous retable by José de Churriguera, the founder of the dynasty. The sacristy and chapterhouse can also be visited.

Adjacent to San Esteban is the convent of **Santa María de las Dueñas**, which, though humbler in proportion, has possibly the most grotesquely decorated cloister in Europe. Contorted forms and faces lunge at you from every side. Skulls, monsters and mythical beasts that lurked so large in the Gothic imagination find here their ultimate release at the hands of the Plateresque masons.

Salamanca has many other sights, too numerous to list. Meriting mention, however, are the façades of the Palacio de Monterrey and the Casa de los Muertos, both west of the Plaza Mayor. A walk beside the river will take you to the Puente Romano and the Mudéjar church of Santiago where, every Sunday, a good flea-market is held.

On the road to Portugal, 88km west of Salamanca, lies **Ciudad Rodrigo** (pop. 16,000), rising from the midst of an expansive plain. This is another of those frontier cities – architecturally proud, but economically forsaken – whose palaces were abandoned decades ago and still lie shuttered up and forgotten. In recent years, Ciudad Rodrigo's fortunes have revived a little through agricultural prosperity, but its years of neglect under a relentless *Meseta* summer and winter have jaded it, albeit graciously.

A visit to the medieval core should begin with the cathedral, which is crowned by the southernmost of the thread of Romanesque lantern domes that begins with Toro and continues in

Zamora and Salamanca. The cathedral of Santa María, founded by Ferdinand II (1157–88) of León in 1170, was consecrated in 1230, the same year as the unification of the kingdoms of Castile and León. The Gothic cloister was not finished until the first quarter of the 16th century. The choirstalls are by Rodrigo Aléman, whose other works at Zamora and Plasencia are all fascinating for their choice of subject matter, best described in detail by a sacristan. Outside, above the west door, stands a line of 12 Old Testament characters, each in his own Gothic window; this is one of the most expressively detailed pieces of masonry in all Castile.

From here, walk through the streets to the *castillo* via the central plaza, enjoying the views from the battlemented walls. On the way a singular collection of **palaces** are to be seen: the Gothic Palacio de los Aguilas, and its three Plateresque counterparts, the Casa de los Cuetos, Palacio del Príncipe and Palacio de los Condes de Montarco. The civil architecture dates mainly from the 15th century, when the border with Portugal was delimited, before the discovery of the Americas. In many ways, it is a wonder that so much has survived, for this is another of the Spanish strategic fortress towns whose citizens' lives were interminably disrupted by the passage of wars. The real charm, as in so much of Castile, is that this is a place seldom visited and, for that reason, you'll probably wish you'd spent more time there.

Ciudad Rodrigo is the southwestern outpost of Castile. To the south spread the last volcanic tendrils of the Sistema Central. This rustic backwater is occupied by a smattering of small fortified *pueblos*, where the inhabitants are almost self-sufficient and travellers are treated with enormous hospitality but a kind incomprehension as to why they would want to visit these parts. The roads twist through miles of mountains into Extremadura: a bleak, dramatic landscape. The best time to visit is in the long spring, from March to June, when the fruit trees, the hillsides of wild thyme and lavender, and the pine forests and cork oaks blaze with colour.

The Sierra de Gata extends into the Portuguese Serra da Estrêla, but it is the Sierra de Francia that is somehow the most Castilian of all these southern mountain ranges. It lies 40km east of Ciudad Rodrigo, but is more impressively entered from the north via Salamanca. It begins with **Tamames**, a low-key place on the edge of the flat *Meseta*, where there's a stuffed bull's head in every bar. From there you begin to climb gently into foothills until, at the turning of a corner, the land falls away into distant waves of mountains. **La Alberca** is where the day-trippers go to marvel at these vestiges of western European agrarian village life, where the hills are too steep for tractors and all farming is still done either by hand or with the aid of mules. More authentic and poorer villages lie in the deeper recesses of the range.

For possibly the greatest view in all Castile, you should drive up the Peña de Francia to the monastery. On a clear day you can see across the great bull pasture plain of Salamanca to the Duero basin; west into Portugal; south across the ominous craters of Las Hurdes to the Embalse de Gabriel y Galán; and east to Béjar across the Sierra de Gredos to Avila.

The road east is slow and it will take a good four hours of steady driving to reach Avila, with not much of interest in between except breathtaking landscape and scenes of rural life. If you want to stay overnight in the Sierra de Francia, modest accommodation can be found at the fortified village of **Miranda de Castañar**, or less exciting alternatives at the run-down milling town of **Béjar** (pop. 18,000). A good two days can be spent exploring the surrounding sierra villages. In the summer the mountain streams are dammed to make freshwater swimming pools and every village, however small, holds a *fiesta* and bullfight.

El Barco de Avila (pop. 3,000) lies below the eastern side of the range and has a *castillo* almost as dominating as the mountains that surround it. The road continues north-east through the boulder-strewn plain of Avila, another heavily depopulated province which, along with Soria, has the most extreme *Meseta* climate of all. Here the landscape again becomes forbidding and bleak, with a few isolated farmhouses surrounded by fieldstone walls and conical haystacks; shepherds and transhumant flocks; buzzards and crows picking at the carcasses of rabbits beside the road. In fact, the terrain has changed little since the Iberian tribes carved their strange bull statues, *verracos*, even before the Romans had settled in this area.

AVILA (pop. 41,000) rises from this breathtaking monotony like a vision in stone. Its modern industrial suburbs disguise one of the most mystical medieval cities in Europe. It is protected by a massive defensive wall, about 3km in circumference, and comprising nine gates and 88 cylindrically fronted towers. Although excavations of the foundations have revealed evidence of earlier civilizations, the old core of Avila dates to the resettlement programme instigated by Alfonso VI after the defeat of Toledo in 1065.

It fell to Alfonso's son-in-law, Count Raymond of Burgundy, to create a new frontier fortress settlement to consolidate the lands between the Duero and Tajo. The wall was erected in just nine years (1090–99), and most of the pinkish-yellow stone Romanesque buildings date to the beginning of the 12th century when favourable *fueros* encouraged people to inhabit the new city.

It is best to park outside the walls and explore the city on foot, unless you prefer to tackle a labyrinthine one-way system, narrow lanes where delivery trucks can block your path for several minutes, and efficient traffic police who are only too happy to tell you where not to park. The narrow lanes and quiet shaded plazas contain a plethora of palaces, churches and convents. Some can be visited, others remain private and closed, but the excitement of Avila is in making your own discoveries at your own pace.

Begin with the fortified Gothic **cathedral**, whose apse is strangely incorporated into the defensive structure of the wall. There are good exterior carvings, in particular around the west door with its two strange *maceros*, or wild-looking macemen, possibly of South American origin, who stand threateningly at the sides. The initial impression of the interior is dominated by the peculiar chequered mix of pink and white stone. This is considered to be the first Gothic cathedral in Castile, though it is not difficult to pick out earlier Romanesque and later Renaissance parts. As one would expect of a good Castilian cathedral, it has a treasury, sacristy and cloister (14th to 15th centuries) and some fine sepulchres, such as that of Bishop Don Alfonso de Madrigal by Vasco de la Zarza, one of the initiators of Renaissance sculpture in Castile whose work is in evidence throughout the city.

The best Romanesque churches lie outside the walls. **San Vicente** is the most impressive of these, and contains a magnificent 13th-century tomb of the saint, with sculpted reliefs depicting his life. **San Pedro**, in the Plaza Santa Teresa, has a magnificent west portal and rose window. The **Museo Provincial** in the Casa de los Deanes is well worth a visit for the medieval paintings and archeological finds on display.

Avila, however, is most closely associated with one particular woman: Teresa Sánchez de Cepeda y Ahumeda, better known as Santa Teresa de Avila (1515–82). She was descended from a rich local family and the convent of Carmelitas Descalzas stands on the site of the house where she was born. Throughout Avila there are museums and reliquaries dedicated to her cult and even the local, rather sickly, delicacy of raw egg yolks rolled in sugar are named in her honour. The majority of Avila's visitors come to pay homage to the shrines that keep the memory of her life and work alive.

At the age of seven she ran away from home to seek martyrdom by converting the Muslim communities still living in Castile, and was subsequently inspired by a succession of visions. In 1537 she entered the Carmelite convent of La Encarnación, where she set out to reform the Carmelite Order, cleansing it of decadence and restoring it to a state of austerity and charity. The convent of San José was the first of 32 foundations that St Teresa established throughout Spain, mainly in Castile and Andalusia. Her Order was called the *Discalced* (Barefoot), and the nuns wear sandals to this day as a sign of their humility.

In addition to her work as a dedicated reformer, she was also a writer of mystical works, poems and letters. The most widely known, the autobiographical *Vida*, was denounced by the Inquisition, who tried to have Teresa deported to the New World but, through the support of powerful friends such as Fray Luis de León and San Juan de la Cruz, she refuted the accusations. Her mysticism, as one of her biographers wrote, was 'simple, pure and spontaneous, easily understood by the average believer yet susceptible of multiple interpretations by the theologians'. She was canonized in 1622, and her remains lie in Alba de Tormes, south-east of Salamanca.

The last important building in Avila, the **Real Monasterio de Santo Tomás**, reflects another, darker side of the city's longstanding and deep religious background. It was founded at the end of the 15th century by the Grand Inquisitor General, Torquemada, under the patronage of *Los Reyes Católicos*, and is interesting for its three cloisters and church. One of Castile's most moving sepulchres, that which marks the tomb of Prince John, the male heir apparent to Ferdinand and Isabel, is to be found here. It was his death in 1497 while studying at Salamanca that laid the way open for the rule of the Habsburgs.

TOURIST OFFICES

SEGOVIA: Pl Mayor 12, tel (911) 43 03 28.

SALAMANCA: Pl Mayor, tel (923) 21 83 42; and España 41, tel (923) 24 37 30.

CIUDAD RODRIGO: Puerta de Amayuelas, tel (923) 46 05 61.

AVILA: Pl de la Catedral 4, tel (918) 21 13 87.

Accommodation, Eating and Drinking

SEGOVIA (tel code 911):

(H)**Parador de Segovia**, Ctra de Valladolid, tel 43 04 62. A modern parador on a promontory overlooking the city. An indoor and outdoor pool and excellent amenities. B.

(H)**Los Linajes**, Doctor Velasco 9, tel 43 17 12. An old palace, beautifully situated overlooking the Eresma valley. Private garden. Very central. C.

(H)**Victoria**, Pl Franco 5, tel 43 57 11. A clean and simple alternative near the cathedral. E–D.

(R)The three restaurants specializing in Castilian cooking (roast suckling pig or lamb) and of a comparable level in old, *mesón*-style, wood-beamed dining rooms are:

Mesón de Candido, Pl del Azoguejo 5, tel 42 59 11.

Casa Duque, Cervantes 12, tel 43 05 37.

José María, Cronista Lecea 11, tel 43 44 84.

They also have bars serving traditional *tapas*. C–B.

PEDRAZA (tel code 911):

(H)**Posada de Don Mariano**, tel 50 98 86. A luxurious and popular weekend retreat. B.

(R)**Hostería Nacional Pintor Zuloaga**, Matadero 1, tel 50 98 35. Part of the parador chain, specializing in Castilian/Segovian cooking. C–B.

(R)**El Jardín**, La Calzada 6, tel 50 98 62. Open only at weekends and festivals. Segovian cuisine. C–B.

SEPÚLVEDA:

(R)**Cristóbal**, Conde de Sepúlveda 9, tel (911) 54 01 00. One of the great restaurants for *corderos lechales* (roast suckling lamb cooked in a wood-burning oven). C.

TURÉGANO:

(H)**Sol y Sombra**, Av General Franco 13, tel (911) 50 00 61. Clean, functional rooms. Good base for exploring north of the province. E.

MADRIGAL DE LAS ALTAS TORRES:

(H&R)**Hostal Madrigal**, Ctra de Peñaranda 10, tel (918) 32 08 78. Basic but good for a night. Good restaurant. E.

SALAMANCA (tel code 923):

(H)**Parador**, Teso de la Fería 2, tel 26 87 00. Modern, functional. Great views but lacks atmosphere. B.

(H)**Gran Hotel**, Plaza del Poeta Iglesias 3–5, tel 21 35 00. Expensive, atmospheric and central with all facilities. B.

(H)**Emperatriz**, Compañia 44, tel 21 92 00. Central situation. A cheaper but equally atmospheric alternative to the Gran Hotel. D–C.

(R)**Río de la Plata**, Pl del Peso 1, tel 21 90 05. Simple but good use of local products. C–B.

(R)**El Mesón**, Pl Poeta Iglesias 10, tel 21 72 22. Simple but good food. D–C.

(B)Plenty of good *tapas* bars in and around the Plaza Mayor.

CIUDAD RODRIGO (tel code 923):

(H)**Parador Enrique II de Trastamara**, Pl del Castillo 1, tel 46 01 50. In the restored 15th-century *castillo* and Torre de Homenaje. Garden overlooking the *vega* to Portugal. Good views from the restaurant. C.

(H)**Conde Rodrigo**, Pl del Salvador 9, tel 46 14 08. In an old palace beside the cathedral. Pleasant atmosphere. Good restaurant.

(R)**Mayton**, La Colada 9, tel 46 07 20. Simple but good food. D–C.

SIERRA DE FRANCIA:

(H)**Las Batuecas**, Av Las Batuecas, La Alberca, tel (923) 43 70 09. Simple but very comfortable. D.

(H)**Paris**, San Antonio, La Alberca, tel (923) 43 70 56. Utterly charming. D.

In **Miranda del Castañar** there are two pensions: one on the outskirts, and another on your right as you enter the Plaza Mayor. The latter has more atmosphere and a good restaurant.

BÉJAR:

(H&R)**Commercio**, Puerta de Avila 5, tel (923) 40 02 19. Adequate hotel with a restaurant. D.

AVILA (tel code 918):

(H)**Parador Raimundo de Borgoña**, Marqués de Canales y Chozas 16, tel 21 13 40. A 15th-century palace, with a good garden giving access to the wall. C.

(H)**Palacio de Valderrábanos**, Pl de la Catedral 9, tel 21 10 23. A magnificent old Gothic palace in the shadow of the cathedral. C–B.

(H)**Continental**, Pl de la Catedral 6, tel 21 15 02. If you can withstand the very run-down atmosphere, peeling paint and so on, this has great views and is central. D.

(R)**Mesón del Rastro**, Pl del Rastro 1, tel 21 12 18. In an old house beside the wall. C.

(R)**Molino de la Losa**, beside the bridge outside town in a converted mill, tel 21 11 01. Regional cooking. B.

Comunidad de Madrid

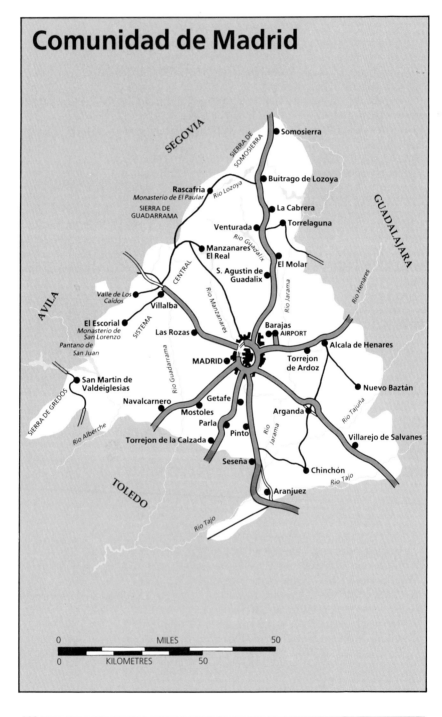

CHAPTER TWELVE

Comunidad de Madrid

MADRID, MOST SPANIARDS would agree, is the centre of Spain – not only its administrative capital, but a place whose radial axes attract migrants from all the different regions. Geographically, the Comunidad (7,995sq km) is bounded by the Guadarrama range across the north-west and the drainage basin of the River Tajo to the south and east. With its population of around five million, it is the most densely populated region in the Peninsula, while its altitude of 667m makes it the highest capital in Europe and accounts for the extreme variations between its dry, hot summers and freezing winters. The best time to visit is in the spring or autumn when days are more temperate and the sky is blue.

Madrid is a modern capital, the historic centre of which is surrounded by interminable residential neighbourhoods and hideous dormitory suburbs thrown up in the last 50 years. The majority of sights of interest can be found in the relatively small centre, and can best be explored on foot or by Metro, bus or taxi. Cars are a nuisance in Madrid and, for security's sake, should be parked underground at the first opportunity.

Several of Madrid's central neighbourhoods retain small-town charms to form a series of intimate Castilian *pueblos* that at night change into centres for its exuberant nightlife; further from the centre, it has much in common with other western European capitals: gimcrack apartment buildings, graffiti, street poverty and drugs.

Madrileños are generally known for their hospitality and pride, and this has helped make their city a place of stylish hedonism to suit any pocket or inclination. You will quickly discern the contrasts between the daytime, when life goes on as in any progressive European capital; and the night, when streetlife takes off and there are traffic jams up to the *madrugada* (early hours).

The origins of Madrid are obscure. Excavations along the River Manzanares have unearthed Paleolithic, Bronze Age and Iron Age artefacts, while proof of some Celtic, Roman and Visigothic settlement has been found in the remains of a forge and fragments of statues and masonry. The earliest standing remains are some ninth- or tenth-century Moorish walls near the royal palace on a promontory referred to as 'Mayrit' in Islamic chronicles, where the Emir Mohammed I constructed an *alcázar* (c. 854). Even after Madrid's capture by Alfonso VI in 1085 it remained an outpost of Toledo; a farming community overshadowed by more important Castilian wool towns such as Segovia, Avila and Valladolid.

The 16th century changed all this. Charles V wrote of Madrid: 'It is an agreeable and healthy place, easily reached, and with a strategic, geographical situation surrounded by fertile fields and abundant water.' Philip II was even more attracted by the proximity of good hunting grounds and by the altitude, which helped to relieve his gout. In 1561 he made Madrid the capital and *única corte* (unique court). He commissioned the building of his palace-monastery of El Escorial in the Sierra de Guadarrama overlooking the villa, which became the seat of New World government.

In the reign of Philip IV the city was extravagantly patronized and became a place of courtly celebration and Baroque elegance. The Palacio del Buen Retiro became a nucleus for artists, including Velázquez, Murillo and Zurbarán and writers such as Lope de Vega, Calderón de la Barca, Quevedo and Tirso de Molina. More palaces and religious buildings in the imported French style were added under the Bourbon Kings, including a new royal palace and academies of learning and science.

From 1759 Charles III 'El Gran Alcalde' (Great Mayor), as Madrileños affectionately refer to him, set about classicizing the city, commissioning architects such as Francisco Sabatini and Juan de Villanueva. The Paseo del Prado became a wide tree-lined boulevard with three great fountains dedicated to Neptune, Cybele and Apollo. He founded the Museum of Natural Sciences (later the Museo del Prado), the Astronomical Observatory, the general hospital, the royal porcelain factory, the church of San Francisco El Grande and the Botanical Gardens.

It is fortunate that so much survived the French occupation of the city, which began with a massacre of Madrileños on 2 May 1808 – a notable day in the Madrid calendar. The French and Joseph Bonaparte nevertheless introduced some conception of urban planning to Madrid, and the city expanded elegantly in well-built suburbs throughout the 19th century. The most remarkable of them was the Barrio de Salamanca, which is the smartest district of the capital. Trams, hydraulic lifts and the construction of the New York-style Gran Via Madrid and of the university (1927) completed its transformation into a progressive European city: an apt setting for the intellectual movements after 1898 that accounted for Madrid's strong Republican stance in the Civil War.

Post-war construction fever and the Nationalist desire to centralize Spain round Madrid brought about the rapid and uncontrolled growth of the city, the unfortunate results of which are all too obvious today. These have been tempered to some extent by the 'green' mayor, Enrique Tierno Galvan and, though the road system has improved, pollution continues to get worse. However, the 1980s did produce a rich *movida* (flourishing) of Madrid artists, writers and film-makers – the successors of the brilliant court of the city's golden age. If Madrid lacks the Mediterranean panache of Barcelona, it thrives on the wide skies and empti-

---

Principal Fiestas and Events of Madrid

Reyes Magos (children's parade on night of 5 January; holiday on the following day). Traditional celebration for children with a parade of *gigantes* (gigantic papier-mâché models), zoo animals, and helicopter displays.

San Isidro (two weeks from 15 May). Traditional week of revelry celebrating the patron saint of Madrid. Bullfighting at Las Ventas.

San Antonio de la Florida (9–13 June). In Moncloa district and around church with the Goya frescoes. Traditionally the beginning of the hot weather in Madrid.

San Lorenzo, San Cayetano y La Virgen de la Paloma (6–15 August). In all central districts, a wild week of drinking and *verbenas* (night festivals), when all the madness of Madrid boils to the surface.

Nochevieja (31 December). The New Year traditionally chimed in at the Puerta del Sol, with everyone eating a grape between chimes.

---

ness of the *Meseta*, which lend it a sombre dignity and style.

Madrid – Capital

The main sights of **MADRID** (pop. c. 4,500,000) lie in a relatively small area in the heart of the capital. It is here you will find the streets of endless bars, the Austrian Quarter, the great monuments of Charles III's reign, the art galleries, the Prado Museum, the Retiro Park and the Royal Palace. Armed with a good map – such as the small pocket Almax map available at all *kioskos* – it is quite simple to find your way about.

Traditionally the **Prado**, on the main north–south axis (Castellana–Paseo de Prado), is the most important cultural introduction to Madrid. If you include in your itinerary the other interesting sights nearby, you will need at least a day to explore this part of the city properly.

In 1785 Charles III commissioned the neoclassical architect Juan de Villanueva (1739–1811) to build a nat-

ural history museum here on the site of a meadow or the 'prado of St Jerónimo'. The Napoleonic Wars intervened before it was inaugurated and, after the war, it was used to exhibit the royal art collection, opening its doors to the public in 1819. The contents of the Prado embody the taste of both the Habsburg and the Bourbon Kings, and you will find here the Venetian masters patronized by Charles V and the Flemish school admired by Philip II (especially Bosch), as well as an unrivalled collection of 16th- to 18th-century Spanish painting (notably Velázquez and Goya), and numerous other Italian, French, German and English masterpieces. Over the years the collection has steadily grown, particularly in 1836, when many monastic collections were added, and more recently through private bequests such as the Thyssen-Bornemisza collection.

The rooms of the Prado are so dauntingly full of exceptional paintings that to give a detailed account of them is impossible here. Visitors should buy the excellent *Guide To The Prado* by Consuelo Luca de Tena and

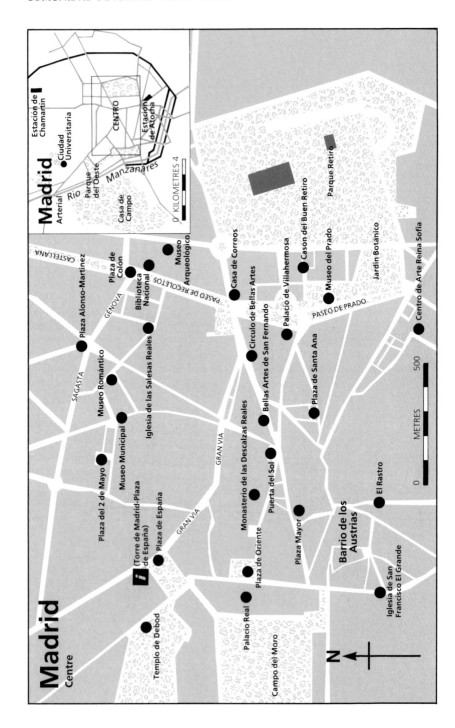

Manuela Mena (available in most European languages at the museum bookshop). Your ticket to the Prado gains you entry to the three Prado annexes: the Palacio de Villahermosa; the Casón de Buen Retiro, a short walk up the hill behind the museum, and containing 19th-century Spanish art; and Picasso's vast monochrome painting, *Guernica*, housed in the same building but entered from the door facing the Retiro park. (Open, all parts: 9am–6.30pm. Cl Sun & Mon.)

Beside the Prado lie the **Botanical Gardens**, which contain around 30,000 varieties of plants, shrubs and trees. Until a few years ago, medicinal plants were dispensed each day at the main gate – another enlightened innovation by Charles III. A small pavilion in the grounds stages frequent exhibitions of a mainly botanical nature. The entrance is via Plaza Murillo (open 10am–1 hour before sunset). A second-hand book market is held daily along the Cuesta de Moyano on the other side of the gardens.

More contemporary art can be found five minutes' walk from the Botanical Gardens, just off Calle de Atocha and the Plaza del Emperador Carlos V, at the **Centro de Arte Reina Sofía**, Calle Santa Isabel 52, in the ancient Hospital General de San Carlos (open 10am–9pm. Cl Tues). This is another building designed by Francisco Sabatani and José de Hermosilla, and constructed on the orders of Charles III in 1776 – the modern perspex lifts were added in 1991. It houses some of Europe's best travelling exhibitions and, since 1992, the contemporary art collection. Also worth knowing about is the Filmoteca Cinema at the other end of Calle Santa Isabel 3, which shows continuous orig-

inal version films. The neighbouring district round Atocha Station has been altered to cater for the high-speed train to Seville, but it is nevertheless quite run-down.

Running parallel, the Calle de Atocha leads directly uphill and ends among the narrow labyrinth of streets surrounding the **Plaza Mayor**, the architectural masterpiece of the Austrian Quarter. This huge rectangular plaza, measuring 120m by 100m, was commissioned by Philip III in 1617, and it is his bronze equestrian statue by Juan de Bolonia that stands at the centre. Though burnt three times, it has seen *autos-da-fé*, bullfights, legal hearings, plays and markets (there is one dedicated to philately every Sunday), and retains a wonderfully picaresque feeling. At more tranquil times it can be appreciated over a drink in one of the open-air cafés, and some of the best hat shops in Spain can be found beneath its arcades.

The narrow streets and diminutive plazas lying to the south-west contain even older aspects of Madrid. Here wide, French-influenced buildings give way to a burrow-like residential neighbourhood situated between the main Metro stations of this area: Lavapiés, La Latina and Tirso de Molina. This is the Austrian Barrio, with its concentration of the oldest and best churches – San Miguel, the Capilla del Obispo and San Francisco El Grande – as well as the beautiful Plaza de la Villa and Plaza de la Paja. Every Sunday and public holiday the area plays host to Madrid's Rastro Market, something of a Madrileño institution, where the smartest auction-house dealers mix with ordinary bargain hunters in search of some uncatalogued surprise. This must be

Principal Museums of Madrid

Prado, Paseo de Prado. (See p. 223.) Tues–Sun 9am–6pm. Cl Mon.

Museo de la Real Academia y de Bellas Artes de San Fernando, Calle Alcalá 13. Housed in the former Palacio Goyeneche, this museum contains a wide selection of Spanish painting from the last five centuries, including important works by Goya, Murillo, Sorolla, plus a set of 20 Picasso etchings and eight remarkable life-size portraits by Zurbarán. There are frequent temporary exhibitions; downstairs is the national print museum. Tues–Sat 9am–7pm. Sun–Mon 9am–2pm.

Monastery of La Descalzas Reales, Plaza Descalzas 3. Former palace built for Philip II's sister, Doña Juana, and turned into a convent for women of the royal household. There is a stunning collection of paintings, including works by Rubens, Murillo, Zurbarán, Tiziano and Carreño. Mon–Sat 10.30am–12.30pm & 4–6pm. Sun 10.30am–12.30pm.

Museo Arqueológico Nacional, Calle Serrano 13. Founded in 1867 by Isabel II, this contains the most complete archeological and historical collection in Spain from Iberian origins to the 19th century. The basement is given over to Paleolithic remains – mammoth tusks, tombs, primitive tools and pots found in caves through-out the Peninsula and Balearic Islands. The ground floor has an absorbing collection of Iberian works: Punic pottery, fertility gods, Visigothic crowns, the mysterious *Dama de Elche*, Roman sarcophagi, Egyptian mummies and Arab, Romanesque and Gothic work. In the grounds is the reconstruction of the Great Hall of the Bisons in the Altamira Cave in Cantabria. Tues–Sun 9am–2pm. Cl Mon.

Museo Romántico, Calle San Mateo. An excellent example of a 19th-century Madrid palace, with a fine collection of furniture and paintings bequeathed to the state by the Marqués of Vega Inclan in 1921. Visconti-like rooms set about a jaded garden courtyard. Tues–Sat 10am–6pm. Sun 10am–2pm. Cl Mon.

Museo Municipal, Calle Fuencarral 78. Dedicated to the history of Madrid, this museum contains exhibits from prehistoric stone implements to artefacts of this century. Magnificent oils of 18th-century Madrid by José del Castillo, as well as architectural drawings, satirical prints of Joseph Bonaparte, painted fans, etc. Tues–Sat 10am–2pm & 5–9pm. Sun 10am–2pm. Cl Mon.

Museo Cerralbo, Calle Ventura Rodriguez 17. Collections bequeathed to the state including works by El Greco, Goya and Zurbarán. In a 19th-century palace. Tues–Sun 10am–2pm & 4–6pm. Cl Mon & Aug.

Museo de América, Avenida de los Reyes Católicos 6. Reopened in 1992. It con-tains the largest single collection of pre-Columbian artefacts in Europe. Started by Philip II, it includes the Tro-Cortesiano Codex and other Mayan, Quimbayan, Colombian and Peruvian exhibits. Tues–Sun 10am–2pm. Cl Mon.

---

one of Europe's most African-looking markets and, if you find yourself in Madrid on a Sunday morning, it's cer-tainly worth heading here for the atmosphere alone. If you're tempted to buy, remember that bargaining is nor-mal and you can expect to achieve a third to a half off the opening price offered. On normal weekdays, numer-ous antique dealers open for business, and more can be found in the new pre-cinct beside the Puerta de Toledo – but prices are even higher. In August the *verbena* is held here too.

Museo Lázaro Galdiano, Calle Serrano 122. One of the great private museums of Europe, assembled by the financier José Lazaro Galdiano, who was an important artistic patron at the end of the 19th century. More than 30 rooms are packed with paintings, ceramics, jewellery, glass, coins, seals, armour and ivory. A small portrait by Leonardo de Vinci of an hermaphroditic Christ stands amid the work of other major painters such as Zurbarán, Ribera, Goya, Bosch and Constable. Daily 10am–2pm. Cl Aug.

Museo Nacional de las Artes Decorativas, Calle Montalbán 12. Textiles, ceramics and industrial arts. Tues–Fri 10am–5pm. Sat–Sun 10am–2pm. Cl Mon, July, Aug, Sept.

Museo Nacional de Etnología, Calle Alfonso XII 68. Religious and ceremonial exhibits from the Spanish colonies, including the crown of King Bulamba. Tues–Sat 10am–2pm & 4–7pm. Sun 10am–2pm. Cl Mon & Aug.

Museo Naval, Calle Montalbán 2/Paseo del Prado 5. Model ships, maps, etc., including the first drawing of the New World by Juan de la Cosa (1500). Tues–Sun 10.30am–1.30pm. Cl Mon & Aug.

Museo Sorolla, Paseo General Martínez Campos 37. The studio and paintings of the great Valencian painter Joaquín Sorolla Bastida (1863–1923). Tues–Sun 10am–2pm. Cl Mon.

Panteón de Goya, San Antonio de la Florida, Paseo de La Florida. Frescoes by Goya (1798). Thurs–Sat & Mon–Tues 10am–1pm & 4–6pm. Sun 10am–1pm. Cl Wed.

Monastery of La Encarnación, Pl de la Encarnación, beside Plaza Oriente. Founded in 1616 by Philip III. Herreran façade. Cloister has been converted into a museum with some impressive painting.

Several important contemporary collections are put on regularly at the:
Centro Cultural de la Villa, Plaza de Colón.
Fundación Caja de Pensiones, Calle Serrano 60.
Circulo de Bellas Artes, Calle Marqués de Casa Riera.
Sala de Exposiciones, Biblioteca Nacional.
Fundación Juan March, Castelló 77.

Notes:
Opening times of some museums such as the Prado and Centro Reina Sofia are detailed in the main text.
 A full weekly listing of what's on in Madrid is published in the cheap and comprehensive *Guía de Ocio* (100 pesetas), available from all kiosks and newsagents.

Three minutes' walk from the Plaza Mayor along Calle Mayor lies the Puerta del Sol – kilometre 0 – from where all distances in Spain are measured. It is a place that attracts every extreme of city life from unemployed gipsies to smart bankers buying city news. The most impressive building is the Casa de Correos, seat of Madrid's *ayuntamiento* (city hall), with a clocktower telling Spain's official time. Now a busy focus for the city, it was here in 1808 that the insurrection against the French began. The statue of

El Oso y el Modroño (Bear and Strawberry Tree) is the symbol of the Comunidad. Within a few minutes' walk of the Plaza are several important museums, including **San Fernando de Bellas Artes** and the monastery of **La Descalzas Reales** (see p. 226).

Calle Alcalá leads east over a hill to the Plaza de Cibeles, and along its route lie some of the city's most impressive palaces. Many of them now serve as banks, and are adorned with looming roof statues that appear to dance in the blue heat of a Madrid summer's day. At No 42, where the road joins the Gran Via, is the Círculo de Bellas Artes, which stages frequent travelling exhibitions and has a particularly grand *Belle Epoque* bar. The outdoor café in the summer is a good place to admire what Richard Ford once described as one of the most beautiful streets in all Europe.

Alcalá divides the Paseo del Prado and Paseo de Recoletos at the Plaza de Cibeles with Madrid's most celebrated fountain. This represents Cybele, Phrygian goddess of nature, riding in a chariot pulled by two lions that symbolize elegance and harmony. It is the most imposing of the many fountains along the Castellana and Paseos de Recoletos and Prado that feed off an underground stream.

On the north-west corner of the Plaza, patrolled by white-gloved guards, is the **Palacio de Goyeneche**, now the Ministry of Defence. This was erected in 1777 by the celebrated Duchess of Alba, Doña María del Pilar. Diagonally opposite, on the far side of the plaza, looms the neo-Plateresque **Palacio de Comunicaciones**, or 'Our Lady of Communications' as Madrileños like to quip, which serves as the central post office and the fastest

place to post a letter (though the stamp-vendors are notoriously fast with tourists, so always check your change). On the other corners lie the Banco de España and the Palacio de Linares, which was recently converted into the Casa de América: an office for the development of Hispanic relations.

Continuing up the hill along Calle Alcalá, you arrive in the Plaza de la Independencia. Its toppling cornucopias and the figure of a naked Mars were sculpted by Francisco Gutierrez and Roberto Michel, who were also responsible for the Cybele fountain. From there you can reach the Retiro Park.

The **Parque del Retiro** is an essential retreat from the bustle of Madrid life, when the streetlife gets too much. It's the place to go when you want open space, shade and cleanish air. There are four main entrances along the west side (C/ Alfonso XII) – the Puerta de Independencia, Puerta de España, Puerta de Felipe IV and Puerta del Angel Caído near the Astronomical Observatory. The Metro entrance is on the north.

The *Estanque* is a large rectangular lake overlooked by a tall Baroque commemoration statue of Alfonso XII on horseback. Along its waterfront, most of the park's amusements take place: tarot-card readers, marionettes, pirate tape salesmen, clowns, magicians and fire-eaters. But the park's other attractions include a 'Zen' garden and rose garden, boat rides, exhibitions in the Palacio de Velázquez, Palacio de Cristal and Casa de Vacas, as well as numerous cafés serving fresh *horchata* (tiger-nut milk), the perfect drink to quench your thirst in the dry summer heat.

The Calle de Serrano leads north

The Retiro Park: Historical Development

It was the idea of Philip IV's chief minister, the Count Duke Olivares, to establish a park in Madrid as a place to celebrate *fiestas*, bullfights and court pageantry, as well as a site for his private aviary full of birds from the New World. Italian landscape gardeners, including Cosme Lotti who had worked on the Boboli Gardens in Florence, were brought in when work began in 1633. Lotti designed the Estanque as a set for *naumaquias* (maritime operas), written by the great playwright of that era, Calderón de la Barca. Special effects included exploding volcanoes, simulated naval battles, floating islands and orchestral barges pulled by dolphins. It was an era of courtly extravagance in Madrid, symbolized by the building of the Palacio del Buen Retiro, the one remaining wing of which now contains the Military Museum.

Philip V, educated at Versailles, commissioned Robert Cotte, landscape gardener to Louis XIV, to build the *parterre* beside the Philip IV gate, and the ornamental bay trees and clipped hedges have survived to this day.

In 1746 Ferdinand VI reintroduced the maritime operas for the great Italian castrato, Farinelli. However, it was in the reign of Charles III that lasting alterations to the park were made. Several new buildings were erected within the confines of the grounds, including the royal porcelain factory, the Astronomical Observatory, the Museum of Natural Sciences (Prado) and the Botanical Gardens.

During the French occupation, the park was used as a garrison and many of the trees were chopped down, and then the liberating British forces destroyed the porcelain factory. With the Bourbon restoration, Ferdinand VII redesigned the gardens along more romantic lines, with a Persian palace and the highly ornamental *templete* (small temple) you can still see today.

In 1868, the park was opened to the public for the first time. The western border with the Paseo del Prado was moved to its present position and a grand residential area built in its place. For the great Exhibition of the Philippines in 1887, two new palaces were constructed by the architect Ricardo Velázquez Bosco. The Palacio de Velázquez was built out of brick and iron in a neo-Mudéjar manner, while the second, the Palacio de Cristal, was constructed in the style of Sir Joseph Caxton's Crystal Palace and palm house in London.

The park has changed little in the last 80 years, except that the gardens of Cecilio Rodríguez, architect of the Parque Oeste, have been added. During the Civil War the park commanded considerable respect from all sides, and emerged from the conflict almost unscathed.

from the Plaza de la Independencia and is the main artery of the Barrio de Salamanca, Madrid's chicest residential and shopping area, with its elegant stores and many good contemporary art galleries. At No 13 is the **Archeological Museum** and, just beyond it, the Plaza Colón and the Jardines del Descubrimiento with a monument to the first voyage of discovery. Beneath Columbus's statue and the great cascade of water, you will encounter the **Centro Cultural de la Villa**, which has frequent exhibitions.

Behind the Archeological Museum and facing the Paseo de Recoletos is the **Biblioteca Nacional**. The complete building was designed by Francisco Jareño and, though not open to the public, the library contains medieval codices, illuminated manuscripts, the complete works of Spain's Golden Age and a collection of *Don Quixote* editions, including one that contains the authentic autograph of Cervantes. You can visit a small gallery space up the main steps to the right, which holds exhibitions generally connected with the library, and gives you the opportunity to see the impressive main staircase.

Leading north from the Plaza de Colón is the Paseo de Castellana, which effectively marks the beginning of the new city with its progressively more modern buildings. Unless you're particularly interested in some quite impressive skyscrapers such as the Torre Picasso, Spain's tallest building, then there's not much to detain you here beyond the open-air sculpture park, built below a flyover and the *terrazas* (outside bars) spread out along the tree-lined avenue, which stay open to the early hours through the summertime.

Just up from the Plaza Colón is the Plaza de la Villa de París, a favourite demonstration spot for any Madrid anti-lobby overlooked by the Palacio de Justicia and the church of Las Salesas Reales. These building were commissioned during the reign of Ferdinand VI (1746–59) who is buried inside beside his wife. The interior frescoes of the church are by the Gonzalez Vázquez brothers, and there are two fine paintings by Zurbarán. Five minutes' walk along Calle Fernando VI lie two interesting but often neglected museums that are worth attention if you're in the neighbourhood: the **Museo Romántico** and the **Museo Municipal** (see p. 226).

Calle Hortaleza, a narrow street famous for its art shops, connects the pivotal Metro stop at Plaza Alonso Martínez to the Gran Via, the most colourful street in the city, where the worst excesses of American-style culture rub shoulders with an inimitably Spanish world. On every side the cultural paradoxes of modern Spain clash: the expensive fashion house 'Loewe' is a close neighbour to fast food restaurants, cinema theatres, shoeshines and mendicants, sleazy bars, transvestite haunts and tourist shops.

The Gran Via ends in the Plaza de España, the most depressing testament to Franco's vision – an overbearing and charmless square surrounded by grim authoritarian architecture, namely the Edificio España and the Torre de Madrid. The fountains and memorial to Cervantes, Don Quixote and Sancho Panza in the centre do nothing to alleviate its lacklustre ambience.

From there it's a short walk to the **Palacio Real** in Calle Bailén. (Open 9.30am–1.30pm & 3.30–6pm. Cl Sun pm and for official use.) This vast Bourbon palace was built on the site of an earlier Moorish *alcázar*, which had been destroyed by fire in 1734. The present building was constructed by Juan Bautista Sachetti from Guadarrama stone. Charles III was the first king to inhabit it and, though it is still used for official functions, you can visit it to admire the work of the many court painters patronized by Charles III: Conrado Giaquinto, Giovanni Battista Tiépolo and the Czech, Anton Mengs, all of whom contributed to the magnificent frescoes.

The statues of the Kings of Spain that were intended for the rooftop were found to be too heavy and now surround the Plaza de Oriente and the north garden. The guide from the Patrimonio Nacional will lead you on the scheduled two-hour visit through seemingly endless rooms in an exuberant and often indigestible parade of interior décor. Outstanding are the Sala de Porcelana, a room encased entirely in porcelain plaques; the frescoes of the Comedor de Gala; the Salón de Carlos II, where Charles III died; the Sala Amarilla, covered in gold and yellow silk tapestries from the tapestry factory in Madrid; the collection of clocks in the Salón de Cine; the private rooms of Alfonso XIII; the throne room, Salón del Trono, with fine chandeliers from La Granja; and the Cámara and Anticamara, with a table given to Ferdinand VII by the British Government in recognition of the aid he sent during a plague in Gibraltar. This and much, much more. . . .

A separate ticket gains you entry to the Armería Real (Royal Armoury), which contains more than 44 suits of armour made for Charles V, a sword credited to Hernan Cortés, and other royal campaigning memorabilia. Also worth a few minutes' attention is the Farmacia, with some interesting pharmaceutical instruments and medicine jars manufactured at Talavera and in the Buen Retiro porcelain factory. Your visit to the palace will take up the best part of a morning or afternoon.

In front of the palace, across Calle Bailén is the Plaza de Oriente with an impressive statue of Philip IV inspired by the Velázquez painting in the Prado. Below the palace to the west stretches the **Campo del Moro**, one of the quietest and most undervisited parks in Spain, which houses the

Museo de Carruajes (Carriage Museum) in the old stables there.

To the north of the palace stretches the **Parque del Oeste**, containing the Temple of Debod, a peculiar Egyptian temple surrounded by water. The views at sunset over the Casa de Campo to the Sierra de Guadarrama are magnificent. A funicular connects it with the Casa de Campo.

The **Casa de Campo**, one of the largest urban parks in Europe, was founded by Philip II on land that originally formed part of the royal hunting grounds. Today it is possible to find wild mushrooms and asparagus here at the right time of year. Among its features are the zoo and the *parque de atracciones* (funfair). Its main purpose, however, is for the trees to turn some of that urban carbon dioxide into oxygen.

For all its cultural highlights, Madrid is just as much a city of the night when the busy daytime neighbourhoods metamorphose into late-night haunts, and Madrileños descend from the suburbs to fill the streets with noise, music and colour. Most of Centro is given over to night entertainment, especially the streets in and around Plaza Santa Ana. A more traditional side of the city can be found near the Plaza Mayor, where the bars play flamenco and the restaurants along Calle Cuchilleros exhale the typical smells of the Castilian table such as roast suckling pig.

For a younger clientele the areas around the Plaza Dos de Mayo and Chueca have literally hundreds of bars and restaurants that stay open until the small hours, but this is certainly not the place to venture if you're wearing or carrying anything valuable as both areas are notorious for drugs.

The monastery of El Escorial to the west of Madrid was built by Juan de Herrera for Philip II and contains the pantheon of almost all the Habsburg and Bourbon kings of Spain. Incafo

TOURIST OFFICES

Main office in the Plaza España at Princesa 1, tel (91) 541 23 25. Others at Barajas Airport and Chamartín Railway Station.

Accommodation, Eating and Drinking (tel code 91)

There is accommodation in Madrid to suit every taste and pocket and lots of it. There is never normally any need to book in advance except during the spring and autumn festivals. Middle-range and cheap tourist accommodation lies all along the Gran Via. Business-class accommodation is concentrated in and around the Castellana. Cheaper alternatives of *hostales* and pensions can be found near the Plaza Mayor and Puerta del Sol.

(H)**Ritz**, Plaza de la Lealtad 5, tel 521 28 57. Considered one of the most exclusive hotels in the world, with a good terrace restaurant serving Sunday brunch. A.
(H)**Palace**, Plaza de las Cortes 7, tel 429 75 51. Overlooking the Cortes. Many great names have stayed here, including J. F. Kennedy and Mata Hari. Dalí used to take a whole floor. Excellent food in the Neptune grill. A.

(H)**Emperatriz**, López de Hoyos 4, tel 563 80 88. A modern hotel with all facilities off the Castellana. B–A.

(H)**Galiano**, Alcala Galiano 6, tel 319 20 00. Quiet and central. Near Plaza Colón. Private garage. No food. B.

(H)**París**, Alcala 2, tel 521 64 96. Overlooking the Puerta del Sol. Functional. C.

(H)**Mónaco**, Barbieri 5, tel 522 46 30. In an old bordello where all the ministers of Alfonso XII used to go and *siesta*. A little run-down, but good atmosphere. C.

(H)**Residencia Santander**, Calle Echegaray 1, tel 429 95 51. Clean and tidy rooms in a lively area at night. D–C.

(H)**Reconquista**, Calle Zorrilla 7–2 (between C/ Alcalá and Carrera de San Jerónimo), tel 429 81 97. D.

(H)**Filo**, Plaza Santa Ana 15–2, tel 522 40 56. Just one of many cheap *hostales* in the area. Family-run, clean and central. E–D.

(R)**Lhardy's**, Carrera de San Jerónimo 8, tel 522 22 07. Founded in 1839. Delicatessen on ground floor. Excellent house wine. A.

(R)**Casa Lucio**, Cava Baja 35, tel 265 62 52. Best Castilian food of highest quality, ingredients cooked without pretension. Good atmosphere, with clientele that includes politicians and American tour parties. B–A.

(R)**El Schotis**, Cava Baja 11, tel 265 32 30. Traditional Madrileñan food. C–B.

(R)**Las Cuevas de Luis Candelas**, Cuchilleros 1, tel 266 54 28. Famous as one of Hemingway's haunts. In a street of traditional restaurants. C–B.

(R)**Casa Botín**, Cuchilleros 17, tel 266 42 17. Another Hemingway haunt. It is unashamedly geared to tour parties, but is still good, serving traditional food. C–B.

(R)**Ribeira Do Miño**, Santa Brígida 1, tel 521 98 54. Good Gallegan cooking. B.

(R)**Currito**, Pabellón de Vizcaya de la Feria del Campo, tel 464 57 04. Quite far out in the Casa de Campo but excellent Basque food and a summer terrace. B.

(R)**La Bola**, Calle La Bola 5, tel 247 69 30. Near the Palacio Real. Has the best *cocido Madrileño* in town. Excellent house wine. C.

(R)**Zara**, Calle Infantas 5, tel 532 20 74. Simple Cuban-based food. D–C.

(R)**La Vascongada**, Plaza Vázquez de Mella 10, Good fresh fish dishes. E–D.

(R)**Vesuvio**, C/ Hortaleza 15, just off the Gran Via. Cheap Italian restaurant. E–D.

(B)**Bocaíto**, Calle Libertad 6. A favourite *tapas* bar among Madrileños. Everything on the menu can be classed a speciality.

(B)**Café Gijón**, Paseo de Recoletos 21. The memory of Spain's great artistic generation of the 1920s still hovers above the hum of conversation, and the *literati* continue to congregate here at lunchtime and in the evening. Simple, traditional *tapas*.

(B)**El Espejo**, Paseo de Recoletos 31. A *tapas* bar a few doors along from Café Gijón, and decorated with all the *Art Nouveau* extravagance normally associated with Barcelona. Try *chipirones en su tinta* (baby squid cooked in their own ink).

(B)**Museo Chicote**, Gran Via 12. A venerated cocktail bar, where old men congregate in the afternoon underneath the hat racks to sip dry martinis mixed to a recipe made famous by the film-maker Luis Buñuel. Around 8pm a younger crowd descend to use up the rest of the night. All drinks are accompanied by dishes of almonds, olives and crisps. Excellent *tapas*-like lunches.

(B)**Mallorca**, Calle Serrano 6. One of a chain of patisseries/*tapas* bars, where the mink-and-Mercedes set converge to guzzle *tapas* and glasses of well-matured Rioja or *cava*. Good place to buy a take-away *tapas* lunch to eat in the Retiro Park.

The Comunidad

The usual places for people to explore from Madrid are the satellite cities of Segovia, Avila and Toledo, but there are several sights within the boundaries of the Comunidad. **El Real Monasterio de San Lorenzo** or **El Escorial** is the most impressive, reached via N-VI La Coruña highway. (Open 10am–1.30pm & 3.30–6pm. Cl on main holidays.) At an altitude of 1,028m on the slopes of the Guadarrama commanding a magnificent view over the west of the Comunidad, it was here that Philip II in 1562 commissioned the royal architects, Juan Bautista de Toledo and Juan de Herrera, to build a monastic palace and permanent resting place for the Kings of Spain to fulfil the conditions of his father Charles V's will. Its dedication to San Lorenzo honours the victory of Philip II's troops at the Battle of San Quentin on St Laurence's Day, 1557.

El Escorial means slagheap, a term that could ironically allude to the building's vast, expressionless form, but actually signifies the old mine on which it was built. Some people consider it the eighth wonder of the world; others are not so complimentary. Nevertheless, the austere majesty of its vast granite dimensions cannot be denied, and it serves to remind its visitors of the great power that Spain once wielded in the world. Philip II boasted that from El Escorial he had ruled the world with a few sheets of parchment and a quill pen.

The western façade is 207m long and 20m high, and its central portal gives access to the Patio de los Reyes. The façade of the church is adorned with gilt and marble statues by Monegro of the Kings of Judea – David, Solomon, Hezekiah, Josiah, Jehosophat and Manasseh. You enter the pietistic Doric interior beneath the horizontal vault: a daring piece of architectural planning by Herrera. Here the profuse ornamentation of marble, bronze, jasper, rare woods and bright frescoing is in stark contrast to the austerity of the monotone granite.

In the centre of the high altar, above the exquisite tabernacle, is a large panel by Tibaldi depicting the ecstatic martyrdom of St Lawrence, who was grilled to death. It is said that, when he felt he was done on one side, he turned onto the other. On the gospel side of the altar are the bronze figures of Charles V and his immediate family at prayer. On the epistle side kneels Philip II with three of his four wives: Mary Tudor is missing. The frescoes of *The Glory* on the vault above the choir are by Luca Cambiasso (1527–85); others are by Luca Giordano.

Entry to the church is free but the tours of the monastery, which begin in the entrance on the north side, require you to obtain a ticket. You are first shown into the Palacio Real, which begins with several 18th-century rooms decorated with tapestries from ceiling to dado, where furniture is placed austerely against the walls. The tapestry rooms end at the Sala de las Batallas, with a vast mural depicting the Battle of Higueruela, fought against the Moors in 1431. This is followed by the Habitaciones de Maderas Finas, with some magnificent marquetry work in rare woods, mainly of German origin. You finish the tour in the exit vestibule that contains Philip II's sedan chair, which supported him through his worst periods of gout.

The Palace of Philip II is on the

ground floor and has some fine 15th- and 16th-century paintings. You can see Philip's bedroom, in which a small window gives directly onto the high altar of the chapel. Here the king died.

The gallery rooms are reached off the palace cloister and contain important works by Bosch, including two *Temptations of St Anthony*; as well as Titian's *Last Supper*; Velázquez's *Joseph's Tunic*; and El Greco's *St Maurice and the Theban Legion*, the masterpiece that failed to find favour with Philip II. This effectively excluded El Greco from becoming court painter, and he was subsequently patronized by the clergy in Toledo. There are other works by Dürer and Tintoretto, and an exceptional *Descent from the Cross* by Veronese.

On the other side of the chapel is the Patio de los Evangelistas, remarkable for the frescoes above the great decorated staircase by Lucas Giordano. Nearby the Salas Capitulares are frescoed in Pompeiian style and hung with works by Ribera.

A doorway leads from the cloister into the antesacristy, where a guide escorts you down the serpentine staircase into the octagonal Panteón de los Reyes. Here all the Spanish monarchs and their mothers since Charles V are buried, with the exception of Philip V (La Granja) and Ferdinand VI (Las Salesas Reales). The coffins are diminutive, considering the stature of many more recent Bourbon kings. The explanation is that, after the death of a monarch, the body was first left to decompose in lime in a small room beside the stairs; and the bones were subsequently dismantled and entombed. Next to the mausoleum is the neo-Gothic Panteón de los Infantes, where other members of the royal household are buried in some finely sculpted Carrara marble tombs.

The last part is the *Biblioteca* (library), reached through a door beside the main west entrance. The original murals by Tibaldi and Carducho depicting the liberal arts – philosophy and theology, grammar, rhetoric, dialectic, arithmetic, music, geometry and astrology – are peculiarly complemented by the austere Doric bookcases designed by Herrera. In the display cases (although the exhibits may change) are facsimile copies of Alfonso X's Book of Chess; autographed manuscripts by Santa Teresa de Avila; a 15th-century Hebrew Bible; the Koran, written in gold letters, of Mulay Zidán, Sultan of Morocco; and the illuminated breviaries of Isabel la Católica, Charles V and Philip II. There is also a *Beatus*, unfortunately not on permanent exhibit.

In the basement is the Museo de Arquitectura, with drawings and instruments used in the construction of the palace. Outside, a walk above the palace takes you to the Casita de Arriba, a neoclassic pavilion built by Villanueva, surrounded by a rose garden and commanding good views of the monastery. The Casita de Abajo, by the same architect, is a 20-minute walk down the hill, and contains frescoes by Lucas Giordano.

To do El Escorial justice, you will need the best part of two days with a night in between. Other places in the area to visit include **Santa Cruz del Valle de Los Caídos**, Franco's memorial to the fallen, which is only 8km away. This subterranean mausoleum contains the tombs of the Nationalist dictator (d. 1975) and his mentor, José Primo de Rivera, buried austerely in the floor next to the high altar.

An impressive highroad continues north through the ski-resort town of Puerto de Navacerrada along the valley of the River Lazoya to the restored 14th-century monastery of El Paular. Half of it serves as a Benedictine monastery, and the rest has been turned into a luxury hotel. The church contains a magnificent 15th-century alabaster retable and wrought-iron *reja* (screen). Good walks can be taken in the surrounding wooded hillside beneath the towering peak of Peñalara.

South of El Paular is the *castillo* of **Manzanares El Real**, beside the Parque Natural de la Cuenca Alta de Manzanares. Apart from supplying much of Madrid's water, this is one of the most unspoilt areas of the region and a favourite haunt of weekend hikers.

The north of the Comunidad is surprisingly wild. The most important village is **Buitrago de Lozoya** that lies just off the main Madrid–Burgos road (N-I). If you're driving either to or from Madrid, it is worth stopping here to see the impressive battlements built around the reservoir, a Mudéjar castle, a restored church with Mudéjar tower, and the peculiar Museo Picasso. The latter is to be found at Plaza Picasso 1, in the basement of the *ayuntamiento* (town hall), and is dedicated to works that the artist gave to his lifelong friend, Eugenio Arias, the barber of Buitrago. (Open Tues–Sun 11am– 1.30pm & 4–6pm. Cl Mon.)

Alcalá de Henares (pop. 153,000) lies east of Madrid, although the urban sprawl, which gets worse as you enter Alcalá, has almost engulfed the distance in between. Before the *desamortización* (dissolution) this was the seat of Madrid's main university, which was founded by the powerful Toledan prelate Cardinal Archbishop Jiménez de Cisneros. He is remembered chiefly for his regency after the death of Ferdinand in 1516, and for commissioning the polyglot Bible. Much of the historic town centre was destroyed in the Civil War, but worth finding are the Plateresque façade of the **university** by Rodrigo Gil De Hontañón, and its three-tiered gallery courtyard. *Cisne* (swans) abound in the decoration, alluding to the name Cisneros. Other university and ecclesiastical buildings, in varying states of restoration but still worth exploring, include the Paraninfo, the chapel of San Ildefonso, the Herreran Iglesia Magistral and Archbishop's Palace. Alcalá's other main attraction is the Casa de Cervantes, a small museum dedicated to memorabilia from the era of Spain's most longstanding and well-known writer, Miguel de Cervantes y Saavedra (1547–1616), who was born on this site.

Just 20km south-east of Alcalá is **Nuevo Baztán**, a village built by José de Churriguera for the rich Navarrese banker, José de Goyeneche, at the beginning of the 18th century and recently spoilt by the growth of an ugly modern suburb. The architecture of the palace is restrained from the exuberance normally expected of this genre, and is currently undergoing restoration. **Loeches**, 16km back towards Madrid, is famous for its medicinal waters and as the resting place of Philip IV's prime minister, the Count Duke Olivares, who is buried in the convent church (d. 1645).

South of Madrid, on the border with Castile–La Mancha, lies the majestic but rather staid royal palace of **Aranjuez**, built on the banks of the River Tajo. It can be visited under the

The Torre Picasso in Madrid is a symbol of post-Franco, democratic Spain. It is one of Europe's largest skyscrapers and the headquarters for two private TV stations. Incafo

guidance of the Patrimonio Nacional if you still have an appetite for Bourbon court taste. The interior is another procession of richly decorated rooms, among which only the Sala de Porcelana and Saleta de Espejos (Hall of Mirrors) and the Sala Arabe, a replica of the Sala de las Dos Hermanas in the Alhambra, stand out as memorably different. (Open 10am–1pm & 4–6.30pm.) Another ticket grants you access to the Museo de Historia del Traje, a costume museum exhibiting mainly court and military uniforms. The collection of fans is interesting.

The gardens built along the banks of the Tajo are Aranjuez's most redeeming feature. The Jardín de la Isla has some fine statues and trees, and the Jardín del Príncipe, which surrounds the Casa del Labrador, built in 1803 for Charles IV and containing more Bourbon finery, is a fine place to relax and enjoy watching local life.

Chinchón, 20km to the north-east, is the Comunidad's most picturesque village. It is famous for its Plaza Mayor, encircled by houses with wooden balconies that double up as boxes during the August bullfights, and its *aguadiente* distilleries that produce a sweet or dry liqueur. There are a number of good restaurants in the village. In the Gothic church the retable frames a Goya depicting the Assumption of the Virgin.

TOURIST OFFICE

ALCALA DE HENARES: Callejón de Santa María 1, tel (91) 889 26 94.

Accommodation, Eating and Drinking

SAN LORENZO DE EL ESCORIAL (tel code 91):

(H)**Victoria Palace**, Juan de Toledo 4, tel 890 15 11. Rather like a central European *schloss*. Quite luxurious, with all facilities. B.

(H)**Cristina**, Juan Toledo 6, tel 890 19 61. A few doors from the Victoria Palace. Central. B–C.

(R)**Charolés**, Floridablanca 24, tel 890 59 75. Slightly *nouvelle cuisine*, but excellent service. Booking necessary. Seasonal menus. A.

(R)**La Cueva**, San Antón 4, tel 890 15 16. In an old 18th-century *posada* (inn). Traditional Castilian food. C.

RASCAFRIA:

(H)**Santa María de El Paular**, tel (91) 869 10 11/12. Luxury hotel in a restored monastery. Magnificent setting in the foothills of the sierra. Almost a health club in the facilities it offers. B–A.

BUITRAGO:

(H)**Casa Pepe**, Ctra Madrid–Burgos km76, tel: (91) 868 02 12. Adequate for a stop going in or out of Madrid.

ALCALA DE HENARES:

(R)**Hostería del Estudiante** Colegios 3, tel (91) 888 03 30. In the former Colegio de San Jerónimo, which specialized in the languages of Greek, Latin and Hebrew. *Artesonado* (inlaid wooden ceiling) and old fireplace add authentic touches. Excellent food. C–B.

ARANJUEZ:

(R)**Casa Pablo**, Almíbar 42, tel (91) 891 14 51. Old bullfighting memorabilia decks every wall of this most traditional bar and restaurant. B.

CHINCHÓN (tel code 91):

(H)**Parador de Chinchón**, Av de Generalisimo 1, tel 894 08 36. In a 17th-century Augustinian monastery. Good restaurant. C–B.
(R)**Mesón Cuevas del Vino**, Benito Hortelano 13, tel 894 02 06. Castilian specialities. C–B.
(R)**El Rincón de Luis**, Grande 31, 8km away in Titulcia, tel 893 10 20. Booking is necessary to enjoy this simple but excellent food. C.

CHAPTER THIRTEEN

Castile – La Mancha
(Castilla–La Mancha)

THE SOUTHERN *Meseta*, once known as 'Castilla–La Nueva' when it included Madrid, is now referred to as 'Castilla– La Mancha' and comprises the five provinces of Guadalajara, Cuenca, Toledo, Ciudad Real and Albacete stretching across 79,226sq km.

Much of the landscape to the west and south is a flat sub-plateau broken up by shallow river valleys and planted with row upon row, field upon field, of olive trees, vines and wheat. To the east are the more mountainous districts bordering upon Aragón and Valencia, where the Rivers Tajo and Guadiana begin their descent towards the Atlantic.

Travellers too often forget about Castile–La Mancha, considering it the barren, characterless country of *Don Quixote*, worth visiting for little other than its capital, Toledo. It is true that you have to look harder and drive further to find places of interest in this region, and the small agricultural *pueblos* are generally not geared to tourism. However, this should not deter travellers from visiting it, as good bases for exploration can be found at Sigüenza, Cuenca, Alarcón, Toledo and Almagro.

The Sierra de Alcarria and Sierra de Alcaraz are both fascinating backwaters of traditional Castilian life, and south of Toledo the memory of the brave hidalgo Don Quixote de la Mancha is everywhere. It was in his imagination that windmills became giants, flocks of sheep turned to hostile armies and the crenellated and craggy escarpment reared across the horizon like impenetrable fortifications. Don Quixote gave mythological status to La Mancha. His gaunt, bearded face glares from stickers on the label of the local Manchegan cheese, his saddled figure and his trusty *escudero*, Sancho Panza, ride into the horizons of Valdepeñas labels, and the *Ruta Turística de Don Quijote* encourages travellers to follow in his footsteps – though no one is sure exactly where his footsteps trod.

High summer is not the most agreeable season to visit the region, when the sun-scorched plateau radiates an interminable heat, and the still, monotonous landscape encourages the mind to crave the sea and shade. Spring is the

Castile–La Mancha

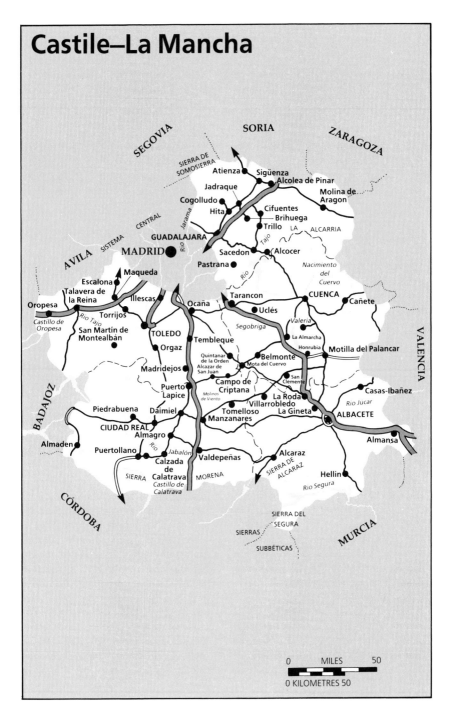

SEGOVIA

SORIA

ZARAGOZA

SIERRA DE SOMOSIERRA

Atienza

Sigüenza

Alcolea de Pinar

Jadraque

Molina de Aragón

Cogolludo

Hita

Cifuentes

Brihuega

Trillo

LA ALCARRIA

CENTRAL

Jarama

GUADALAJARA

AVILA

SISTEMA

MADRID

Río Tajo

Sacedon

Alcocer

Pastrana

Nacimiento del Cuervo

Maqueda

Río

Tarancon

CUENCA

Cañete

Escalona

Ocaña

Uclés

Talavera de la Reina

Illescas

Valeria

Oropesa

Torrijos

Río Tajo

Segobriga

La Almarcha

Castillo de Oropesa

San Martín de Montealbán

TOLEDO

Tembleque

Honrubia

Motilla del Palancar

Orgaz

Quintanar de la Orden

Belmonte

VALENCIA

Madridejos

Alcazar de San Juan

Mota del Cuervo

BADAJOZ

Puerto Lapice

Campo de Criptana

San Clemente

Casas-Ibañez

Molinos de Viento

La Roda

Piedrabuena

Dáimiel

Villarrobledo

Río Jucar

Tomelloso

La Gineta

ALBACETE

CIUDAD REAL

Manzanares

Almagro

Almaden

Puertollano

Almansa

Calzada de Calatrava

Valdepeñas

Alcaraz

SIERRA

Jabalon

SIERRA DE ALCARAZ

Hellin

Castillo de Calatrava

MORENA

Río Segura

CÓRDOBA

SIERRA DEL SEGURA

SIERRAS

SUBBÉTICAS

MURCIA

0 MILES 50

0 KILOMETRES 50

best time, when the great geometric shapes of the landscape are divided by fields and hedges of red poppies; the wheat plains of Guadalajara are verdant; clouds roll across the immense blue horizons; and raptors hunt over the Montes de Toledo and Serranía de Cuenca.

The historical significance of the region has always focused on its capital, Toledo: a great city under Roman, Visigothic, Arab and Christian rule. The surrounding lands were variously ruled by *taifas*, crusading Orders and powerful local families. The concentration of castles and fortified villages in Guadalajara and Cuenca defended the passes into central Castile from the Mediterranean. In the south of the region, along the border with Andalusia, the lands were governed after the Reconquest by the crusading Orders of Santiago, Calatrava and Alcántara until their disbandment towards the end of the 15th century.

Guadalajara and Cuenca

The provincial capital of **GUADA-LAJARA** (pop. 62,000) – in Arabic, Uad-al-Hayar (River of Stones) – lies 58km north-east of Madrid. In the last few decades, after near-total desecration in the Civil War, it has turned into something of a high-rise dormitory suburb, but there is one building very well worth a visit.

The Palacio del Duques del Infantado, the magnificent Plateresque palace with Gothic and Mudéjar touches, was built towards the end of the 15th century by the architect Juan Guas for the Mendoza family, one of the aspiring Renaissance dynasties of the age and powerful landowners in this area. The dressed-stone façade is richly studded with diamond-shaped bosses, and the Gothic loggia running just below the roof is a rare and impressive touch. The main patio is a riot of sculptural fantasy and is currently undergoing restoration, though the small but undistinguished museum can be visited. (Open Tues–Sat 10am–2pm & 4–6pm. Sun 10am–2pm. Cl Mon.) The *artesonados* (inlaid wooden ceilings) of the main rooms were once unrivalled for their splendour, but were sadly destroyed by fire in 1936. The royal marriages of Philip II to Isabel de Valois and Philip V to Isabel Farnese took place here. In the 15th-century church of San Francisco is the Panteón de los Duques de Infantado.

Continuing north-east from Guadalajara, turn left off the main N11 after 6km and take the C101 via **Hita**. This small, rather woebegone *pueblo*, with an impressive Renaissance gateway leading into a small arcaded plaza, is associated with Juan Ruiz, Archpriest of Hita (1283?–1350?), author of the *Libro del Buen Amor*, which, along with the *Poem of the Cid*, is the most important poem of medieval Spain. It is a ribald, often Rabelaisian saga about the success and, more often, failings of love. The main – possibly autobiographical – character, Don Melón de la Huerta, has 12 different attempts at seduction, including an encounter with four shepherdesses who rape him, and a platonic affair with a nun.

Jadraque is easily identifiable from a distance by its looming Castillo del Cid on a conical spur, commanding spectacular views over the Valle de Henares – a 15th-century stronghold built by Cardinal Mendoza. The 16th-century parish church was once worth visiting for a beautiful *Flagellation of Christ* by Zurbarán, but this was sold recently to pay for redecoration work that includes some rather cheap and ugly pine stalls.

Cogolludo lies 20km west of Jadraque, and is worth the detour for the flamboyant Gothic–Plateresque palace, built in 1495 for the first Duke of Medinaceli, Luis de la Cerda y Mendoza. The Mendozas were instrumental in introducing the Renaissance to Spain, through Iñigo Lopez de Mendoza, who served as ambassador to the Holy See. Here in the Plaza Mayor the strong Italianate characteristics of the palace are obvious, particularly in the façade of the rectangular quarry stones and Tuscan-style patio, with the large sculptured fireplace within.

Turning north, the GU151 skirts the Embalse de Alcorio to **Atienza**, surrounded by some impressive 11th- to 13th-century walls. This fortified village contains several well-preserved Romanesque churches built about sleepy arcaded plazas. Each year at Pentecost there is a strange *fiesta* known as La Caballada, when the men dress in black capes and gallop around the walls to commemorate the day when the local inhabitants prevented the young son of Sancho III and Blanche of Navarre from falling into the hands of his uncle, Fernando de León, who had laid siege to the place.

West of Atienza lies the Reserva Nacional de Sorsaz, a desolate sierra bordering on the Comunidad de Madrid, where slate villages such as **Majaelrayo** and **Campillo de Ranas** lie in the shadows of windswept mountains. The scenery is magnificent,

though the roads are variable. Further to the north in the Sierra de Pela, bordering with Soria, lie the villages of **Albendiego**. **Campisábalos** and **Villacadima**, all with Romanesque churches.

From Atienza it is 30km along the C114, beside another walled *pueblo* at Palazuelos, to **Sigüenza** (pop. 5,000). Known as 'Ciudad de los Obispos', and one of the most charming monumental cities of Castile, Sigüenza is tastefully geared towards tourism and particularly beautiful in the spring and autumn. All approaches are dominated by the view of the Bishops' Castle, which now serves as a parador and makes an excellent base from which to explore the province and parts of southern Soria (see p. 248).

The fortified **cathedral** became the nucleus for a powerful medieval bishopric. Work started in the mid-12th century and the twin battlemented towers on either side of a tremendous rose window are a testament to the defensive and sometimes aggressive stance of Sigüenza's bishops. Architecturally, the cathedral has a feeling of Cistercian austerity that is lightened by the pink hue of the stone, although later Gothic, Plateresque and classical features are all discernible.

Inside, the dim but elevated space is broken up by the clustered columns supporting some fine vaulting. Two Gothic pulpits, the 15th-century choirstalls and their canopy attributed to Rodrigo Alemán are worth attention, but the cathedral's showpiece lies in the Capilla de San Juan y Santa Cantalina, the pantheon of the Arce family. The late Gothic sculpture here, familiarly referred to as 'El Doncel', of a young knight nonchalantly reading is, in fact, the resting place of Don Martín

Toledo, built on a steep rise above the River Tajo, was the Visigothic capital of Spain, and centre of a flourishing medieval translation school and Sephardic community. Incafo

Vázquez de Arce, killed in action in 1486 during the last campaign against the Moors of Granada. The sculptor is unknown. In the sacristy there is a unique panelled ceiling studded with 300 medallion heads designed by Alonso de Covarrubias.

In front of the cathedral the Museo Diocesano de Arte exhibits local archeological finds, sacred art, bronze crucifixes and a couple of fine paintings by El Greco and Zurbarán. (Open Tues–Sat 11.30am–2pm & 3.30–6pm. Sun 11.30am–2pm. Cl Mon.) Calle Mayor leads uphill from the plaza, past the convent of Clarisas de Santiago to the Castillo de Los Obispos, built over

an earlier Moorish fortification and now adapted to the needs of a luxury hotel. From there it is worth wandering back down through the streets below the castle, which contain other important monuments such as the Casa del Doncel, the 15th-century palace formerly of the Bedmar family, and the church of San Vicente, with a fine carved doorway.

At almost every other shop in Sigüenza you can buy the cured ham or honey produced in the Alcarria, a succession of high grazing plains and rolling sierras to the south running across the provincial border between Guadalajara and Cuenca. Here villages are noted for their wickerwork, honey or wild herbs, and any are worth stopping at to experience the slow, unaffected pace of rural life. The two main towns of the Alcarria, **Brihuega** and **Cifuentes**, are interesting for their vernacular architecture.

Pastrana, further to the south, is more grandiose and has a stronger señorial history. In the Plaza Mayor stands the Palacio de los Duques de Pastrana, where Philip II's mistress, the one-eyed Duchess of Eboli, was banished and died, having fallen from favour for alleged infidelity with the King's minister, Antonio Pérez. From Pastrana there is a 15-minute drive to the Mar de Castilla, where you can swim if the heat gets too much. The Alcarria can be pleasantly explored in a day out from Sigüenza.

East of Alcarria lies the Parque Natural del Alto Tajo, where the River Tajo, from its source in the Montes Universales, is already powerful enough to cut a deep limestone gorge on its way to Lisbon. The landscape surrounding the upper Tajo is magnificent, and from here you can clearly see the *Meseta*'s ragged pockmarked roads and tracks running through the scraggy escarpment, and the bleak pine forests known well by only a few shepherds and wild boar hunters. **Molina de Aragón**, an ancient Moorish outpost but now somewhat forsaken, lies on the far side of the park under the semi-restored fortifications of a five-towered *castillo*.

The mountains extend south over the provincial line to become the Serranía de Cuenca, source of many rivers and, like the upper Ebro or the Duero border with Portugal, a place where the true meaning of the tableland can be understood. Raptors circle

in the sky, cars become rare and forestry helicopters buzz overhead looking for forest fires in summer. Windbeaten karstic formations rise and die along every horizon. The Serranía is the heart of the eastern *Meseta* border where Aragón, Castile and Valencia meet; the soul of the Iberian mountains.

The Serranía is best entered from the north-west through **Priego**, a picturesque hillside village well known for its yellow and green glazed ceramic pots. From there the road climbs east past the turning for the royal spa of Solan de Cabras, through the towering Desfiladero de Hoz de Beteta and the ruined *castillo* at **Beteta** before cutting south to the Nacimiento del Cuervo, near the eastern border with Teruel. This is the spectacular source of the River Cuervo, which begins in a succession of waterfalls tumbling over moss-enveloped rock into pools; a popular spot in the summer, frozen and more imposing out of season. **Cañete** lies 60km to the south, still preserving part of its Arab wall and the southern entrance to the mountains.

There are several parts of the Serranía where erosion has sculpted the land into fabulous, often surreal shapes. The Ciudad Encantada (enchanted city), near the Sierra de Valdecabras 25km north of Cuenca, has several examples of Jurassic and Cretaceous limestone erosion with odd formations mushrooming from among the pine forest over an area of 20sq km. To the north, part of the landscape around **El Hosquillo** has been transformed into a wildlife park and the caves and defiles used to create a natural zoo. At **Las Torcas**, lying southeast of Cuenca off the main N240, you can walk among the craters.

CUENCA (pop. 43,000), the capital of the province, is the most spectacularly sited of all *Meseta* cities, on a dramatic promontory overlooking the Rivers Júcar and Huécar. Its *casas colgadas* (hanging houses), as their name suggests, cling to the red cliffsides as if to defy gravity, which they have achieved successfully since the 14th century. Avoid the modern environs and drive into the centre of the old city, parking in or near to the Plaza Mayor. Cuenca itself has enough of interest to warrant an overnight stay and the best part of a day to visit.

The **cathedral** is unique of its style, with a neo-Gothic front and a 12th- and 13th-century interior with features associated with Anglo–French Norman architecture of the same period. The retable above the high altar is the work of that tireless neoclassical architect, Ventura Rodríguez, and is protected by an exceptional wrought-iron *reja* (screen) by the local craftsman, Hernando de Arenas. There are several side-chapels of interest for their flamboyant Gothic decoration. Some of the cathedral's more valuable objects are exhibited in the sacristy. The Sala Capitular is crowned by a fine *artesonado* ceiling, although the garish polychrome finish was a later addition.

Cuenca's importance can be gauged from the fact that a castle existed on this promontory as far back as the ninth century, and by the 14th century the city lay at the head of the largest diocese in Spain. This was the age when its great cardinal, Gil Alborñoz, was a key figure in the restoration of the papacy's power in Rome during its exile in Avignon. He is buried in Toledo cathedral (see p. 251). The 16th-century bishop's palace has been converted into the **Museo Diocesano-Catedralico**, and contains work by El Greco, a Calvary by Gerard David, a 14th-century Byzantine diptych and fine examples of tapestries and carpets that were once woven in Cuenca. (Open Tues–Sat 11am–2pm & 4–6pm. Sun 11am–2pm. Cl Mon.)

The Calle Obispo Valero leads downhill beside the cathedral to the Casa Colgadas and the **Museo de Arte Abstracto**. This is the most important museum of its genre and contains work by Chillida, Tapiès, Saura, Sempère and Zobel, among others. The museum also preserves a fine *artesonado* Mudéjar ceiling. (Open Tues–Sat 11am–2pm & 4–6pm. Mon 11am–2pm. Cl Sun.) Just up from there in the Casa del Curato is the **Museo de Cuenca**, with interesting Iberian, Roman and Visigothic artefacts from the province. (Open Tues–Sun 10am–2pm & 4–7pm. Cl Mon.) Another part of Cuenca's charm is appreciating the hanging houses from a distance, from one of the paths that lead to the good walkways along the riverbanks.

Cuenca is the ideal place from which to explore the Serranía and the northern perimeters of the province; while the southern zone, where the sierras give way to wheat prairies and agricultural steppes, is more easily tackled from Alarcón.

Alarcón, on a rise above the River Júcar, was a site conquered and reconquered throughout the crusade against the Moors. It was part of the dowry given by Al-Mutamid of Seville when his daughter married Alfonso VI, and later fell into the hands of the Order of Santiago. The *castillo* is now a parador and the village has one church of importance, Santa María La Mayor, which has a classical façade resembling a triumphal arch.

The Knights of Calatrava

The Campo de Calatrava is the name given to the lands that fell within the defensive jurisdiction of the Knights of Calatrava. Throughout the 11th century the territory was controlled by the Knights Templar but, when they were forced to retreat towards the end of the 12th century, the lands were offered by the crown to anyone who would protect them against Moorish incursions.

The task was undertaken by a warrior-monk from Navarre, who established an ascetic Order of Knights that were given papal sanction and called the Knights of Calatrava in 1164. Like the Knights of Santiago and Alcántara, whose Orders were established at about the same time, the Calatrava Order was ruled by a council presided over by a Grand Master and his subordinate commanders from the different territories.

The temporal power of the Grand Masters expanded so widely throughout the Peninsula between the 13th and 15th centuries that they became virtually petty princes. Among the many reforms undertaken by Isabel la Católica was the disbandment of the Order's effective military rule, which she achieved by manipulating the grandmasterships into the hands of her husband and then diminishing their effective power until their role was merely ceremonial.

The ruined Roman settlement of **Valeria** lies in between Alarcón and Cuenca, but **Segóbriga**, 80km west of Alarcón just off the N111 at Saelices, is better excavated. It rises from the Cigüela plain, a place inhabited from Iberian times although its fortunes reached their zenith during the Roman occupation. A small museum exists on the site, exhibiting objects and sculpture found during the excavation of the theatre and amphitheatre. The small Visigothic basilica on a hill beside the ruins was once the seat of a bishopric.

Uclés, a fast 15km north of Segóbriga, has an impressive monastery, discernible from afar, that closer inspection shows to combine, with surprising fluency and effect, Gothic, Plateresque, Herreran and classical features. It was here that Isabel la Católica managed to persuade the chapter of the Knights of Santiago to relinquish their authority and influ-

ence to the crown. This effected the virtual demise of the power of the warrior-monks of Santiago and, soon after, of their rivals of Alcántara and Calatrava. One reason why so many *castillos* lie in ruins today was because of the disbandment of the crusading Orders by *Los Reyes Católicos*, as they concentrated sovereignty into the hands of the monarchy; any threatening *castillos* were demolished by royal command.

Fortunately **Belmonte**, lying 100km west of Alarcón, has survived intact and is one of the best preserved Gothic *castillos* of the region. In the 14th century Pedro I 'the Cruel' conferred the status of a town on Belmonte; it subsequently served as a fortress-palace for the Marqueses de Villena. The village has a marked señorial quality with large doorways, stone *emblasonadas* (coats-of-arms) and daunting protective grilles across the windows. This was the birthplace of the great Renaissance poet and translator, Fray Luis de León (1527?–91).

South-east of Belmonte is the equally beautiful village of **San Clemente**, once again developed by the Order of Santiago and the Villena dynasty in the 15th century. Most of its larger monuments, such as the Plateresque Casa Consistorial in the Plaza Mayor, are examples of fine parochial Renaissance architecture. It lies a few miles from the provincial border between Cuenca and Albacete.

ALBACETE (pop. 126,000) is the undistinguished capital of a seldom-visited province that historically has always belonged to Murcia, but was incorporated into Castile with the redrawing of the regional boundaries following the new constitution in 1978. It is an agro-industrial area with some beautiful stretches of road in the north-east running along the Júcar valley. The single reason to cross the province is to reach the Sierra de Alcaraz, sometimes referred to as the Switzerland of La Mancha, bordering on the Sierra de Segura – if not the most beautiful, then certainly the most obscure, route into Andalusia.

The most monumental town is **Alcaraz** (pop. 2,000), a burrow of whitewashed houses built beneath a ruined *castillo*. Of interest are the magnificent Plaza Mayor and the church of La Trinidad with a twin-arched Gothic doorway. **Ayna**, on the eastern side of the *massif*, is a humbler place but spectacularly positioned on the side of a steep river valley aptly named Garganta del Mundo (the world's ravine).

TOURIST OFFICE

GUADALAJARA: Travesía de Beladíez 5.

Accommodation, Eating and Drinking

GUADALAJARA:

(R)**Minaya**, Mayor 23, tel (911) 21 22 53. You eat upstairs quite elegantly beneath a painted *artesonado* ceiling. Good local manchego wine. C–B.

SIGÜENZA (tel code 911):

(H)**Castillo de Sigüenza**, Plaza del Castillo s/n, tel 39 01 00. One of the older Franco-era paradors. Commanding magnificent views over the river valley. Luxurious and peaceful. Ideal for exploring as far north as Soria and the province of Guadalajara. B.

CUENCA (tel code 966):

(H)**Posada de San José**, Julián Romero 4, tel 21 13 00. In a restored *posada* (inn). Intimate and relaxed atmosphere. C.
(R)**Mesón Casas Colgadas**, Canónigos s/n, tel 22 35 09. This is the most authentic

place to eat in a hanging house, with views over the Huécar gorge. The food is excellent.

ALARCÓN:

(H)**Parador Marqués de Villena**, Avda Amigos del Castillo, s/n, tel (966) 33 13 50. Excellent for exploring the south-east. Belonged to Enrique de Villena (1384–1434), Marquis of Villena, who wrote the first book of Spanish cooking, *Arte Cisoria* (The Art of Carving). Parador food suffices. Locally shot *perdiz* (partridge) is always good in La Mancha, especially served *en escabeche* (pickled in wine vinegar and herbs). B.

(R)**Don Pepe**, Desvío de Valverde de Júcar, Olmedilla de Alarcón, tel (966) 33 22 94. A rural alternative to the Alarcón parador. C.

Toledo and Ciudad Real

TOLEDO (pop. 58,000), built on a steep promontory overlooking the River Tajo, was an important Roman settlement and capital for various periods of Visigothic, Moorish and Christian Spain. It remains the seat of Castile's archbishopric and is a magical, sometimes mysterious city geared these days unashamedly to the day-tripper. For more than a merely superficial understanding of its former imperial greatness, you should try to spend at least a couple of days and nights here to explore it.

The main road from Madrid enters the city through the grand Renaissance Visagra Gate. Continue up the hill, through the Plaza de Zocodover and past the *alcázar*; on the far side as you start to descend is a car park, where you should leave your vehicle and explore on foot. It is pointless trying to drive anywhere inside the old city, but be warned that the streets are narrow, hilly and labyrinthine, and continuous attention should be paid to the map.

The **alcázar** stands at the highest point of the city. Other fortresses existed on the site before the present building was commissioned by Charles V, and though it was sacked four times it has been restored in line with the drawings of the original architects, Alonso de Covarrubias and Juan de Herrera.

Down from the *alcázar* in Calle de Cervantes leading into the Plaza de Zocodover is the hospital of **Santa Cruz**, a fine Plateresque building by Enrique de Egas. The building now houses the main museum in Toledo, containing a good archeological section with Roman and Visigothic remains. Other rooms are devoted to tapestries, paintings, furniture, sacred art and the damascened 'blades' and armour for which Toledo is still famous.

The Plaza de Zocodover, the centre of café life, contains patisseries selling the very finest of Toledo's famous marzipans and is the most atmospheric place to stop for a drink. From there the narrow shopping thoroughfare, Calle de Comercio, leads to the **cathedral**. The first stone was laid in 1227

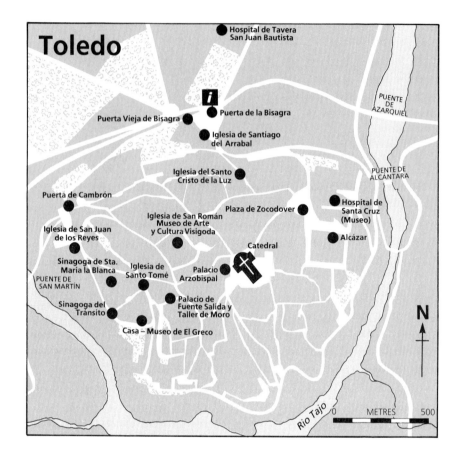

Toledo

Hospital de Tavera
San Juan Bautista

PUENTE DE AZARQUIEL

Puerta Vieja de Bisagra

Puerta de la Bisagra

Iglesia de Santiago
del Arrabal

Iglesia del Santo
Cristo de la Luz

PUENTE DE
ALCANTARA

Puerta de Cambrón

Plaza de Zocodover

Hospital de
Santa Cruz
(Museo)

Iglesia de San Román
Museo de Arte
y Cultura Visigoda

Iglesia de San Juan
de los Reyes

Alcázar

Catedral

Sinagoga de Sta.
Maria la Blanca

PUENTE DE
SAN MARTIN

Iglesia de
Santo Tomé

Palacio
Arzobispal

Sinagoga del
Tránsito

Palacio de
Fuente Salida y
Taller de Moro

N

Casa – Museo de El Greco

Rio Tajo

0   METRES   500

but the building took more than two and a half centuries to complete. There are eight different doorways, all notable for their carvings, and access is through the *Puerta de Mollete* (door of rolls), where bread was once distributed to the poor. You arrive in the ogival twin-storey cloister, with frescoes by Francisco Bayeu depicting the martyrdom of the saints, which joins the Bishop's Palace via a passageway over the street. A ticket grants you entrance to the sacristy, treasury, choirstalls and side-chapels.

Eighty-eight columns support the dim but immense interior of the cathedral. In the centre, as with almost all Spanish cathedrals, are the choirstalls and Capilla Mayor, enclosed by magnificent *rejas* (screens) by Domingo de Céspedes and Francisco de Villapando respectively. The lower choirstalls by Rodrigo Alemán are carved with scenes from the fall of Granada, punctuated with a few of his more licentious whims.

The wood and gilt Gothic altarpiece of the Capilla Mayor can be illuminated by feeding a 25-peseta coin into the box to the left of the *reja*. This also enables you to see the tombs of the *Reyes Viejos* (old kings) buried on each side in Gothic niches: Alfonso VII (1126–57), gospel side; Sancho III (1157–8) and Sancho IV (1284–95), epistle side. But it is the monumental sepulchre of Cardinal Cisneros, tutor to Isabel la Católica and founder of the hospital of Santa Cruz, that upstages them all and was installed against the will of the cathedral ministry one night on the orders of Her Majesty in fulfilment of the great prelate's dying words. Part of the original Gothic screen had to be knocked down to accommodate it.

Behind the Capilla Mayor, in bursts of fluffy cherubs, waves, flames and clouds, stands one of the most outrageous pieces of Churrigueresque structures in existence: the *Transparente* by Narcis Tomé. Composed of coloured marbles, bronze and stucco, it was built to bring more light into the back of the altar and lends what someone once described as 'a sensation of carefree artistic disorder. It is heaven.'

Among the most important sidechapels is the Capilla de San Ildefonso, containing the tomb of the warriorarchbishop, Gil Alvarez de Alborñoz (1310–67). He campaigned in Africa, saved the life of Alfonso XI at the siege of Tarifa, and renounced his archbishopric in order to command the forces of Pope Innocent VI and reconquer the papal state. After his death in Italy, his body was carried overland back to Toledo to be buried.

In the Capilla de los Reyes Nuevos lie three more Trastamaran kings: on the right upon entering, Henry II (1369–79) with his wife Doña Juana; opposite, with Catherine of Lancaster, Henry III (1390–1406); beside the altar, John I (1379–90) and his wife Leonor of Aragón.

The story of the Capilla de la Descensión contains mythical elements. It is related that the Virgin appeared to Bishop San Ildefonso in this place in the year 666, a story depicted in the panels of the retable by Juan de Borgoña. A piece of the rock that touched her foot is preserved behind a grille to the left of the altar. The Capilla Mozárabe, guarded by a *reja* by Juan Francés, still celebrates the Mozarabic liturgy which began in Visigothic times and is independent of later Roman liturgical reforms. Its most obvious characteristics are the blue vestments of its celebrants, not used outside Spain.

The Plateresque Sala Capitular is interesting for its Mudéjar *artesonado* (inlaid ceiling), and the sacristy has a fine ceiling by Lucas Giordano and works by El Greco. The treasury contains the great monstrance by Enrique de Arfe, a 15th-century cross painted by Fray Angélico and the rock-crystal jewelbox of Juana 'La Loca', among many other priceless artefacts.

From the cathedral, take the Calle de la Trinidad leading into the Calle de Santo Tomé in the south-west corner of Toledo. In an annexe beside the church of Santo Tomé hangs El Greco's imaginative masterpiece, *The Entombment of Gonzalo Ruiz, Conde de Orgaz*, showing the appearance of St Stephen and St Augustine at the philanthropic Count's burial.

Behind the church, take a look at the patio in the Palacio de Fuentesalida and the Taller de Moro, an old workshop used by the cathedral masons, now housing a small **Museum of Sculpture and Tiles**. Continuing downhill you should eventually emerge into Calle de Los Reyes Católicos, where you will find the two magnificent synagogues that are enduring testaments to the power and importance of the Sephardic Jews of medieval Toledo.

In the **Sinagoga del Tránsito** (1357–60), built by Pedro I's treasurer, Samuel ha-Levi, is a small museum dedicated to Sephardic manuscripts. The newly restored prayer hall, with stucco-latticed windows, a gallery and Hebraic inscriptions around the wall, appears almost austere in comparison to the **Sinagoga Santa Maria la Blanca** (c. 1203), its counterpart just down the road. More Arabic in style, like a mini-mosque, this synagogue's sensation of space is enhanced by the 32 octagonal columns with stucco capitals and horseshoe arches.

It would have been a cruel irony if the Catholic Kings, who expelled the Jews from Spain in 1492, had been buried in nearby **San Juan de los Reyes** as they intended when they commissioned its construction in commemoration of Isabel's victory over Juana La Beltraneja and the Portuguese at the Battle of Toro in 1476. Nevertheless, this remains one of the best examples of late Gothic–Plateresque architecture, and is the work of Juan Guas and a troop of stonemasons judging by the amount and quality of the sculpture. Both the church and cloister merit a visit, the latter for the *artesonado* ceiling covering the upper level with the royal coat-of-arms endlessly repeated.

The most tourist-orientated place in this area is the **Casa-Museo de El Greco**, back near the Sinagoga Tránsito. This is a reconstruction of the house where El Greco lived and worked, and is of interest more for its patio, tiles and archeological finds than as a reconstruction of a 16th-century dwelling. Among the paintings are several works and copies by El Greco, Velázquez, Murillo, and others.

El Greco was born in Crete in about 1541, when the island was part of the Venetian Empire. He studied painting in Venice under Titian and Tintoretto before making his way to Spain via Rome. His aspirations to work as a court painter to Philip II at El Escorial were dashed when his work *St Maurice and the Theban Legion* found disfavour with his patron (see p. 235). From there he left for Toledo and made a living from mainly ecclesiastical commissions until his death in 1614.

The Paseo de Recaredo joins the south-west corner of Toledo with the north and the Visagra Gate, the main entrance to the city and the point at which this itinerary began. Just along from here, but outside the city confines, stands the hospital of **Tavera/San Juan Bautista**, commissioned by Cardinal Tavera. This was the first great Renaissance building of Castile and its main architect was the Cardinal's secretary, Bartolomé de Bustamante. However, many of the central figures associated with 16th-century building were involved in its construction, particularly Covarrubias, Vergaras and Villalpondo.

The guided tour of the palace rooms is interesting as this is one of the only authentic reconstructions of a palatial Renaissance interior where much of the original art collection is still intact. This includes exceptional works by El Greco, Tintoretto and Caravaggio, and Ribera's peculiar painting of a bearded woman breastfeeding her child. The library is the most memorable room, and contains some beautiful examples of Mudéjar bookbinding that recall the

The large green and glazed façade of the Plaza Mayor at Almagro was built on the proceeds from the mines of southern Castile–La Mancha, exploited in the 16th century by the Dutch banker, Jakob Fugger, and his descendants. Angus Mitchell

age when Toledo housed the most important translation school of the 12th and 13th centuries. Your visit also includes a tour of the chapel, pharmacy and the semi-circular underground crypt of the Dukes of Medinaceli.

Walking back into the city through the Visagra Gate, you pass the church of **Santiago del Arrabal**, founded shortly after the reconquest of Toledo in 1085 and one of the finest examples of Toledan Mudéjar–Romanesque with elegant *ajimez* (twin-arched windows) and a Moorish tower. Continuing uphill, you pass through the Mudéjar horseshoe arch of the Puerta del Sol, and into Calle del Cristo de la Luz to the dusty little brick church of **Santo Cristo de la Luz**, formerly the

mosque of Bib-al-Mardón. It was here, so the story goes, that the horse of Alfonso VI collapsed to its knees as the conquering king entered the city in 1085, and refused to move until part of the wall of the church had been removed. Here the discovery was made of a crucifix and candle that had burnt unceasingly for 373 years, the period of Moorish occupation.

More frescoes of the period can be found in the Mudéjar church of **San Roman**, now serving as a Museum of Visigothic Art that contains mainly stone carvings and a fragment of the Apostles' Creed – the main testimony of Reccared's (586–601) conversion from Arianism to Catholicism.

These are the main sights of Toledo,

but there are countless others that clearly bear the evidence of the city's long and unique history. At sunset when the air cools and the swallows dive through the sky, walk around the perimeter walls overlooking the Tajo and savour the Grecoean red and purple hues of the city reflected in the slow waters of the river. By driving or walking in between the two main bridges crossing the Tajo – the Puente de Alcántara (east) and the Puente de San Martín (west), it is not hard to understand why this remains one of the most attractive medieval cities of Europe.

For more panoramic views, follow the signs to the modern parador, from where Greco was supposed to have painted his famous cityscape. In the hills adjoining you can see the *cigarrales* (country houses), some of which date back to the Arab occupation but are now private summer retreats hidden along shaded driveways.

From Toledo the normal route south is to rejoin the fast N-IV at **Tembleque**, stopping for a drink in its elegant Plaza Mayor, before continuing on to Andalusia. This route offers little beyond the Flemish-looking windmills and the endless lines of vines and olives around **Valdepeñas** (pop. 25,000) – the largest single wine-growing region in the world.

The character of the province of Toledo is defined by the rugged plain of the River Tajo bordered to the north by the Sierra de Gredos and to the south by the Montes de Toledo. **Talavera de la Reina** (pop. 70,000) is the only town of any significant size and remains the centre of a large ceramics and lustreware industry. Here you will find a few dusty Mudéjar

churches and countless shops and warehouses selling the brightly coloured handpainted pottery. *Castillos* worth making a detour for are at **Malpica de Tajo**, **Escalona**, **Guadamur** and **Oropesa** (parador). There are also Iberian remains, including the haunting Iberian Bulls, at **Guisando**, just over the border in Avila; and Ibero–Roman ruins beside the Tajo near the provincial boundary with Extremadura.

The Montes de Toledo are desolate mountains with neatly farmed olive groves on their periphery slopes and mainly private hunting estates higher up. The villages of **Consuegra** and **Campo de Criptana** are notable for their windmills, and the former celebrates the largest saffron harvest in the world each year in the last week of October. The mountains divide the Tajo basin from the basin of the River Guadiana, which is currently drying up badly in many places due to the toll of irrigation required by farmers in the area.

The **Parque Nacional Tablas de Daimiel**, once Nueva Castilla's most important wetland, is now almost dry and the thousands of birds that once migrated through the area have been forced in the last few years to find alternative breeding and feeding grounds. It is sad that even when an area has been designated a national park, it can be allowed to deteriorate in this way. But, as you will discover throughout Spain, any national understanding of conservation has a long way to go before it reaches a comparable standard with other western European countries.

The Parque Natural de Las Lagunas de Ruidera, 80km to the south-east, has fortunately fared better. There you can explore a succession of lakes stepped up the hillsides that feed off the Embalse de Peñarroya. For the more romantically minded there is also the Cueva de Montesinos, where Don Quixote had one of his most hallucinatory experiences:

> There appeared before my eyes the most royal and sumptuous palace on earth, whose walls and battlements appeared to be formed of clear transparent crystal; and when two great doors opened in them I saw coming out towards me a venerable old man, in a cloak of purple serge which trailed on the ground. (Part II, Chs. 22 and 23)

The character in question is Montesinos, one of Quixote's imaginary heroes, who relates how the lakes are in fact Ruidera, her seven daughters and two nieces who were transformed by Merlin the Magician.

If you decide to explore this part of La Mancha it is best to base yourself at **Almagro** (pop. 8,000), one of the finest and most thoughtfully preserved Renaissance towns in Castile. It rises anonymously from the fertile plain known as the Campo de Calatrava, and contains a unique *Casco Antiguo* (Old Quarter): tractor-wide streets of farmhouses on the outskirts and streets of whitewashed mansions inside.

It was 16th-century Dutch banking money belongly mainly to the Fugger family that generated Almagro's prosperity, and this northern European influence explains the glazed and green Plaza Mayor, which contains the patio-theatre or Corral de la Comedias, still used in the summer as a stage for a theatre festival. At the open end of the Plaza is the equestrian statue of Diego de Almagro (1478–1538), conqueror of Chile.

The drive south to **Calzada de Calatrava** takes you through less pampered *pueblos*, where the rule of the Knights of Calatrava can be partly understood by visiting the magnificent ruins of the Castillo de Salvatierra/de Calatrava, facing on the far side of the valley the ruins of a convent that also belonged to the Order. This was the great military stronghold of the crusading Order, whose purpose was to defend these southern marches against Al-Andalus.

A dirt track leads up to the *castillo*, but you may prefer to leave your car at the bottom of the hill and walk up to the ruins. Only the church has so far been restored, but the views across the surrounding plain to the Sierra Morena are magnificent. The Sierra Morena (dark sierra) alludes to the colour of its hills and sparsely populated grazing ground, where cork oak pastures are separated by stone walls and private farming *pueblos* – not unlike parts of Extremadura.

A road cuts through the plain from Calatrava through the sierra to Córdoba via the ecologically disgraceful chemical works at **Puertollano** (pop. 53,000), one of the most depressing towns in Iberia. It was built to mine the coal hills to the west and now serves as a vast settlement for workers in the plant. After Puertollano the road south, worn badly in places, takes you over a miniature *Meseta* and thence into Andalusia, where you eventually meet the Guadalquivir at Montoro.

TOURIST OFFICE

TOLEDO: Puerta Bisagra s/n, tel (925) 22 08 43.

Accommodation, Eating and Drinking

TOLEDO (tel code 925):

(H)**Conde de Orgaz**, Paseo de Cigarrales, tel 22 18 50/54. Modern parador on the other side of the Tajo, overlooking the city. Clean and luxurious. B.

(H&R)**Hostal Cardenal**, Paseo de Recaredo 24, tel 22 08 62. In the 17th-century Lorenzana Palace, just beside the Visagra Gate. Very central for exploring the old city. Family-run country hotel atmosphere. Air-conditioned restaurant with summer terrace serving local specialities cooked in old wood-burning ovens. C & C–B.

(H)**María Cristina**, Marqués de Mendigorria 1, tel 21 32 02. Recently opened. Good value for money. Parking. Air-conditioning. C–B.

(R)**Adolfo**, Granada 6, tel 22 73 21. Backed up with an excellent cellar, this is the most lavish dining room in Toledo. Cl Sun evenings. B.

(R)**Horno La Catedral**, Nuncio Viejo 1, tel 22 42 44. Specialities include *jabalí en adobo a la parilla* (wild boar smoked and marinated with garlic, then grilled). C–B.

PUERTO LAPICE:

(R)**Venta El Quixote**, just off the N-IV. Traditional Manchegan *venta* painted in bright blue and whitewash with the bar built among the vast wine *tinajas* (vats). Excellent restaurant. Specialities include *migas de pastor* (breadcrumbs fried with garlic) and *flores Manchegas* (fried flower-shaped pastries with ice-cream). Shop selling local wine and cheese. C.

MANZANARES:

(H)**Parador de Manzanares**, tel (926) 61 04 00. Good for a night if you're driving straight through to Andalusia. Modern and functional. C.

ALMAGRO: (tel code 926):

(H)**Parador de Almagro**, tel 86 01 00. Built on the ground plan of a 16th-century Franciscan convent. Brightly painted rooms overlooking 16 patios. Excellent for exploring the south of the region. Cosy. C–B.

(R)**El Corregidor**, Plaza Fray Fernando Fernández de Córdoba 2, tel 86 06 48. Bar with upstairs summer terrace and blue-beamed restaurant. Good use of figs and almonds in many of the dishes. B.

CHAPTER FOURTEEN

Extremadura

EXTREMADURA IS A REGION of desolate beauty – flat and mountainous, arable and barren, bleak and spectacular. Protected by a yoke of obscure sierras to the north, the land descends through a series of fertile valleys running into the river basins of the Tajo and Guadiana, where the roads straighten and cut their way through expansive prairies to the white villages and rolling hills along the border with Andalusia.

The history of Extremadura is one of near-continuous isolation. Under the Romans it enjoyed a period of relative prosperity on account of the *Via Plata* (Silver Road), which joined the rich mines of Rio Tinto with the Atlantic coast of the north. Evidence of this affluence can be seen in the *balnearios* (thermal baths) at Baños de Montemayor, Alange and El Raposo; or in the great Teatro Romano in Mérida. Moreover, the countryside was opened up and navigated by a series of stone bridges, many of them extant though water has long ceased to flow beneath their arches.

During the *Reconquista* the region became a no man's land and war zone between the expanding kingdom of León and the *taifa* states of the south. The name Extremadura originated at that time to describe the 'Lands beyond the Duero' (non-Christian Spain lying south of the River Duero). The crenellated *castillo* ruins crowning so many hilltops remind you of this state of perpetual frontier skirmish. The founding of the military Order of Alcántara in the 12th century marked a more disciplined attempt to encroach on Moorish territory.

After the fall of Granada in 1492, the crusading zealotry of the Extremeños found a new outlet in the subjugation of the Americas. Rumours circulating from Seville of the New World spoke of fabled kingdoms such as El Dorado, and the sons of Extremadura left in droves to seek their fortunes overseas. Among their number were Hernán Cortés, the Pizarro brothers and Núñez de Bilboa. As you drive between villages and cities you'll undoubtedly recognize places for their namesakes on the far side of the Atlantic. Yet, even though the Extremeños laid the foundation-stone of Spanish imperialism, little remains to remind you of their glory days except the exquisite Renaissance palaces – some

Extremadura

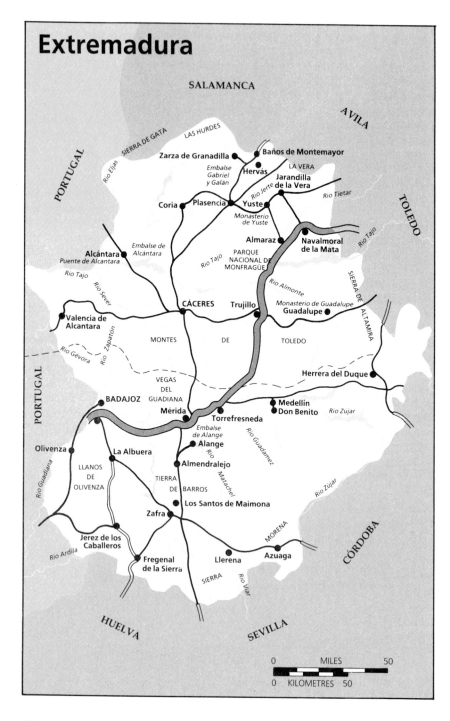

SALAMANCA

AVILA

PORTUGAL

SIERRA DE GATA

LAS HURDES

Río Eljas

Zarza de Granadilla

Baños de Montemayor

LA VERA

Embalse Gabriel y Galán

Hervás

Jarandilla de la Vera

Río Jerte

Río Tietar

TOLEDO

Coria

Plasencia

Yuste

Monasterio de Yuste

Almaraz

Navalmoral de la Mata

Río Tajo

Embalse de Alcántara

Alcántara

Puente de Alcántara

Río Tajo

PARQUE NACIONAL DE MONFRAGÜE

Río Almonte

SIERRA DE ALTAMIRA

Río Sever

CÁCERES

Trujillo

Monasterio de Guadalupe

Guadalupe

Valencia de Alcántara

MONTES

DE

TOLEDO

Río Zapatón

Río Gévora

PORTUGAL

VEGAS DEL GUADIANA

Herrera del Duque

BADAJOZ

Mérida

Torrefresneda

Medellín

Don Benito

Río Zújar

Olivenza

La Albuera

Embalse de Alange

Alange

Almendralejo

Río

LLANOS DE OLIVENZA

TIERRA DE BARROS

Río Matachel

Río Guadámez

Río Zújar

Los Santos de Maimona

Río Guadiana

Zafra

Jerez de los Caballeros

Río Ardila

Fregenal de la Sierra

Llerena

Azuaga

MORENA

CÓRDOBA

SIERRA

Río Viar

HUELVA

SEVILLA

0   MILES   50

0   KILOMETRES   50

neglected, some restored – built from the local granite.

With the decline in Spain's empire, Extremadura sank back into a state of proud indifference as a dust-blown frontier: a refuge for minorities, gipsies and Bible salesmen. George Borrow based much of his 19th-century study on the Zincalis and gipsies on his experiences among their counterparts in Extremadura. The abject poverty of the region has only partially been eased in the last four decades by a concerted governmental effort to 'modernize' the region. But the images of old Spain, such as farming by mule, or driving sheep out of the burning plains in the spring are still familiar. Old men pass their days in bars between games of dominoes and shots of brandy, while widows dressed in black sit crocheting and chatting on doorsteps until sunset. It's a hermetic world, which the young still desert to seek fortune elsewhere.

The environment continues to support one of the most untamed ecosystems remaining in Europe. Numerous different species of raptor, eagle, vulture, peregrine and kite fly overhead. In springtime the mountainsides are covered in wild flowers and the air fills with the smell of lavender and thyme. By August, everything but the cork, oak and eucalyptus trees has been burnt a pale brown by the merciless sun. Autumn brings the sheep back to the cork and oak *dehesa* (grazing land) to graze before the lambs are born in December.

The Northern Sierras and River Valleys

The fastest road into Extremadura from the east is the N-V-E4 from Madrid to Navalmoral de la Mata. From Navalmoral de la Mata the CC904 leads north through Talayuela across the River Tiétar. This area is given over to tobacco plantations, and you see the huge hole-ridden barns built beside the stream for drying the leaves. Continue on the road winding up the foothills of the Sierra de Gredos to Jarandilla de la Vera.

Jarandilla de la Vera, surrounded by thick deciduous woodlands on a site overlooking the River Vera, is renowned for its *pimentón* factories, which grind red peppers into a bright orange powder used as a cooking spice. On the promontory above the village stands an early 15th-century fortress-palace, once owned by the Counts of Oropesa, but now graciously converted into a national parador. Vast cylindrical towers surround a rectangular interior and beautiful courtyard with a two-storey gallery. It was here that the Emperor Charles V (1516–58) waited while his deathbed was prepared in the nearby monastery of Yuste. The village is composed of the typical popular architecture of the area, crooked old adobe and painted houses with wooden balconies built about the church of Nuestra Señora de la Torre, the crenellated rooftop of which has a blatantly defensive structure.

The Valley of La Vera contains several other villages of a similar dilapidated charm with narrow porticoed lanes emanating from the wooden and granite arcades of the Plaza Mayor and the occasional fine parochial church or palace. Other villages worth visiting near Jarandilla include **Pasarón de la Vera** and **Losar de la Vera**. In the surrounding countryside there is a thriving, self-contained world of fruit orchards, wild herbs, grazing animals and trout streams, while the soil each year yields an important cherry harvest. In spring, with the snow still lying on the Sierra de Gredos, and the terraces of cherries in full blossom, it is not difficult to understand why the Holy Roman Emperor Charles I of Spain, chose this valley and the silence of its monastery for his retirement and death.

The monastery of **Yuste** lies a few kilometres up a side road leading out of **Cuacos de Yuste** and is set in a forest of oak trees in the shadow of the sierra. It was destroyed by the occupying French army in 1809, and fell into a state of ruin until restoration work began in 1958 to mark the 400th anniversary of the Emperor's death. The rooms are still draped in black muslin and a mournful atmosphere pervades, especially when the two great cloisters echo with the sound of chanting monks. You will be shown around by an official guide, who will point out the chair specially designed to ease the strain on Charles's gout-swollen legs; the pool where he used to bathe during the summer, now filled with golden carp; the platform he used for mounting his horse; and the crypt that housed the coffin before his body was transferred to the mausoleum of the Kings of Spain at El Escorial.

Continuing from Yuste along roads in varying states of disrepair, you come to **Garganta la Olla**, where the route twists through the Gredos via the quiet hamlets of **Piornal** and **Valdastillas** before reaching the main Plasencia–Avila N110 following the course of the River Jerte. This is another serene valley of stone walls, crystal-clear rock pools and terraced orchards. In spring or autumn when the landscape is at its best, you'll find it difficult not to spend a few days here soaking up the rural lethargy.

Hervás, locked away among olive groves and cherry orchards in the highlands of Extremadura, has remained a refuge for Sephardic Jews since their expulsion from Spain in 1492. It is typical of the persecuted communities who found refuge in these wild outbacks, and contains probably the most authentic *aljama* anywhere in Spain, with its whitewashed and timbered houses cascading with geraniums and a diminutive synagogue that is still used today. Some 10km further north, on the border with Castile, is the old Roman spa town of **Baños de Montemayor** with a well-preserved town centre and leaning church tower.

Driving south from the Gredos foothills, you arrive in under an hour at **Plasencia** (pop. 31,000): the transport capital of the Extremaduran highlands built around a bend in the River Jerte. The dusty outskirts hide a well-preserved centre, which is surrounded by the remnants of vast walls studded with six gates and 68 semicircular towers. It is another of those strategically placed siege cities that was continually sacked and rebuilt throughout the Reconquest until its final resettlement during the reign of Alfonso VIII (1158–1214) who said of it, in an attempt to attract settlers: *'placeat Deo et hominibus'* (that it may please God and men). The name Plasencia supposedly derives from this pronouncement.

Life revolves around the busy Plaza Mayor where time is kept on the *ayuntamiento* (town hall) by the Bavarian-looking clock inhabited by a mechanical marionette who strikes the hour. Market days are particularly lively, when farmers descend from the sierras to sell everything from dried figs to mountain honey. Austere, noble mansions – some with wrought-iron balconies and others with sculpted corner windows – lie neglected in the backstreets of the Old Quarter around the Gothic and Romanesque churches of **San Nicolás**, **San Martín**, **San Vicente** and **San Pedro**. Your first objective, however, should be to visit the **cathedral**, the eccentric silhouette of which looms majestically above the Placentina skyline and hints at the importance of Plasencia as an early Renaissance city – an edifice that in today's context appears as overstated and undervisited as the surrounding town.

It is, in fact, two unfinished cathedrals built between the 13th and 16th centuries and constructed around a remarkable proto-Gothic cloister. Entry is through the north door, which is surrounded by a richly ornamented Plateresque façade of carved skulls and bas-reliefs. Inside, fluted pillars with weave-patterned bases support a canopy of stellar vaulting. The cathedral is a collaborative effort by masters of late Gothic and early Renaissance Castilian architecture: Juan de Alava, Enrique Egas, Diego de Siloé, Gil de Hontañon and Alonso de Covarrubias. The oak *sillería* (choirstalls) are the work of Rodrigo Alemán, whose wicked humour in this instance mixes scenes from the Old Testament with more profane subjects such as bullfighting and hairdressing.

Passing through into the cloister, designed by an Arab architect named Asoyte, you can seen the remains of the Romanesque nave and the *Melón*-dome over the chapterhouse, reminiscent of the late Romanesque style to be seen in the cathedrals in the southern reaches of the kingdom of León. A spiral staircase leads to a terrace overlooking the rooftops of the city.

Leaving Plasencia southbound for Trujillo, turn left after about 2km along the C524. On this road you'll get your first real taste of the Extremaduran plateau: vultures and eagles circling above the oak and cork *dehesa*, woebegone farmsteads, and pigs grazing for windfall acorns. After about 20km a sign marks your entry into the **Parque Natural de Monfragüe**, one of the most fiercely protected wildlife sanctuaries in the Peninsula, which stretches either side of the vast rocky ravine carved out by the Tajo. In the tiny hamlet of **Villarreal de San Carlos** there is a park centre with books and information on the area, where wardens will advise you about hides and observation-points. The road continues out of the park to Trujillo. (See p. 266.)

Before leaving northern Extremadura, a few words should be said of the other sierras, which again are rarely visited by travellers and comprise some of the most desolate but beautiful mountain scenery in the country. In the extreme north-western corner of the region lie the five peaceful valleys beneath the Sierra de Gata, the last mountain range before Portugal in the great central range – the Sistema Central – that cuts across the *Meseta*. This is an area of vast pine forests and small intimate villages huddled up the steep inclines, where the worn stone streets flanked by wood and wattle houses hide in their midst some architectural relic or are protected from on high by the ruins of a *castillo*.

Adjoining the Sierra de Gata to the east are the peaks of Las Hurdes, one of the most legendary sierras in Spain, where the dearth of churches in many of the small hamlets led to a surge of mythomania about the inhabitants, together with a folklore centred around devils, witches, cannibalism and banditry. There were even far-fetched claims that the Hurdanos did not know of the existence of God until the end of the last century. In 1932 Luis Buñuel made a film of the area, *Tierra Sin Pan* (Land without Bread), whose theme revealed the near-surreal poverty of the people. The crooked concentration of ironstone houses capped with slate roofs still upholds a remarkably primitive way of life: where the subsistence level of each *pueblo* depends on the goats, almond crop, honey, windfall chestnuts and wild chickpeas. At the centre of the range lies the village of **El Gasco** meekly positioned beneath a soaring volcano covered in rockrose and juniper, where you can still buy primitive pipes hewn from the lava.

The waters from these sierras flow between steep hills terraced with almond and olive trees, into the Embalse de Gabriel y Galán, a huge reservoir named after the poet, José María Gabriel y Galán (1870–1905), who wrote in the old dialect of Leonese. Traces of this tongue can still be detected in the everyday conversation of the people of these sierras. On the banks of the reservoir, and reached by a dirt road from **Zarza de Granadilla**, are the picturesque remains of the walled town of **Granadilla**, deserted except for a caretaker, his family and a few free-range turkeys. Its situation could not be more idyllic: perched on the tip of a small peninsula between the horizon of mountains to the north and the wild *dehesa* to the south, with a

daunting granite *castillo* on the site of an Arab *alcázar*. Few ruins can boast of such a romantic position.

Following the River Alagón south along a series of quiet, unmarked country roads, you pass the busy, dilapidated agricultural town of **Coria** (pop. 10,000), founded by the Celts, with a large 15th-century *castillo* built for the Dukes of Alba. This is fortified by an impressive pentagonal tower and a hybrid cathedral that mixes all styles between late Gothic and Baroque. At the confluence of the Alagón and Tajo, 50km further south, lies the town of **Alcántara**, perched serenely on a barren promontory.

The magnificent bridge crossing the Tajo at Alcántara was constructed in the age of Trajan (AD 98–103) by the architect Cayus Julius Lacer. It is a wonder of Roman engineering, forged in uncemented granite blocks, 71m high and 194m long, with a triumphal arch in the middle emblazoned with the Habsburg and Bourbon coats-of-arms. Alcántara ('bridge' in Arabic) became an important defensive site during the Reconquest and headquarters for the military Order of the Knights of Alcántara. You can walk around the ruins of the hilltop *castillo* where the Order was founded in 1218 and see the Plateresque marble tomb of Bravo de Jerez, one of its Grand Masters, in the church of Santa María de Almocóbar. You should also be sure to visit the ruins of the Monastery of San Benito with its beautiful twin-storey Gothic cloister. To the east of Alcántara the charming village of **Garrovillas**, an ancient Iberian settlement, contains a superb, whitewashed arcaded plaza where the ease of Extremeña life can be savoured over a quiet and leisurely drink.

Accommodation, Eating and Drinking

NAVARREDONDA:

(H)**Parador de Gredos**, village of Navarredonda, tel (918) 34 80 48. Although in Castile, this is a good place from which to explore the pine-covered Gredos mountains. C.

JARANDILLA DE LA VERA (tel code 927):

(H)**Parador Carlos V**, in the *castillo* above the village, tel 56 01 17. Rooms overlook a beautiful Renaissance courtyard and fountain in this magnificent *castillo*, built for the Counts of Oropesa and Marqueses de Jarandilla. C.
(R)**Cueva de Puta Parió**, Francisco Pizarro 10, tel 56 01 32. Despite its name, meaning 'the cave where the whore gave birth' – a common swearing sentence in Spanish – this is a simple tavern serving local specialities. D.

HERVÁS:

(H)**Hostal Montecristo**, Av de la Provincia 2, tel (927) 48 11 91. Basic but clean. E–D.

PLASENCIA (tel code 927):

(H&R)**Hotel Alfonso VIII**, C/ Alfonso VIII 34, tel 41 02 50. A central and modern hotel. The restaurant is the best in town, serving excellent Extremeña cuisine. C&B.
(H)**Hostal Los Alamos**, Ctra N630 km131.7, tel 41 15 50. There are several cheaper *hostales* in the centre of town, but this has good facilities and is popular with drivers, especially truckers. E–D.

Conquistador Country

Entering Extremadura along the C401 from Toledo, this route takes you through the central plateau of the region and the great conquistador memorial cities of Guadalupe, Trujillo and Cáceres.

Guadalupe (pop. 2,765) was the spiritual mecca of the conquistadors, and became the most universal name of Extremadura. You need only look at the index of an atlas to see its influence in the naming of settlements throughout the New World. Moreover, the monastery became an important missionary training school directed towards the Catholic conversion of the Americas. Christopher Columbus made a pilgrimage here after his first voyage before continuing his journey to break the news of his discovery to *Los Reyes Católicos* at Barcelona, in order to fulfil a vow he had made when riding out a near-catastrophic storm on his voyage back to Spain in 1493.

Hernán Cortés spent nine days praying to the Virgin of Guadalupe before embarking on his expedition to conquer Mexico, and he rededicated the holy city of Tepeyac in her honour. The riches of the Virgin remained legendary until the monastery was sacked by the French in 1808, when much of the treasure was stolen, but it was beautifully restored a century later and the majority of art was returned.

The small medieval town is situated in the heart of the fertile Sierra de Guadalupe: yet another self-contained valley of green hill pastures, vineyards and olive groves. From the hive of red-tiled rooftops rises the impressive mass of the Hieronymite monastery. Easygoing local life hums around the bars and shops in the arcaded plaza and between the narrow alleyways of whitewashed houses.

The **monastery of Guadalupe** was founded by Alfonso XI in 1340 in thanksgiving for his victory at the Battle of Salado, and quickly grew in stature thanks to a small charred image of the Virgin, carved in holm oak, Nuestra Señora de Guadalupe, Patroness of the Hispanic World. Blessed with miraculous powers to keep kings from making wrong decisions, sailors from drowning and soldiers safe in war, her popularity spread far and wide and Guadalupe was steadily enriched and venerated until the 17th century, by which time it had become one of the most affluent foundations in Europe. Three hospitals, a medical school and several important workshops were established within the humble confines of the town and the Hospedería served as a school for the royal Infantas.

In the centre of the plaza stands the carved font where the first Indian cap-

tives from the New World were baptized. The flamboyant façade of the church is laced with imposing Mudéjar–Gothic stone tracery. You enter the church through one of the corroded-green bronze doors with finely moulded scenes depicting the life of Christ and Mary being crowned by angels. Inside, gold glitters out of the gloom. On a pedestal above the high altar is the 12th-century Madonna, dressed so extravagantly as to be hardly visible. The nave is divided by an exquisite wrought-iron *reja* (screen); and the 17th-century retable, carved in parts by Jorge Manuel Theotocopuli, El Greco's son, is a bewildering assembly of enamel, polychrome and gilt sculpture.

Entry to the monastery is through a ticket room adjoining the church, where you're obliged to join a small party conducted by a guide. The tour begins in the **Embroidery Museum**, lined with cabinets displaying minutely stitched, *haute couture* vestments and altar covers. From there you walk around the Mudéjar brick-built cloister (1402–12) with a two-storey gallery of horseshoe arches, and a Gothic–Mudéjar water pavilion that rises from the trimmed hedges and citrus trees of the patio garden. This is a unique Mudéjar construction, whereby the Arabian veneration for water has been ingeniously incorporated into the basic design of the monastic cloister. Beside the brightly tiled fountain and basin – another example of the strong Muslim influence – there is a connecting door leading to a Gothic cloister, now the monastery's hotel.

Up a spiral flight of red jasper stairs, you are next conducted to the *Camarín* (robing room), where the Virgin

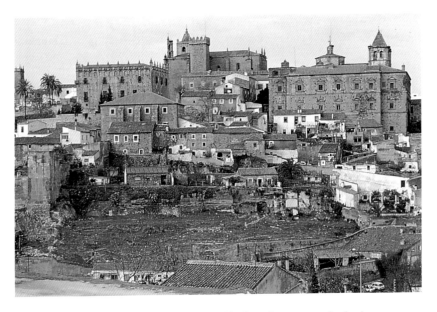

The crenellated horizon of Cáceres, surrounded by less picturesque suburbs, is a testimony to the important role of Extremadura in the conquest of the Americas and its subsequent decline into poverty. Incafo

appears once more, seated on her swivel throne and surrounded by an indigestible Baroque mass of religious paintings by Luca Giordano, gilded marquetry and an ivory Christ. Here, the Virgin is dressed for processional occasions and you have a chance to study her face in close proximity and wonder at her wardrobe, which includes a coat stitched by Isabel Eugenia, the daughter of Philip II.

Back on the ground floor you pass into the **sacristy**, which is lined with a series of paintings by Francisco Zurbarán (1598–1664) illustrating scenes from the life of St Jerome. The strangest portrait shows a monk being insulted by a lion-tamer with rather long, knife-like fingernails. These works were originally commissioned

for the room, and you will notice how the frames for the pictures and the windows are the same size. Above the altar, in the adjoining chapel, hangs one of Zurbarán's most accomplished works: *The Apotheosis of St Jerome*. The guide will also point to the navigation lantern captured from the Turkish flagship at the Battle of Lepanto (1571). The tour ends with a visit to the Reliquary Chamber, which contains strange rock crystal mirrors and countless relics preserved in the most extravagant gold and silver designs.

As you leave Guadalupe it is hard not to marvel that such an isolated village with its majestic and oversized monastery should have had such a massive and widespread spiritual influence throughout South America.

After Santiago de Compostela, Montserrat in Catalonia and El Pilar in Zaragoza, Guadalupe is the next most important religious shrine in Spain, and it is difficult to escape the mystical charm of such a place, which drove those few successive generations of Extremeños to conquest in the name of holy crusade.

The road west meanders quietly out of the sparse and jagged Sierra de las Villuercas onto a fallow, boulder-strewn plain, where strange granite formations haunt the landscape and buzzards hunt above the ditches along the roadside. **Trujillo** (pop. 10,000), 'the Cradle of the Conquistadors', is a magnificent memorial town built upon the proceeds of conquest – a breath-taking assembly of Renaissance palaces, fortress-churches, convents and battlements on a promontory overlooking the bleak Extremeñan plain. From the ring road, head uphill into the huge, arcaded Plaza Mayor, from where the whole town can be explored easily on foot.

The Plaza Mayor is the heart of the town, and contains the most atmospheric bars where every afternoon the locals come to play cards and talk. The irregular pattern of steps, arcaded fronts and whitewashed houses in the shadow of imposing señorial palaces invests it with a unique personality that is both mundane and majestic. Beneath the lichen-covered exterior of the church of San Martín stands a daunting bronze statue of Francisco Pizarro (1475?–1541) on horseback and dressed in full conquistador regalia. It was he, along with his brothers and a small army of compatriots, who conquered Peru and so destroyed Inca civilization. On the opposite side of the plaza stands the 16th-century Palacio del Marqués de la Conquista, with heavy wrought-iron *rejas* (gratings) protecting the windows and the Pizarro coat-of-arms above the *balcón en ángulo* (angular balcony), a peculiar architectural detail common to many 16th-century palaces in this part of the country. Carved into the façade are the faces of Francisco and Hernando Pizarro above their respective Inca princess wives. The tourist office in the Plaza Mayor will supply you with a good town map, which gives short histories of the other main palaces in the surrounding streets and the families who commissioned them.

Forming a solid backdrop on the crest of rock above Trujillo stands the Moorish *castillo*. A wall encircles the old half of the town and four of the seven gates are still preserved. At its heart stands the Romanesque–Gothic church of Santa María la Mayor, built on the site of an Arab mosque and containing Roman sarcophagi. Here, too, are the tombs of the Pizarros and of García de Paredes, the 'Spanish Samson', who supposedly held whole armies at bay with nothing but his strength and his sword. Of great artistic interest is the winged retable by Fernando Gallego, composed of 25 panels depicting everything from the Descent into Hell to the Adoration of the Kings. If the church is locked, ask for the sacristan who lives nearby and has a key.

In the streets south of the church lie other important *casas solariegas* (noble palaces), some in a sad state of neglect, others privately restored but most inlaid with carved *emblasonadas* (coats-of-arms) above the austere Renaissance doorways. On Calle Palomas stands the house where Francisco Orellana (1511–46) was born, the first

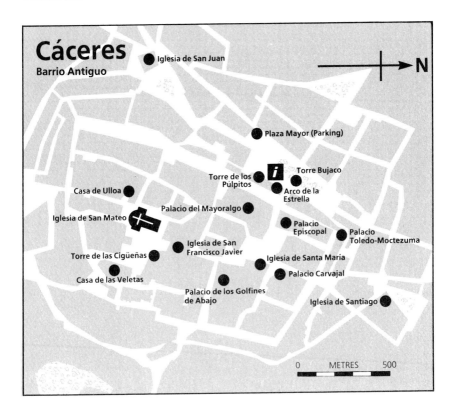

Cáceres
Barrio Antiguo

Iglesia de San Juan

N

Plaza Mayor (Parking)

Torre de los Púlpitos

Torre Bujaco

Casa de Ulloa

Arco de la Estrella

Iglesia de San Mateo

Palacio del Mayoralgo

Palacio Episcopal

Palacio Toledo-Moctezuma

Torre de las Cigüeñas

Iglesia de San Francisco Javier

Iglesia de Santa Maria

Casa de las Veletas

Palacio Carvajal

Palacio de los Golfines de Abajo

Iglesia de Santiago

0   METRES   500

man to navigate the Amazon. Trujillo is a sedentary place that remains semi-ruinous yet rather lovingly neglected. Like a cemetery, it has a sombre and melancholic air but there are palaces here instead of headstones.

On a fast flat road through prairieland and grazing pasture 50km to the west, you arrive in the more progressive city of **CÁCERES** (pop. 68,000), a place embellished and patronized in each era. Perfect examples of Roman, Moorish and Christian art are walled up tightly in an architectural inner sanctum where the white storks – which nest in profusion across the rooftops and on the towers – have an undisturbed view of the garden patios

and well-preserved buildings of the monumental core.

Like Trujillo, this is a city strategically placed on a rise overlooking the central Extremaduran plain but with a far more modernized atmosphere, created by a large student population and Cáceres' role as provincial capital. The shops are smarter, the buildings restored and the character almost cosmopolitan in comparison to the rest of Extremadura. From the outskirts, follow the signs towards la *Ciudad Monumental*, which should take you to the Plaza Mayor: another general rendezvous, full of outside cafés in the shade of the whitewashed arcades.

The old city, which has served as a

location for films such as Franco Zeffirelli's *Romeo and Juliet*, is an intense concentration of narrow cobbled streets, candlelit churches, discreet plazas and sombre but sumptuous palaces, all densely packed within a Roman and later Arabian wall that still has 12 of its original towers. When Alfonso IX captured the city on 23 April 1229 and rededicated it to St George, Cáceres became an urban fortress for chivalric knights and an important outpost for the great reconquest of southern Spain. The late medieval architecture evident in many of the palaces dates from the succeeding centuries of warring prosperity, when noble families fought as much among themselves as against the Muslims. As a result of wealth derived from Spanish expansion into South and Central America, architectural affluence continued: façades were given Renaissance facelifts, and the churches were embellished with important works of art.

Enter the monumental city up the staircase and through the *Arco de la Estrella* (Arch of the Star) on the east side of the Plaza Mayor between the Towers of Bujaco and Púlpitos. Carry on up the lane between the Mayoralgo and Bishop's Palace, on the right and left respectively, to the Plaza de Santa María. Facing you is the cathedral church of **Santa María**, with a bronze statue of San Pedro de Alcántara embedded in a curved niche at the base of the tower. The Gothic interior protects important memorial stones, sarcophagi and a Renaissance retable depicting the Assumption of the Virgin.

Engraved into the façade of the Bishop's Palace is the face of an Indian princess; and the small alley winding

north from the plaza leads to the *Palacio Toledo-Monteçuçuma*, named after the daughter of the Aztec emperor who married Juan Cano de Saavedra, a colonizer of Mexico after Cortés. Back in the Plaza de Santa María, on the corner next to the church, is the **Palacio Carvajal**, easily distinguishable by its corner balcony and framed stone *escudo* (shield) above the arched doorway. After lying in ruins for many years it was recently restored and now houses the tourism and craft council. You can visit the courtyard and private chapel on the ground floor before ascending to the first floor gallery where the rooms have been decorated in the style of the 19th century and contain interesting paintings, porcelain and furniture.

Continuing out of the plaza on the other side of the church, you arrive in the Plaza de San Jorge, with the imposing Baroque church of **San Francisco Javier** and its adjoining student residence. Opposite is the **Casa de los Becerra** with simple windows interspersed by imposing coats-of-arms and strange gargoyles staring down from the roof – another perfect example of late medieval/early Renaissance civic architecture. Down the hill on the left is the **Palacio de los Golfines de Abajo** with vast defensive towers and twin-arched Romanesque windows.

Climbing further, you arrive at the top of the old city, crowned by the church of **San Mateo**, where some of the great Cacereñan nobility are buried. Surrounding other sides of the plaza, you see the *casa solariega* of the Ulloa family, the convent of **San Pablo**, where a hidden nun behind a revolving screen sells home-made cakes and biscuits, and the **Torre de las Cigüeñas**, still standing thanks to a special dispensation granted by the Catholic Kings, who ordered all others to be pulled down in an attempt to stop local feuding at the end of the 1400s.

The adjacent Plaza Valetas houses the **Museo de Las Valetas**, built on the site of the Arab *alcázar*. It contains interesting archeological finds from the area, including Bronze Age funerary steles and objects found in the local Paleolithic Cave of Maltravieso. In the basement, looking rather like a subterranean mosque, are the horseshoe arches of the *aljibe* (old Moorish water cistern).

The monumental city is a place that can be visited again and again as there's always something new to discover. Around sunset, the first streetlamps light up and a warm desert wind fills the palm trees with movement. The stone turns a deep russet-gold, and the aeronautical act of the swallows is gradually replaced by the silent swooping of bats. When the walls are floodlit you should return to the old city and walk once more through its medieval lanes, where the silence hangs like a mantle.

TOURIST OFFICES

TRUJILLO: Plaza Mayor 18, tel (927) 32 06 53.

CÁCERES: Plaza del General Mola 33, tel (927) 24 63 47.

Accommodation, Eating and Drinking

GUADALUPE (tel code 927):

(H)**Parador de Guadalupe**, Pl Santa María de Guadalupe, tel 36 70 75. In the former 15th-century hospital. Swimming pool and all the comforts expected of the parador chain. C.
(H)**Hospedería Real Monasterio**, Pl Don Juan Carlos I, tel 36 70 00. A more monastic atmosphere around the Gothic plant-filled courtyard. Good restaurant. For the pilgrim rather than the pleasure-seeker. D–C.
(R)**Mesón El Cordero**, Convento 11, tel 36 71 31. Excellent regional cooking. D–C.

TRUJILLO: (tel code 927):

(H)**Parador de Trujillo**, Plaza de Santa Clara, tel 32 13 50. Around the gracious patio of the convent of St Clare. Medieval interior, good furniture and paintings. C–B.
(H&R)**Hostal Pizarro**, Pl Mayor 13, tel 32 02 55. Overlooking the plaza. Worth ringing to reserve in the summer. Good restaurant. D&C.

CÁCERES (tel code 927):

(H)**Parador del Comendador**, Ancha 6, tel 21 17 59. In the former 14th-century

Palacio del Comendador. Porticoed patio and tower. C–B.

(H)**Goya**, Plaza General Mola 33, tel 24 99 50. Of the couple of cheap pensions in the plaza with the most basic of facilities, this is the best. D–E.

(R)**El Figón de Eustaquio**, Pl de San Juan 12, tel 24 81 94. Traditional *mesón* decoration. C–B.

(R)**Bodega Medieval**, Orellana 1, tel 24 54 58. In the monumental city; 16th-century dining room. C.

(B)**Corral de las Cigüeñas**, Cuesta Aldana 6. A noisy outdoor bar in an ivy-clad courtyard with palm trees. In the Old Quarter. Good for local atmosphere. C.

Pueblos Blancos and Roman Bridges

The Vegas de Guadiana is the name given to the commercial farmland lying on either side of the River Guadiana after it is disgorged by the network of reservoirs in central eastern Extremadura, on the border between the provinces of Cáceres and Badajoz. Here, irrigated fields, fruit trees, crops of olives and figs are interspersed by stock farms and modernized agricultural villages – all part of the successful Badajoz Plan, inaugurated in the 1960s to stimulate the local economy.

The route begins in **Medellín**: a small dust-blown *pueblo* on the southern banks of the river, tucked beneath the shadow of a 14th-century *castillo*. In the plaza stands a memorial to Hernán Cortés who was born here in 1485. On a plaque beneath the statue the words Méjico, Tlaxcala, Otumba and Tabasco commemorate the victories that led him to the conquest of Mexico. From Medellín, alternative routes lie north and south of the river to Mérida.

MÉRIDA has changed quite considerably from the days when it was the capital of the Roman province of Lusitania, and an important road junction between Sevilla and Salamanca, Lisbon and Toledo. The original city of Augusta Emerita was founded by the legate Publius Carisius in 23 BC and served as a retirement settlement for loyal legionaries before becoming a bishopric under the Visigoths. The Moors made it the military centre of their southern kingdom until its capture by Alfonso IX in 1228. From then on, Mérida fell into a period of decline from which it has never escaped.

Enter Mérida over the magnificent Roman bridge built of granite blocks with 64 arches spanning the river. On your right stand the ruins of the **Alcazaba** which, for the last four years at least, have been in a permanent state of restoration with little progress. The Visigothic cistern with geometric friezes is the most interesting part so far excavated. Continue uphill into the Plaza España with its open-air cafés, flowerbeds and a bandstand, which all combine to create a jaded, Hispanic feel like the setting in a novel by Gabriel García Márquez. Up a sidestreet, installed in the church of

Santa Clara, is the Visigothic annexe to the **Archeological Museum**, with a small but exceptional collection of stone carvings from the fourth to the seventh centuries. Also within easy walking distance of the centre are the Arc de Trajan; the Parador Nacional, situated in a beautiful convent; and the Temple of Diana, hidden among rather dusty back alleys.

The main body of ruins is focused further up the hill virtually on the outskirts of town. A ticket gains you entry into the gardens that contain the **theatre** built by Agrippa, with a split-level, galleried stage supported by Corinthian columns and interspersed by marble statues. The semicircular auditorium surrounding it fills with over 5,000 people each night during August when the town hosts an important festival.

A short distance away is the much larger, elliptical **amphitheatre** where gladiatorial shows and mock naval battles were staged. Outside the grounds, on the other side of the car park, is the **Casa del Anfiteatro**, a well-preserved Roman villa with a ground plan of galleries surrounding a patio. Look for the beautiful mosaic depicting grapes being trampled into wine, and the original irrigation channels that brought water from the San Lázaro aqueduct on the northern edge of town. Turn left out of the villa and continue to the bottom of the road, where you come to the Circus Maximus – traces of the huge hippodrome can still be seen here, encircled by an even larger but hardly distinguishable stadium.

However, the new focal point of interest in Mérida is without doubt the **Museo Nacional de Arte Romano**, where three open-plan floors dis-playing statues, columns, pottery, jewellery, coins, funerary busts and sensational mosaics are all effectively offset against the soaring red brick walls. When the foundations were laid at the beginning of the 1980s, the architects discovered a Roman road running across the site, and subsequently incorporated it into their basement design. Guided tours of the crypt usually leave every hour from the ground floor.

Back down by the river, next to the bullring, is the **Casa de Mitra**, with an exceptional turquoise mosaic that depicts mythical fish and river gods. The villa once belonged to Caius Accius Hedychus, the high priest of an important Mithraic community that flourished in Mérida during the second century AD. The Cult of Mithra was closely associated with the sacrifice of bulls and in the house you can still see the *spelaea*: a sunken chamber where animals were sacrificed to the pagan sun-god.

On the Avenida de Extremadura, the dusty ringroad circling the northern end of town, stands the church of **Santa Eulalia**, built around the ruins of an old temple dedicated to Mars. A local legend relates how during the reign of Diocletian a young girl spat in the eye of an official who had ordered her to renounce Christianity, whereupon she was put in an oven. The way in which she was martyred is recalled in the small chapel in front of the church: it is still called the *Horno* (Oven) *de Santa Eulalia*.

Continuing south along the N630 towards Zafra, there is an interesting detour on the way to the village of **Alange** with a Roman spa and notable *castillo* ruins. Midway you pass the farming town of **Almendralejo** standing in the centre of the region known as the *Tierra de Barros*, a fertile landscape of figs and vineyards producing aromatic *cavas* and white wines.

Zafra (pop. 14,000), one of the oldest towns in Extremadura, has a run-down charm best experienced during the cattle fair of San Miguel, which is held in the first week of October when a huge harvest festival takes place. The whitewashed houses offset the menagerie of plants spilling from the wrought-iron balconies, and the fuelled conversations of local farmers reverberate through the bricked arcades.

The heart of the community centres about the palm avenue in the solemn Plaza Grande surrounded by 18th-century señorial mansions. Adjoining it is the humble Plaza Chica with an iron cross on a granite column at its centre. In the surrounding streets the collegiate church of Nuestra Señora de la Candelaria is worth a visit for the side-chapel with a retable by Francisco de Zurbarán. Head then for the Parador Nacional Hernán Cortés: a majestic palace rising above the roof-line of the town and formerly the ancestral home of the Dukes of Feria. Nine perfectly cylindrical towers enclose an austere central garden-patio with two floors of open-air marble galleries designed by Juan de Herrera, the architect of El Escorial. If you're not a guest, ask the desk porter if you can see the small private Gothic chapel and the carved polychrome walls of the Sala Dorada, now rather inappropriately used as a guest television room.

The N435 and then the N431 leads south-west from Zafra through wild-looking olive groves and cork forests haunted by *castillo* carcasses, the most impressive of which looms above **Burguillos del Cerro**, a former Templar stronghold. Most of the many bridges round here date from the Roman occupation, when the woods were felled to feed the fires of the Río Tinto mines in the Sierra Morena to the south. The Dolmen of Toriñuelo, signposted just off the road beside a barn as you climb the last sierra surrounding Jerez de los Caballeros, is just part of a whole network of megalithic tombs scattered about this territory.

Your first view of **Jerez de los Caballeros** (pop. 10,000), sitting compactly among the sierras and glorified by the great Baroque belltowers rising like jewelled candelabra from its midst, will undoubtedly cause surprise. A dozen convents, four important Baroque churches, and an immaculately restored *castillo* seems quite an accomplished legacy for a town with only one small hotel.

The *Caballeros Templarios* (Knights Templar) who helped Alfonso IX wrest Jerez from the Moors in 1230 were given custody and defence of the stronghold in return for their loyalty. In 1312 a Papal Bull demanded the dissolution of the crusading Order but the knights stood firm and met their end through mass decapitation in a corner of the *castillo* still remembered as the *Torre Sangrienta* (Bloody Tower). In 1362 Jerez passed out of crown hands and became the property of the Order of Santiago. Under their protection, peaceful religious foundations arose about the perimeter walls, and the influx of riches from the New World led to the construction of civic buildings, fountains and signorial mansions throughout the 16th and 17th centuries.

The Roman theatre at Mérida is the most elegant classical reminder of the 'centuries of Roman rule in Spain'. It is still used every August for its intended purpose. Incato

With its myriad of steep cobbled lanes, Jerez is one of those quiet, understated *pueblos blancos,* preserved because many of the streets are too narrow for traffic. From the well-groomed gardens of the *castillo,* you have commanding views of the town's layout, and the church towers act as a compass if you get lost in the maze of tall, whitewashed lanes. The Torre de San Bartolomé, with a fallen angel atop its weathervane, is even more distinguishable by the blue-and-yellow glazed mosaics studded between the statuettes, columns, balconies and voluted carvings embellishing the façade. Inside lies the macabre glass-covered coffin of Vasco de Jerez, a local nobleman, who has been unabashedly decomposing in public for the last four centuries. Many of the silver and gilt floats used during *Semana Santa* wait patiently in the side-chapels for the next Holy Week procession, when they're polished up, garlanded in flowers and carried through the streets in one of the most spectacular Easter parades to be experienced outside Seville.

In the Plaza de España, surrounded by cafés and palm trees, is the church of **San Miguel**. This has an extravagant Baroque belfry of carved brick, the decorations on which grow progressively richer as the tiers of the tower get higher. Inside, there are some interesting frescoes and a notable wrought-iron pulpit. Just beneath the castle stands the parish church of **Santa María**, considered to be the oldest church in Extremadura on account of a Visigothic inscription on one of the columns that claims 24 December 556 as the day of consecration.

Ambling through the streets of Jerez, you will eventually come upon the house of Núñez de Balboa (1475–1519) who, like so many of his generation, sailed to the Americas and ended up being the first Spaniard to dip his toe in the Pacific Ocean, before he was murdered by his compatriots. An equally famous contemporary of Balboa, commemorated with a statue beside the Puerta de Burgos, was Hernándo de Soto (1500–42), who helped the Pizarro brothers roll through Peru before going on to make his own conquest in Florida.

From Jerez you can either continue south to **Fregenal de la Sierra**, with its unhurried farming community that clusters around another bold Templar *castillo* and plaza; or follow the small country roads north to Olivenza. The dramatic city walls surrounding **Olivenza** bear witness to its history as a frontier community continuously involved in the territorial struggles between Spain and Portugal. In 1298 the town was part of the dowry settlement in the marriage of Beatrice of Castille to the Infante Don Alonso of Portugal, whose fief it remained almost without interruption until 1801. During the course of the 'Orange War' it was recaptured by the troops of Godoy, since when it has remained under Spanish sovereignty.

Years of Portuguese control left their mark on Olivenza. Many important buildings bear strong traces of the 'Manuelino style': an architectural technique rooted in late Gothic and early Renaissance, which developed in line with Portugal's rapid 16th-century colonial expansion. It is in many ways the Portuguese form of Plateresque. Around the finialed doorway of the municipal library, armillary spheres and other nautical motifs form part of the general decoration. Glazed tiles were used in several of the churches and the Hospital de la Caridad as a colourful embellishment for rooms and walls and a sobering foil to the vast gilt retables. In the church of Santa María Magdalena the full personality of 'Manueline' architecture is felt. The west door is an intricate ensemble of elegant pillars surrounded by bas-reliefs, while the interior Gothic vaulting is supported by an avenue of spiralling marble columns.

The C436 heads north through the fertile *vegas* of the Guadiana plateau with the hills of Portuguese Estremadura rising in the distance beyond the river. Fields of fruit orchards, vine and cereals line the road to Badajoz, where disturbing high-rise suburbs warn you away from the busy southern provincial capital.

BADAJOZ (pop. 123,000) has never had an easy time, stuck as it is on the main overland route between the Mediterranean and Lisbon. Wars have been fought over this strategic spur of land for the last 2,000 years – with Badajoz always coming off worst. The old city assembled about the remains of the Arab Alcazaba was the scene of continuous fighting with the Portuguese, who considered it the 'key to their kingdom'. During the War of Independence, Wellington lost 15,000 men in a single afternoon spent storming the city. Again, in 1936, it was the scene of a brutal massacre of thousands of Republican refugees, who were lined up in the bullring and shot. The early Gothic cathedral of San Juan is the main reason for visiting the city; but if you like Zurbarán and Morales then examples of their work, along with that of other Extremaduran artists, can be seen in the Museo de Bellas Artes, which can provide a relaxing break before crossing the border into Portugal.

TOURIST OFFICES

MÉRIDA: El Puente 9, tel (924) 31 53 53.

ZAFRA: Pl de España, tel (924) 55 10 36.

BADAJOZ: Pasaje de San Juan 2, tel (924) 22 27 63.

Accommodation, Eating and Drinking

MÉRIDA (tel code 924):

(H&R)**Via de la Plata**, Pl de la Constitución 3, tel 31 38 00. Built above a Roman temple. Has variously served as a convent, hospital and jail before becoming a parador. Beautiful patio. Restaurant is good. B.
(H)**Hotel Emperatriz**, Pl de España 19, tel 31 31 11. In another medieval palace overlooking the busy main plaza. Beautiful courtyard and excellent value. D–C.
(H)**Senero**, Holguin 12, tel 31 72 07. Quiet and simple rooms. E–D.
(R)**Nicolás**, Felix Valverde 13, tel 31 96 10. Local food. C.

ZAFRA (tel code 924):

(H)**Parador de Hernán Cortés**, Pl Corazón de María, tel 55 02 00. Beautiful 15th-century residence of the Dukes of Feria. Superb marble patio. C.
(R)**La Posada** in the (H)**Huerta Honda**, López Asme, tel 55 08 00. Good restaurant in an Andalusian *posada* (inn). C–B.

JEREZ DE LOS CABALLEROS (tel code 924):

(H&R)**La Cancela**, Corazón de María 6, tel 73 10 48. Very basic accommodation and better food. D–C.
(H)**Oasis**, El Campo 18, tel 73 14 53. A slightly more upmarket hotel. D–C.

BADAJOZ (tel code 924):

(H)**Cervantes**, Tercio 2, tel 22 51 10. Central. In the only hotel in an old building in the city. D.
(R)**La Toja**, Av de Elvás 22, tel 23 74 77. A menu mixing Gallegan and Extremaduran food. B.
(R)**Los Gabrieles**, Vicente Barrantes 21, tel 22 00 01. Good local food. C.

CHAPTER FIFTEEN

Andalusia

(Andalucía)

ANDALUSIA IS THE SECOND-LARGEST region of Spain, and comprises eight provinces – Huelva, Sevilla, Cádiz, Córdoba, Málaga, Granada, Jaen and Almería – that together stretch across 87,299sq km. The region is characterized by whitewashed mountain *pueblos* juxtaposed with the crowded holiday metropoli of the south and miles of dry olive groves growing beside the fertile plain of the great River Guadalquivir.

Water is possibly the area's essential physical feature. Not only is Andalusia the narrowest divide between Continental Europe and Africa, but it is also the harbour bridging the Mediterranean and Atlantic. For a time it was the catalyst between Islam and Christianity and later between the Atlantic and Pacific, and for the last 500 years it has remained a stepping-stone from the Old World into the New.

Andalusian culture is understandably difficult to pinpoint, for it has absorbed features from a number of other countries over the years. It could be expressed through its orators, philosophers and poets such as Seneca, Maimónides or Lorca; the artistic brilliance of its Arab and Moorish *taifa* kingdoms; the rhythm of its flamenco music; the colours of its ceramics and landscape. Roots can be traced from the numerous cultures that have inhabited these parts since the Phoenicians. The Romans called it Baetica, but its present name derives from the centuries of Islamic government from 711 to 1492, when the territory was known as Al-Andalus.

With the fall of the Nasrid kingdom of Granada, the active Muslim civilization was extinguished. Many Moors fled back to North Africa, others remained. But the Arab and North African influence is still profound. Only in Aragón is the juxtaposition of the two civilizations so marked, and there remains in the place-names, the vernacular architecture, food, music, and even the agricultural traditions, strong derivations from both the Arabs and the Moors.

The Islamic civilization of Al-Andalus produced a succession of some of the most brilliant societies Europe has ever known, politically based upon racial and religious

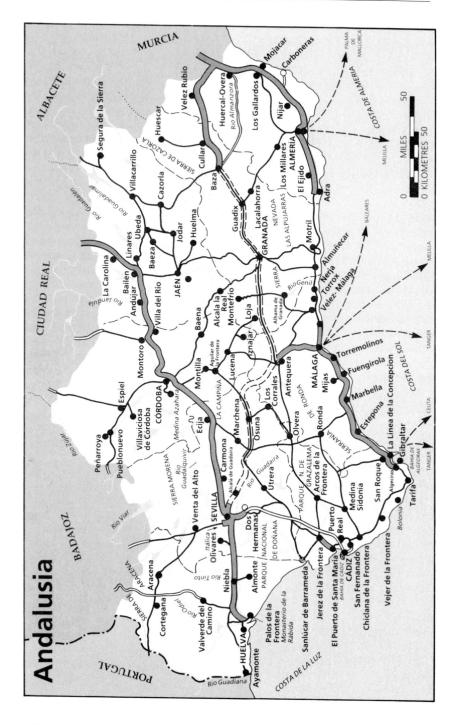

toleration, or *convivencia*. The state encouraged crucial developments in the fields of arts, astronomy, medicine, botany, architecture, translation, philosophy, poetry and artisanal skills such as pottery and carpentry. When its cities were first enriched with New World money, its ports and capital Seville became centres of the Renaissance and Baroque.

As the New World resources drained away, Andalusia went into steady decline, and the land fell into the hands of relatively few families. Villages survived through the strong sense of solidarity, and local communities were ruled in the absence of landowning families by local dynastic families or the church.

In the 18th century the *hermandades* (brotherhoods) raised the status of many villages by competing among themselves through the patronage of church and lay building. By the 19th century Andalusia was one of the poorest and least developed regions of Europe, almost untouched by the industrial revolution.

The great Andalusian traditions that survive are most passionately expressed through the region's *fiestas*. The *Semana Santa* (Holy Week) festivities are celebrated everywhere, but most majestically in Seville, where the sense of solemnity is overpowered by the magnificent spectacle. This *fiesta* is followed by the *Fería de Abril*, which is, in essence, a fervent thanksgiving for spring. The procession to El Rocío and the February carnival in Cádiz are equally hedonistic, but in a way that is livelier than almost anywhere else.

The fact that Andalusians are the brunt of much national humour does not stop most Spaniards from secretly envying their way of life. The pulse,

even the light, of Andalusia is different. Andalusians retain unashamedly romantic notions about life that derive in part from the several hundred thousand gipsies who live there and keep the musical soul of the region, flamenco music, alive. Even the new communities of foreigners along the coast have found their place and purpose in the order of life. It is a place where communities of different beliefs, needs and desires have always managed to mix: sometimes in a state of war, but more often at peace.

The physiography of the region is both mountainous and flat in turn. The River Guadalquivir and tributaries irrigate a great fertile agricultural plain that lies between the rather desolate heights of the Sierra Morena to the north and the mountains that rise steeply from the coast in the south. The landscape varies from the monotonous miles of olive groves to the delicately rolling agricultural plains surrounding Seville. Sub-tropical valleys and glaciated mountain peaks, valleys of citrus fruit, desert wilderness, river delta, paddyfields and orchid farms all have their place in Andalusia. Olives, wheat, grapes and citrus have been farmed here for centuries, but in recent years the climate has allowed the successful cultivation of avocados, mangoes, and even papaya.

Córdoba, Seville and the Guadalquivir Basin

Andalusia is reached from Madrid in about four hours along the main N-IV via Valdepeñas. At the Desfiladero de

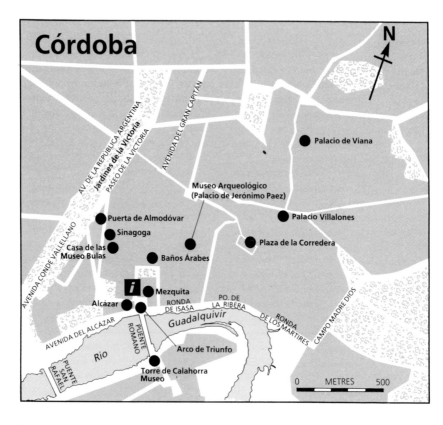

Córdoba

N

Palacio de Viana

AV. DE LA REPÚBLICA ARGENTINA
Jardines de la Victoria
PASEO DE LA VICTORIA
AVENIDA DEL GRAN CAPITÁN

Museo Arqueológico
(Palacio de Jerónimo Paez)

Puerta de Almodóvar

Sinagoga

Casa de las
Museo Bulas

Baños Árabes

Palacio Villalones

Plaza de la Corredera

AVENIDA CONDE DE VALLELLANO

i Mezquita

Alcázar

RONDA
DE ISASA

PO. DE
LA RIBERA

RONDA
DE LOS MARTIRES

CAMPO MADRE DIOS

PUENTE
ROMANO

Guadalquivir

AVENIDA DEL ALCAZAR

Rio

PUENTE
SAN
RAFAEL

Arco de Triunfo

Torre de Calahorra
Museo

0   METRES   500

Despeñaperros the road splits and the oncoming traffic disappears. This is the most traditional entry to the south over the bleak goat-grazing heights of the Sierra Morena.

The Guadalquivir (Big River, in Arabic) is joined at the industrial town of **Bailén** (pop. 17,000), scene of a battle against the French in 1808 when the invading general, Dupont, with 20 campaign victories to his name, surrendered to the Seville junta, who had never before staged a pitched battle. It was an event that made the French realize that the resistance of the May uprising in Madrid could be repeated in the south.

The river then drifts in and out of sight along agro-industrial roadsides. **Montoro** is worth a short detour for its bridge and riverbank houses hanging over the cliffsides. Beyond it, **CÓRDOBA** (pop. 300,000) rises from the plain, protected from the north by the mantle of its grey sierra.

If you've never been before, then you should start understanding Andalusia by spending a couple of days, at least, in Córdoba. Continue into the city along the river, turning off at the Roman bridge and triumphal arch. In front of you should be the **Mezquita**, a building comparable with any of the greatest shrines of worship in the world. It is 174m in length and 137m in width, and is protected by a vast defensive wall and dominated by a Renaissance belfry on the northern side. The influence of this mosque diffused into several later European architectural movements, including Mozarabic, Romanesque, Mudéjar and Gothic. It is as outstanding as the Gran Mezquita de Sammarra in Mesopotamia, and became a prototype for mosques throughout Islam. There is no clearer statement than this of the great Cordoban civilization: the most artistically progressive city west of Constantinople from the ninth to early 11th century. When Córdoba became the refuge of the surviving Ummayad dynasty after their flight from Damascus, the mosque was founded by Abd-ah-Raman I (756–88) to be the main temple for his new emirate.

It was built on a Roman temple to Janus and the old Visigothic cathedral of San Vicente, and was finished under Hishâm I (788–96). Later enlargements were undertaken by Abd-ah-Raman II (822–52), Mohammed I (852–86) and Al-Hakem II (961–76), who added 12 new bays and built the present *mihrab* (prayer niche) that normally shows the direction of Mecca, but here points towards Damascus, the city from which the Ummayads were exiled. The exterior is interesting for the different styles of door and window art, so characteristic of Spanish architecture. Here Islamic elements such as horseshoe arches and Moorish decorations mingle with Gothic intrusions. The combination is fascinating.

You enter the sanctuary in the midst

The Mezquita at Córdoba, extended between the eighth and 11th centuries, was the centre of the most brilliant culture of western Europe during that period – a catalyst of learning, astrology, poetry, medicine and mathematics.   Angus Mitchell

of the fountains and water channels of the Patio de los Naranjos, the oldest surviving patio-garden in the Islamic world, where purification rituals took place before prayer. The orange trees become a natural extension of the avenues of different coloured marble columns within, which were pillaged from the far corners of the Roman Empire. Double tiers of arches, made from alternating white stone and red brick, sometimes decorated with *atauriques* (interlacing floral patterns) were a form that originated in Damascus and spread via Córdoba into the Romanesque of the Camino de Santiago and as far north as the Auvergne. Other innovations that spread to the rest of Europe whose origins can be traced to the Mezquita include the multifoil arch, intersecting rib vaulting and the shell-shaped dome of the prayer niche used to amplify the sound of a single voice.

In terms of decoration, the mosque is as rich and exquisite as both the Dome on the Rock in Jerusalem and the Mezquita Azul in Istanbul. Typically Islamic is the geometric patterning created by interwoven arabesques; and the *mihrab* with its gold Cufic lettering, jewel linings and intricate Mudéjar stuccowork.

The 16th-century cathedral towering in the middle is for most people a rather horrendous intrusion of Plateresque bad taste; a brutal and ineffective attempt to make height conquer the horizontal. It was commissioned by Charles V, but met with his later disapproval – a sentiment that most have shared ever since. The attempt to Christianize the mosque never really worked and, even though side-chapels are protected by screens and there is a small treasury of cathedral art, the Islamic spirit prevails.

By contrast, the Andalusian spirit has turned the buildings immediately facing the mosque into enterprises unashamedly geared to making money from tourists. Souvenirs and tourist shops of every description are found here selling ceramics, jewellery, film, Moroccan *taracea* (inlay) and gold-plated mementobilia. Overlooking the Mezquita are hotels of varying prices, the more expensive of which have underground car parks reached down tunnels dug at perilous-looking angles.

After the Mezquita you should make your way into the alleyways surrounding the **Barrio de la Judería**. There you glimpse the patio courtyards protected by the patterns of wrought-iron gates and window *rejas* (grilles), hear the soft splash of fountains, and smell the jasmine-scented air – all recurring sensations of Andalusia.

Balconies explode with colour above the narrow cobbled streets, which once lay at the centre of some 80,000 shops and workshops. After the capture of Córdoba by Ferdinand III in 1236 many beautiful Romanesque–Gothic churches were founded in the area on the site of former mosques. Some buildings have since had Renaissance facelifts, but the confused maze of well-kept alleys still retains the feel of the Arabian *souk* rather than the European city.

The 11th-century **Arab baths** in Calle Velázquez Bosco; the elegant Mudéjar **synagogue**, with a memorial plaque to the Jewish scholar Maimónides; and the beautiful Arab palace, the **Casa de las Bulas**, containing a small museum dedicated to Córdoba's great bullfighting past, should be chanced upon as you find your way around. The Judería is closed off on the western side by the battle-ments of the old city wall and the Jardines de la Victoria – an avenue of fountains, magnolias and orange trees, with a statue of the mathematician and astrologer Averröes beside the impressive horseshoe Puerta de Almodóvar.

At the southern end of this walkway is the **Alcázar de los Reyes Cristianos**, which should absorb another half-day of your attention. Its rooms have been filled with some impressive Roman and Paleo-Christian remains from earlier settlements in Córdoba. The gardens are a beautiful expression of the Islamic desire to integrate water and nature. Between the topiaries and clipped cypresses rise statues of the late medieval Kings of Spain and a memorial to Columbus in audience before *Los Reyes Católicos*.

From the towers and battlements there are magnificent views across the river to the Torre de la Calahorra that once protected the southern entrance to the Puente Romano. It now houses the city museum, which contains exhibits relating to the Cordobese poet Luis de Góngora (1561–1627). A little way downstream are the old mills that once supported the great wheel that fed the *alcázar* gardens with water but was dismantled because its noise disturbed the sleep of Isabel la Católica. On the north bank a smaller scoop wheel has survived.

The **Museo Arqueológico**, housed in the impressive Palacio de Jerónimo Paéz, is one of the most important in the Peninsula. Several rooms are dedicated to fine Roman mosaics and sculpture, but the bulk of the collection has been taken from Medina az-Zahra on the outskirts of Córdoba and bears witness to the artistic brilliance of that

short-lived court.

Leaving the Old Quarter surrounding the Mezquita, it is worth taking a look at the Plaza de la Corredera, which stages an open-air market on Saturdays. To the north, lost among the crooked streets of the Bullfighters' Quarter surrounding Plaza Don Goméz, is the **Palacio de Viana**. This is one of the finest examples of a señorial palace, and is open morning and afternoon to the public. The large Renaissance doorway leads into a patio with a palm tree at its centre, an ancient Islamic symbol of reason overpowering doubt, and a frequent sight throughout Andalusia.

The rooms of the palace are filled with examples of furniture, paintings and ceramics from almost every period since the 16th century, and can be visited in small guided tours. Of particular interest are the Flemish tapestries, pottery from Talavera de la Reina and Puente del Obispo, paintings depicting the five senses by Jan Breughel, and the examples of stamped leather for which Córdoba was once famous. From many rooms you get a view of the 14 exquisite patio gardens that can be explored at your leisure. They are an example of the importance in Andalusian architecture of the balance between house and garden – one being an extension of the other.

Córdoba takes a certain amount of perseverance to understand with any degree of thoroughness, and the Cordobeses are quite private and guarded in their manner. But if you form a palate for the local Montilla wine and enjoy the noisy life of the crowded bars, then it can be a hard city to leave.

The province of Córdoba is mainly agricultural. To the north, in the Sierra

---

Medina az-Zahra

Medina az-Zahra (City of Flowers) was founded during the reign of Abd-ah-Raman III in 936. It lay a few miles west of Córdoba in the foothills of the Sierra Morena and, judging by reports from contemporary Muslim chroniclers, it was one of the most luxurious palaces that ever existed even though it survived for just 40 years and today lies in semi-excavated ruins.

Architects were commissioned from Constantinople and Baghdad to help in the construction of the royal palace, schools, barracks and mosque. The grounds graduate down a hillside, across a surface area of about 2.5sq km. At the top stood the distinctive horseshoe arches of the palace façade, behind which stretched a succession of courtyards, chambers for entertaining and royal apartment rooms, with tracery windows looking across the gardens. Forming a central axis to these buildings was the chamber of the Caliphs, entered by one of 32 doors carved from ivory and rock crystal and damascened with gold, silver and bronze. A transparent alabaster ceiling might well have covered the patio area. In the centre stood a great fountain filled with mercury, which astounded visiting Christian kings. Precious stones and metals were imported from the far reaches of the Islamic empire to decorate the interior. Emeralds and rubies were set into the stuccowork and the floors littered with the finest silks, cushions and rugs.

The middle terraces were given over to gardens, patios and orchards carpeted with aromatic violets. The golden carp in the ponds allegedly consumed 12,000 loaves of bread each day and at night 1,000 Nubian slaves dressed in gold and silver brocade lit the tiled pavilions with torches.

On the lowest level, hidden from the palace by an avenue of palm trees, lay the barracks, offices, mint, armoury and baths. An aqueduct was constructed to feed the underground *aljibe* (cistern) with fresh water. But the whole place was sacked and destroyed by Berber soldiers in 1013 and was never reoccupied.

Morena, is the Valle de los Pedroches with some peaceful run-down farming villages that survive mainly from sheep and goat grazing. To the south is Montilla country, where the dry and delicate local table wine is fermented around several impressive towns. They can be explored on a leisurely day out from the provincial capital.

Montilla (pop. 25,000) is the heart of Córdoba's wine-making industry and the birthplace of Gonzalo Fernández y Aguilar, whose successful campaign against the French in Italy between 1495 and 1498 led to his being created first Viceroy of Naples. **Aguilar** is smaller but has a fine octagonal plaza and Moorish *castillo* ruins. **Lucena** is an ancient Jewish village and was once the centre of a thriving school of Talmudic philosophy. All three towns have some fine Renaissance churches and señorial palaces built by local families flush with fortunes made in the New World.

If you're heading on to Seville, then an alternative to the main road via Ecija and Carmona is to take the slow route hugging the northern bank of the Guadalquivir, where the extraordinary fertility of the land can be appreciated.

Ecija (pop. 38,000), *La Ciudad del Sol y Las Torres* (City of the Sun and Towers), is a place too often passed by – perhaps understandably in the height of summer, when it is so unbearably hot that you can supposedly fry eggs on the flagstones. The heart of the town is beautiful – sleepy, confident and tranquil – and the Ecijans are justifiably proud of their *pueblo*, which is as good an example as any of a large and thriving *pueblo blanco*.

Its 11 Renaissance/Baroque towers, 15 belltowers and more than 20 señorial palaces comprise one of the most densely packed and well-kept areas of Andalusian Baroque architecture outside Seville. They were mainly built during the 18th century owing to the power and patronage of the *hermandades*, the artisanal brotherhoods like local trade unions whose influence increased as the power of the local landed families declined. The *hermandades* are still in evidence today; if you visit at Easter or Christmas you will see posted on any church door the programme of events for each brotherhood.

Make first for the Plaza Mayor with the *ayuntamiento* (town hall) occupying one end. From there walk through the Plaza to the Palacio de los Marqueses de Peñaflor, a palace that will be found in any anthology of 18th-century Baroque architecture. The polychromed curvilineal façade with a wrought-iron balcony running right across the first floor shows above all the versatility of the local architects who had to work within the confines imposed by the irregular groundplan inherited from Moorish times. The twin-storey pink marble doorway

leads into a *zaguán* (entrance hall), from where you gain access to the patios and flamboyantly decorated staircase. The palace today serves as a cultural centre.

The churches in Ecija are too numerous to list and should perhaps be explored by chance rather than in any specific order. Most have rich Baroque–neoclassic interiors, but generally it is their dimensions and exterior decorations that are of most aesthetic interest. A good local map giving exact names and locations can be obtained from the tourist office.

Ecija's importance is mainly due to its position on the River Genil: one of the Guadalquivir's great tributaries that springs from the northern face of the Sierra Nevada and then irrigates the *vega-Meseta* to the west of Granada before it eventually meets the Guadalquivir at Palma del Río.

If you're heading south from Ecija, take the road to Osuna through the area known as La Campiña. This comprises the five fortified *pueblos* of Ecija, Osuna, Marchena, Utrera and Carmona. Their role has always been the defence and maintenance of this exceptionally fertile farmland of soft prairies that are a dazzling green in spring. For those seeking a few days of rural exploration, it is best to visit these towns from Carmona.

There is a Roman acropolis at **Osuna** (pop. 17,000), as well as a 16th-century university and Baroque señorial palaces. The small Archeological Museum in the Torre del Agua will fill in the town's historical background for you. Of the churches the most impressive is the Colegiata, at the highest point in the town, containing the pantheon of the Dukes of Osuna and a Museum of Sacred Art.

Marchena (pop. 18,000) has a 12th-century Almohad walled-in core reached through the impressive battlemented gate known as the Arco de la Rosa. From Marchena, Carmona can be reached by a direct road along the Corbones valley or through **Paradas, Arahall** and the fortified town of **Alcalá de Guadaira** beneath the ruins of an Almohad *castillo*.

Carmona (pop. 25,000) is the most imposing of all these towns, with two impressive Roman gateways – Puerta de Córdoba and Puerta de Sevilla – at the eastern and western ends of the *Barrio Antiguo* (Old Quarter). For an understanding of Cormona's formidable defensive importance, head first for the Alcázar del Rey Don Pedro, now restored and serving as a parador. The location commands magnificent views for miles around over the coloured patchwork plain of La Campiña.

A Roman Museum has been created on the site of the Roman necropolis and is one of the better displayed excavations in the region, showing how the town – Carmo to the Romans – was an important centre of political activity in the region of Baetica. The most impressive tombs are the Triclinio del Elefante, which includes a kitchen where the funerary wake was held, and the mausoleum of the Servilia family, which is constructed like a small country house with a domed burial chamber cut out of the rock. (Open Tues–Sun 10am–2pm & 4–6pm. Cl Mon.)

Carmona's architecture bears traces of almost every subsequent period, although, as in Córdoba, its narrow *souk*-like lanes give it a predominantly Arab touch. The main church of Santa María La Mayor is mainly a 14th-century Gothic construction. The horseshoe arches around the Patio de los Naranjas are all that remain of an earlier mosque that once stood on the site, and carved on one of the columns is a peculiar series of sixth-century inscriptions, thought to be some sort of Visigothic calendar.

The Mudéjar church of San Felipe has a beautiful *artesonado* (inlaid wooden ceiling), and the mighty belltower of San Pedro is an imitation of the Giralda beside Seville cathedral. Otherwise, 18th-century Baroque influences prevail although the structures are quite often earlier. Baroque church interiors are something you quickly get used to in southern Spain; here, flamboyantly adorned interiors with gilt and polychromed altarpieces, and huge unrestored canvases are in stark contrast to the more austere and quite often worse-kept church interiors of the north.

SEVILLE/SEVILLA (pop. 710,000) is the capital of Andalusia, the seat of an archbishopric, a university city, the most important industrial centre of the Andalusian autonomy, and generally considered to be the most vibrant city in the Peninsula. It spawned two of the most exotic characters of fiction: the insatiable womanizer, Don Juan, and the personification of the *femme fatale*: Carmen.

The three most important spring *fiestas* – *Semana Santa*, the *Feria de Abril* and pilgrimage to *El Rocío* – are among the wildest in Spain, when confraternities, *hermandades*, landowners, the devout, horsemen and gipsies mingle together to celebrate their enjoyment of life. Such celebrations are the outward expression of the anarchic spirit of Andalusia, but in Seville the sense of energetic activity can be found at almost any time of year.

The historical importance of Seville has always been due to its navigable position on the Guadalquivir. Known to the Romans as Hispalis, the city thrived under their rule, fell later beneath the Visigothic government from Toledo, and produced the great bishop San Isidoro who with St Leander established Christianity here and was considered the last of the great humanist minds. Under caliphate rule it equalled Córdoba in its artistic and intellectual power, and later reached a peak of prosperity during the reign of the poet king Al-Mutamid (1068–95). The Almohads bequeathed it a fabulous minaret, which is one of the finest pieces of Maghribian architecture to survive.

In 1248 the key to the city was handed over to the conquering Ferdinand III. Christian Seville became a venue for the itinerant Spanish court, especially during the reigns of Alfonso X and Pedro I 'the Cruel', who lived in Arabian-style luxury in the greatest surviving statement of Mudéjar court architecture, the *alcázar*.

Seville's initial trading monopoly with the New World ensured its immediate status as a Renaissance centre and the most affluent port in Spain. A naval college was founded, and the city produced painters such as Diego Velázquez (1599–1660), Bartolomé Murillo (1618–82) and Juan de Valdés Leal (1622–90), whose work is still in evidence everywhere. When the New World funds ebbed and were diverted towards northern Europe, Seville declined economically, but it never lost its pride or place as one of the most romantically conceived cities of Europe.

Any tour should begin with the cathedral, *alcázar* and maze-like Barrio de Santa Cruz, the inner square mile whose concentrated trove of monuments will take the best part of two days to explore. Remember, though, that the one-way system is impossible and the roads are too congested. Cars should be parked, preferably out of sight underground, and then walk everywhere you need to go.

The cathedral of **Santa María** is built over a Roman temple, Visigothic cathedral and 12th-century Almohad mosque. It is the largest Gothic building in Christendom and was constructed between 1402 and 1506. (Open Mon–Sat 10.30am–1.30pm & 4.30–6.30pm. Sun 10.30am–1.30pm. Cl holiday afternoons.) When the chapter of Seville decided to build the cathedral they were determined to 'construct a church so great that it never should have its equal. Let posterity say that those who dared to devise such a work must have been mad.' It is arguably the most impressive cathedral anywhere in Spain. Though Gothic in style, it better reflects the Renaissance spirit of 16th-century Spain – solemn and majestic.

The imposing bronze Mudéjar doorway of the Puerta del Perdón, stamped with Cufic lettering and Christian escutcheons, leads into the horseshoe arcades of the Patio de los Naranjos, the oldest surviving part of the mosque. At its centre stands a fine octagonal Visigothic fountain used by Muslims for their ablution rites. Entry from the patio is through a small church known as the Sagrario and, on the western side, the Biblioteca Colombina, which contains much of the great classical library collected by Columbus, including his copy of the *Tablas Alfonsinas* – a wealth of astronomical science compiled by astronomers under the auspices of Alfonso X (1252–84).

The Giralda that towers above the cathedral and most of the city was originally a minaret built in 1184 by the Maghribian architect, Ahmad Ibn Baso, who is also credited with the *muezzin* towers in Rabat and Kutubiya in Marrakesh. Almohad architecture concentrated on essential geometric forms that in many ways mirrored those of the Cistercian builders of northern Spain at about the same time. Decoratively the most interesting feature is the trelliswork relief of intersecting arches: the practical architectural phenomenon of the Mezquita in Córdoba. In the 16th century the Giralda was extended with a Renaissance belfry and topped by a copper weathervane depicting faith. You can climb up the tower for an unprecedented view over the city.

The interior of the cathedral is a mighty 117m long by 76m wide by 56m high at the crossing, with five aisles most probably based upon the same groundplan as the mosque. Light shines through some brilliant Renaissance stained glass by Enrique Alemán and Arnold of Flanders to illuminate the dim and cool interior, with its

The stately sarcophagus containing the remains of Columbus, beside a large mural of St Christopher in the cathedral of Seville. Some historians claim, however, that Columbus still rests in the cathedral at Santo Domingo. Incafo

superabundance of figurative sculptures, retables, gilded *rejas* (screens) and rich religious paraphernalia. There is a small royal pantheon; the tomb of Christopher Columbus, brought from Havana to Seville in 1899 after the granting of Cuban independence; sculpture by the Baroque master Montañes and paintings by Murillo, Velázquez and Zurbarán; the exceptional alabaster tomb of Archbishop Juan de Cervantes; and terracotta from the della Robbia workshops. Among the cathedral treasures kept in the Plateresque Sacritía Mayor is a fine ivory Christ by Alonso Cano. Like Toledo cathedral, the treasures here are rich and varied and far too numerous to describe in detail.

The Coro and Capilla Mayor are surrounded by magnificent wrought-iron and gold *rejas*, the work of Fray Francisco de Salamanca and Sancho Muñoz. The vast altarpiece, composed of 45 carved polychromed and gilded panels, depicts the life of Christ and Mary and is the work of the Flemish painter, Pieter Dancart.

The Plateresque Capilla Real (Royal Pantheon), finished by Juan de Maeda, contains the tombs of Alfonso X and his mother, Beatrice of Swabia. The remains of Ferdinand 'El Santo' are embalmed in a silver shrine. On the high altar stands the Virgin de los Reyes, a Romanesque Madonna and the patron of Seville, used as a talisman in Ferdinand's conquest of the city.

On the two main plazas surrounding the cathedral, the Plaza de los Reyes and the Plaza del Triunfo, there are several other buildings that should attract your attention. The Churrigueresque façade of the **Archbishop's Palace** has some fine 17th-century paintings in the main hall. More impressive is the Herreran *lonja* (exchange) (1584–98), built to accommodate the overflow of merchants from the Patio de los Naranjos during Seville's period of commercial prosperity. It is an isolated quadrangular building with a fine Doric and Ionic patio and a marble and alabaster staircase leading to the small museum annexed to the Archivo de las Indias. (Open Mon–Fri 10am–1pm.) The manuscripts and documentations were gathered from the scattered archives and papers relating to the New World, and were housed here on the orders of Charles III in 1758. Considering their importance, they are still hardly touched upon by research. There is generally some kind of exhibition in the main rooms showing urban developments of early South American settlements.

Also on the Plaza del Triunfo is the **Real Alcázar**, originally a well-fortified Arab palace, which was extended under the rule of Abd-ah-Raman II and by the Almohads. It was inhabited in the 14th century by the court of Pedro I, who had the rooms redecorated in Mudéjar court style by architects and artisans hired from Toledo and from Yusuf I in the neighbouring kingdom of Granada. Subsequent alterations were undertaken by *Los Reyes Católicos*, who built the oratory; in 1526 Charles V was married to Isabel of Portugal in the Great Hall of the Ambassadors, and commissioned extensive work on the gardens. Later Frenchification by Philip V is fortunately understated. Despite these changes, the *alcázar* remains the most obvious proof of the desire of the medieval Kings of Spain to emulate the luxurious lifestyle of their Islamic neighbours. Here there is

Columbus to 1492

Columbus has been so mythicized that it is difficult to say anything about him that does not arouse controversy of some kind. His birthplace, for one, has for long been a cause for regional and national debate: Greece, Portugal, Catalunya, Galicia, Castile, Corsica, Switzerland and England have all come up with different theories suggesting that he was their native son. But Columbus was, in fact, born in the Italian city republic of Genoa in 1451, one of the richest mercantile corners of Europe and locked at that time in a battle with the Aragonese–Catalan Empire for supremacy of the western Mediterranean.

The sea was home for Columbus. In 1474 he went on his first long voyage to Chios, which encouraged an understanding of the Mediterranean and an interest in subjects such as botany and geography. In 1476 he was shipwrecked after a naval skirmish off Cape St Vincent in Portugal, and he stayed there for a while, fascinated by the findings of the maritime court founded by Henry the Navigator at Sagres. In the next couple of years, he embarked on journeys to England, Iceland and Madeira.

In 1479 he took up residence in Lisbon, following his marriage to Felipa Moniz de Perestrello. In 1482 he sailed to Guinea, most probably in search of gold. It was a voyage that gave him his first taste of dense virgin jungle and his first sighting of the southern cross. In the following years he steeped himself in Atlantic culture, and made trading voyages to the archipelagos of the Azores and Canary Islands to consolidate his belief that new lands existed to the west.

He began a correspondence with the Italian humanist and scientist Toscanelli and in 1484 proposed to King John II of Portugal his plan to *'buscar el Levante por El Poniente'* (to search for the Levant by way of the West). His proposals were turned down and he journeyed to the monastery of La Rábida in southern Spain, where he befriended Fray Marchena, a Franciscan monk with court connections.

From 1486 until 1492 Columbus continued his pressure upon *Los Reyes Católicos* to have faith in his plan. They eventually approved it, together with all his privileges, rights and prerogatives, on 17 April 1492. Columbus then assembled a crew and three caravels – the *Santa María, Pinta* and *Niña* – and set sail from the small port of Palos on 3 August 1492.

a blend of elements that bridge faith and time in a way that can only be discovered in Spain: Roman columns, Gothic carving, *ajimez* (twin-light windows), and the Moorish decorative ingenuity of *artesonados* (inlaid wooden ceilings), iridescent tiles and rich stuccowork inscribed with Cufic inlay.

You enter via the Puerta de los Leones, through a complex pattern of passageways, vestibule and ante-patios that survived from the Almohad palace and were later extended to include the Casa de Contratación, which was established in 1503 to administer trading relations with the New World. You arrive in the public entertaining chambers centred around the Patio de la Doncellas. This two-storeyed patio, restored in the time of Charles V, is decorated in delicately carved friezes of stucco and tiling, and its name (meaning patio of the handmaidens) supposedly derives from a story about the Asturian king Mauregatus (783–88) who supplied Abd-ah-Raman I with virgins in return for his military support. Surrounding the patio are the chapel and official entertaining chambers. The Salón del Techo de Carlos V, with a sumptuous carved and polychromed coffered ceiling, connects with the Habitaciones de María de Padilla and from there to the Salón de Embajadores, the most impressive and intrinsically Mudéjar room in the palace. Continuing through the Dormitorio de Felipe II you arrive in the more private quarters adjoining the Patio de las Muñecas, whose supporting columns were perhaps pillaged from the palace of Medina az-Zahra. Here the rooms, including the Salón de Principe and Dormitorio de los Reyes Moros, are less formal, lighter and more private. A staircase ascends to more royal apartments with some fine tapestries and rooms decorated in typically courtly fashion; the style here is less noticeably Mudéjar, although there are more examples of *artesonado* ceilings and stucco arabesque decoration.

The views you get from the palace will soon entice you into the garden, laid to a Moorish groundplan, enlarged by Charles V and destroyed by earthquakes in the 18th century. Though, in places, it remains in disgraceful disrepair, there are corners where the air is 'jasmine-laden' and the sound of water splashing into brightly tiled fountains so enticing that a *siesta* whatever time of day is unavoidable. Parts of the garden are 11th- and 12th-century, and recent excavations have uncovered a sunken quadripartite flowerbed with a circular intersection at the axes from the period of Almohad

rule. The dividing walls were supported by arcades and could be used as walkways.

The walls of the *alcázar* border to the north with the **Barrio de Santa Cruz**, which, like the Judería in Córdoba, is a densely packed hive of whitewashed streets, with wrought-iron balconies overflowing with flowers. The names of the alleys alone go far to explaining the sensuous mood of the Quarter: there are 'Callejón de vida' (alleyway of life), 'del agua' (of water), 'de la pimienta' (of pepper), 'de mármol' (of marble) and 'de la gloria' (of glory), leading into small plazas shaded with palms and orange trees. At its heart is the Plaza de Santa Cruz, where the remains of the painter Murillo supposedly lie.

The main building of interest is the church of **Santa María la Blanca**, originally a synagogue that was given a Baroque overhaul in the 17th century, although some Visigothic capitals are still discernible. It contains works by three of Seville's most prolific painters: Murillo, Morales and Luis de Vargas. The unrestored **Hospicio de Venerables Sacerdotes**, an ecclesiastical retreat, has a Baroque patio with a fine 18th-century tiled dado, and a richly decorated chapel with frescoes in the dome by Valdés Leal and walls by Lucas Valdés.

On the southern side of the *alcázar* lie the **Palacio de San Telmo** and the **university**. The San Telmo Palace is a fine example of southern Baroque architecture, a style that can be traced from southern Italy to the churches of Mexico. The palace once served as a naval college and is now a priests' seminary.

The university is the second-largest

edifice in Spain after El Escorial, and was built in 1757 originally to house the *fábrica de tabacos* (tobacco factory). This was the setting for Prosper Merimée's book *Carmen*, which was given a musical score by Georges Bizet. Inside, there is an impressive succession of courtyards and interior patios. Richard Ford observed in the mid-19th century that 'the many thousands of pairs of hands employed [at the factory] are principally female . . . they are reputed to be more impertinent than chaste and . . . undergo an ingeniously minute search on leaving their work, for they sometimes carry off the filthy weed in a manner Her Most Catholic Majesty never dreamt of.'

North of the university is the Prado de San Sebastián, a principal meeting point for the April *Fería*; and the Parque de María Luisa, a place to escape from the heat and hassle. This is one of the great urban parks of Spain, laid out at the end of the 19th century by the French landscaper, J. Forestier, in a style that might be termed neo-Mudéjar. He adopted the materials common to the Moorish garden – bricks, lustrous ceramics and whitewash – and created avenues lined with magnolias, palms, chestnuts, pecans and even banana trees. Open spaces were embellished with marble statues of local writers and poets, and water was used to provide a source of serenity. The park was finished for the Ibero-American exhibition staged in Seville in 1929. The central attraction for this event was the Plaza de España: something of a neo-Mudéjar folly, Baroque in its proportions, this is a vast semi-circle of buildings where bricks, decorative paving, water, arched pedestrian bridges, coffered ceilings

and tiling were used in the overall design. It incorporated a mixture of all the traditional elements of Andalusian architecture updated using the industrial methods of the time, and is now used for governmental purposes.

The two main pavilions within the park still serve as museums. The Archeological Museum in the 'Renaissance' pavilion, Plaza América, covers Andalusia's history from the Phoenicians and includes funerary objects from the kingdom of Tartessos, as well as a large collection of Roman sculpture and mosaics, plus glass from Itálica and Arva. Opposite is the Museo de las Artes y Costumbres Populares in the 'Mudéjar' pavilion. Here you will find Andalusian folk costumes, old flamenco dresses and *mantas*, musical instruments and agricultural implements, pottery and local crafts. (Both museums open Tues–Sun 10am–2pm. Cl Mon.)

You should try to spend half a day exploring the sites of interest along the Guadalquivir and the Paseo de San Cristóbal. Here the *cofradías* rehearse for the April *Fería* during the long winter evenings, when the sounds of their drums and brass instruments echo across the water. The most notorious building stands beside the Puente de San Telmo and is known as the **Torre de Oro**. This 12-sided building is another masterpiece of 12th-century Almohad ingenuity and was once covered with the golden metalliferous tiles that gave it its name. It was built by Yusuf II to protect Seville against the Christians after the Battle of Las Navas de Tolosa in 1212 when the Christians gained the upper hand strategically in the Reconquest. Today it contains a small Naval Museum. (Open 10am–2pm. Cl Mon.) A little further on is the

Real Maestranza, Seville's legendary bullring.

By crossing the river at the Puente de Isabel II, you will arrive in the **Barrio de Triana**. Tradition has always considered this to be Seville's gipsy neighbourhood and today the local way of life still survives, although the gipsies have dispersed but not disappeared. Indeed the Trianians quip that Seville is a world away and consider a trip across the bridge as a journey rather than an excursion. Triana shows another aspect of Seville, with its small covered markets and dusty shops selling ceramics, tiles and pottery: the traditional local industry of Triana. In the brightly painted backstreets it is an experience to explore the simple fishermen's bars, or visit bakeries smelling of local delicacies such as the anis pastries called *tortas*.

The western and northern neighbourhoods of Sevilla Centro, once bounded by the great Almoravid wall, are divided by the main streets of Avenida de la Constitución and the covered shopping walkway of Calle Sierpes. This takes you into a more respectable urbanized area that was developed during the 18th century, largely through the patronage of the *hermandades* (see p. 285). Here gracious apartment buildings are interspersed with convents and Baroque churches, and it is within this main residential neighbourhood that several palaces and religious buildings of an earlier period are to be found. Several contain many fine examples of *artesonados* (inlaid wooden ceilings), local tiling and terracotta work.

Unfortunately, lack of space precludes much detail about these religious foundations, many of which keep erratic hours, but worth searching out is the convent of **Santa Clara**, with Mudéjar remnants discernible in a Renaissance structure with a beautiful patio and fine tilework. In the garden you will see the Torre de Don Fadrique, which once formed part of the palace of Don Fadrique, son of Alfonso X. The church of **San Lorenzo**, in the plaza of the same name, is built on the site of a mosque. It is a Gothic structure with a Baroque interior and fine altarpiece by Montañés. In the treasury you can find some fine sacred art belonging to the Hermanadad del Gran Poder. The monastery of **San Clemente** is a 13th-century monastery built over an earlier mosque, and has 16th-century *azulejos* (glazed tiles) and a magnificent *artesonado* ceiling.

Of the civic buildings in this area, the *ayuntamiento* (town hall) in the Plaza Nueva at the end of Avenida de la Constitución was built between 1527 and 1564 and is a fine example of the Plateresque style. The design for the façade is the work of Diego de Riaño. The Museo de Bellas Artes in the old convent of Merced at Plaza Museo 9, is mainly dedicated to 13th- to 19th-century paintings and has some good examples of the 16th-century Seville school, as well as some interesting tiling, furniture, ceramics and sculpture. (Open Tues–Fri 10am–2pm & 4–9pm. Sat–Sun 10am–2pm. Cl Mon.)

The architectural highlights of this area are the two Renaissance–Mudéjar palaces belonging to the two most powerful landowning families in Spain today: the Casa Pilatos, which belongs to the Dukes of Medinaceli; and the Casa de las Dueñas. The latter is the April residence of the Duchess of Alba, and can be visited by previous appointment in writing to Duques de Alba, Calle Dueñas 5, 41003 Sevilla.

The **Casa Pilatos**, at Plaza Pilatos 1, was founded by the 1st Marqués de Tarifa, Don Fadrique de Ribera, following his return from a pilgrimage to Jerusalem in 1520. Gossip quickly circulated among the Sevillians that the plans were copies of those used for the praetorium where Christ was sentenced. The new property was thereafter referred to as the Casa de Pilato (House of Pilate), a title that became official in the 19th century. (Open daily, winter 10am–1pm & 3–7pm; summer 9am–1pm & 3–9pm.) Early Gothic, Plateresque and Mudéjar elements harmonize well here. The pervasive atmosphere surrounding courtyards, galleries, public rooms and gardens alike is both lavishly Moorish and magnificently Renaissance in style. From 1534 to 1539 carpenters, painters and glaziers from Genoa were commissioned to work with local artisans on the structure. On the death of Don Fadrique in 1539, when he left two illegitimate daughters and no direct heir, the house passed to his cousin, Per Afán Ribera III. His position as Viceroy of Naples enabled him to fill the palace with many important classical antiquities that remain on display to this day. Under the third Duke of Alcalá the house became a favourite setting for humanist gatherings.

The outlying suburbs of Seville have little to detain the traveller except for the ruins of the Roman city of **Itálica**, 8km north near **Santiponce**. This was Iberia's first purpose-built Roman colony, and was founded by Scipio Africanus in 206 BC as a resettlement area for veterans of the Second Punic War. Two of Rome's greatest emperors, Trajan and Hadrian, were born here and the city's fortunes peaked in the second century AD before it fell to the ravages of the central and eastern European migrations.

Apart from the huge amphitheatre, with the capacity for seating 25,000 spectators, excavations have revealed a large arcaded plaza, defensive wall and urban settlements. This was a thriving imperial city set back from the Guadalquivir on a promontory above what 2,000 years ago would have been marshes but now forms a rather dirt-swept industrial suburb.

Unfortunately many of the better objects from Itálica fell prey to pillaging in the last century and are now to be found in private collections such as the Palacio de Lebrija in Seville. A small on-site museum has maps and a few objects to help you envisage more clearly this once thriving settlement, and more artefacts can be seen in the Archeological Museum (see p. 293).

Itálica now lies overlooking vast expanses of wheat and orange groves that feed off the tributaries running out of the Sierra Morena into the Guadalquivir plain. The land is sculpted into soft, voluptuous lines in a way that only centuries of farming can do. In the winter and spring gipsies sell sacks of oranges beside the road. Once it has passed through Seville, the Guadalquivir becomes a vast delta, as it collects the waters of the Rivers Guadaira and Guadiamar, which is siphoned off to feed miles of paddyfields. It then enters the marshes and becomes the spine of the Parque Nacional del Coto de Doñana, a wetland considered by environmentalists to be the most important in Europe. The park centre is at Ctra Del Rocío a Torre la Higuera, Almonte, tel (955) 23 23 40.

The reserve constitutes several different ecosystems – scrubland, abundant with wild herbs, virgin pine and cork oak forests; 40km of deserted beach and dunes; and inland marshes and lagoons that dry to mudflats in the summer. There is concern because the water level subsides each year. The last few pairs of European lynxes live here, along with herds of red deer, badgers, foxes, wild boar and a few stray camels. More significant is the park's situation as a nesting ground and sanctuary for birds migrating between Asia, Africa and Europe. More than 150 different species of birds pass through this wild and volatile wilderness from places as distant as Siberia, China and Trinidad. These include geese from Scandinavia, bee-eaters from Ethiopia, woodcock from the west coast of Scotland, purple herons from Central Africa, egrets from Nigeria, flamingoes from Kenya – all of which can be seen feeding and congregating at different times of the year.

The delta spans out in a great triangle that stretches from Huelva to Sanlúcar de Barrameda. Safaris are conducted through the park in Land-Rovers, but otherwise the area is rather inaccessible, dangerous and best left alone to the few settlers who eke out a living from selling wild honey, collecting pine cones, making charcoal and fishing.

TOURIST OFFICES

CÓRDOBA: Torrijos 10 (opposite Mezquita) & Plaza de Judá Leví, tel (957) 47 20 00 ext 209.

ECIJA: Avda de Andalucía, tel (957) 483 30 62.

CARMONA: Plaza de Judá Leví, tel (95) 47 20 00.

SEVILLE: Avda de la Constitución 3, tel (95) 424 14 04.

Accommodation, Eating and Drinking

CÓRDOBA (tel code 957):

(H)**Hotel Maimónides**, Torrijos 4, tel 47 15 00. Opposite the cathedral. Glassed-in patio, quiet rooms and underground parking. B–A.
(H)**Parador Arruzafa**, Ctra de El Brillante, tel 27 59 00. Overlooking the city, 15 minutes from the mosque. A luxury modern parador set in large grounds with swimming pool. Particularly beautiful at night. B–A.
(H)**Séneca**, Conde y Luque 7, tel 47 32 34. In an old flower-filled patio house. Cheap but efficiently run. D–C.
(R)**El Churrasco**, Romero 16, tel 29 08 19. In an old palace, the tables downstairs are situated in a patio cooled by fountains in summer, heated by *braseros* when cold. Very popular locally. Excellent *ajo blanco* (almond and garlic soup) and *rabo de toro* (bull's tail). Cl Thurs & Aug. C–B.
(R)**El Caballo Rojo**, Cardenal Herrero 28, tel 47 53 75. In an alley beside the cathedral, this has a unique Mozarabic menu using subtle amounts of honey, nuts, raisin and fig sauces. Try the *salmorejo* (thick cold soup). B–A.

ECIJA:

(R)**Casa Pirula & Astiga**, both on the main N-IV Madrid–Seville route; serve good gazpacho and *cocido Andaluz* (casserole) depending on the time of year.

CARMONA:

(H)**Parador Alcazar del Rey Don Pedro**, tel (95) 414 10 10. Well-restored rooms in the *castillo* situated around an Arab patio. Best rooms look out over the *huerta* of La Campiña. Good restaurant. B–A.

MARCHENA:

(R)**Venta de los Muleros**, Travesía de San Ignacio 52, tel (95) 484 31 99. Home cooking. C.

OSUNA:

(R)**Mesón del Duque**, Plaza de la Duquesa 2, tel (95) 481 13 01. Good home cooking. C–B.

SEVILLE (tel code 95):

(H)**Alfonso XII**, San Fernando 2, tel 422 28 50. The city's great symbol of luxury: a 1920s neo-Mudéjar palace-hotel. A little worn at the edges but gracefully. A.

(H&R)**Hotel Colón**, Canalejas 1, tel 422 29 00. Recently redecorated. An old favourite for bullfighters and aficionados. (R)**El Burladero**, tel 422 29 00, can also be recommended. A. Meals A.

(H)**Doña María**, Don Remondo 19, tel 422 49 90. Directly in front of the Giralda. Summer terrace. Convenient and luxurious. B–A.

(H)**Simón**, García de Vinuesa 19, tel 422 66 60. Only 2 minutes from the cathedral. Large, old-style rooms and a feeling of faded luxury that is not reflected in the price. Atmospheric patio. C.

(H)**Mauricio**, Lope de Rueda 7, tel 421 60 95. In the heart of the Barrio Santa Cruz, this is well decorated, with some exceptional woodwork. The most homely of the more luxurious hotels. Cars must be parked some distance away but a porter with trolley helps you with your bags. C–B.

(H)**Córdoba**, Farnesio 12, tel 422 74 98. Old mansion house. Efficiently run and good value. D.

(R)**La Albahaca**, Plaza de Santa Cruz, tel 422 07 14. Dining in the plaza in the summer. A beautiful 18th-century mansion house. Delicate seasonal cooking using freshest ingredients. B–A.

(R)**La Dorada**, Virgen de Aguas Santas 6, tel 445 51 00. A classic fish restaurant. B–A.

(R)**Punta de El Diamante**, Avda de la Constitución. Beside the cathedral. Geared to tourists, but good nevertheless. C.

(R)**Bodegón Torre del Oro**, Santander 15, tel 21 42 41. Beside Torre de Oro. Large traditional dining room with coffered ceiling and good atmosphere. C.

(R)**Río Grande**, c/ Betis s/n, tel 427 39 56. Opposite Torre de Oro, on edge of the Triana. Good Andalusian food and a good *tapas* bar. C–B.

(B)**El Riconcillo**, C/ Genoa 42. Many good fried-fish places in the Triana, but this is a slightly more up-market version in an old mansion house.

SANLÚCAR LA MAYOR (tel code 955):

(H)**Hacienda Benazuza**. Luxurious and exclusive hotel in the old farm of the bullfighter Pablo Romero. Indoor and outdoor heated pools. Scheduled to open in March 1992. A.

(H)**Buen Vino**, Los Marines, Huelva, tel 12 40 34. In the heart of the Sierra Morena, this private guest house is run by an English family. Friendly, country life atmosphere. Small pool. B.

New World Ports and the Costa del Sol

Andalusia borders both the Mediterranean and Atlantic and has a total of 886km of coastline. This route takes you through the four capitals and main ports lying along the seaboard: Huelva, Cádiz, Málaga and Almería. In the last decade there has been massive coastal development along the Costa del Sol that has helped bolster tourism but also destroyed the traditional seafaring way of life.

Climatically, this is a coastline of great differences, from the aridity of Cabo de Gata with 200mm of rainfall to the 800mm that falls along the coast of Cádiz. The region has areas of delta marshes, beaches of volcanic sand, long stretches of dunes and cliffs, and only two areas of heavy industry, which are concentrated at Algeciras and Huelva.

HUELVA (pop. 128,000), the most western of the provincial capitals, is a rather bland town built around the delta confluence of the Rivers Odiel and Tinto. Its prosperity has always been dependent upon the exploitation of the mines in the sierras to the north. Archeological excavation of a burial ground in recent years has revealed that this was the site of a prosperous Tartessian settlement, possibly the capital of the kingdom. For those with an archeological interest, there's a good Museo de Huelva at Alameda Sundheim 13, where the exhibits are mainly local finds, Romanesque sculpture and some paintings. (Open Tues–Sat 10am–2pm & 5–7pm. Sun 10am–2pm. Cl Mon.) Apart from this museum, the essentially industrial nature of the city makes buildings such as the Baroque cathedral appear rather dull.

The monastery of La Rábida, 10km south-east of Huelva, is a plain white-washed Franciscan monastery where Columbus said his final Mass before embarking on his voyage of discovery from the nearest port at **Palos de la Frontera**. There is a small museum in the monastery with letters and artefacts pertaining to this event, and you can visit the rooms where Columbus lived. (Open Tues–Sun 10am–1pm & 4–6.30pm. Cl Mon.)

Moguer, just to the north of Palos de la Frontera, is a busy white village built around a large parochial church. Apart from this, the lower flats of western Huelva bordering the coast have been mainly given over to agro-industrial farming in the last few years, and miles of plastic scars the country. **Niebla**, just off the main road between Seville and Huelva, was once an important walled settlement on the banks of the River Tinto, with a Roman bridge, ruined *castillo* and a rather decayed but nevertheless señorial old centre with some Mozarabic details in its church of Santa María.

The more mountainous northern parts of the province contain some of the least-known corners of Andalusia. There are several beautiful villages in the chestnut- and olive-covered hills of the Sierra de Aracena. **Aracena** (pop. 6,500) itself sits beneath the ruins of an Almohad fort and has a fine 13th-century Templar church. You can also see the remains of a brick minaret, the Torre Ariosa – a common feature of several villages in this region. Nearby **Jabugo** is famous for its cured ham, and **Alájar** is the most picturesquely maintained and situated white village in this intense hive of mountain *pueblos*.

If you're heading west to Portugal, the most impressive frontier crossing is at **Ayamonte**, where an old car ferry chugs its way across the mouth of the River Guadiana. The town is a small understated resort with a few old convents, churches and mansions in the *Barrio Antiguo* (Old Quarter).

By comparison, the province of Cádiz is beautiful. The mountainous interior is littered with white villages and the coast has been spared development, perhaps ironically, because much of it is still a military zone. The countryside contains some of the most imposing *fincas* (country estates) in all Andalusia, many of them centres for bull-breeding and horse-rearing.

Sanlúcar de Barrameda (pop. 48,000) is the port and resort town at the mouth of the River Guadalquivir, which is almost 2km wide when it reaches the sea. The town is well known for its manzanilla sherry-wine that tastes slightly of the salt breeze. This was the place from which Columbus embarked on his third voyage in 1498, and from which the ships of Magellan's fleet set sail on the first circumnavigation of the world in 1519. It is a pleasant town to spend a few days exploring, with its quiet streets lined with *bodegas* and abundance of bars serving king prawns. At the harbour a ferry crosses the river mouth to the Coto Doñana where there are short excursions on foot into the National Park (see p. 295). In August the town's beach is turned into a racecourse, and locals and visitors alike celebrate five days of horse racing.

Continuing south around the headland the old lighthouses and beaches at **Chipiona** and **Rota** are now surrounded by inferior resort architecture. The US naval base at Rota was given by General Franco to President Eisenhower in 1953 and has remained a bone of local contention ever since. From Rota there is a good view across the bay to Cádiz.

CÁDIZ (pop. 158,000) was the end of the ancient world, the 'ladder of the outer sea', described by Richard Ford as a 'rock-built city, sparkling like a line of ivory palaces, rising on its headland from the dark blue sea'.

It has become a little jaded since then but maintains what historical tradition considers to be the oldest urban foundations in western Europe, built more than three centuries before Rome, by Phoenician sailors from Tyre in the 12th century BC. The place has remained vital for exploiting the tin, silver and gold mines of the interior, and the sherry export industry of the 18th and 19th centuries.

Cádiz centre lies within the maze of streets connecting the five-pointed headland and the *faro* (lighthouse). Here are the fishermen's bars exuding the smell of frying; the snaking narrow streets that sell cheap summer clothes and heavy woollen sweaters; the fish market where sharks, swordfish and tuna are thrown around like sardines; and the ocean promenades, which the sea has never ceased to engulf with its sound.

Traditional Gaditano family life has always been closely interwoven with the transient life of sailors and seafarers. There are always big boats anchored off the *dársena*: tankers, naval ships, trawling fleets, and passenger yachts. It is a neighbourhood whose fables have moved many, and the town's greatest living poet is the flamenco singer Camarón de la Isla whose voice is as dry as the Solano wind that blows sharply from the east.

Cádiz has some of the most rundown *hostales* in Spain, but the wine is cheap and the general mood rough, amiable and easygoing. In the summer you eat outside at night in makeshift restaurants set up in the plazas, and choose your fish fresh from the marble slab beside the charcoal *brasero* where it is cooked. Streetlife includes boardgames, cards and wall football, and children play outside well into the night. An old tourist brochure claims that 'Cádiz is, above all, the physical manifestation of the joy of living' which, though perhaps exaggerated, is certainly true at carnival time in February.

The Museo de Cádiz in Plaza Mina has been well restored and contains an archeological section with a pair of magnificent fifth-century BC sarcophagi with a man and woman carved in life-size horizontal relief on the lids. Upstairs, there are 18th-century puppet theatres, and the fine arts collection, which includes the series of monk portraits by Zurbarán, commissioned originally by the Cartuja in Jerez that fell victim to *desamortización* (dissolution) in the 1830s. It is ironic that Juan Alvarez Mendizábal, responsible for this act of expropriation, was born in Cádiz in 1790. (Open Tues–Sat 10am–2pm & 4–6pm. Sun 10am–2pm. Cl Mon.)

You should allow a day and two nights to see Cádiz, and a visit to the fish market should not be missed if you're there during the week. Some sights of interest include the neoclassical cathedral with the tomb of Manuel de Falla, born here in 1876; the oratory of Santa Cueva with Goya frescoes; and the oratory of San Felipe Neri, where the liberal manifesto called the Constitution of 1812 was pronounced – a political act that remained a symbol of liberal manifestations until the Constitution of 1978 was declared.

A short ferry crossing connects Cádiz with **Puerto de Santa María** (pop. 55,750), a town that grew rich from the exportation of sherry. Many Irish and English settlers came to exploit the local wine industries in the 18th century, and families such as

Cádiz, founded by Phoenicians, and considered by classicists to be the oldest surviving settlement in western Europe, is one of the most beautiful coastal cities of Spain. Incato

Osborne and Harvey have become national brand-names. Along with Sanlúcar, this town, with its many streets of urban palaces hidden behind *rejas* (grilles) and whitewashed façades, has remained the main sherry port for Jerez to the north.

Jerez de la Frontera (pop. 200,000) – 72km south of Seville and 36km north from Cádiz – is a place synonymous with sherry and the art of its fermentation. It rises from the midst of the rich farmland of the lower Guadalquivir depression, whose mild and precipitous climate and *albariza* (chalky soil) are ideal for growing the Fino grape.

Jerez's industrialized and developed suburbs hide within their historic centre many of the great *bodegas* belonging to the families who make the wine, including Domecq, González Byass, and Terry. They can be visited by making a courteous prior arrangement, and are interesting for the great casks and traditional method of pouring the liquid from a height. The Spaniards are equally familiar with Jerez for its distillation of cheap strong brandy.

Besides alcohol, Jerezandos are well loved for their annual horsefair in May, when you can see some of the most controlled dressage imaginable, which most probably descends from the horse-handling traditions of the Arabs.

The *Alcázar* in this monumental city was once the residence of the Caliphs of Seville, and contains an Arab *mezquita* that was transformed into a church by Alfonso X. In the narrow alleys of the old town are several impressive mansions with peaceful garden-patios, and the great Italianate neoclassical palaces such as the 18th-century Palacio Domecq and the Casa-Palacio de los Dávila, both in Plaza Domecq.

Of the many churches, several have Mudéjar features incorporated into later Baroque and neoclassical structures. The Gothic **cathedral** looks its best during *Semana Santa* (Holy Week) and the *Vendimia* (wine harvest festival) in September, when it is the centre for local celebrations. The **Colegiata de San Salvador** (1696-1795) is more impressive for the Plateresque sculpture of its west door and the isolated campanile.

The large Renaissance *ayuntamiento* (town hall) known as the **Casa del Cabildo Viejo**, in the Plaza de la Asunción, was built by Andrés de Ribera, and houses the Archeological Museum. A collection of mainly European clocks of the 16th to 19th centuries can be seen in **La Atalaya**, Calle Cervantes. (Open Sun–Fri 9am–2pm. Cl Sat, holidays & Aug.) A **Museo del Vino** in the Casa del Vino on Avenida Domecq looks at the development and methods of making sherry. (Open Sun–Fri 10am–1pm. Cl Sat & holidays.) A new **Museum of Flamenco Art**, in the Palacio Pemartín, Calle Quintos 1, contains a flamenco archive and musical instruments associated with this music. The **Botanical Garden** in Calle Taxdirt has plants that come mainly from the Guadalquivir delta, and a good reptilarium. (Open daily 10am–6pm.)

Returning to the coast, **San Fernando** (pop. 80,000) has become a rather run-down modern extension of Cádiz and is surrounded by a popular beach on the coastal side and some junk-littered salt marshes inland. The Costa de la Luz continues south of here in wide expanses of sand interspersed by areas of crags and cliffs.

Cabo de Trafalgar is the cape where the decisive naval battle was fought in

1805. Several villages in this area maintain their coastal charm, despite their increased populations in the summer. **Vejer de la Frontera** is a white *pueblo* built on a hilltop and has a busy central hive of streets. In the village of **Barbate**, tuna fishermen trail a net across 7km of the river mouth weighted with hundreds of anchors to catch just as many of the 90-kilogram fish on a single excursion. The majority are sold to Japanese and Korean freezer ships, but in the restaurants at night you understand better the meaning of fresh tuna.

To the south **Zahara de los Atunes** is a quiet resort with a couple of *hostales* that are booked solidly throughout the summer and a rather haunting holiday condominium that was only ever half-built and is now covered in graffiti and broken glass – something of a monument to the determination of a local lobby fighting against *costa*-ization. The Roman ruins of Bolonia and old guns washed up along the shores after the Battle of Trafalgar are other relics of the past that can be found by walking along the beach and up into the dunes for a few hours in the direction of Tarifa.

Tarifa (pop. 16,000) is the most southerly point of mainland Europe, about 13km from Africa. The old Arab walled town built by Abd-ah-Raman III is nowadays a popular haunt of a dedicated wind-surfing community, attracted here by the strong sea breezes. It is a strange corner of the world where an ocean absorbs a sea in what is known as the Estrecho de Gibraltar, one of the ancient pillars of Hercules. The strait has two main ports: Algeciras and Gibraltar, which face each other on either side of the Bahía de Algeciras.

Algeciras (pop. 100,000), like many ports of southern Spain, has survived by moving the goods produced in Andalusia: oil, wine and pottery in the past and, more recently, cars and chemicals. Here there is a strong North African atmosphere due to the connections with Ceuta and Tangier on the North African coast. It is a low-key place, with plenty of action around the port, train or bus station, but otherwise not worth a detour.

Gibraltar is where the great tourist emporiums begin. The name derives from Gebel-al-Tarik (Hill of Tarik), which is where the Arab lieutenant crossed in 710 and sparked the Muslim conquest of Spain. Here the Arabs built their first mainland fortification.

British forces captured Gibraltar in 1704 and in 1713 it was ceded to them in the Treaty of Utrecht, whereupon it became one of the most strategic points for 19th-century imperial expansion. In 1969 it was isolated behind the 'Garlic Wall' when the barrier was closed as a result of Spain's claim over the area, but when Spain became an EEC member the border was opened.

Gibraltar is an anomaly that could only have developed out of the last two centuries of Anglo–Spanish politics. As a place to visit, it has two sides. One is fast and financial and to some extent responsible for much speculation along the coast. The other side is its Britishness: Marks and Spencer, red pillarboxes and BBC TV: all signs of the amazing determination of the British to hold on to it. A cable car takes you up onto the rock and rests mid-way at the feeding den of the Barbary apes that live there. At the top are the remains of a Moorish wall and a rather antiquated wax museum.

From Gibraltar begin the place-names that have become part of travel agents' parlance in most north European countries, particularly the UK, Germany and Scandinavia. Places that a mere two decades ago were docile fishing villages are now package-tour condominium cities. The urbanization along the Costa del Sol varies from the opulent luxury villas to the sad exploitation of the package-tour, high-rise apartments where thousands of sun-worshippers congregate in the summer.

Not so long ago the coastal plain was connected by a small road, and many of the inland villages could be reached only by mule. But fast profit economics have been taken to the extreme: makeshift plastic greenhouses scar the coast, riverbeds are bone dry, and the original road – the N340 – is considered one of the most dangerous in Europe. The way of life in just two decades has been turned upside down and the strong social order that once existed has been suffocated by cultural cross-fertilization. Today the majority of the male workforce works in the construction industry rather than farming or fishing as did their ancestors. One saving grace lies behind the old fortified town of **Estepona** (pop. 35,000) and **Sotogrande**: the beautiful white-washed village of **Casares**, which is a popular day-trip for people wishing to escape the coast.

Marbella (pop. 85,000) and **Puerta Banús**, spread beneath the peaks of the Sierra Blanca, are the most exclusive and expensive resorts along the Costa del Sol. Here paparazzi photo-journalists track every movement of 'La Jet' – Marbella's international jet-set, consisting of royals in exile, different branches of European aristocratic families, Saudi Arabian princes, and even ex-cons and arms-dealers. Marbella is a European Beverly Hills with immaculately maintained residential neighbourhoods, where the rich drive their open-topped jeeps between their luxury apartments and the large private yachts anchored in the harbour. Along with St Tropez, Monaco and Capri, Puerto Banús is one of the most exclusive yachting harbours in the Mediterranean.

The old centre of Marbella has retained some of its charm, as is the case with many of these *pueblos*-turned-resorts. With its Arab banks and the exorbitantly priced restaurants, it is an area that is more of interest to the curious day-tripper who wants to see how the other half live.

Fuengirola (pop. 48,000) spreads beneath a 12th-century *castillo* and has a large British ex-pat population, but it is at **Torremolinos** (pop. 28,000) where the worst excesses of the budget end of the tourist industry have been perpetrated, and the town's heart has been lost amid dozens of high-rise apartments built to accommodate the millions of sun-seekers. The urbanization continues all the way to Málaga.

MÁLAGA (pop. 590,000), once the centre of a great Moorish pottery industry, is now a mainly modern city that has grown rich from tourism. It retains a certain charm along its wide palm-lined avenues and sub-tropical gardens near the port, but little of the thriving 18th-century town survives and those buildings that do are in a sorry state of repair. Much of the old fishermen's quarter was destroyed by a torrential flood in 1989.

The principal monuments are the Baroque Corinthian cathedral founded by the Catholic Kings at the end of the

15th century, which was a fine marble stairway ascending to the west door. The Castillo de Gibralfaro is connected by a tunnel to the ninth-century *alcazaba*, and both these structures have well-maintained interior patios and are fine examples of the Moorish ability to blend architectural features that are both defensive and recreational. The *alcazaba* was extended by the Nasrids of Granada at the beginning of the 14th century and has an Alhambra-like feel. Also worth a visit is the Archeological Museum, which contains good Phoenician and Roman exhibits and Malagueño lustreware. Of the other museums, the Museo de Bellas Artes in the beautiful Palacio de Buenavista in Calle San Agustin merits attention. It has exhibition rooms surrounding Mudéjar and Renaissance patios, and some fine works by Morales, Murillo, Zurbarán and early sketches by Picasso (who was born in Málaga in 1881) and his teacher, Muñoz Degrain.

Continuing east from Málaga along the seafront you will notice the ruins of the old coastal watchtowers overlooking the Mediterranean. A turning at Torre del Mar takes you inland to **Vélez Málaga** (pop. 48,000) in the shadow of Moorish fortifications. The town has an impressive señorial Old Quarter, which is admittedly now a little dishevelled. Lost among the recently developed outskirts are small factories that still produce the red-baked floor tiles, which are one of the most predominant architectural features of southern patio architecture. To the east and north of Vélez Málaga lies the Sierra de Almijara, whose remote and wild mountains offered sanctuary to anti-Franco guerrillas until the 1950s. A beautiful mountain road crosses the heights to Alhama de Granada on the far side.

Back on the coast, **Nerja** (pop. 18,000) has expanded rapidly in the last few years, and the little beach where the fishermen used to moor their boats is now surrounded by modern tourist architecture, although there are still a few fine private houses built along the cliffs. A new mountain road has recently opened that joins Nerja to **Torrox** and goes through the Sierra de Tejeda via **Frigiliana**, an ancient Phoenician settlement and still one of the most atmospheric *pueblos blancos* along the southern coast. Avocado and mango plantations have replaced the old olive groves.

The Cueva de Nerja is a welcome escape from the relentless summer heat and is interesting for its cathedral-like underground spaces. The coast lying below the caves remains the property of the gin-distilling Larios family and has been spared development. The terraces are still farmed in the traditional way and here you can get some indication of how the Costa del Sol must once have looked.

The coast road becomes progressively more twisted as Almuñecar and Motril approach. At both of these towns different roads lead up through the western side of the Sierra Nevada to Granada. The road from Almuñecar is particularly impressive as it winds through the sub-tropical Verde valley, before traversing a bleak mountain wilderness of rocks, wild herbs and scrub and finally reaches the fertile plain surrounding the *vega* of Granada.

There are the remains of a Phoenician necropolis at **Almuñecar** (pop. 18,000), as well as the *Cuevas de Siete Palacios*, once used by the Romans, but it has otherwise suffered the curse of too much modernization. **Motril** (pop. 46,000) is equally badly scarred. At the ancient Phoenician **Puerto de Adra**, the Costa del Sol becomes the Costa de Almería.

Owing to the lack of water in Almería and its arid climate, the coastal developers have been thwarted at least temporarily, and the Costa de Almería has some of the quietest and least disturbed beaches on the Spanish coast. Development has been allowed in some areas, such as **Almerimar**, **Roquetas de Mar** and **Mojacar** towards the regional border with Murcia, but there are long stretches of sand here where seclusion can still be found.

ALMERÍA (pop. 155,000), rather like Málaga, is a facilities capital with an airport, train station and road junctions. A run-down Old Quarter that retains some atmosphere sits beneath the towers and battlements of the Arab *alcazaba*, erected in the eighth century and extended by Abd-ah-Raman III and Hayrán, the first independent Emir of Almería. There is a small botanical garden of Saharan flora and fauna in Calle Chamberí at the foot of the *alcazaba*.

Work began on the Gothic–Renaissance cathedral in 1524 in accordance with plans drawn up by Diego de Siloé and was eventually finished in the 18th century. There is a significant archeological collection with a good ceramics section in the Museo de Almería. (Open Mon–Sat 10am–2pm. Cl Sun & holidays.)

West of Almería stretch the bleak mountains falling towards the Cabo de Gata. The interior of Almería has some of the wildest mountain scenery in Spain, used in the last three decades as a location for the shooting of films varying from David Lean's *Lawrence of Arabia* to the great spaghetti westerns of Sergio Leone. The locals of Tabernas near Mini Hollywood still remember with pride the days when its locals were used as extras in films with stars such as Clint Eastwood and Lee Van Cleef. The ruined sets of Mexican fortresses and even petrol-pump stations still rise from the hinterland and a typical western-style saloon town, complete with gunslinging theatrics, can still be visited.

In the last decades Almería has adopted a new role as Europe's winter garden. Miles of plastic greenhouses grow tomatoes and cucumbers that ripen under Almería's December sun. Plastic covers many of the inner valleys, and shanty villages have grown up beside several traditional settlements to accommodate the itinerant and temporary workforce of pickers and fertilizer sprayers.

To the north-west the desolate heights of the Sierra Nevada are crisscrossed by fertile river valleys that irrigate large citrus plantations. The Sierra de las Filabres, the heartland of Almería, is more deserted and a few isolated roads weave their way up and over the heights, where there is little to see but the odd farmhouse and gliding vulture.

TOURIST OFFICE

HUELVA: Plus Ultra 10, tel (955) 24 50 92.

Accommodation, Eating and Drinking

AYAMONTE (tel code 955):

(H)**Costa de la Luz**, El Castillo, tel 32 07 00. Modern and good for a few days by the sea.
(H)**Parador Cristobal Colón**, Magazón, near Huelva, tel 37 60 00. C.

HUELVA:

(R)**Las Candelas**, at the Aljarque junction on the Punta Umbría road, tel (955) 31 83 01. Good seafood. C–B.

MOGUER:

(R)**La Parrala**, Plaza de las Monjas 22, tel (955) 37 04 52. Simple but good cooking. C–B.

SANLÚCAR DE BARRAMEDA (tel code 956):

(H)**Palacio de Medina Sidonia**, Condes de Niebla 1, tel 36 01 61. Only three rooms and one suite have so far been completed in this beautifully restored palace. Run by the Duqesa de Medina Sidonia with charm and eccentricity. Essential to book. D–C.
(H)**Posada de Palacio**, Caballeros 11, tel 36 48 40. In a patio-garden palace. Cl Jan and Feb. B.
(R)**Venta Antonio**, Ctra Jerez–Sanlúcar km7, tel 33 05 35. Excellent shrimps and shellfish. Unpretentious. Modern ambience. B.

CÁDIZ (tel code 956):

(H)**Hotel Atlántico**, Duque de Nájera 9, tel 22 69 05. Efficient, modern and central. Garage and swimming pool. Good restaurant. B.
(H)**Imares**, San Francisco 9, tel 21 22 57. In the centre of the old city. Atmospheric and good value for money. D–C.
(R)**El Faro**, San Félix 15, tel 21 10 68. Excellent fish dishes. B–A.
(B)**Taberna La Manzanilla**, Feduchy 19, tel 28 54 01. *Tapas* and sherry.

JEREZ DE LA FRONTERA (tel code 956):

(H)**Jerez**, Avda Alcalde Alvaro Domecq 35, tel 30 06 00. Where the bullfighters stay. Traditional and in front of the *feria*-ground. A.
(R)**Gaitán**, Gaitán 3, tel 34 58 59. Central. Specialities include *lenguado vendimia* (sole in sherry). B.

VEJER DE LA FRONTERA:

(H&R)**Hospedería del Convento de San Francisco**, Ctra Málaga–Cádiz, km 48, tel (956) 45 10 01. In an ancient 17th-century Franciscan convent. Horse-riding, hunting, trekking and flamenco are all organized from here. Restaurant (**El Refectorio**) serves local specialities. C–B.

ZAHARA DE LOS ATUNES:

(H)**Hostal Castro**, Gobernador s/n. tel (956) 43 02 48. Good value. Simple rooms near the sea. Excellent restaurant. C.

TARIFA (tel code 956):

(H)**Dos Mares**, Ctra Cádiz km78, tel 68 40 35. On the beach, the Continent's most southern hotel. Excellent atmosphere. C–B.
(R&B)**Tasca de Chan**, Batalla del Salado 57, tel 68 42 23. Good seafood at bar or in restaurant. C.

MARBELLA (tel code 956):

(H)**Marbella Club**, Ctra de Cádiz, km 178.2, tel 77 13 00. Where 'La Jet' hang out. Luxury to the last detail. Beautiful gardens and pool. A.
(H)**Guadalpin**, Ctra de Cádiz, km 179, tel 77 11 00. A cheaper alternative just down the road from the Marbella Club. Pool and all amenities. C–B.
(R)**La Hacienda**, Ctra Málaga–Cádiz, km193, tel 83 11 16. Eating can be outrageously expensive in Marbella, and price does not necessarily mean quality. This is excellent for a special night out.

PUERTO BANÚS:

(R)**Antonio**, Muelle Ribera, tel (956) 81 10 91. On the harbour front. Good fried fish. B–A.

MÁLAGA (tel code 952):

(H)**Parador de Gibralfaro**, Monte de Gibralfaro, tel 22 19 02. In a prime position overlooking the city. Set amid a pine forest near the fortress. C–B.
(R)**Antonio Martín**, Plaza de Malagueta s/n, tel 22 21 13. Seafood and *rabo de toro* (bull's tail) are its specialities. B.

NERJA:

(H)**Parador**, Avda Rodríguez Acosta, tel (952) 522 00 50. Modern parador set in cliffside gardens overlooking the beach.
(R)Eat in Frigiliana, where there are several good restaurants on the main road into the village.

ALMERÍA (tel code 951):

(H)**Gran Hotel Almería**, Avda Reina Regente 8, tel 23 80 11. Where all the movie stars used to stay. Comfortable and central. B.
(R)**Bellavista**, on the road to the airport, in Los Llanos del Alquian, tel 22 71 56. Good fresh fish. C–B.

MOJACAR (tel code 951):

(H)**Reyes Católicos**, Playa, tel 47 82 50. On the beach. Large, modern and air-conditioned. Good pool. B.
(R)**Elizabeth**, Aire s/n, tel 47 80 14. Strange blend of North African dishes. C.

Granada and the Pueblos Blancos

From Arcos de la Frontera a road runs virtually parallel to the coast through the continuous band of mountains dividing the sea from the Guadalquivir depression. At Granada they rise into the Sierra Nevada, with the highest peak in Iberia, where the landscape is as desolate as the moon.

All the towns and villages of this area once formed the heartland of the Nasrid kingdom of Granada that lasted from the 13th to the 15th century. Their great band of defensive fortifications stretched between *pueblos*, ports and the capital. The kingdom was founded on the back of the Almohad demise and the unsettled period after the Battle of Navas de Tolosa in 1212. In 1239 Ben al-Ahmar established his first court in the Alhambra, and this eventually fell to *Los Reyes Católicos* on 2 January 1492.

Of the many sierras that graduate away from the Sierra Nevada into the distance towards the sea or the *Meseta*, many are striking for their isolated beauty, not unlike the mountain ridge stretching across the north Atlantic coast, the Cordillera Cantábrica. Habitation has never been easy in this territory, yet throughout these desolate highlands are spread the *pueblos blancos* (white villages), one of the oldest and deepest reserves of traditional rural life left in Europe.

These were originally frontier settlements and the many crumbling fortifications extant attest to their role as the last line of Moorish defence, no different to earlier lines of fortifications along the Rivers Duero and Tajo. By the mid-13th century Islamic territory had been reduced to a small mountain enclave based around its capital of Granada, and supplied by a few southern ports such as Málaga and Almería. These *pueblos blancos* were the first line of inland defence that progressively fell into Christian hands until Granada's surrender.

The close-knit societies that have survived in these quite hostile and isolated parts have always depended on local solidarity. The houses are built closely together and from an aerial point of view look as if they have been drawn together like iron shavings to a magnet. Here the links of religion and

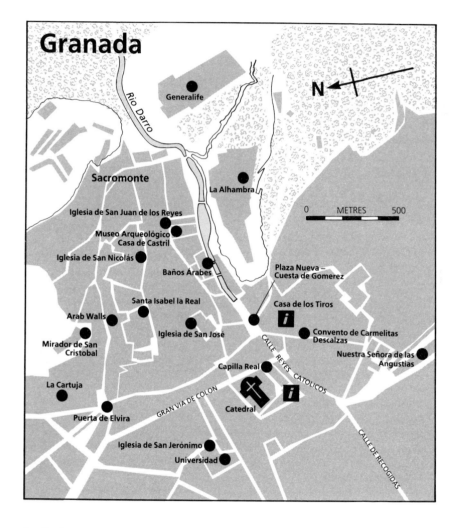

Granada

Generalife

Río Darro

N

Sacromonte

La Alhambra

0   METRES   500

Iglesia de San Juan de los Reyes

Museo Arqueológico
Casa de Castril

Iglesia de San Nicolás

Baños Árabes

Plaza Nueva –
Cuesta de Gomerez

Santa Isabel la Real

Casa de los Tiros

Arab Walls

Iglesia de San José

Convento de Carmelitas
Descalzas

Mirador de San
Cristobal

Nuestra Señora de las
Angustias

Capilla Real

CALLE REYES CATOLICOS

La Cartuja

GRAN VIA DE COLON

Catedral

Puerta de Elvira

Iglesia de San Jerónimo

Universidad

CALLE DE RECOGIDAS

family, heaven and earth, faith and science have helped the inhabitants survive through the generations.

Architecturally they have characteristics in common with the shining white villages dotted throughout the Mediterranean, and with the mud-and-wattle villages of the Atlas mountains in Morocco. The great Baroque campaniles that rise from so many of these *pueblos* are also a familiar sight,

even as far away as Mexico.

The province of Cádiz has the greatest concentration and many of the best examples of the *pueblo blanco*. They perch languidly in the landscape, rolling down slopes like ivory dice, fortified and peaceful in the afternoon sun. The roads joining these villages can be quite nerve-racking and they should be handled carefully. Walking is the best way to see this country.

Arcos de la Frontera (pop. 28,000) lies one hour south of the Giralda in Seville, and perches like an eyrie on a vertical promontory to the north of the River Guadalete. There are two main centres in the town: firstly, the *Barrio Antiguo* (Old Quarter), built across an undulating summit and including the main concentration of narrow cobbled streets and buttressed houses, diminutive plazas and ruins of the ancient Arab walls. A second whitewashed *barrio* stands outside the old walls, where you find the artisanal workrooms and shops selling crafts such as wicker, pottery and blankets.

The campaniles of the two Isabelline Gothic churches of Santa María de la Asunción and San Pedro are where the heart of the old town lies. As with many white villages, this is best not entered by car as the narrow lanes were never designed for such use. Cars should be parked before the streets begin to get too narrow. It is also worth finding the municipal tourist office to the west of the *castillo*, because Arcos has a large selection of monuments and the local tourist map is invaluable.

From the *mirador* (lookout point) you get a fair idea of the town' strategic importance and near-impregnable position. The original 11th-century *castillo* was the residence of the Ben Jazrum *taifa* dynasty and looks south across the Peña de Berlanga. Alfonso X captured it in 1264. Beside the *castillo* is the *ayuntamiento* (town hall), where there are fine *artesonados* (inlaid ceilings) and a portrait of Charles IV attributed to Goya. Arcos has several señorial palaces: the Mudéjar Palacio del Conde del Aguila and the Renaissance façade of the Palacio del Mayorazgo are two of the most impressive.

From Arcos the mountain road starts to ascend to **El Bosque** beside the most southerly trout stream in Europe. To the south beneath the towering Sierra de Ubrique is **Ubrique** (pop. 17,000), a *pueblo* long famous for its leatherware and where hand-tooled work is still made in its modernized workshops. Turning north-east, you arrive in 20km at **Grazalema**, in the Parque Natural de Grazalema, with a microclimate that makes it one of the wettest districts of Andalusia. The scree mountains above the village, rising to the highest peak of El Pinar (1,644m), catch the clouds as they blow off the sea and the valleys catch the rain. From the village you look west over the Mirador for miles down the valley.

On the outskirts of the *pueblo* there is a good hotel, from which the mountains can be explored on foot. In the restricted areas there are the last few surviving Spanish *pinsapos* (literally, pine saps) left over from the last Ice Age, and other rare plant species. Information on horseback excursions through the park is available at the Ronda tourist office.

A day's ride to the north is **Zahara**, which is equally impressively positioned. You should also visit **Setenil**, where the houses huddle for shelter beneath the overhanging rocks, and pots of geraniums cascade from every available upper-storey *reja* (grating). Further north, **Olvera** (pop. 12,000) spreads beneath *castillo* ruins. There are many other similar villages to be explored, and the more you take the small roads, the more of them you are likely to discover.

Ronda (pop. 34,000) is the nerve-centre for many villages in this area. Its ancient centre is to be found on a fortified promontory girdled by the River Guadalevín that irrigates the surrounding cherry and peach orchards crisscrossing the high plains of the serranía. The Tajo gorge is Ronda's outstanding feature. The Puente Nuevo built in 1761 spans the two sides of the gorge 90m above the river and divides the old Moorish part from the later Christian quarter, built after the surrender of the city in 1485.

Ronda's post-Moorish prosperity was due to the Real Maestranza de Ronda, a local noble brotherhood established in 1573 by Philip II chiefly to defend Ronda and the serranía from attacks by Moors or bandits. Several palaces belonging to important Maestranza families can be admired in the Moorish quarter, and include the Casa de Marqués de Salvatierra, the Palacio de Mondragón and the Casa del Rey Moro.

Also within the intricate Moorish centre of burrow-like sloping limewashed lanes and mansion houses are the remains of the Arab baths, situated in the town centre beside the old bridge and the Plateresque Colegiata de Santa María la Mayor, which still retains the 12th-century minaret of the mosque it is built upon. The *alcazaba* and Arabic Puerta Almocobar are further to the south.

The Plaza de Toros (1784) lies just up from the Puente Nuevo in the New Quarter, and is a neoclassical jewel whose ringside woodwork is strikingly painted in the national colours of yellow and red. This is one of the homes of bullfighting and a small museum of the art is mainly dedicated to the 18th-century *torrero*, Pedro Romero, who defined and standardized the *corrida*. Beyond the bullring you can walk down the Alameda or

terracing that climbs steeply up the face of the gorge and from there gain fine views of the town.

In the 19th century north European romantics had a predilection for walking in the surrounding countryside near Ronda, as much for the joys of nature as for the thrill of banditry. Today the banditry is controlled but the serranía remains an inspiring place to walk. One possibility takes you north of the town to the ruins of Ronda la Vieja, on a promontory to the southwest of Setenil.

Two beautiful drives connect Ronda to the coast. The longer route to Algeciras goes via the impressive white village of **Jimena de la Frontera**. There is a faster connection with the sea at **San Pedro de Alcántara** near Marbella that traverses the Sierra de Bermeja.

Continuing east from Ronda, there are two alternative routes to Antequera. The southern route travels via **El Burgo** and the enchanting *pueblo* of **Casarabonela** – where every available patch of wall, and even the campanile, gleams with calcimine – to the ruined Moorish castle of **Alora**, which now serves as a cemetery. The road then cuts north through the Garganta del Chorro, vast limestone gorges that border the wildlife park of El Torcal de Antequera, and one of the most important karstic landscapes of southern Europe. It is well worth a day's excursion.

The faster northern route to Antequera passes by **Teba**, another Moorish town and scene of a strange event related in the chronicles of Froissart. As Robert the Bruce lay dying, he called for his faithful Lord James of Douglas and asked him to take his heart after his death on cru-

Pueblos blancos *are scattered throughout the mountainous interior of Andalusia. Many were founded as frontier villages by the Moors to defend the medieval Nasrid kingdom of Granada.*   Spanish Tourist Office

sade to the Holy Land. Douglas chose to fight the Muslims in Spain and at the siege of Teba he staged a brave last stand and was killed while using the heart preserved in a silver casket as a talisman. A short way beyond Teba

you join the main road and soon arrive in Antequera.

Antequera (pop. 41,000) sits on a promontory in the middle of a small agricultural plain. You can drive through the narrow streets up to the

Moorish *alcazaba*. The Torre Mocha commands views in all directions over the irregular pattern of terracotta rooftops and the limestone heights containing El Torcal. The gardens are currently undergoing restoration.

There are several fine churches here, including that of Carmen, with a Churrigueresque retable and magnificent *artesonado* ceiling. In the Renaissance Palacio Nájera is an interesting archeological collection from local excavations. But Antequera's great remains are its dolmens of Menga, Viera and El Romeral that once formed part of a Megalithic or late Stone Age burial ground (2,500–1,800 BC). All of them lie on the north-eastern outskirts of town and are well signposted. El Romeral, in the grounds of a sugar refinery, contains a fascinating subterranean chamber with a cupola roof.

A fast road connects Antequera to Málaga, a beautiful detour takes you further east through the Sierra de Tejada and the fertile valley, emerging at Vélez Málaga (see p. 305). Just 24km north-east of Antequera is the bird sanctuary surrounding Fuente de Piedra, the largest lake in the region, the slightly salty waters of which were used by the Romans to cure gall- and kidney-stone complaints. In the spring, flamingoes nest on the Isla de La Colonia, hoping that their chicks can hatch and grow before the waters subside and vermin can ravage the young.

The road east to Granada passes **Archidona** (pop. 10,500), where a fine octagonal plaza stands at the centre of its *Casco Antiguo* (Old Quarter). To the north just across the border into Córdoba and overlooking the Embalse de Iznájar is the white *pueblo* of **Iznájar**, with a huge parochial church, *castillo*

ruins and houses that appear to slide down the limestone gradients towards the placid water.

Here you enter the fertile *vega* of olive groves and fruit orchards watered by the tributaries of the River Genil. A series of fortifications that formed the last line of defence before Granada rise from the plain and include Illora, Moclin, Piñar, Salar, Tajarja and, the most impressive of them all, at Montefrío, where the ruins are overpowered by the church perched on the steep projection of rock above the cluster of white houses below.

To the south, **GRANADA** (pop. 265,000) is protected by the snow-capped peaks of the Sierra Nevada. Above the city rises the Alhambra, in an imposing situation comparable to that of any building of an Islamic court that has survived between the Agra, Kashmir, Baghdad, Marrakesh, Mecca and Turkey. In the way that Covadonga was the last refuge for the Christians in 711, so the Alhambra was the last stronghold of the Moors until the Nasrids retreated into Africa in January 1492.

Head first for the centre of town and park your car as close as possible to the Plaza Nueva, the geographical nucleus for the main sights and for the majority of hotels and outside cafés. From there the Cuesta de Gomerez leads steeply uphill to the Alhambra.

The **Alhambra** (Red Palace) and **Generalife** sit on a natural acropolis above the town. The walls are almost irrelevant to the defence of the place and might rather be considered as adobe canvases upon which the interior is hung. It is best visited in late spring–early summer, when the snows of the mountains are thawing, water is plentiful and the irises are in bloom. Autumn and winter can be equally spectacular when the mountains are covered in snow. During the summer it can be uncomfortably crowded. (Open daily 9am–8pm in summer, 9am–7pm in winter. Free on Sunday afternoons and 2 Jan. Some evenings the palace is floodlit and can also be visited.)

You enter through the vast horse-shoe arch of the Puerta de la Justicia into a plaza bounded by the Palacio de Carlos V, a large Renaissance building constructed by Muslim workmen in return for the privilege of being allowed to wear their turbans. Its robust façade and interior circular court of Doric and Ionic columns are the antitheses of Moorish architecture. A Museo de Bellas Artes (Cl Mon) and the Museo Nacional de Arte Hispano-Musulman are both exhibited on different floors within the palace. (Open 10am–2pm. Cl Sun & local holidays.)

Facing the palace is the *Alcazaba*, a plain fortification where the foundations have been excavated. It is worth walking around the walls and climbing the stairs of the Torre de la Vela for the views over the houses, palm trees and gardens nestled in the Albaicín.

The Royal Palace is entered beside the palace of Charles V. Here the main body of courtyards are richly decorated in tiles, stucco and carving that all lend such harmony to the pattern of garden patios. Ultimately, however, it is the use of water that gives the Alhambra life, and this is the most ingenious and vibrant example of Moorish aquatic engineering. The waters of the Darro and Genil surrounding the spur on which the palace was built were drawn off by a series of canals dug high up near their sources to allow enough pressure to feed the fountains, pools and baths of the Alhambra. Around every corner here, water adopts a different role.

In the great Court of the Myrtles it reflects the interplay of sky and architecture. In the Patio of the Lions it forms the active centrepiece, with the central basin symbolizing the reservoir of the heavenly ocean supported on the backs of 12 lions representing the signs of the zodiac.

The palace is divided into three main areas: one for governmental purposes, another for entertaining, and the third for private use. You enter the public rooms that once surrounded the Patio de Meswar, but were knocked down to make room for the palace of Charles V. From there you reach the *Patio de Arrayanes* (Court of the Myrtles) with the richly adorned Sala de la Barca and Salon de Embajadores at the northern end, both with exceptional *artesonados* (inlaid wooden ceilings). From here you gain access to the underground domed crypt commissioned by Charles V, with its strange acoustical effects, and the Arab baths with stars drilled into the ceiling to allow light but not heat to filter inside.

The royal apartments were built around the Patio de los Leones, and include the Sala de los Dos Hermanas, the Salón de los Abencerrajes, and the Patio de Lindaraja. Verses from the Koran are inscribed across the *azulejos* (glazed tiles), and water is channelled between the slender columns. The desire to create a paradise on earth was surely achieved here by the Nasrids.

Walkways of cypress trees, rose gardens, magnolias and lily ponds continue up the hill, with the parador of San Francisco in their midst. Parts of the outlying areas are being excavated, and the views from the walls are breathtaking. Sitting on the crest of the hill above the Alhambra and reached across a bridge over the ravine is the summer palace known as the **Generalife** – a word that derives from the Arabic *djannat al-'arif* (garden of the architect) – which served as the summer palace of the Nasrids. The main courtyards date from the reign of Ismail (1315–25) and were built earlier than the lower palace, which was constructed during the reign of Mohammed V (1354–91). You enter the Patio de la Acequia, where a canal and arcade of fountains divide the quadripartite garden. The royal residences overlook this and another patio behind.

Returning down the hill, the oldest quarter of Granada is found in the **Albaicín**, a gracious neighbourhood of tight alleys and walls hiding palm-shaded gardens. The Carretera del Duero crosses the valley Darro, which provides the network of private patio-garden houses with water. Worth visiting are the **Moorish baths** on the corner of Calle Baruelo and the **Archeological Museum** in the Plateresque Casa de Castril, which has some exceptional ceramics. (Open daily 10am–2pm.) The earliest 16th-century churches, such as San Juan de los Reyes and San José, are also found in the maze of narrow alleys here. The heart of the neighbourhood is near the church of San Nicolás, which gives the most-photographed view of the Alhambra, impressively sited beneath the Sierra Nevada. Beyond the Albaicín is the Gipsy Quarter known as Sacromonte, which you should explore with caution. It has an active gipsy community that still survives in part from the exploitation of strangers.

Granada's cathedral rises behind Plaza de Isabel la Católica and is built on the foundations of a former mosque. It is a fine Gothic structure with a flamboyant Plateresque façade, and contains the marble sarcophagi of the Catholic Kings in the Capilla Real behind a magnificent *reja* (screen) by Juan de Zagala. (Open daily 11am–1pm & 4–7pm.) The basement treasury has some vestments with Mudéjar embroidery, and the sacristy houses the private art collection of Isabel, including works by Berruguete and Botticelli.

Along San Jerónimo leading from behind the cathedral is the church of San Jerónimo, where you can see the tomb of Gonzalo de Córdoba, the great commander of the Catholic Kings in Italy. The Baroque buildings of the **university** are also interesting, although the campus has been moved to the outskirts of the city. Day and night the outside cafés and local bars are alive with students, and the area has the highest concentration of markets, shops and restaurants.

The last great sight of the city is **La Cartuja**, reached along the Calle Real de Cartuja that leads from the Plaza del Triunfo beside the Puerta de Elvira, one of the surviving Arab gates into the city. The 18th-century Carthusian monastery has a cloister and chapel, but it merits attention for its sacristy, which is the most dazzling example of a Baroque interior in the country: an exuberant congregation of marble, stucco and polychrome inlaid with ivory, precious stones and tortoise-shell. Every available area of wall space is covered.

From Granada, the small GR420 road snakes eastwards and upwards into the Sierra Nevada, via Europe's most southerly ski resort. In the summer when the snow has melted you can cross beneath the scree slopes of Mount Mulhacén (3,482m), the highest peak in Iberia, and wind your way into the villages of the Alpujarras. Otherwise the villages should be approached via the spa town of **Lanjarón**, the best base for exploring the area.

Until the last few decades the Alpujarras contained some of the most inaccessible mountains in Europe. The villages are surrounded by *huertas* of vegetables and terraces of oranges, vines, lemons, figs, almonds and olives that are built steeply along the stream valleys. Village traditions such as *esparto* weaving, pottery, carpentry and leatherwork have been kept alive throughout succeeding generations.

The local need for self-sufficiency keeps these people hardy, although the area was 'discovered' in the 1970s by European hippies, who still maintain quite a large presence in the area. The next Dalai Lama was born to a couple who live in a Buddhist community here. All the villages between **Orgiva** and **Trévelez** are nevertheless beautiful, and each one is different on account of the variation in altitude. The mountains themselves are beautifully peaceful, their stillness and silence broken only by the sound of goat and sheep bells.

The eastern approaches to the Sierra Nevada and Granada are defended by the magnificent Renaissance castle at **Localahorra**, which is imposingly positioned on a steep hill overlooking the dilapidated village and the surrounding wheat plain and reached by a dirt track. Unfortunately, the castle is kept under lock and key. Continuing north, you arrive in **Guadix**, a rather dust-blown town with a ruined *alcazaba* and

an enormous Renaissance hall-church at its centre. The strange Troglodyte quarter is still inhabited by gipsies and albinos.

The road continues north from Guadix through villages selling ceramics and animal hides into the province of Jaén, where the extensive olive groves typifying this area extend monotonously to every horizon. The provincial capital of **JAÉN** (pop. 105,000) has grown rapidly in the last few years. Here you will find the ruins of an *alcazaba* and curtain wall on the mountain behind the town. In the town centre a 15th- and 16th-century cathedral stands amid several religious buildings of the same period, some beautifully restored Moorish baths and a good Museo Provincial. (Open Tues–Sun 10am–2pm & 4–7pm. Cl Mon.)

North-east of Jaén lie the limestone Sierras de Segura and Cazorla where the Guadalquivir rises. The scenery is beautiful but wild and is of interest more to those in search of nature rather than culture. The fortified señorial villages of **Cazorla** (pop. 9,000) and **Segura de la Sierra** (pop. 2,700), situated in the south-western and north-eastern parts of the range, are the best places to base yourself. In 1179 the Treaty of Cazorla was signed, which checked the expansion of the Aragonese–Catalan empire southwards and laid open the way for their Mediterranean expansion.

The towns of Baeza and Ubeda are more accessible, slightly larger and only 40km from the main Madrid–Córdoba road. Together they certainly deserve a day of your attention to explore their fascinating señorial centres. **Baeza** (pop. 15,000) is the smaller of the two; follow the signs into the *Barrio Antiguo* (Old Quarter) and park beside the cathedral of Santa María, built on the site of a mosque. It is a plain but large 16th-century Gothic construction with a cloister. Just below this is the Plateresque Palacio de Jabalquinto, with an ornamental Plateresque façade and top-floor loggia. In front is the Romanesque church of Santa Cruz and, just down the hill beside the main road, the Plaza de los Leones, with the city's old slaughterhouse adorned with the imperial coat-of-arms of Charles V. Beside it the 16th-century Casa del Populo joins the Arco de Jaén. On the far side of the road is the main arcaded plaza, close to which many impressive mansions are to be found in the surrounding streets.

At **Ubeda** (pop. 31,000) follow the signs to the parador and park in the monumental Plaza de Vázquez de Molina. Ubeda is another busy town whose centre contains some of the finest Renaissance architecture in Andalusia. This is mainly the work of the architect Andrés de Vandelvira, who built the hospital of Santiago, and the portal to San Nicolás de Beri. Much of the building work was paid for out of the generous purse of Charles V's secretary of Castile, Francisco de los Cobos, who ran the country during the Emperor's frequent absences. The town has a faintly Italianate feel and few relics of its Moorish past remain, although a thriving settlement certainly existed here.

Francisco de los Cobos is buried in the lavishly decorated Sacra Capilla del Salvador at the far end of the Plaza de Vázquez de Molina. This grand basilica-church, still privately owned, also contains a superb carved altar by Alonso Berruguete, which is protected by a large 16th-century *reja*. Also in the plaze is St María de los Reales Alcazares, a predominantly 15th-century church with a later, classically-inspired façade. Directly in front is the *ayuntamiento* (town hall) in the former *Palacio de las Cadenas* (Palace of Chains), residence of Francisco de los Cobos and his heirs. You can walk discreetly through the building and courtyard, which contains the municipal police station and information office in the plaza on the far side.

In the Plaza Mayor further to the north stands the 13th-century church of San Pablo, with a fine tympanum and good carving inside on the capital heads. In the surrounding streets the main concentration of palaces stretches right up to the Plaza de Andalucía: the axis between the old and new neighbourhoods. Here you can admire the Torre de Reloj, a defensive tower now serving as a campanile, and the bullet-riddled statue of the Nationalist general, Sero, which remains as a local reminder of Ubeda's mainly Republican stance during the Civil War.

An Archeological Museum has been installed in the Palacio Mudéjar on Calle Cervantes, which has a good collection of local artefacts. Also of interest is the Museo San Juan de la Cruz, with a monograph of the life of the mystical poet and monastic reformer, St John of the Cross, who was born in Fontiveros, Avila, in 1542 and died in Ubeda in 1591.

TOURIST OFFICE

GRANADA: Plaza de Padre Suárez 19, tel (958) 22 10 22.

Accommodation, Eating and Drinking

ARCOS DE LA FRONTERA (tel code 956):

(H)**Parador Casa del Corregidor**, Plaza del Cabildo s/n, tel 70 05 00. Perched on top of the fortified promontory in the centre of town. A well-restored mansion house filled with antiques. Patio and terrace. Best rooms have terraces overlooking the valley. C–B.
(R)**El Convento**, Maldonado 2, tel 70 23 33. In a restored convent. Home cooking. D–C.
(R)**El Brigadier**, Ctra Arcos–El Bosque Presa de Arcos s/n, tel 70 10 03. Good local food, including *adobo a la Andaluza* (fish in spicy batter), *cordero al Jerez* (lamb in sherry). C–B.

GRAZELEMA:

(H)**Grazelema**, Ctra Comarcal, tel (956) 14 11 87. A modern hotel on the outskirts of town. Excellent views. A peaceful base from which to explore the area. C.

RONDA (tel code 952):

(H)**Hotel Reina Victoria**, Doctor Fleming 25, tel 87 12 40. The longstanding favourite. Magnificent views. A little worn but still stylish. B.
(R)**Don Miguel**, Plaza de España 3, tel 87 10 90. A large dining room catering mainly for tourists. Some traditional Ronda dishes include *pierna de venado* (venison), cakes made by the local monastery and local cheeses. Good wine. C.
(R)**Pedro Romero**, Virgen de la Paz 18, tel 87 10 61. Local dishes. C.

ANTEQUERA:

(H)**Parador de Antequera**, Parque de María Cristina s/n, tel (952) 84 02 61. A modern parador within a large garden. Good for an overnight stay to explore the *pueblo* and surrounding nature parks. Good regional cooking. C–B.

LA BOBADILLA:

(H&R)**Hotel La Bobadilla**, just off the road between Archidona and Loja, tel (958) 32 18 61. An intelligent modern hotel development, set amid rolling countryside. All luxuries such as golf course, hunting, health club, tennis are included. Restaurant (**La Finca**). A.

GRANADA (tel code 958):

(H)**Parador de San Francisco**, Real de la Alhambra s/n, tel 22 14 41. The most heavily booked hotel in Spain. Within the grounds of the Alhambra, on the site of a mosque and palace. Beautiful courtyard and outside restaurant. B.

(H)**Alhambra Palace**, Peña Partida 2, tel 22 14 68. Beautiful gardens, Arab grill and theatre. B.

(H)**Washington Irving**, Paseo del Generalife 2, tel 22 75 50. Faded but atmospheric and conveniently placed beside the Alhambra. C–B.

(H)**Niza**, Navas 16, tel 22 54 30. Some rooms with wonderful views to the Alhambra. In the middle of the lower town. C.

(R)**Mirador de Morayma**, Pianista García Carrillo 2. In an old *carmen* (villa) in the Albaicín, this specializes in traditional Granadina cooking. Local dishes include *tortilla Sacromonte* (sheep brains omelette), *guiso de pescuezo de borrego* (mutton stew) and *dulce de membrillo* (quince pie). B.

(R)**Velázquez**, Emilio Orozco 1, tel 28 01 09. Regional cuisine. Cl Sun & Aug. B–A.

(R)**Sevilla**, C/ Oficios 12, tel 22 12 23. Founded by the bullfighter, Lagartijo Chico. Something of a tourist classic. B–A.

GUADIX:

(H&R)**Comercio**, Mira de Amescua 3, tel (958) 66 05 00. Functional hotel, with restaurant. D.

CAZORLA:

(H)**El Adelantado**, Sacejo–Sierra de Cazorla, tel (953) 72 10 75. Stunning situation amid the mountains and freshwater streams of the sierra. Good pool and local fishing. Cl second half of Jan and all of Feb. Restaurant recommended. C–B.

UBEDA:

(H)**Parador Condestable Dávalos**, Plaza Vázquez de Molina 1, tel (953) 75 03 45. In a beautiful 16th-century palace in this stunning Renaissance plaza. Ideal for exploring the province of Jaén. Good restaurant with local cooking. C–B.

CHAPTER SIXTEEN

Murcia

THE INDEPENDENT MOORISH KINGDOM of Murcia lasted just 19 years from 1224–1243, after which it was incorporated into the kingdom of Castile and repopulated by Catalans. It is a place seldom visited for its own sake, but is more often passed through by people on their way further south. However, since it became autonomous in 1978 and lost Albacete to Castile, it has done well to establish a regional identity for itself. Murcia has been quick to revive its old traditions and market its local produce of canned fruit and strong red table wine.

Geographically, the interior is something of a no man's land: a continuation of the wild Sierras Subéticas that stretch over the border with Almería, Granada and Albacete, and were once mined for their rich mineral deposits. It does, however, have one of the most active agricultural industries on the Levant, and produces and exports almost 50 per cent of Spain's lemon harvest, as well as tons of marmalade and preserves.

Its fertile coastal plain and river valleys have been irrigated and farmed by successive conquerors over the centuries, and the *vega* of the River Segura is one of the most intensely cultivated valleys of southern Spain. Much of the irrigation in this area can be traced back to the Moors, who developed a large silk-growing industry in Murcia during the tenth and 11th centuries.

The idyllic climate of Murcia's coast, the Costa Cálida, has led to the area being quite heavily popularized, with little aesthetic regard, most of which is concentrated around the Mar Menor. Better beaches can be found between the fortified town of Aguilas and Cartagena, where there are quieter stretches of sand and a healthy tourist infrastructure geared to water sports and scuba diving. The seabed all along the Levant coast is like a lost city of Poseidon owing to the many trading ships that have sunk in these waters from the time of the Phoenicians and Carthaginians.

In contrast, the wild and mountainous inland districts have strong groups of old fortified settlements where more traditional industries such as pottery and weaving have survived, and the mountains and forest are used as grazing land for sheep and goats.

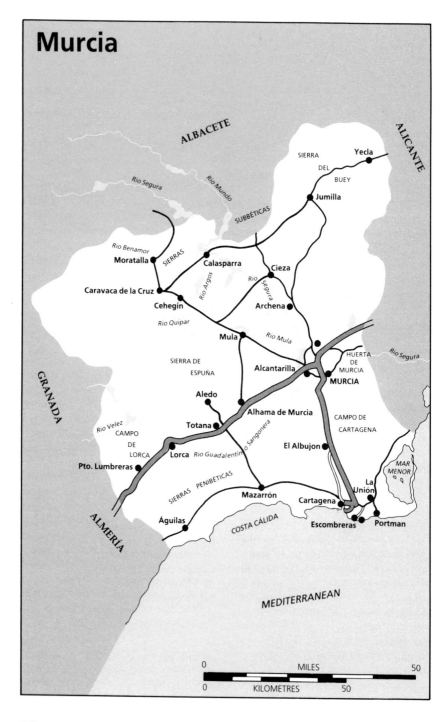

Murcia

ALBACETE

ALICANTE

Rio Segura

Rio Mundo

SIERRA

DEL

BUEY

Yecla

Jumilla

SUBBÉTICAS

Rio Benamor

SIERRAS

Moratalla

Calasparra

Cieza

Rio Argos

Rio Segura

Caravaca de la Cruz

Cehegin

Archena

Rio Quipar

Mula

Rio Mula

Rio Segura

SIERRA DE

ESPUÑA

Alcantarilla

HUERTA

DE

MURCIA

MURCIA

Aledo

Alhama de Murcia

CAMPO DE

CARTAGENA

GRANADA

Rio Velez

CAMPO

DE

LORCA

Totana

Rio Sangonera

El Albujon

MAR

MENOR

Pto. Lumbreras

Lorca

Rio Guadalentin

SIERRAS   PENIBÉTICAS

Mazarrón

La

Unión

ALMERÍA

Águilas

COSTA CÁLIDA

Cartagena

Escombreras

Portman

MEDITERRANEAN

| 0 | MILES | 50 |
| 0 | KILOMETRES | 50 |

Important areas of wildlife survive particularly in the Parque Natural Sierra Espuña above the spa town of **Alhama de Murcia**.

Murcia city and its suburbs, stretching as far as **Alcantarilla**, are where the bulk of the agro-industrial business is done – the canning factories for peaches and apricots, the jam-making and *pimentón* industries. **MURCIA** (pop. 308,000) was founded by Abd-ah-Raman in 831, although earlier settlements probably existed in this place. It is a prosperous and efficient modern town that has been thoughtfully developed in the last decade or so, and has made itself attractive to the tourist industry while remaining the main transport axis of the region.

It is the town's Baroque architecture, comprising some of the most important urban examples of this style in the country, that is its most appealing feature. The *Trapería* (Old Quarter) is on the north bank and has a web of interesting streets bisected by the Gran Via. The main concentration of buildings lie near the Puente Viejo, the old bridge crossing the River Segura.

Murcia's cathedral is one of the great specimens of southern Baroque architecture: a style that stretches from Italy to Mexico, and entered Spain through the Levant region. The main cathedral façade was completed between 1737 and 1792 and is attributed to the Valencian architect Jaime Bort i Melía. Few buildings mix so many styles with such conviction. This cross-breeding is most evident in the vast diminutive campanile that is more than 91m tall. The base is Renaissance, the middle tier Herreran, and the top Baroque turning into Rococo. You can climb a circular staircase inside for an overall panorama of the city and river.

The cathedral's interior is mainly Gothic with Plateresque decoration. The most striking side-chapels, many of which show Spanish dexterity in ironwork and polychrome sculpture, include the Capilla de los Junterones with an exceptional Italian retable and the Gothic–Plateresque Capilla de los Vélez.

Several other churches in Murcia show clearly the influence of southern Baroque, and the tourist office offers a good map with an itinerary showing the different buildings and styles. Those of most interest include Santo Domingo, San Andrés, La Merced, San Bartolomé and the Ermita de Jesús, transformed into an Archeological Museum with a Bellas Artes section and the largest single collection of Holy Week *pasos* (processional floats) by the local sculptor Francisco Salzillo (1707–81). Salzillo remains the recognized master of this art and the *pasos* are polished every Easter and used for some of the most moving Holy Week processions in the country. Salzillo's work can be admired in churches throughout the region.

Murcia is generally a prosperous city in comparison to the port of **Cartagena** (pop. 175,000) – a large Spanish naval base that has seen better days and is somewhat run-down and dirty. A few buildings are worth visiting, however, such as the cathedral-church of Santa María la Vieja and the Castillo de la Concepción with a Torre de Homenaje that once served as a lighthouse when this was an Arab harbour.

Its natural outer harbour with an inner lagoon protected by two fortifications has always made Cartagena one of the most prized ports in the western Mediterranean and it was for this reason that it became the capital of the Carthaginian empire in 228 BC. Cartago Nova, as it was known, was the base from which Hasdrubal launched his attacks on the Iberian interior as far as Salamanca, and the place from which the gold and silver mined in the interior was exported.

Its archeological heritage is understandably large. There are excavations of a Roman amphitheatre and a magnificent series of exhibits in the Museo Arqueológico Municipal at Calle Santiago Ramón y Cajal 45, and the Museo Nacional de Arqueología Marítima in the Faro de Navidad with good exhibits rescued in underwater excavations. (Open Tues–Sat 10am–2pm & 4–6pm. Sun 10am–2pm. Cl Mon.) Processional floats by Salzillo can be seen in the churches of La Caridad and Santa María de Gracia.

The most attractive parts of Murcia, however, are not its cities and coastline but the towns and *pueblos* of its interior. The fortified town of **Lorca** (pop. 70,000) is an agricultural and quarrying town in the south-east of the region and stands amid another rich *vega* irrigated by the River Guadalentín. Park in the Plaza de España, from where you can walk to the main sights such as the Baroque Colegiata de San Patricio, the Palacio de los Guevara and the Centro Regional de Artesanía in Calle Lope Gisbert, which has a permanent exhibition of local *artesanía* (crafts), including embroidery and rugs.

Smaller and less modernized villages lie in the heart of the Sierra de Espuña. **Mula** crouches around a *castillo* and has a picturesque pattern of streets that burst with noise during Holy Week when drumming drowns out the racket of the crowds who come to watch. West of Mula there is an interesting network of traditional villages in the upper reaches of the Segura valley and along its tributaries.

The Templar Knights and Order of Santiago held sway over the area from the fortified sanctuary at **Caravaca de la Cruz** (pop. 22,000) where the *Vera Cruz* (True Cross) appeared in 1232, an

---

Ibn Al-'Arabi

Muhyi-d-din Ibn Al-'Arabi is still considered the greatest sufi mystic of the Islamic west, whose doctrine was derived from the mystical interpretation of the Koran and Platonic traditions. He spent his youth in Seville, during the greatest era of Muslim culture, where his father was a high-ranking court official.

From there he travelled through North Africa to Mecca, where he met a girl whose beauty and saintliness would become his symbol for love, divine wisdom and the muse for his poetry. He then became closely involved with the world of sufi teaching, which he pursued through the east until he himself had become 'the greatest master'. He finally settled in Damascus, where he died in 1240. His mosque-tomb at the foot of Mount Kasyun remains one of the most sacred shrines after Mecca of the Muslim world.

Apart from his poetry, he wrote copiously upon many subjects including astrology and psychology. His most innovative work was *The Revelations of Mecca* – an analysis and summary of spiritual matters that was to affect later philosophers such as Ramón Lull.

Moratella in Murcia, with a medieval castle and austere Renaissance church. Incafo

event celebrated each year with a May *fiesta*. In the network of streets below the *castillo* there are several fine Baroque palaces and the Carmelite convent of San José, founded by Santa Teresa de Avila. The local red marble that typifies the architecture of this area can also be seen in the other picturesque *pueblos* nearby, which include **Calasparra**, **Cehegín** and **Moratalla**, all of which have castle ruins and Baroque churches.

The Segura valley has always been of strategic importance as a pass into the southern *Meseta*, and evidence of this can be seen in the ruined defences of such agricultural villages as **Cieza**, **Blanca**, **Ricote** and **Ojos** spread along the *vega*. **Archena** (pop. 12,000) can boast the remains of Roman and Arabic baths and is well geared towards hydrotherapeutic holidays. The water is allegedly good for the respiratory system, rheumatism and skin.

The north of the region is more mountainous and contains the main wine-growing area, centred around the town of **Jumilla** (pop. 21,000). It is a busy place that is of some interest because of its 15th-century *castillo* and church of Santiago, another great church with hybrid elements bridging all architectural movements between Gothic and the neoclassic. The August wine festival is the time to see the locality in full swing.

Further to the north-east, almost on the border with Valencia, is **Yecla** (pop. 27,000), another old stronghold for Moors and then Christians that now survives from its annual harvest of grapes and wine-making. The most memorable feature here is the blue-and-white striped cupola tower of the Basilica Concepción. In the Museo Arqueológico Municipal in the Casa de Cultura there are mainly Iberian artefacts and objects from the rupestrian caves at Los Cantos de la Visera and the Cueva del Mediodía situated in the surrounding Sierra Salinas. (Open Tues & Thurs 5–9pm.)

TOURIST OFFICES

MURCIA: Alejandro Seiquer 4, tel (968) 21 37 16.

CARTAGENA: Plaza Ayuntamiento s/n, tel (968) 50 64 83.

MURCIA:

(H&R)**Rincón de Pepe**, Apóstoles 34, tel (968) 21 22 39. This large hotel has good, well-restored rooms and a restaurant that spearheaded a revival in Murcian regional cooking. B–A.

CARTAGENA:

(H)**Cartagonova**, Marcos Redondo 3, tel (968) 50 42 00. Large and functional. C.

ARCHENA (tel code 968):

(H)This is a spa resort with three hotels, all offering hydrotherapy using the medicinal waters first exploited by the Romans and widely known for their medicinal qualities. **Termas**, **León** and **Levante**, tel 67 01 00. All three are situated around the Balneario and offer the same facilities and well-sited gardens. C.
(R)**Viruta**, Jacinto Benavente 12, tel 67 05 34. Serves the best local food. B.

LORCA:

(R)**Cándido**, Santo Domingo 13, tel (968) 46 69 07. A long-established local favourite. Simple home cooking. C.

CARAVACA DE LA CRUZ:

(H&R)**Caballos del Vino**, Ctra de Murcia, km63, tel (968) 70 22 19. Adequate rooms and better restaurant. C.

JUMILLA:

(R)**Casa Sebastián**, Mercado de Abastos, tel (968) 78 01 94. Open only for lunch. C.

CHAPTER SEVENTEEN

Comunidad Valenciana

FEW LANDSCAPES HAVE CHANGED so drastically in the last three decades as the great coastal plain of the Comunidad Valenciana. The vast irrigated *huerta* of citrus groves, and idyllic little trading and fishing ports backed by scree-grey mountains, has been shattered by the worst excesses of modern mass tourism. Each summer the Costa Blanca and Costa Azahara are invaded by millions of sun-worshippers and, if you come in search of the rich Levantine heritage, then you must be prepared to accept these excesses of the leisure industry.

The history of the western Mediterranean coast, known as the Levant, is far removed from its modern context. Valencianos were by nature traders, artisans and farmers. In the sierras behind the coast scattered agrarian communities developed in the Bronze Age and were gradually refined through the influence of foreign civilizations, especially Phoenician; even today the Comunidad has one of the densest rural populations in Europe.

The Comunidad Valenciana is comprised of three provinces: Alicante in the south, Valencia the capital, and Castellón, bordering with Catalunya in the north. The intense cultivation of citrus fruits is concentrated mainly along the coastal plain. Mountains rise steeply a few kilometres inland from the sea to meet the *Meseta*. Modern irrigation has to some extent ruined the old Moorish system; few riverbeds contain water, and many have been dammed inland to generate the electricity required to fuel the coast.

Autonomy has encouraged a revival in Valenciano, a dialect of Catalán, which developed when Valencia became part of the Aragonese–Catalan empire after it was reconquered by James I in the 13th century. It is, however, the earliest history of the region that is most fascinating. Throughout the Comunidad are rupestrian or troglodyte caves, many of them with drawings; the best are the Cuevas de la Araña near **Bicorp** in the Reserva Nacional de la Muela de Cortes. Testament to the high artistic level reached by the indigenous Iberian tribes of this region is borne by the hoard of jewellery found in a riverbank near **Villena** in 1963, which consisted of an exceptional collection of Iberian gold bracelets and plates; and by the 'enthroned

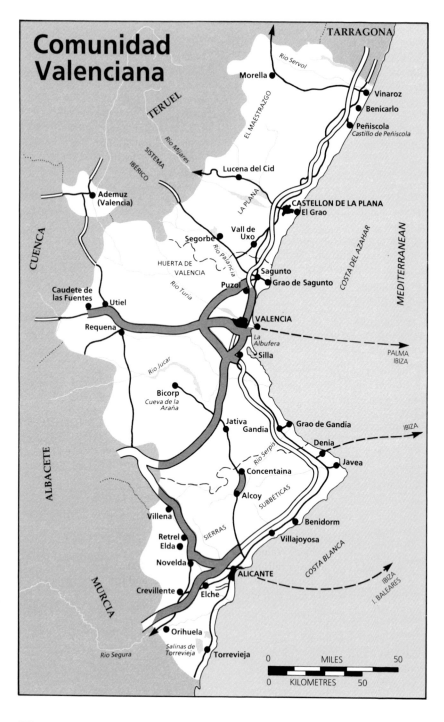

Comunidad Valenciana

TARRAGONA

Rio Servol

Morella

Vinaroz

Benicarlo

Peñiscola
Castillo de Peñiscola

TERUEL

EL MAESTRAZGO

Rio Mijares

SISTEMA

IBÉRICO

Lucena del Cid

LA PLANA

CASTELLON DE LA PLANA
El Grao

Ademuz
(Valencia)

CUENCA

Segorbe

Vall de
Uxo

Rio Palancia

HUERTA DE
VALENCIA

Rio Turia

Sagunto

Puzol

Grao de Sagunto

COSTA DEL AZAHAR

MEDITERRANEAN

Caudete de
las Fuentes

Utiel

Requena

VALENCIA

*La
Albufera*

Silla

PALMA
IBIZA

Rio Jucar

Bicorp
*Cueva de la
Araña*

Jativa

Gandia

Grao de Gandia

IBIZA

Denia

Rio Serpis

Concentaina

Javea

Alcoy

SUBBÉTICAS

Villena

Benidorm

Retrel
Elda

Villajoyosa

SIERRAS

Novelda

COSTA BLANCA

IBIZA
I. BALEARES

ALICANTE

Crevillente

Elche

MURCIA

Orihuela

*Salinas de
Torrevieja*

Rio Segura

Torrevieja

| 0 | MILES | 50 |
| 0 | KILOMETRES | 50 |

ladies' such as the 'Dama de Elche', now permanently exhibited in the Archeology Museum in Madrid. Almost every large town and many small villages have an archeological museum with Phoenician, Iberian, Carthaginian, Roman and Moorish artefacts, and interesting sites and monuments from these periods are strung out all along the coast and interior.

Inland, a series of fortified towns to be found on promontories defending the mountain passes include **Onda**, **Segorbe**, **Liria**, **Buñol**, **Játiva**, **Bañeres**, **Villena**, **Elda**, **Elche** and **Orihuela**. If you are driving from north to south and wish to avoid the crowded coastal route in the summer, then this is the recommended itinerary.

VALENCIA (pop. 750,000), the capital of the Comunidad, is an established European city with an airport and university. It flourished towards the end of the last century, when it was one of the most elegant resorts of the Mediterranean, filled with orange blossoms and magnolia trees along its riverside *paseos* and fountain-filled plazas. Today, it functions as a busy regional capital, an important international convention and trade fair centre, and is the third-largest city by population in Spain. At night it is an exciting place, with a lively streetlife and good restaurants.

As might be expected, Valencia's sprawling and ugly suburbs veil an historic core of interest that indicates its prosperity as a Mediterranean trading capital. The city was probably founded by defeated Roman legionaires who named it Valentia Edetanorum. Subsequent Moorish irrigation of the surrounding *huerta* made it a prosperous area agriculturally. In 1094 it was cap-tured by the Cid, who ruled it until his death. Of Arab Valencia, the main remains are the Baños del Almirante.

In 1238 the city was incorporated into the Aragonese–Catalan Empire but, like Aragón, was bankrupted by the expulsion of the Moriscos in 1609. In 1707 its rights were abolished as a result of local support for Archduke Charles of Austria in the War of Spanish Succession, and in the last century it adopted a strongly Republican stance. However, during the abortive coup in the Cortes in 1981 led by General Tejero, his side-kick, General Milans del Bosch, launched a tank attack from his headquarters in the Gothic church of Santo Domingo in Valencia.

The ruins of the two main gates into the city – the Torre de Serrano near the River Turia and the Torres de Quart, beside the botanical gardens – are all that remain of what must have been a magnificent city wall, which was destroyed in the 1870s and now lies beneath an inner urban ring-road.

The heart of the old city is centred around three plazas within the old confines. The Plaza de Zaragoza is a good place to park; from there you get a view of the octagonal *micalet* (belltower) beside the cathedral, the main urban landmark. It's normally open during cathedral hours and you can climb a spiral staircase inside for the panorama.

The **cathedral** is stylistically rather indefinable, and from the outside several different movements from Gothic to Baroque are apparent. The most impressive entrance is the Puerta de los Apóstoles, which is the meeting-place every Thursday at noon of the local water tribune, the 'Tribunal de las Aguas', a body founded in the tenth century to settle irrigation disputes in the *huerta*.

Inside the cathedral, the alabaster windows of the *cimborio* (dome) filter a cool light across the Gothic vaulting. In the **Museo Catedralicio-Dicesano**, situated in the old chapterhouse, there is a first-century agate chalice taken from San Juan de la Pena in Aragón and acclaimed locally to be the Holy Grail. (Open Mon–Sat 10am–1pm & 4.30–7pm.)

Beside the cathedral, in the Plaza de la Virgen, is the Basílica of **Nuestra Señora de los Desamparados**, containing the Gothic statue of the Virgin who is patron of the city. Also in the plaza is the **Palau de Generalitat** (1510), the headquarters of the regional government, with some excellent *artesonados* (inlaid wooden ceilings) in the main entertaining salons.

A few streets down in Plaza de Mercado is the Lonja de Seda, an elegant 15th-century silk and commodity exchange. It is a fine example of civic architecture, bridging the Gothic and Renaissance with helicoidal columns and elegant ribbed vaulting. Opposite is the **market**, with a magnificent stained-glass ceiling: a great masterpiece of Modernist civic architecture, as well as an excellent source of the choicest produce from the *huerta*.

From the Plaza del Mercado a road leads down to the Plaza de País Valenciano, where you will find the tourist office and the main urban facilities. If you head further east through the streets behind the *lonja* (exchange) you will pass the Baroque Torre de Santa Catalina, a polygonal tower with good reliefwork of sculpted flowers. You should then arrive in the Plaza de Patriarca, containing the main university building and the Colegio

del Patriarca, founded by Juan de Ribera. It was his paranoia about a Moorish–Turkish invasion at the beginning of the 17th century that led to the expulsion of the Moriscos.

Just behind the plaza is the **Palacio de Dos Aguas**, with an outstanding Churriguera portal carved in translucent alabaster by Ignacio Vergara. On either side of the door, two semi-naked slaves guard the jars containing the *dos aquas*, and above the entrance stands a Madonna and Child surrounded by angels and streams of light. It is a fitting entrance into Valencia's **Ceramics Museum**, which contains many fine examples of medieval Mudéjar pottery from the factory at Manises, nowadays a run-down village on the way to the airport.

Valencia has several good museums, but the **Museo de Bellas Artes** at calle San Pío 9 is excellent. Among its treasures are good archeological items, paintings by Bosch, El Greco, Velázquez and Goya, and important sculpture. (Open Tues–Sun 10am–2pm & 4–6pm. Cl Mon.) It is reached across the Puente Trinidad spanning the dry riverbed of the Turia, blocked up and diverted after the tragic floods in 1957. Several sections of the riverbed have now been converted into different garden promenades with cafés and palm-shaded walkways – all features that are part of the plan to breathe new life into Valencia's urban centre. There are several good parks where the city's 19th-century elegance can still be touched upon, and in the Viveros Gardens is a small but charming zoo with mainly Iberian animals and birds.

The last museum of note is devoted exclusively to the *Fallas* – Valencia's big annual *fiesta* held between 13 and

20 March. It is located on Plaza Monteolivete 4 and contains the best *ninots* (gigantic papier-mâché dolls) of recent years. (Open Tues–Sun 10am–2pm & 4–7pm. Cl Mon.)

The *Fallas* are the most important celebrations of the spring equinox held in Spain, and one of the largest annual fireworks displays in the world. The neighbourhoods of Valencia compete for the prize of the best *ninot*, and all the entries are paraded through the streets before being ceremonially burnt in a huge urban bonfire on the *Nit de Foc* (Night of Fire). This is undoubtedly the most exhilarating time to see Valencia, when the city is caught up in a week of incessant celebration, music, gunpowder and paella.

To the north of Valencia, the main coastal relics are at **Sagunto** (pop. 58,000), on the banks of the River Palancia. Here you will find the ruins of a Roman amphitheatre and the cyclopean *alcázar* on the foundations of earlier fortifications that lie across a narrow promontory overlooking the mainly modern town. The dispute over Sagunto between Rome and Carthage was the main cause of the Second Punic War that ousted the Carthaginians from Spain and inaugurated the centuries of Roman occupation. It was here in 1873 that Alfonso XII proclaimed himself king and restored the Bourbon monarchy.

The coast of the province of Castellón de la Plana, the Costa del Azahar (Orange Blossom Coast) further to the north has more old settlements hidden within holiday apartment blocks, but the long sandy beaches are the main attraction here. The provincial capital, **CASTELLÓN DE LA PLANA** (pop. 132,000), has a Gothic cathedral, which was rebuilt in the 1950s after it was destroyed in the Civil War. The heart of the town is similarly modern. Only the Museo de Bellas Artes is of much interest.

The great fortress of this coast is **Peñiscola** that sits on a small peninsula connected to the mainland by a thin spit of land. The setting is magnificent and the small whitewashed houses surrounding the *castillo* have been spared development because there is no space to expand, although the surrounding beaches are heavily built up. The castle was one of the great strongholds of the Knights Templar and was later expanded by Pedro de Luna, who was elected Pope Benedict XIII but was deposed and took refuge in Peñiscola until his death in 1423.

Returning down the coast 12km south of Valencia, between the villages of **Saler** and **El Perellolies**, some respite from the development can be found in La Albufera – a large lagoon of freshwater separated from the Mediterranean by a narrow sandbar. It has shrunk through development and water-siphoning to a tenth of the size that it once was, and is now controlled by a series of sluice gates that regulate the intensive cultivation of rice fields. Its delicate ecosystem is threatened on all sides from pollution but it remains one of the most important wetlands in the Peninsula.

Traditional methods of fishing are used by the local fishermen, who motor through the shallow waters in flat-bottomed boats. The local villages are composed of *barracas* – small whitewashed houses with sharply slanting thatched roofs and often with their foundations supported on stilts. The area is now a protected wildlife sanctuary and is an abundant reserve for aquatic birds and freshwater plantlife.

Boats can be hired at **Silla** for excursions through the lagoon.

The coast further south of Valencia and continuing into the province of Alicante has the main concentration of tourist developments and beaches stretching around the headland at Cabo de la Nao. **Gandía** has maintained an old historic core a little inland from the beach hotels. **Oliva** is a small and comparatively quiet and unspoilt resort. **Denía** is much larger and uglier, and **Jávea** is attractive by comparison.

Calpe spreads beneath a dramatic rock and magnificent views can be admired from the hilltop village of **Altea**. **Benidorm**'s resident population of 42,000 swells to a quarter of a million in July and August and is the most extreme example of high-rise condominium architecture. The local authorities have to import new sand from Africa each year to keep the 6km beach looking clean. In the sierra behind Benidorm rises the **Castillo de Guadalest** which is reached through a rock-hewn tunnel. From its towers the views across the headland are unsurpassed, although the coaches do a good trade keeping the battlements filled with tourists in the summer and terrorizing traffic on the twisting mountain roads.

ALICANTE (pop. 270,000) is perhaps the most interesting stop along the Costa Blanca and, because of its size, is better able to absorb the annual summer invasion. The city spreads around the promontory that supports the Castillo de Santa Bárbara, which is reached by a lift cut through the rock. There is an excellent contemporary art museum – the Colección de Arte Del Siglo XX – in the Casa de la Asegurada in Calle Villavieja. It contains work by many of Spain's finest modern painters and sculptors of this century (Open daily 10.30am–1.30pm & 6–9pm.) Otherwise Alicante is well known for its sybaritic nightlife, centred around the *Barrio Santa Cruz.*

Alicante province has several places of interest in the interior. To the north **Alcoy** (pop. 67,000), at the head of the Valle de Torremanzanas, has an interesting *Casco Antiguo* (Old Quarter), with some fine Baroque churches. In the last ten days of April, the victory over the Muslims is celebrated in the *fiesta* of the 'Moros y Cristianos', when the locals dress up in theatrical-looking medieval armour and stage a mock battle to celebrate the part played by St George in the victory over the Moors in 1227.

West of Alcoy on the road to Yecla, is **Villena** (pop. 30,000), standing amid its own *vega*, with a mainly 15th-century *castillo* belonging to the Villena family whose territories once stretched across much of south-east La Mancha as far as the coast. The highlight of this small prosperous town is the José María Soler Museum in the local *ayuntamiento* (town hall), which contains many archeological artefacts from the region, found mainly by the local archeologist in whose honour the museum is named. In 1963 Soler was excavating a Bronze Age village at El Cabeza Redondo when he discovered 35 pieces of gold jewellery. A few months later he came upon a pot buried in a riverbank with another 65 pieces. The finds substantiated his theory that this was a prosperous gold-mining district during Iberian times. The private archeological collection belonging to José Maria Soler can be seen if he is telephoned in advance on (96) 580 04 29.

The small agricultural farms lying amidst the fertile river valleys of the Valencian interior are a very different aspect to the swarming coast of summertime.   Veronica Janssen

To the south of Villena on the road to Alicante is **Elche/Elx** (pop. 185,000), an Iberian settlement that is now a shoemaking town, known for its salted almonds and with an African-looking urban core of narrow whitewashed alleys. It is best known for the 'Dama de Elche', the enthroned priestess who now takes pride of place in the first Iberian room in Madrid's archeological museum (see p. 226).

Of more immediate interest is El Palmeral, the forest of palm trees that stretches across one side of the town and contains between 350,000 palm trees. It is unique to Europe and, though there are botanical gardens and palm trees all along the Levantine seaboard, this is the most exotic. It seems probable that it was planted

by the Phoenicians and was later expanded by the Arabs. Walking through the shade of its gently swaying palms and between the beds planted with cactus, the meaning of the oasis takes on a European dimension. To the Arabs the palm represented the power of reason overcoming doubt, which may explain why many single trees rise from patio-gardens throughout the south.

The palms live between 200 and 300 years and reach heights of up to 30m. Not only do they produce a rich annual harvest of dates, but their branches are dried and then woven and their trunks sized down and used for supporting arcades which can be seen in El Huerto del Cura in the middle of the forest. The 'palm de resistance' is referred to locally as the 'imperial palm' and is composed of eight separate trunks.

Leaving Elche on the road for Murcia, you enter the fertile plain of the River Segura, planted with citrus groves. **Orihuela** (pop. 49,000) stands at its centre and has a cultural tradition more in common with Murcia than Alicante. This was the birthplace of Miguel Hernández, a contemporary of the poet Lorca, who died while in prison in 1942.

Both the cathedral and the church of Santiago have striking Gothic and Plateresque details, although the architectural highlight is the Colegio de Santo Domingo, which is perhaps the grandest Renaissance building in Valencia and the seat of a former university. The interior cloisters have 18th-century dados made of tiles from Manises and Alcora. In the surrounding streets there are many señorial mansions and other Gothic and Renaissance churches worthy of attention, as well as a good Diocesan Museum that has been installed around the transitional Gothic cloister of the Bishop's Palace.

The inland regions of the Comunidad de Valencia have many similar fortified agricultural towns. **Játiva**, 56km south of Valencia, is another stronghold that rises amid vines and orange groves that are watered by tributaries of the River Júcar. This was once the property of the Borgia family, who moved from Aragón to this region before continuing to play havoc within the Holy See. Like many towns in this area, Játiva is characterized by its señorial mansion houses in the midst of its jaded Old Quarter.

The most unspoilt villages are to be found back in the north-east of Castellón in the area known as **El Maestrazgo**, which stretches across the regional border between Castellón and Teruel in Aragón (see p. 174). It is a mountainous district dotted with small fortified villages; another no man's land of sleepy *pueblos* generally presided over by some kind of looming ruin. **Morella** lies at the centre of the area and has a strong likeness to the *bastide* towns of the Dordogne with sturdy stone-built houses radiating from an arcaded Plaza Mayor.

There are several villages in this area worth seeking out: **Forcall**, **Traiguera**, **San Mateo**, **Ares del Maestrazgo** and **Zorita del Maestrazgo** are the most picturesque, falling within the Castellón frontier. This is once again an area with a strong medieval atmosphere, with Crusader frontier architecture protecting the roads between the coast and Castile.

TOURIST OFFICE

VALENCIA: Paz 46, tel (96) 352 28 97; Plaza País Valenciano 1, tel (96) 351 04 17.

From the port, car ferries depart daily for Mallorca and less frequently for Ibiza. Information and tickets: Transmediterranea, Avda Manuel Ingeniero 15.

Accommodation, Eating and Drinking

LA ALBUFERA (tel code 96)

(H)**Luis Vives**, El Saler, tel 323 68 50. A better alternative than staying in the city is the parador set among pines and sand dunes at El Saler, a few miles to the south. B. (H)**Casino Monte Picayo**, Puzoi, tel 142 12 11. A gaming casino is joined to the hotel. C.

Acknowledgements

The greatest debt of thanks must extend to Jeremy Catto for his constant guidance and suggestions with the first draft; to Vicky Hayward for her profound knowledge of regional cooking; to Antonio Lobato for his mine of anecdotes about more obscure aspects of Spanish folklore; to Valeria Miñaur for her patience over the maps; to Fania Miñaur for her work on the final draft and index; to Pedro Muñoz for his wisdom; and to Atico Uno for the space.

This guide was otherwise researched and the places visited independently by the author, with the loan of a car by Avis.

Of the many books that were read and referred to, the most dog-eared left on the shelves in English are: Richard Ford's three-volume classic *Handbook for Spain 1845*; Bernard Bevan's *History of Spanish Architecture*; Titus Burckhardt's *Moorish Culture in Spain*; *The Oxford Companion to Spanish Literature*; Alistair Boyd's *Companions to Castile and Central Spain* and *The Essence of Catalonia*; Frederic Grunfeld's *Wild Spain*; Ian Robertson's *Blue Guide* and the three-volume *Naval Intelligence Division Geographical Handbook Series: The Peninsula*.

Index to Place Names

(Individual buildings inside towns are not indexed, nor are names of people)

* Stopping places on the Camino de Santiago.